Local Content Requirements

As anti-globalization and geopolitical tensions continue to rise, the use of local content requirements (LCRs) around the world has become more noticeable than ever before.

The reasons for adopting LCRs range from ensuring domestic supply availability, job creation, and increasing value added to safeguarding national security. Ing and Grossman examine country-specific as well as firm-product level exercises to explain how LCRs reduce fair competition, resulting in lower trade and productivity, which ultimately lowers world economic output and overall human welfare. Countries around the world are investigated with specific attention to the US, China, Indonesia, and resource-intensive countries, including mining-intensive ones. The book also presents product- and firm-level analyses, answering the question of why countries adopted LCRs and how LCRs affect the world economy.

This book is a useful resource that will interest policymakers, researchers, and advanced undergraduates interested in international trade, industrial policy, political economy, labour economics, and development economics.

Lili Yan Ing is a lead advisor (Southeast Asia Region) at the Economic Research Institute for ASEAN and East Asia (ERIA). She also serves as secretary general of the International Economic Association (IEA).

Gene M. Grossman is the Jacob Viner Professor of International Economics in the Department of Economics and the School of Public and International Affairs at Princeton University.

Routledge-ERIA Studies in Development Economics

Production Networks in Southeast Asia
Edited by Lili Yan Ing and Fukunari Kimura

The Indonesian Economy
Trade and Industrial Policies
Edited by Lili Yan Ing, Gordon H. Hanson, and Sri Mulyani Indrawati

World Trade Evolution
Growth, Productivity and Employment
Edited by Lili Yan Ing and Miaojie Yu

East Asian Integration
Goods, Services, and Investment
Edited by Lili Yan Ing, Martin Richardson and Shujiro Urata

Developing the Digital Economy in ASEAN
Edited by Lurong Chen and Fukunari Kimura

COVID-19 in Indonesia
Impacts on the Economy and Ways to Recovery
Edited by Lili Yan Ing and M. Chatib Basri

Robots and AI
A New Economic Era
Edited by Lili Yan Ing and Gene M. Grossman

Local Content Requirements
Promises and Pitfalls
Edited by Lili Yan Ing and Gene M. Grossman

For more information about this series, please visit: www.routledge.com/Routledge-ERIA-Studies-in-Development-Economics/book-series/ERIA

Local Content Requirements

Promises and Pitfalls

Edited by
Lili Yan Ing and Gene M. Grossman

Routledge
Taylor & Francis Group
LONDON AND NEW YORK

First published 2024
by Routledge
4 Park Square, Milton Park, Abingdon, Oxon OX14 4RN

and by Routledge
605 Third Avenue, New York, NY 10158

Routledge is an imprint of the Taylor & Francis Group, an informa business

Funded by Economic Research Institute for ASEAN and East Asia (ERIA).

British Library Cataloguing-in-Publication Data
A catalogue record for this book is available from the British Library

Library of Congress Cataloging-in-Publication Data
Names: Ing, Lili Yan, editor. | Grossman, Gene M., editor.
Title: Local content requirements : promises and pitfalls / edited by Lili Yan Ing and Gene M. Grossman.
Description: Abingdon, Oxon ; New York, NY : Routledge, 2024. | Series: Routledge-ERIA studies in development economics | Includes bibliographical references and index.
Identifiers: LCCN 2023029276 (print) | LCCN 2023029277 (ebook) | ISBN 9781032542232 (hardback) | ISBN 9781032542218 (paperback) | ISBN 9781003415794 (ebook)
Subjects: LCSH: International trade. | Foreign trade regulation. | Commercial policy. | Economic development.
Classification: LCC HF1379 .L625 2024 (print) | LCC HF1379 (ebook) | DDC 382—dc23/eng/20230629
LC record available at https://lccn.loc.gov/2023029276
LC ebook record available at https://lccn.loc.gov/2023029277

ISBN: 978-1-032-54223-2 (hbk)
ISBN: 978-1-032-54221-8 (pbk)
ISBN: 978-1-003-41579-4 (ebk)

DOI: 10.4324/9781003415794

Typeset in Galliard
by Apex CoVantage, LLC

Protection for sale. Love is not

Michelle and Han Na

LYI

Nick, Dina, Rob, Shari, and Sam

GMG

Contents

Figures

Tables

Contributors

Kun Cai, University of International Business and Economics (UIBE), China

David Christian, Economic Research Institute for ASEAN and East Asia (ERIA)

Paulo De Sa, Independent Senior Consultant

Oscar Fernando, Young Professionals 2021, the World Trade Organization (WTO)

Dorothee Flaig, University of Hohenheim

Gene M. Grossman, Princeton University

Keith Head, University of British Columbia

Lili Yan Ing, Economic Research Institute for ASEAN and East Asia (ERIA) and International Economic Association (IEA)

Jane Korinek, Organization for Economic Cooperation and Development (OECD)

Michelle Limenta, University of Pelita Harapan

Junianto James Losari, City University of Hong Kong

Thierry Mayer, Paris Institute of Political Studies (Sciences Po)

Marc Melitz, Harvard University

Susan F. Stone, University of South Australia

Yessi Vadila, the Ministry of Trade of the Republic of Indonesia

Zhi Wang, University of International Business and Economics (UIBE) China and George Mason University

Rui Zhang, Business School, Sun Yat-Sen University

Acknowledgements

We specially thank Chatib Basri, Ernawati Munadi, Siwage Dharma, Dani Rodrik, Justin Yifu Lin, Miaojie Yu, Elhanan Helpman, Hal Hill, Tetsuya Watanabe, Shujiro Urata, Haryo Aswicahyono, Kiki Verico, Fauziah Zen, Iman Pambagyo, Mari Pangestu, and colleagues at the Ministry of Trade of Indonesia, the Ministry of Finance of Indonesia, CEPR, OECD, University of Indonesia, CSIS, Gadjah Mada University, Peking University, Sun Yat Sen University, Liaoning University, and University of Pelita Harapan for sharing their insights on LCRs. Ivana Markus and Livia Nazara provided excellent research assistance and Catherin Safitri provided generous administration support. We also thank Gilbert Gnanarathinam, Kendrick Loo, and Chelsea Low from Routledge, and Fadriani Trianingsih from ERIA.

1 Introduction

Gene M. Grossman and Lili Yan Ing

Local content requirements in theory and practice

Local content requirements (LCRs) have been used by many countries, both developed and developing, to promote the use of local inputs and support the growth of domestic industries. Initially, the term LCR (or, equivalently, "content protection") was used to refer to a mandate that a certain fraction of domestically produced inputs, by value or by volume, be incorporated in any final good sold in the domestic market. Over time, the range of policies covered by the term has expanded alongside the increased range of localization practices used by various national and local governments. Now, outcomes may be legally mandated or aspirational. The outcomes may reference input shares, employment, firm-ownership shares, location of R&D, or technology transfer. LCRs may include restrictions on the provision of certain services, eligibility for government contracts, local performance of compliance tests, or the location of data storage. Aspirational targets might be incentivized with subsidized export or investment financing, with tax breaks, with price concessions for government-supplied energy or infrastructure, with conditional bailouts, or with other financial inducements. In this book, we use the term LCR broadly to include any laws or regulations that require or encourages the use of locally produced inputs or services in a multi-stage production process.

LCRs also play a role in bilateral and regional trade agreements, where they are known as "rules of origin" (RoOs). Trade agreements generally call for preferential tariff treatment of goods emanating from a partner country. But such agreements must define what it means to "emanate from," or else goods imported from outside the member countries may enter the region in a low-tariff country and then be shipped on to a high-tariff country after the addition of only minimal or negligible local value added. RoOs specify what fraction of the value added of an internally traded good must originate within the region in order that the good qualify for preferential treatment. RoOs might also further stipulate minimum percentages from each of the various countries within the region, as with certain provisions of the United States-Mexico-Canada Trade Agreement (USMCA). While perhaps originally

DOI: 10.4324/9781003415794-1

intended to thwart transshipment, RoOs are regularly used now to encourage regional production.

LCRs first entered the arsenal of trade instruments in Australia, which, in 1948, restricted the use of imported car parts in the local assembly operations of British multinationals while offering concessionary financing based on the fraction of Australian value added to encourage the production of "Australia's own car" (Pursell, 2001). Several countries quickly followed suit, including Canada, which instituted LCRs to shield domestic parts producers from American competition prior to the conclusion of the Canada-American Automotive Agreement in 1965 (Wonnacott and Wonnacott, 1967; Johnson, 1971). LCR policies to foster import substitution in the automobile industry soon became commonplace in Latin America, where they were introduced in Chile, Argentina, Mexico, and Brazil (Munk, 1969; Johnson, 1967). Moreover, Australia quickly extended its use of this new instrument well beyond the automobile sector, implementing policies to encourage or require use of local inputs in industries as disparate as petrochemicals, tobacco, peanut oil, coffee, fruit juices, industrial machinery, and agricultural tractors (Lloyd, 1971). Still, LCRs were relatively uncommon when Corden (1971) and Grossman (1981) first analyzed their economic consequences. Their popularity waned in the 1980s as more and more countries became disillusioned with using a strategy of import substitution to promote development.

LCRs have made a roaring comeback, particularly after the Global Financial Crisis in 2008. Between 2008 and 2013, almost 200 new LCR measures were introduced, according to the Global Trade Alert. This figure grew to more than 500 measures that were put into place during the period from 2014 to 2020. Moreover, the implementation of these policies has been widespread, ranging across developed and developing economies. Quite prominently, the United States has made LCRs a cornerstone of its recent policy to promote the development of electric vehicles as part of the Inflation Reduction Act of 2022. The range of economic activities targeted by LCR policies around the globe has expanded to include many resource-extracting sectors, information technology, healthcare goods and services, financial services, agricultural products, and others.

Why do countries adopt LCRs that favor local sourcing of intermediate inputs and services? The list of arguments to support such policies mirrors those offered for protectionist trade policies more generally. First, LCRs might afford new job opportunities in certain sectors or regions of the economy. These jobs, in turn, might boost wages, reduce unemployment, or encourage investments in human capital. Second, LCRs, by encouraging specific local activities, might provide spillover benefits to other activities and sectors via research and development or learning by doing. Third, localization policies might encourage or mandate greater foreign direct investment, joint-venture partnerships, or technology transfer on terms favorable to the host country or at the expense of alternative hosts. LCRs applied to primary products are often intended to encourage higher value-added activities, with the aim of promoting indigenous management skills and technological knowhow.

Of course, LCRs, like other forms of protection, often fail to achieve these lofty goals. Whether introduced by well-meaning leaders or in response to special-interest lobbying, such policies often fail to generate positive spillovers of sufficient magnitude to justify the higher costs of domestic sourcing. The desired jobs may not materialize due to inadequate management, lack of requisite skills, unavailability of complementary inputs, or other reasons. Even if new job opportunities are generated in targeted sectors, they may come at the expense of employment in other sectors that potentially offer greater economic benefit. In short, policies that discriminate in favor of local producers of inputs and services may be subject to the same, unfavorable cost-benefit analysis as with other forms of trade protection. Numerous tales of disadvantageous LCRs are told in Hufbauer et al. (2013), Stone et al. (2015), and elsewhere in literature. Similar critiques of RoOs in bilateral and regional trade agreements may be found in Cadot et al. (2006), Krueger (2012), Conconi et al. (2018), Cadot and Ing (2019), and elsewhere.

The theoretical literature, beginning with Grossman (1981) and Dixit and Grossman (1982), has identified a particular risk associated with LCRs that distinguishes these policies from tariffs and other forms of protection for domestic industries. Whereas tariffs on final goods boost local demand for the protected goods and thereby demand for all inputs (including those produced locally) used in the production of these goods, LCRs that raise the cost of inputs can easily have unintended consequences. Alongside the import substitution mandated or encouraged by these policies comes an adverse "output effect"; as costs for downstream producers rise, these firms likely will scale back production and reduce their demand for inputs in the process. The offsetting substitution and output effects of LCRs may help to explain why empirical studies often find disappointing or even adverse effects of these policies on employment, value added, and foreign investment in targeted industries.

Our book

This book is intended to update the literature on local content requirements and rules of origin and to further understanding of the experience with and consequences of such policies and their consistency or not with the rules established by the world trading system.

The distinctive features of our book are twofold. First, the research reported here uses the most up-to-date catalogs of LCRs that have been growing rapidly since the Global Financial Crisis of 2008. Second, the research complements analysis of LCRs at the global level with country- and firm-specific exercises.

The remainder of this book contains seven chapters that can loosely be divided into three parts. The first part, comprising Chapters 2 and 3, provides an overview of major LCR policies used globally (Chapter 2) and in mineral exporting countries (Chapter 3). The second part focuses on important recent LCR policies in the world's two largest economies, the United States and China. Chapter 4 concerns the effects on the organization of the North American automobile sector of the new RoOs in the USMCA while touching also on the implications for the car industry of Britain's exit from the European Union. Chapter 5 addresses China's industrial policy initiatives such as "Made in China 2025" that are intended to promote further industrialization and innovation in that country. The final three chapters shine a spotlight on Indonesia, a large, emerging economy that is a major exporter of natural resources. Indonesia is interesting for our purposes because its laws and regulations include a variety of LCR policies and because it provides a test case for the consistency of such policies with the rules agreed by members of the World Trade Organization (WTO).

We proceed now to describe the contents and main contributions of these chapters in somewhat greater detail.

Chapter 2 by Dorothee Flaig and Susan F. Stone discusses the recent experience with LCRs in the world economy. They begin by reviewing the reasons why countries implement policies that stipulate or incentivize the use of domestic inputs in local production. Among the most prominent objectives that they cite are employment objectives and technology transfer. Next, the authors discuss trends in the implementation of LCRs, pointing to an acceleration of usage from the period of 2008–2013 to the more recent period of 2014–2020, as reported by Global Trade Alert. The authors cite India, Germany, and the United Kingdom as the most intensive users of LCRs, but they qualify this observation by pointing out that counts of usage do not account for heterogenous impact and that the Global Trade Alert tallies LCRs in multiple jurisdictions within a country, so that more decentralized polities are likely to have higher counts.

The heart of the chapter uses the OECD Trade Model, METRO, to provide a quantitative evaluation of seven major instances of new LCR policies, chosen from a sample of 565 measures that were considered for the purpose. The measures under review were selected as those that could be modeled quantitatively and that were likely to be among the most trade distorting. In order to apply the METRO model, a policy must specify an identifiable sector and an identifiable restriction that could be meaningfully enforced, it must affect a sufficiently large sector or region of the economy, and it must be a binding measure applied where the domestic sector has capacity to meet the required demand. Application of these criteria yields a good sample of the types of LCR measures that have been applied recently and of the types of economies that have applied them. Specifically, the authors focus on (i) tax credits available to Argentinian car producers that use specified percentages of local content; (ii) a requirement imposed by Brazil on the telecommunications sector that they use a minimum of local content in their 4G networks; (iii) the preference margins allowed by the Brazilian government for public procurement of a variety of nationally produced goods; (iv) regulations introduced by the Indonesian government that essentially require the entire assembly process of motor vehicles and motorcycles to take place locally; (v) a regulation that makes it mandatory for Saudi Arabian governmental agencies to purchase their medical supplies from the local industry; (vi) a Mining Charter in South Africa that establishes a minimum local content requirement for mining goods and for total services used by firms in the domestic mining industry; and (vii) the Buy America program that is required of U.S. states that receive grants for transportation funding from the federal government.

METRO is a static, global, computable general equilibrium (CGE) model. It incorporates many countries, sectors, and factors of production and distinguishes output from each sector according to its end use. The authors model each of the LCR measures as a restriction of calibrated magnitude on the input choices of sectors in the affected countries. After solving the baseline model under the assumption that the LCR policies are not binding, they resolve the model imposing their calibrated restrictions. The simulations provide estimates of the effects of the seven policies on real GDP, trade flows, labor income, total disposable income, and the terms of trade. They also generate disaggregated estimates of the effects of the policies on imports and production in the 27 sectors captured by the model.

Flaig and Stone estimate that the economic impacts of the seven LCR measures they study are modest but generally negative. The LCRs tend to undermine the long-run competitiveness of the sectors in which they are applied while having limited or negligible spillover effects on the broader economies. Since the model assumes full employment, where the policy targets a large sector – such as the LCRs in the automobile industries in Argentina and Indonesia – the expanded use of local inputs necessarily comes at the expense of other sectors of the economy. As the non-targeted industries substitute away from domestic inputs, their demand for imports grows, with a potentially negative (albeit small) effect on the terms of trade.

Chapter 3 by Jane Korinek and Paolo De Sa builds on Korinek and Ramdoo (2017) and focuses on laws on regulations that seek to stimulate growth of local industries upstream and downstream from the mining sectors in resource-rich economies. The chapter begins with a typology of LCRs that distinguishes mandatory measures from incentives-based policies and supply-side policies from demand-side policies. Demand-side policies intended to promote backward linkages between mining firms and their suppliers include preferences for local suppliers of inputs used in mining and numerical targets for employment by extractive firms. Supply-side policies with upstream suppliers include requirements to provide training, fund capacity development, and conduct awareness campaigns about procurement opportunities. Demand-side policies aimed at increasing interactions with firms and industries downstream from the mining sector include restrictions or taxes on mineral exports beyond those on processed products, requirements that extractive firms sell a specified share of their output domestically, or tax concessions that favor local sales. On the supply side, LCRs might require extractive firms to invest in downstream processing facilities or to collaborate with training institutions to promote the development of needed skills. Incentive-based policies to encourage forward linkages might include tax concessions based on domestic sales of mined materials or subsidized loans for capacity investments. The authors note that mandates have been more popular in African countries such as Ghana, South Africa, Tanzania, and Zambia, whereas more developed economies such as Australia, Canada, and Chile have relied more heavily on an incentive-based approach.

Korinek and De Sa go on to highlight a number of common reasons LCRs in the mining industries have generated disappointing results. First, an inadequate appreciation of mining firms' inputs needs and of the absorptive capacity of local suppliers has led many countries to set unrealistic targets for local procurement that domestic firms have been unable to satisfy. Second, some countries have employed broad definitions of local content, which provides flexibility to the sector but makes it difficult to assess gains in value added and spillovers to the rest of the economy. The available evidence suggests that mandatory, quantitative LCRs have failed to generate significant growth in the use of locally sourced inputs by the mining sector, nor have they strengthened linkages with upstream industries. Meanwhile, requirements or incentives for downstream processing have failed in the long run when processing firms have not been able to produce goods of sufficient quality or to achieve international cost competitiveness. Finally, the authors note, LCRs have contributed to government deficits even when they appear on paper to be fiscally neutral, because they decrease profitability in the mining sectors and thereby reduce the governments' receipts from corporate taxes and royalty payments.

The authors conclude that when used at all, LCRs should be part of a comprehensive policy to promote institutional development and to foster intersectoral partnerships. They note that government support for sectors that rely on local mineral extraction may exacerbate the impacts of materials price fluctuations, harm the local ecology, and interfere with diversification of the broader economy. Instead, Korinek and De Sa suggest that resource-rich countries devote greater attention to promoting macroeconomic stability, removing barriers to entry, providing a transparent and stable regulatory environment, and improving local infrastructure, institutions, and skill levels.

Chapter 4 by Keith Head, Thierry Mayer, and Marc Melitz analyzes the tighter rules of origin that now apply to the North American automobile industry following the renegotiation of the regional trade agreement that was formerly NAFTA and now is USMCA. NAFTA required regional content of 62.5% of value for cars to qualify for duty-free entry into one of its members. The USMCA raised this regional content requirement to 75% and introduced additional, binding requirements. The tightening of the RoOs and the adding of additional requirements clearly were intended to discourage firms from sourcing parts from outside North America, which the parties (and especially the United States) hoped would bolster demand for North American parts.

In a companion paper, Head et al. (2022), the authors extend the one-input Grossman (1981) model to include many inputs. However, their main result, unlike what was emphasized by Grossman, does not rely on a reduction in the number of completed automobiles. Instead, they make another important observation. Firms in the automobile industry retain the option to choose the cost-minimizing source of parts, provided they are willing to sacrifice the treaty's tariff benefit and pay the MFN tariff whenever a completed car crosses a border. Indeed, Head et al. document in Chapter 4 that compliance with the RoOs has declined since the introduction of the stricter USMCA rules. If compliance rates fall sufficiently, a tighter RoO intended to expand value added within the region might have the opposite effect. The authors term the inverted-U shape relationship between the strictness of RoOs and the regional value added a "Laffer curve for RoOs."

The authors take their model to the data, using detailed information on the source of engines and transmissions for all car models assembled in North America. Since the U.S. MFN tariff on automobiles is only 2.5% and only a fraction of the cars assembled in Mexico are exported (a fraction that varies by model), it stands to reason that some producers will be willing to pay the tariff in lieu of sourcing more expensive parts. Simulation of the model predicts that 16.9% of models that complied with a binding RoO under NAFTA will become non-compliant under the tighter RoOs of USMCA. These firms account for a predicted 11.9% fall in employment in plants that manufacture parts, offsetting the 23.6% rise in employment that the model predicts for plants that choose to comply with a binding RoO ex post. Overall, the model predicts employment gains of only 2.3% in plants that manufacture parts, much smaller than the 20% gains that would have been expected had they assumed that all carlines comply with the new RoOs. Had the new RoOs been set at 85%, as the United States had initially demanded, employment in parts manufacturing actually would have declined, according to the model's estimates.

The authors also simulate the effects of BREXIT on the European car industry. After Britain's withdrawal from the European Union, the country negotiated a new pact known as the European Union and United Kingdom Trade and Cooperation Act. The TCA requires regional content of 55% for British cars to enter duty free into the European Union and for EU cars to enter similarly into Great Britain. The authors note that 85% of carlines already satisfied this requirement prior to TCA, suggesting that the plants manufacturing these models will be little affected. On the other hand, the MFN tariff in both Britain and the European Union is 10%, much higher than the level in the United States, suggesting that firms that did not already satisfy the new RoOs beforehand may well choose not to comply. The simulations again indicate that a fall in employment in parts manufacturers serving firms that choose not to comply will offset the employment gains in firms that comply with a newly binding constraint. Overall, the gains in employment are predicted to be less than 1%.

The analysis by Head et al. in Chapter 4 emphasizes that overly strict LCRs that are not subject to mandate but rather are supported by fiscal incentives may be counterproductive. Firms that would have complied with a milder restriction may opt out once the requirements become too severe.

Chapter 5 by Kun Cai and Zhi Wang analyzes LCR policies in China, with a particular emphasis on the Made in China 2025 policy. The chapter begins with an overview of China's LCR framework, noting that these policies were explicit prior to China's accession to the WTO but became more opaque afterward. Although the legally mandated LCR percentages for goods or services were gradually lifted, implicit localization biases ingrained in the implementation of industrial policies took their place. On the surface, these policies treat producers similarly regardless of nationality, but in practice, only indigenous firms can benefit from many of the preferential policies, and when foreign producers are able to participate, often they are "encouraged" to transfer technology or to source locally. The opaque nature of the current LCR policies makes them difficult to measure precisely, but the authors argue that their effects are very heterogeneous across sectors. Moreover, Beijing has launched a recent campaign to encourage the development of more advanced technologies at home to rely less on the United States and other Western suppliers. China aims to bolster indigenous firms' capacity for innovation and to have them become global leaders in advanced technologies. To further these objectives, various government agencies in China at different levels have implemented a series of industrial policies, including some implicit LCRs that benefit local firms.

Cai and Wang are especially interested in the impacts of China's LCR policies on the domestic value added embodied in exports. They extend the Koopman et al. (2012) methodology for using world input-output matrices to attribute value added in exports to source countries so as to allow for circumstances as in China, where a sizable fraction of exported goods is produced in export processing facilities that are able to import their raw materials and components duty free. The authors use the input-output matrices published by China's National Bureau of Statistics for 2007, 2012, and 2017, along with detailed trade statistics from China Customs. Using the changes that occurred during the periods between the publication of these data, they estimate the impact of China's LCR policies on the fraction of domestic value added in total exports, manufacturing exports, and exports of foreign-owned firms. In the aggregate, domestic value added in exports rose from 64.6% in 2007 to 65.3% in 2012 and to 69.9% in 2017. The estimated gains are smaller when only manufacturing is considered, and they mask opposing trends for normal and processing exports. Whereas the domestic value-added share in normal manufacturing exports increased from 2007 to 2017, the share in processing exports actually declined. Focusing only on foreign owned firms, they find a slight decline over the period.

The authors also study changes in domestic value added in exports at the industry level, comparing only 2012 with 2017, because industry definitions changed after 2007. Roughly one-third of the 68 industries, accounting for 20% of total exports, had a domestic value-added share in exports between 51% and 75% in 2012. These were mostly capital-intensive industries such as basic chemicals, iron and steel, lifting and handling equipment, pumps, generators, and batteries. Roughly half of the industries, accounting for 25% of total exports, had a domestic value share in the earlier year greater than 75%. These industries were more labor intensive, including textiles, apparel, footwear, leather, and furniture. The lowest domestic value-added shares were found in the more technologically sophisticated industries, such as computers, communication equipment, and electronic components, where foreign ownership plays a major role. Comparing the estimates for 2012 and 2017, 15 of the 68 industries saw their domestic value-added share in exports rise by more than 5%, and 4 experienced an increase of greater than 9%.

Cai and Wang concede that their methodology does not allow them to test for a causal relationship between LCR policies and domestic content outcomes. Still, their accounting decomposition leads them to conclude that the various LCR policies implicit in China's industrial strategy did not seem to play a significant role in promoting increased local content in China's exports between 2007 and 2017.

Chapter 6 by Michelle Limenta, Lili Yan Ing, Junianto James Losari, and Oscar Fernando is the first of three that focuses on LCRs in Indonesia. Indonesia is among the countries with the highest incidence of local content restrictions, with LCR policies dating back to the 1950s. LCRs have long appealed to Indonesian policymakers who are keen to encourage domestic value added and expand employment in the industrial sector.

Limenta et al. consider in detail whether Indonesia's LCR policies are consistent with its commitments under its various multilateral and regional trade and investment agreements. They begin by outlining the justifications offered by the Indonesian government for its various policies. These include the country's goal of upgrading competitiveness and eliminating its trade deficit, which the government believes can be achieved by increasing local value added in traded sectors.

The use of LCRs began in Indonesia with the "Benteng Program" (1950–1957), followed by the "Deletion Program" (1974–1993) and the "National Car Program" (1996). After a period of dormancy, Indonesia resumed in 2009 a local content strategy with the implementation of the "Increased Use of Domestic Production" program. This policy introduced local content requirements for goods and services purchased by the government. In 2013, Indonesia implemented the aforementioned regulation stipulating a minimum percentage of domestic oil and gas as input into the local production of many goods. Since that time, many members of the WTO have challenged Indonesia's policies in the Trade-Related Investment Measures (TRIMS) Committee, claiming that they run counter to commitments that Indonesia made to its trade and investment partners. Of particular concern to the WTO members have been policies regulating the use of domestically produced energy, as well as policies addressed to the telecommunications, pharmaceutical, and retail sectors.

The authors proceed to review Indonesia's relevant commitments under TRIMS, the General Agreement on Tariffs and Trade (GATT), the General

Agreement on Trade in Services (GATS), and the Subsidies and Countervailing Measures (SCM). They also outline commitments under Indonesia's various regional and bilateral trade agreements and its comprehensive economic partnership agreement (CEPA). Finally, they discuss commitments under investment agreements such as its bilateral investment treaties (BITS) and the investment chapters in its regional trade agreements and CEPA. Next, they review the case law in the WTO Dispute Settlement Body and in the Investment-State Dispute Settlement (ISDS) that addresses LCR policies implemented by other countries, in particular the United States, China, Japan and South Korea.

Limenta et al. conclude that Indonesia's various trade and investment agreements do impose disciplines on its use of LCRs. They argue that the LCRs that Indonesia has used to target strategic sectors likely violate the terms of the WTO treaty. Indonesia provides fiscal and other benefits to firms based on their use of domestic input and services, which negatively impacts competitive opportunities of foreign producers of like products. Such policies run counter to the principle of national treatment that lies at the core of the TRIMS and the GATT, even if compliance is voluntary. The government of Indonesia should be more aware of the risk it takes in violating its international commitments, even if challenges to its LCR policies do not appear to be imminent. It should consider replacing its LCRs with other policies that encouraged increased domestic value added that do not run counter to its international commitments.

Chapter 7 by Yessi Vadila and David Christian examines the dynamic impacts of LCRs in Indonesia on its trade flows between 2004 and 2020. The authors identify 16 regulatory documents that contain LCRs and map these to the product codes that are affected each year. When they merge the LCR dataset with Indonesia's trade data at the 8-digit HS level, they find that as many as 740 products, or roughly 8% of all products, received an LCR policy treatment during the period under review.

Using an event-study methodology, the authors apply a difference-in-differences (DID) estimator to assess whether the presence of an LCR on a product lead to a different trade outcome up to five years following the implementation compared to products that are not subject to such a restriction. The study focuses on LCRs with backward consequences, i.e., those that are imposed on producers of final goods that use other products as inputs. The study includes some covariates in the regressions, such as tariff rates imposed by Indonesia and its trading partners at the product level, economic and trade variables that characterize the demands by its leading trading partners for each product in each year, and several gravity variables corresponding to the primary trade partners for each product.

Vadila and Christian find a negative and significant association between the implementation of an LCR and the growth of exports within five years, especially as concerns manufacturing products. Their results point to a steeper relative decline in export value than in export volume, which is suggestive of a loss in competitiveness due to the LCR. In contrast, the results tend to suggest a positive relationship between LCRs and product-level imports, albeit not one that is statistically significant. In further analysis by product group, one of their key findings is that LCRs are associated with a decline in both imports and exports of products that are highly linked to other sectors that are subject to LCRs, which suggests that Indonesian industry has relocated resources to satisfy the LCRs. The findings in this chapter serve as a timely reminder for policymakers to exercise caution when introducing LCRs, given the potentially harmful consequences for trade and competitiveness that LCRs may generate, especially in sectors that produce and export manufactures.

Chapter 8 by Lili Yan Ing and Rui Zhang quantifies the impacts of LCRs on costs, sales, employment, and prices in Indonesia. They focus on a single regulation, namely the Ministry of Energy and Mineral Resources Regulation No. 15/2013, which imposes penalties on suppliers of the upstream oil and gas sector that do not comply with specified minimum percentages of domestic content.

Ing and Zhang introduce a compliance decision into the input-sourcing model developed by Blaum et al. (2018). As in Head et al., firms trade off the higher unit costs they face if they choose to comply against a penalty that is imposed for non-compliance when selling to the upstream oil and gas sector. The model allows for firm heterogeneity in reliance on imported inputs in the production process. The more dependent is a firm on imported inputs in the unconstrained equilibrium, the greater will be the burden imposed by complying with the LCR and the less likely it is that the firm will comply. The model allows the authors to measure the cost of compliance for each firm as functions of their local content, production parameters, and non-compliance fees. Then the equilibrium model can be used to estimate the effects on production costs in firms that are not bound by an LCR in response to the changes in product and factor demands by the firms that do choose to comply.

Ing and Zhang calibrate the model's parameters so that its equilibrium matches data for 2012, just prior to when the LCR policy was first introduced. Then they simulate a counterfactual that represents the LCR that regulates the use of domestic content in the upstream oil and gas sector. They find that the LCR is binding for larger manufacturing firms that have higher import shares and that the LCR-bound firms that import the most are less likely to comply, because they face the highest compliance costs, which, on average, amount to 24% of their original unit costs.

Next, the authors examine the impact of the LCR on firms in different sectors, decomposing the effects according to whether firms were constrained compliers, unconstrained compliers (non-binding firms), and non-compliers. Although the LCR is estimated to have generated an increase in the local contents of compliers, they find that the effect on the local content of non-compliers and unconstrained is negative (but small). This surprising outcome reflects that firms for which the LCR was not binding or not applicable substituted away from local content in response to higher domestic input costs induced by the LCR. The estimates suggest that the higher domestic input costs that resulted from the regulation depress aggregate output and employment by 0.2% and 0.1%, respectively. The estimates also suggest substantial reallocation of sales to the upstream oil and gas sector between compliers and non-compliers. Compliers see an average increase in their sales to the upstream oil and gas sector of 13%, whereas non-compliers experience an average decrease in their sales to the same sector of 34%. The LCR in the oil and gas sector is estimated to increase the consumer price by 0.4% and thus reduce consumer welfare.

The chapter by Ing and Zhang in particular highlights the importance of recognizing firm heterogeneity when evaluating the impacts of LCR policies.

References

Blaum, J., C. Lelarge, and M. Peters. 2018. The Gains from Input Trade with Heterogeneous Importers. *American Economic Journal: Macroeconomics*, 10, pp. 77–127.

Cadot, O., and L. Y. Ing. 2019. How Restrictive are ASEAN's Rules of Origin?, in *East Asian Integration: Goods, Services and Investment*, eds. Lili Yan Ing, Martin Richardson, and Shujiro Urata, https://doi.org/10.4324/9780429433603

Cadot, O., and others (eds). 2006. *The Origin of Goods: Rules of Origin in Regional Trade Agreements*, 1 May, online edn. Oxford: Oxford Academic, https://doi.org/10.1093/0199290482.001.0001

Conconi, P., M. García-Santana, L. Puccio, and R. Venturini. 2018. From Final Goods to Inputs: The Protectionist Effect of Rules of Origin, *American Economic Review*, 108 (8), pp. 2335–2365.

Corden, W. M. 1971. The Theory of Protection, *The Economic Journal*, 82 (325), pp. 261–262, https://doi.org/10.2307/2230241

Dixit, A. K., and G. M. Grossman. 1982. Trade and Protection with Multistage Production, *The Review of Economic Studies*, 49 (4), October, pp. 583–594, https://doi.org/10.2307/2297288

Grossman, G. M. 1981. The Theory of Domestic Content Protection and Content Preference, *The Quarterly Journal of Economics*, 96 (4), pp. 583–603.

Head, K., T. Mayer, and M. Melitz. 2022. *The Laffer Curve for Rules of Origin*. Manuscript.

Hufbauer, G. C., J. J. Schott, C. Cimino-Isaacs, M. Vieiro, and E. Wada. 2013. *Local Content Requirements: A Global Problem*. Washington, DC: Peterson Institute for International Economics.

Johnson, H. G. 1971. The Theory of Content Protection, in *Aspects of the Theory of Tariffs*, https://doi.org/10.4324/9780203491560

Johnson, L. J. 1967. Problems of Import Substitution: The Chilean Automobile Industry, *Economic Development and Cultural Change*, 15 (2), pp. 202–216.

Koopman, R., Z. Wang, S. J. Wei. 2012. Estimating Domestic Content in Exports when Processing Trade is Pervasive[J]. *Journal of development economics*, 99 (1) pp. 178–189.

Korinek, J., and I. Ramdoo. 2017. Local Content Policies in Mineral-Exporting Countries. *OECD Trade Policy Papers*. No. 209. Paris: Organisation for Economic Co-operation and Development. http://dx.doi.org/10.1787/4b9b2617-en

Krueger, A. O. 2012. Struggling with Success: Challenges Facing the International Economy, January, https://doi.org/10.1142/8307

Lloyd, P. J. 1971. The Value of Tariff Preferences for the Developing Countries: Australian Experience. *Economic Record*, https://doi.org/10.1111/j.1475-4932.1971.tb00742.x

Munk, B. 1969. The Welfare Costs of Content Protection: The Automotive Industry in Latin America. *Journal of Political Economy*, 77 (1), pp. 85–98.

Pursell, G. 2001. Australia's Experience with Local Content Programs in the Auto Industry: Lessons for India and Other Developing Countries. *World Bank Policy Research Working Papers*. https://doi.org/10.1596/1813-9450-2625

Stone, S., J. Messent, and D. Flaig. 2015. Emerging Policy Issues: Localisation Barriers to Trade. *OECD Trade Policy Papers*. No. 180. Paris: Organisation for Economic Co-operation and Development.

Wonnacott, R. J., and P. Wonnacott 1967. *Free Trade Between the United States and Canada: The Potential Economic Effects*. Cambridge: Harvard University Press.

2 Localization measures

A global perspective

Dorothee Flaig and Susan F. Stone

1 Introduction

In the ongoing effort by countries to provide a conducive environment for economic growth, a measure that remains quite popular with policymakers is a localization requirement or local content requirement (LCR). Generally, these measures have been defined as an industrial policy that requires a given percentage of domestic value added or domestic intermediate inputs to be embodied in final goods (Grossman, 1981). While localization barriers can cover a variety of specific measures (notably involving government procurement), in general, they refer to measures that favor domestic input-producing industries at the expense of foreign competitors.

While LCRs have been traditionally associated with the extractive sectors, they have been applied in several other sectors, including automobiles, information technology (IT), health care, and agriculture (Hufbauer et al., 2013). Energy and IT show a particularly frequent use of LCRs (Cimino-Isaacs, Hufbauer, and Schott, 2014). The design of each LCR determines its ultimate impact. Many measures have a very sector-focused design, while others are more broadly defined.

Examples of localization barriers include:

- Requirements to purchase domestically manufactured goods or domestically supplied services.
- Subsidies or other preferences, including tax breaks and below-market financing, tied to the use of local goods, locally owned service providers, or domestically owned or developed intellectual property (IP), or IP that is first registered in that country.
- Requirements to provide services using local facilities or infrastructure.
- Measures to force the transfer of technology or IP.
- Unjustified requirements to conduct or carry out duplicative conformity-assessment procedures in the country. These LCRs, especially applied in the technology sector, have attracted a great deal of attention lately.

DOI: 10.4324/9781003415794-2

The overarching policy goal of an LCR is to stimulate the domestic economy by increasing investment, training, employment, and tax revenue. For example, extractive industries use them to try to protect emerging downstream operations to increase the domestic share of higher value-added activities. LCRs have also been put in place to create opportunities for local companies to benefit from large-scale foreign investments. It is hoped that these foreign-funded projects will fuel local small and medium-sized enterprise (SME) development. The idea is that by requiring domestic participation, the local economy will benefit through increased demand.

Why use local content requirements?

Countries implement policies that give some sort of preference to domestic inputs for several reasons. These include political pressure from constituents to ensure that domestic businesses do not lose their market share and jobs to overseas competitors. Governments often use LCRs to promote or establish a key sector (e.g., information and communication technology equipment, automobiles, or financial services). Despite the large number of studies examining LCRs, a consensus on the merits of these policies has yet to be reached. Typically, the domestic input producers gain from the LCR, but for a net increase in economic welfare to be realized, these gains need to outweigh the losses not just to domestic final good producers and consumers but to other sectors in the economy. These losses tend to be larger when the policy results in market power in either input or final good markets.

Several factors can influence the extent to which these policies benefit the domestic economy. When countries expand opportunities for trade, there are two opposing effects on domestic firms. One is that the cost of exporting decreases, leading to greater sales for domestic firms that export. The second is that domestic competition increases as imports rise, leading to a reduction in the sales of domestic firms. Which outcome dominates depends on individual firm characteristics. While the short-term impact of LCRs often makes them politically attractive, over the longer run, it is hoped that the industry will become a self-sustaining source of jobs and exports, a conduit for technology, or an inroad to global supply chains (Tordo et al., 2013; Kuntze and Moerenhout, 2013; Hufbauer et al., 2013; Stephenson, 2013). However, the more common outcome is that firms incorporate these government incentives into their long-run cost structures and rarely reach the self-sufficiency stage.

Firms receiving preferential treatment in the domestic market can then use that position to cross-subsidize their exported goods – i.e., making higher profits than would otherwise be the case (without the LCR policy) allows these firms to charge lower prices in export markets. This can potentially undercut competitors in global markets and lead to global trade conflicts that hurt other domestic exporters (Ettmayr and Lloyd, 2017). Moreover, LCRs can limit competition for the target industry and lead to a deterioration in product quality, as they reduce access to technologically advanced inputs and provide little incentive for internal innovation (Hufbauer et al., 2013). Corruption and favoritism from opaque and ad hoc policy design can also increase the long-run negative impact of these policies (Kuntze and Moerenhout, 2013; Weiss, 2016). The objectives of LCRs – such as building up a competitive industry through stronger industrial links, creating new suppliers and backward linkages – is rarely obtained (Hufbauer et al., 2013). In most cases, LCRs isolate high-cost producers from global competition and innovation and result in insufficient incentives for research and development (R&D) investments.

Most LCRs implemented have employment as their primary objective, explicitly or implicitly stated. The use of domestic suppliers has an immediate job effect that can be particularly powerful during economic downturns. LCRs with employment objectives encompass goals such as creating new jobs, creating higher-skilled jobs, and increasing national income. However, these policies often sacrifice job growth in the general economy for job growth in the targeted sector. The United States (US) Buy American Act, 1933, is estimated to have cost about 360,000 jobs in non-targeted sectors throughout the US economy (Dixon, Rimmer, and Waschik, 2018).

Measures targeting technological development tend to require foreign firms to transfer technology to domestic operations or domestic suppliers. To the implementing economy, this technology transfer is seen as an efficient way of increasing competitiveness in world markets. The specific goals of technological development can include improving technological capacity and spurring innovation at the national, regional, or industry level. However, these goals are often undermined by a lack of available skills.

Factors that impact the ability to meet an LCR's stated policy objective can be characterized across four areas: (i) market size and stability, (ii) policy design and coherence, (iii) the restrictiveness of the LCRs, and (iv) the domestic industrial base (Kaziboni and Stern, 2021). If the domestic market is small or unstable and cannot meet the demands of the local producers, there is a risk that these local producers exit the market, defeating any employment or technology-transfer goals. A policy that is too vague is usually unenforceable, and it will not be effective. Moreover, if the LCR is set at a level that does not have a meaningful impact on the sourcing decisions of the importer, no change will occur. Some LCRs are set below existing sourcing levels, having no impact on market decisions. Finally, if there are no credible producers of the input, then any LCR policy will simply lead to firms exiting the market.

Governments often attempt to achieve several policy objectives with one LCR (e.g., increase output and employment along with technology transfer). In these instances, the policy often ends up having contradictory outcomes (e.g., increasing production but decreasing productivity if labor is unable to implement the transferred technology). Subsequent productivity declines, coupled with shortages of sufficiently skilled labor, may lead to an overall lower level of labor demand, showing that one policy is often unable to hit two targets (Fang, 2020). Policymakers often neglect to identify practical challenges that might negatively impact the efficiency and effectiveness of LCRs when adopting these measures. There is limited consideration of the fact that the economic impact of LCRs is complex and depends on several variables, including their interaction across policy areas (Lin and Weng, 2020). The political influence of producers can also affect the level of local participation. Ablo (2017) shows that while LCRs have the potential to promote links between some sectors and the rest of the economy, the degree to which producers support the government may limit the extent to which significant local content can be achieved. Thus, the political relationship between the government and industry, the capacity of local SMEs, and the techniques and practices of multinational companies will all have a bearing on the effectiveness of any LCR policy.

By limiting competition and input choices, the target firm faces a limited, if not single, supplier – leading to higher input costs along the production line. This can also affect the quality of the material/input, which can further impact costs. These higher costs are then passed on, in whole or in part, downstream, increasing costs to both the consumer and producer. This ultimately means higher prices for the end user.

Another way LCRs can have a detrimental effect on the domestic market is through resource allocation effects. Resources being shifted to the targeted firm/industry become scarcer elsewhere in the domestic market, raising costs to other firms. Another longer-term spillover in the domestic economy relates to innovation and skills development. While evidence shows that targeted firms will undertake training and development of local firms to meet LCR targets (Ramdoo, 2015), this leaves little motivation in the domestic firms to innovate, as they have little or no competition to spur such innovation. This can affect the degree to which firms across the economy engage in innovative behavior. This lack of innovation can create the longest-lasting, most detrimental effects of an LCR. A recent study (Kingiri and Okemwa, 2022) shows that local content policies have not had a positive impact on technology development in the Kenyan renewable energy sector.

From the perspective of public expenditures, LCRs reduce import tariff revenue as well as potential corporate tax revenue by increasing the operating costs and reducing the profitability of multinational companies (Kolstad and Kinyondo, 2017). Imposing LCRs has the opportunity cost of forgone taxes, which could be used in more effective ways to improve development prospects. In the case of incentive-based LCRs, governments often forego revenue from or provide incentive payments to these ventures, which has direct public expenditure implications. In addition, past experiences of resource-rich developing countries indicate that local content policies can exacerbate key problems of patronage and rent-seeking, increasing the danger that the resource wealth will undermine rather than help development (Kolstad and Kinyondo, 2017).

This chapter extends and updates our earlier study from 2015 (Stone, Messent, and Flaig, 2015). It discusses recent instances of LCRs and, by modeling representative examples of the policy, provides some insights on the impact they have on the economy. Section 2 examines recent trends in their implementation. Section 3 outlines the measures examined for this study and the modeling approach adopted. Section 4 provides the simulation results, while Section 5 presents some concluding thoughts.

2 Recent LCR implementation

The use of LCRs has been accelerating in recent years. According to Global Trade Alert,[1] countries put in place more than 500 individual local content measures from 2014 to 2020 compared with less than 200 measures from 2008 to 2013 – a 155% increase (Figure 2.1). Not only has the number of measures increased, the way in which they have been implemented has changed. The less transparent types of instruments have risen, with the Global Trade Alert measures rated amber ("likely" to cause discrimination) increasing significantly over those rated red ("almost certainly" causing discrimination against foreign companies). That is, the number of measures that clearly state the type and requirements of an LCR restriction has declined as a share of the total number of LCRs imposed. Only 6% of the measures were rated amber during 2008–2013, whereas 32% of the measures were rated amber during 2014–2020.

On the surface, India, Germany, and the United Kingdom appear to be the main users of LCRs (Figure 2.1). However, the actual impact of these measures is much more complex. First, as noted, Global Trade Alert provides a count of the incidence of a measure, not its impact. Thus, a measure affecting a specific small sector (e.g., Argentina's LCR on certain types of medicines from Spain) counts the same as a general measure affecting a much larger sector (e.g., Russian restrictions on auto parts to the automotive sector for all trade partners). Second, a tightly binding measure counts the same as one that is only partially binding or not binding at all.

In addition, many economies implement these measures at a variety of jurisdictional levels. Larger economies with decentralized economies (e.g., the US and India) have many measures implemented at the level of the individual state or even the local level of government. Others have a much more centralized approach, while still others (e.g., France and Germany) have policies implemented at the supranational level. The variety of instances makes identifying and measuring LCRs challenging.

Global Trade Alert reports LCRs across four intervention types: labor, operations, sourcing, and incentivizing. Labor generally refers to LCRs tied directly to hiring and employment requirements. Operations are LCRs that have requirements concerning a firm's ability/permission to operate in the domestic market. Sourcing refers to the requirements to source inputs (parts and components) from local manufacturers. Incentives are tax or other government benefits received when buying or using local inputs, operations, or labor.

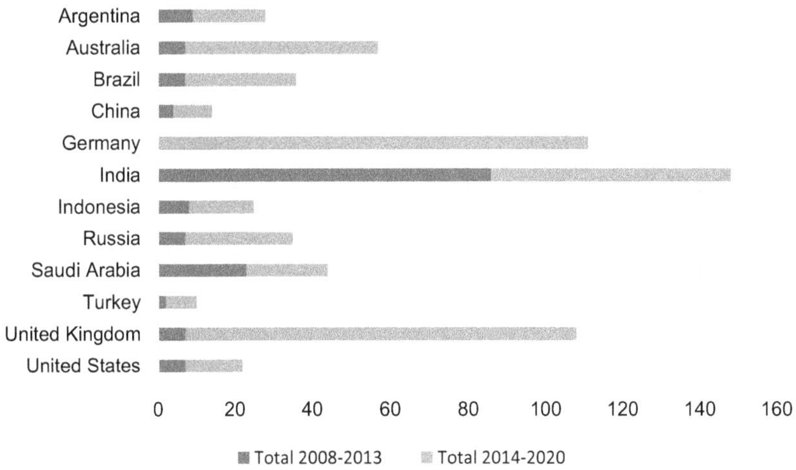

Figure 2.1 Incidence of Local Content Requirements, 2008–2020* (Selected Economies)

BNDES = The Brazilian Development Bank, LCR = local content requirement.

Note: The numbers represent individual instances of LCRs, so their actual impact is not directly comparable. For example, in 2015, BNDES financed three wind parks with $260 million. As these measures affected different trading partners and different sectors within wind turbines, they accounted for 57 of the 594 measures of local sourcing for Brazil. Argentina's LCR on mining counts as one measure yet affects more than 10 sectors measured at the 2-digit level across all trading partners.

* The large number of LCRs attributed to Germany all relate to support given under Germany's Export Credits program.

Source: Global Trade Alert (2022).

Figure 2.2 shows how the types of LCRs used by governments have changed over time. Whereas in the period right after the Global Financial Crisis (2008–2013) LCRs focused on ensuring that inputs and labor were sourced locally, the later period (2014–2020) switched to incentivizing firms by offering tax breaks, preferential lending, or other perks tied to using local inputs or establishing local production. The number of measures offering incentives more than doubled from less than 6% of all measures in 2008–2013 to more than 12% in 2014–2020.

As described by Deringer et al. (2018), Global Trade Alert ranked tracked policy interventions by their possible damage to foreign trade and investment. According to this ranking, LCRs representing public procurement localization are ranked fifth, and measures representing other localization requirements are ranked seventh (Evenett and Fritz, 2021). Ranking ahead of LCRs are (i) state aid, (ii) trade defense, (iii) import tariffs, and (iv) export taxes or restrictions, with trade finance measures in sixth place (Evenett and Fritz, 2021). LCRs

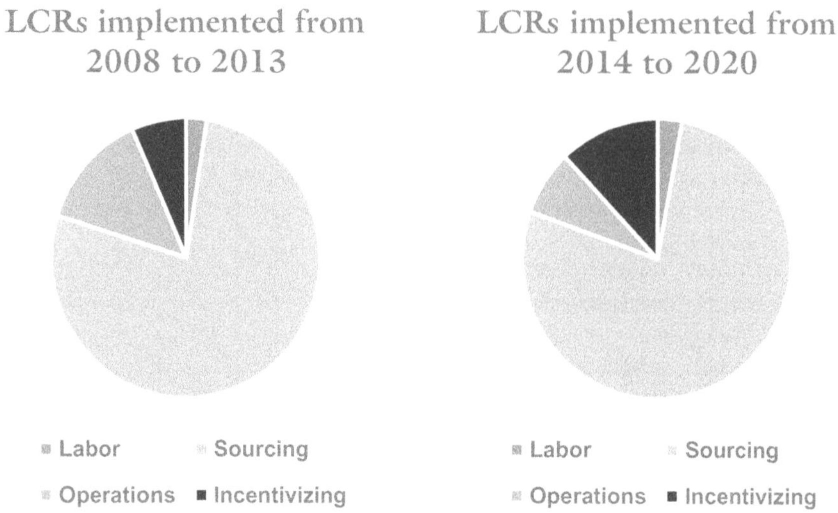

Figure 2.2 Type of Local Content Requirements

LCR = local content requirement.

Source: Global Trade Alert (2022).

are also frequently implemented in the form of discriminatory government procurement. These measures reduce the number of eligible firms allowed to compete in a market and thus decrease output and employment while increasing procurement costs and market power (OECD, 2020).

Measures related to data localization are among the fastest-growing types of LCR measures. Such measures attempt to control the movement of personal data and local storage and processing of data (López González, Casalini, and Porras, 2022). As data flow is becoming an essential aspect of trade, related LCR measures affect most sectors within an economy (OECD, 2020). Some experts perceive this type of protectionism as "perhaps today's greatest threat to the further liberalization of the global trading system" (Ezell, Atkinson, and Wein, 2013).[2] At the same time, the increasing connection of trade and data flows may also provide a stronger rationale for such measures to ensure privacy and identity security.

3 Defining measures to be addressed

It has been argued that localization barriers add to the cost of doing business domestically and internationally, leading to a distortion of world trade flows and lost market opportunities. However, the studies attempting to quantify these impacts across global markets have been limited. This chapter will update one such attempt (Stone, Messent, and Flaig, 2015) by estimating the impact of a set of LCRs on international trade, using the Organisation for Economic Co-operation and Development (OECD) trade model, METRO. This set of LCRs is defined from information taken from several data sources and constitutes current in-force LCR policies that were put in place from 2014 to 2020.[3] Similar to the work undertaken in Stone, Messent, and Flaig (2015), several sources were consulted. These include the following:

- Peterson Institute for International Economics *Local Content Requirements: A Global Problem* (Hufbauer et al., 2013)
- Global Trade Alert online database
- European Commission (2022) Market Access Database
- World Bank (2022) Temporary Trade Barriers Database
- World Trade Organization (2022) Trade Monitoring Database

More than 565 measures were considered for the study. All the identified LCRs were then reviewed to assess their affinity to quantification. The quantitative analysis presented here focuses on measures that tend to be the most trade distorting. These are measures that restrict access to markets and measures that render price preferences tied to a specific level of domestic content. Input measures that determine market access accounted for most of the measures examined for this report. To arrive at a list of measures whose impacts could be quantified, several criteria had to be met. Following the discussion on localization characteristics already, four characteristics can be identified:

1 Identifiable sector – many of the LCRs were broad statements about "supporting" domestic sourcing without direct reference to a particular sector or region of economic activity. For example, countries put in place LCRs for government procurement. These are blanket policies that may or may not be implemented in any specific sector. Given that there is no way to identify which, if any, sectors were affected by these policies, these measures were excluded from the analysis.
2 Identifiable restriction – if the restriction is not clearly indicated, it cannot be meaningfully enforced and thus cannot be modeled. For example, Turkey introduced localization requirements on remote programmable e-SIM technologies without stipulating the size of these requirements.
3 Sufficient size – if the sector or region is not significant, it will have little impact on the market. An example is an Argentine law obliging automobile fuel producers to use bioethanol from the northeast of the country. Neither the bioethanol market nor the northeast region is sufficiently large to be captured in an economy-wide model.
4 Enforceable restriction – there must be a domestic sector that can meet the required demand, and the restriction must be binding (i.e., the measure is excluded if the domestic content already meets or exceeds the level called for in the LCR).

Many of the instruments examined were implemented at the subnational level, which the model does not cover. As noted above, policies related to broad goals such as national security or government procurement can be applied over multiple sectors or not and are at the discretion of government agents. Finally, for many of the measures reported, we were unable to determine if they are still in force. Thus, these were also dropped from the analysis.

Applying these criteria, we were able to identify seven LCRs that meet the conditions necessary for modeling. They provide a good sample of the types of LCR measures applied and the economies applying them. Both developed and developing countries are included in the analysis. This study estimates the economic impact of LCRs imposed in selected subsectors of automobiles, mining, medical supplies, telecommunications, and transport. Finally, some "buy local" procurement provisions are at such a level that noncompliance would undermine a firm's competitive position, making them a "requirement." Thus, we include examples of two such government procurement provisions.

Argentine automotive sector. Since 2016, Argentine car producers can obtain a tax credit, allowing them to defer value-added tax (VAT). This tax credit is conditional on a minimum LCR in the final product. The minimum LCR is 30% for cars, trailers, engines, and agricultural vehicles; 25% for trucks; and 10% for automobile parts. The tax benefit is dependent on the level of local content and ranges from 4% to 15% of the sales value. The Argentine motor vehicle industry has an approximate sales value of $4.5 billion, so the value of this credit is $180 million to $675 million.

Brazilian telecommunications sector. In 2017, Brazil implemented a requirement that the overall level of local content in the equipment used in its 4G networks must be at least 70%. The estimated size of the telecommunications sector in Brazil is more than $8.5 million, with almost 200 million 4G broadband subscribers. The estimated investment in telecommunications equipment was about $5.8 billion in 2018, implying a potential market of more than $4 billion solely available to domestic suppliers. This requirement comes on top of existing LCRs in the Brazilian telecommunications sector (Stone, Messent, and Flaig, 2015).

Brazilian government procurement. In 2013 and 2014, the government of Brazil increased the preference margins for the public procurement of a variety of nationally produced goods. Preference margins are the maximum extent to which the price quoted by a local supplier may be above that of a competitor. The new margins range between 9% and 25% and include IT (15%), tractors (20%), airplanes (9%–25%), various IT-related goods and services (15%–25%), capital goods (15%–20%), and toys (10%). These margins were deemed sufficiently high, given the various market sizes, for firms to be compelled to use local suppliers to remain competitive.

Indonesian automotive industry. To promote the Indonesian motor vehicle components industry, several regulations implemented from 2014 to 2017 require de facto the entire assembly process of motor vehicles and motorcycles to take place locally. To have access to the Indonesian market, the LCR requires all major vehicle components and related services to take place within Indonesia. The Indonesian automotive market accounts for about 10% of Indonesia's gross domestic product (GDP), or roughly $10 billion, with almost 25% destined for export markets.

Saudi Arabian medical supplies. Since 2020, it is mandatory for government agencies to procure a range of medical supplies domestically, such as sterilizers, face masks, personal protective equipment for health practitioners, sterilization supplies for medical tools, and other medical supplies. The market for medical supplies in Saudi Arabia is estimated to be more than $2 billion.

South African mining. The Mining Charter adopted in 2018 by South Africa establishes a minimum LCR of at least 70% for mining goods and 80% for total service expenditure in the sector. In addition, at least 21% of mining goods and 50% of services must be produced by a domestic company owned and controlled by "Historically Disadvantaged Persons," another 5% (goods)/5%–15% (services) must be produced by companies owned by women or youth, and 44% (goods)/10% (services) by companies compliant with local Black Economic Empowerment (BEE). In 2018, the mining sector accounted for $22.5 billion of South African GDP and employed an estimated 456,000 workers.

US Buy America. This far-reaching program has many provisions implemented on a preferential-treatment basis. However, transportation grants across many US states have a specific requirement for local content to be eligible to receive funding. Given that the main source of transportation funding is the federal government, for most US states, this amounts to an LCR. These programs stipulate that any public project funded by Transportation Investment Generating Economic Recovery (TIGER) grants must use some level of domestically produced iron, steel, and other manufactured goods. The amounts of both the grants and the LCR vary by individual states and projects within states but are estimated to be worth more than $4 billion.

Model and data

LCRs may have short-term benefits in terms of specific policy objectives, but adverse effects develop over time and often outweigh the short-term benefits. As with any model, not all the impacts of the policy will be fully reflected in the results. However, using a computable general equilibrium (CGE) model allows for the capture of these longer-run impacts, not to mention the effect these policies have on broader economic activity. The benefit of using a CGE model in this analysis is its ability to capture impacts beyond the targeted sector, showing the effects these measures have on the rest of the economy as well as the global trade environment.

The METRO model (Arriola et al., 2020) is based on empirical data and incorporates unique features of each region's economic system. The model is calibrated to an augmented Social Accounting Matrix (SAM) version of the Global Trade Analysis Project (GTAP) version 10 database (Aguiar et al., 2019). The database features trade flows disaggregated by use categories derived from the OECD Trade in Value Added (TiVA) database as well as United Nations (UN) sources and bilateral remittance data from GTAP satellite data, i.e., GMIG2 (Walmsley, Winters, and Ahmed, 2007).[4] These categories are intermediate use, use by households, use by government, and use by business/investment.

The sector detail depends on the sector coverage in the GTAP database, which distinguishes 65 sectors with more detail in agri-food, and other sectors depicted largely on the International Standard Industrial Classification of All Economic Activities (ISIC) 2-digit level. This sector coverage does not allow modeling of LCR measures at a detailed sector level. The database is aggregated for this study, as detailed in Table 2.A1. The agriculture, food, and textile sectors in the GTAP database are aggregated; the study features 43 sectors, of which 4 are related to the extraction industries, 17 are related to manufacturing, and 20 are in the service sector. The database distinguishes eight factors of production, two skilled and three skilled labor types, capital, land, and natural resources. Countries are aggregated to larger regional composites, singling out the relevant countries of the selected policies examined.

METRO is a comparative static global CGE model.[5] Global CGE models link various markets, economies, and sectors – employing economic theory to show interlinkages between agents, sectors, and economies by simultaneously determining prices and quantities. The strength of METRO lies in the detailed trade structure and the differentiation of production and consumption commodities by use – intermediate, household, government, and capital consumption. The differentiation of commodity supply, and thus the resulting trade flows, by use category improves the ability to depict and analyze specific policy instruments such as LCRs. The remainder of this section gives an overview of key features of the model. Please refer to the METRO model documentation (Arriola et al., 2020) for a detailed and complete description of the model data and equations.

The model is based on a series of regional SAMs, which are linked through trade relationships. Table 2.1 depicts the structure of the database, where income flows are read across rows and columns depict expenditures. Households, for example, receive income from factor services and remittance inflows and spend this income on private consumption, direct taxes, remittance outflows, and savings. Following accounting rules and depicting a complete and circular system, row and column sums must equalize. Thus, the total income

Table 2.1 METRO Model – Structure of the Database and Behavioral Relationships

Expenditure *Income flow*	*Commodities (by sector, imported and domestic, by use category)*	Use category: *Activities (by sector)*	*Factors*	Use category: *Household*	Use category: *Government*	Use category: *Capital*	*Margins (bilateral, by use category)*	*Rest of the world (bilateral, by use category)*
Commodities (by sector, imported and domestic, by use category)		Intermediate inputs: *Leontief input-output coefficients*		Private consumption: *Stone-Geary utility functions*	Public consumption: *Fixed shares*	Investment: *Fixed shares*	Margins exports: *Three-stage CET functions*	Exports: *Three-stage CET functions*
***Use category:* Activities (by sector)**	Domestic supply: *Total supply from domestic production*							
Factors (5 labor types, capital, land, and natural resources)		Value added: *multi-level CES production functions*						
***Use category:* Household**			Factor income: *Fixed shares of factor income*					Remittance inflows
***Use category:* Government**	Import tariffs, export taxes, sales taxes: *Ad valorem and specific*	Production taxes: *Ad valorem*	Factor taxes: *Average tax rates*	Direct taxes: *Average tax rates*				
***Use category:* Capital**			Depreciation: *Shares of factor income*	Private savings: *Shares of household income*	Public savings: *Residual*		*Current account balance on margins trade*	Foreign savings: *Current account balance*
Margins (bilateral, by use category)	Trade and transport margins: *Fixed coefficients*							
Rest of the world (bilateral, by use category)	Imports: *Three-level CES*			Remittance outflows: *Fixed proportion of disposable income*				

CES = constant elasticity of substitution, CET = constant elasticity of transformation.

Source: Adapted from McDonald and Thierfelder (2013).

of each entity must match the total expenditure. Commodities are differentiated by sector and further distinguished by imported and domestic and use category; producing activities are distinguished by sector; and the trading accounts (margins and rest of the world) are distinguished by partner region and use category.

Each economy is represented by a mix of linear and nonlinear relationships, outlined in Table 2.1. Domestic production is depicted by a multilevel nested production tree, assuming perfect competition and profit maximization of a representative firm. Intermediate inputs and value added form the output, assuming constant elasticity of substitution (CES) technology; intermediate input demand is in fixed proportions, assuming Leontief technology. Value added is formed by a nested CES structure by land, an unskilled labor aggregate, and a capital-skilled labor aggregate. All factors – labor, capital, and natural resources – are fully mobile across sectors and fully employed, and wages/returns adjust to changing factor demand.

The model distinguishes four types of commodities according to their use. These are commodities designed for (i) intermediate use, (ii) household consumption, (iii) government consumption, and (iv) investment. The supply to a specific use category is determined by demand, and domestic production supplies the four use categories, assuming perfect substitutability.

Exports are modeled as imperfect substitutes to supply for domestic markets, applying a two-level constant elasticity of transformation (CET) structure that allows firms to differentiate prices in the domestic and export markets, depending on the market shares and price elasticities. On the first level, supply is distributed between domestic and aggregate foreign markets, and it is allocated to different foreign regions on the second level.

On the import side, each region employs the assumption of imperfect substitutability between different source regions and domestically produced commodities and imported commodities, depicted by a two-level CES function. Like the export structure, the composition of domestic and imported commodities is determined, first, by the relative price for the domestic commodity and aggregate import commodity, and second, by bilateral prices determining demand by partner region. Trade elasticities employed in the model are sourced from the GTAP.

Each region's representative household obtains income from sales of factor services and remittance inflows. After paying taxes, remittances, and saving, this income is spent on consumption, assuming the maximization of a Stone-Geary utility function. Each government's income consists of taxes, and all governments consume commodities in fixed shares. Capital resources are from household and government savings, depreciation, and the balance of payments. Investment demand is assumed to be in fixed shares.

The model contains five markets for each region that clearly follow the logic of the SAM structure of a complete and circular system. In factor markets, a region's factor demand equals exogenous factor supply. In the commodity markets, the domestic and import supply is equal to domestic demand for that commodity in a specific use category. Bilateral import flows match the respective export flows. Government savings, the residual of government income and government expenditure, clear the government account. Similarly, the balance of trade, defined as the aggregate of bilateral trade balances, clears the rest of the world account. If all other accounts balance, then so must the final account (Walras's law), and savings equal investment.

The model closure determines how markets are cleared. The closure is selected to incorporate all welfare effects in the period under consideration, i.e., the investment volume does not change, and the savings rate adjusts to equalize savings and investment. The government balance and expenditures are stable, and the income tax adjusts to maintain the internal balance. On the foreign exchange market, the exchange rate, depicting relative price changes between regions, adjusts to balance the current account. An exchange rate index for reference regions is fixed and serves as global numeraire; in addition, each region's consumer price index serves as regional numeraire.

The model features a set of policy instruments, including different taxes and tariffs and specific instruments for nontariff measures. LCRs can be modeled as quantitative restrictions (Flaig and Stone, 2017), as depicted in Figure 2.3. Domestically produced and supplied commodities (QD) are supplied in two homogenous components – the quantity that would be supplied without the LCR (QDNL) and the quantity that is additionally needed to fulfill the LCR (QDLCR). Total supply is likewise broken into two components – the quantity that is supplied through competition (QQARM) and the additional quantity required to fulfill the LCR (QDLCR).

The LCR is modeled as a mixed complementarity problem, with a regime switch between the situation in which the LCR is not binding and where it becomes binding. If domestic sources meet or surpass the LCR, QD equals QDNL, and all goods are supplied through competition. If an LCR is binding, a part is supplied through the LCR channel. Relative prices adjust, leading to changes in the mix of competitively supplied imports and domestic quantities. As the competitive domestic supply and total supply are subject to change, the amount channeled through the LCR channel (QDLCR) is variable and defines the additional domestic supply necessary to fulfill the LCR in the new equilibrium.

In addition, a specific price preferences instrument allows the depiction of policies where sales taxes are differentiated between imported and domestic commodities. In this instrument, sales taxes are rearranged to enter the price system before the Armington nest, i.e., the CES aggregate of imports and domestic produce, allowing for different tax rates between local and imported products.

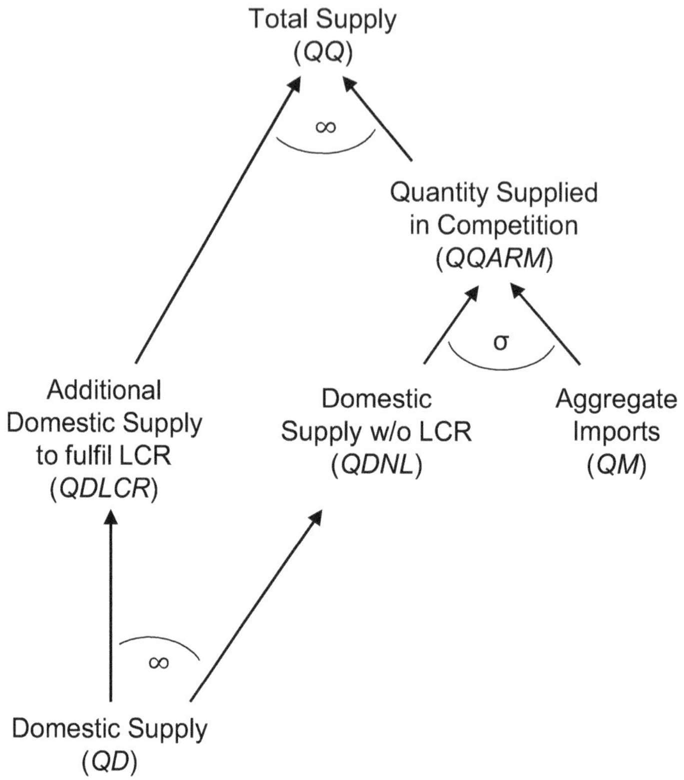

Figure 2.3 Quantitative Local Content Requirement Measure in the Model

Source: Flaig and Stone (2017).

4 Simulations

To understand the impact LCRs may have on the rest of the economy, we modeled seven different policies in the METRO model. As outlined earlier, the LCRs were chosen based on the transparency of the measure and the ability to identify the sectors involved and represent the different types of LCRs discussed. The movement toward the use of incentive-based LCRs in recent years and the nontransparent nature of these LCRs make them difficult to model. This paper identifies two LCR regimes that rely on incentives to raise the content of domestic production: Argentina's tax credit for automotive LCRs and the US grant incentives for state infrastructure projects. Saudi Arabia's medical goods LCR, Brazil's LCR in telecommunications, and Indonesia's automotive LCR are examples of operations LCRs, while the South African LCR in mining is a good example of the traditional input LCR.

Table 2.2 presents the macro-level impacts of the LCRs modeled in this chapter. As described, seven different policies were analyzed to determine

Table 2.2 Country-Level Effects and LCR Related Indicators

Item	*Argentina – automobiles*	*Brazil – telecommunications*	*Brazil–GP*	*Indonesia – automobiles*	*Saudi Arabia – GP medicals*	*South Africa – mining*	*United States–GP transportation*
Real *GDP*	0.1%	0.0%	0.0%	–0.1%	0.0%	0.0%	0.0%
# *Final domestic demand*	0.0%	0.0%	0.0%	0.0%	0.0%	0.0%	0.0%
# *Import demand*	1.7%	0.0%	0.0%	–2.3%	–0.1%	–0.1%	0.0%
# *Export demand*	2.0%	0.0%	0.0%	–2.5%	–0.1%	–0.1%	0.0%
Labor income	0.1%	0.0%	0.0%	0.2%	0.0%	0.0%	0.0%
Disposable income	–0.1%	0.0%	0.0%	0.0%	0.0%	0.0%	0.0%
Terms of trade	–0.1%	0.0%	0.0%	0.6%	0.0%	0.0%	0.0%
LCR related indicators:							
– *GDP share of targeted sector*	3.3%	8.6%	0.0%	4.2%	0.7%	4.0%	0.0%
– *Import share related to LCR*	41.8% (a)	7.9% (a)	8.7% (b)	31.5% (c)	20.1% (b)	17.4% (a)	49.4% (b)
Import share of (a) sector's input, (b) relevant government demand, (c) total demand							

GDP = gross domestic product, GP = government procurement, LCR = local content requirement.

Sources: Model results and METRO database.

both their direct as well as their indirect impact on the countries' economy. The general macroeconomic impacts highlight the relatively small effects these measures tend to have on broad economy-wide measures such as GDP but the more significant impacts they have on trade. The analysis demonstrates that a more in-depth look at their effects shows the impacts are not quite so benign.

Argentina: tax benefit package to boost the automobile industry

The measure is implemented as a quantitative LCR, which ensures that 30% of all intermediate commodities used in the automobile industry, represented in the model database by two sectors – motor vehicles and transport equipment – are domestically sourced. This LCR is combined with a tax reduction on inputs, domestic and imported, equivalent to 10% of the sales value. This amount represents an average tax reduction, assuming firms opt into the tax credit. As outlined, the METRO model works based on a representative firm and assumes that competitive pressures will force firms to choose to adhere to the LCR conditions to qualify for the tax benefit. To the extent that not all firms opt in for the tax benefit, or the LCR applied entitles them to a larger tax credit than the 10% modeled, the actual impact of the LCR will vary. The results presented below provide an indication of the magnitude of the impact on average.

Results

The automotive industry in Argentina accounts for 3.3% of GDP, and 41.8% of its total inputs are imported (Table 2.2). An LCR that requires producers to source 30% of their intermediate inputs from domestic sources, however, is binding for several specific inputs to the automotive sector. These are, most notably, computer, electronic, and optical products (domestic inputs account for 5% of the total inputs of these goods); electrical equipment (2%); machinery and equipment (5%); and motor vehicles and parts (7%). These four inputs account for one-third of inputs in motor vehicle production and one-eighth in transport equipment. The policy therefore results in decreases in imports from the automobile industry and the transport sector.

Broad measures of GDP and final demand are not materially affected by the simulated policy change (Table 2.2). Labor income, a measure of the overall welfare effects of the policy, declines. However, overall Argentine imports and exports increase by 1.7% and 2.0%, respectively (Table 2.2). The export increase is carried by three sectors – motor vehicles, transport equipment, and electrical equipment. Two of these sectors experience the tax break – motor vehicles, where exports increase 52%, and transport equipment, where exports rise by 41%. Electrical equipment benefits from demand by the automotive industry and a relatively high import share of intermediates (43%), resulting in decreasing production costs as import prices decrease, and exports increase 5%.

Motor vehicles and transport equipment benefit, in addition to the import restriction, from a reduction in tax expenditures. Thus, while the policy restricting imports raises costs, the associated tax break decreases costs in the automotive sector by 10%, leaving operators in the sector better-off overall. This is demonstrated by declines in overall production costs in the automotive and transport equipment industry of –5% and –4%, respectively (Table 2.4). This cost advantage allows domestic producers to expand export markets, which, in turn, translates into a boost in production by 39% and 17% in auto and transport equipment, respectively.

While total domestic output does not change, there are significant differences between sectors. Table 2.3 depicts effects on production by sector that range from a decline of 5% in metals and 4% in machinery and pharmaceuticals to an increase of 39% in motor vehicles. Increases in the production of those expanding sectors, predominantly in automotive production, lead to increases in wages of 0.1% to 0.2%.

The exchange rate appreciation (Table 2.2) makes imports more attractive for other activities, except automobiles, and other agents, while decreasing the competitiveness of exports of non-automobile sectors. Imports increase in all non-targeted sectors. Imports in targeted sectors (indicated by an asterisk in Table 2.3) are affected by two opposing effects: the exchange rate effect, which triggers increasing import demand in non-automotive industries, and the LCR, which triggers decreasing demand for imported inputs by the automotive industry. The net effect depends on the relative importance of automotive demand in the imported intermediate inputs of each sector. In addition to decreasing import prices, the LCR increases costs for domestic inputs, which makes imports more attractive.

Unlike the other measures analyzed in this chapter, not all sectors that benefit from a binding LCR for their inputs into automobiles experience a positive net effect on production (Table 2.3). On the contrary, the production of machinery and equipment decreases by 4.2%, driven by decreasing demand for exports and domestic investment, where domestic machinery is substituted for now-cheaper imported goods. In general, sectors that are important inputs into motor vehicles and transport equipment experience a positive effect on production, while for other sectors, negative effects from decreasing demand, import substitution, and lower competitiveness in export markets dominate.

While there appears to be a positive impact on the automotive sector due to this policy, the tax break means reduced revenue for government. The shortfall is financed by increasing revenues derived from households, which leads to a fall in the disposable income of households (–0.1%). This decline amounts to a transfer from households to businesses.

Table 2.3 Model Results – Effects on Imports and Production by Sector, Percentage Changes

	Argentina–automobiles		*Brazil–telecom*		*Indonesia–automobiles*		*Saudi Arabia–GP medicals*		*South Africa–Mining*	
	Imports	*Production*	*Imports*	*Production*	*Imports*	*Production*	*Imports*	*Production*	*Imports*	*Production*
Agriculture	2.0	−1.8	0.0	0.0	0.9	−0.6	0.0	0.0	0.0*	0.0
Coal	-0.2	-3.2	0.0	0.0	0.9	−1.4	0.0	-0.1	-0.1*	0.1
Oil	2.7	−1.3	0.0	0.0	1.1	−1.2	0.1	-0.1	0.0*	0.4
Gas	7.6	-5.4	0.1	-0.1	7.3	-6.1	0.2	0.1	-0.5*	1.4
Minerals	0.8	-0.7	0.0	0.0	0.5	-1.9	0.0	0.0	-0.8*	-0.8
Food	3.6	-1.7	0.0	0.0	1.9	-0.8	0.0	0.0	0.0*	0.0
Textiles	6.0	-0.8	0.0	0.0	1.3	-2.9	0.0*	-0.1	0.0*	0.0
Wood products	4.8	-0.2	0.0	0.0	3.8	-1.1	0.0*	0.0	0.0*	-0.1
Paper production, publishing	3.7	-0.9	0.0	0.0	1.1	-2.0	0.1*	0.0	0.0*	0.0
Petroleum, coal products	1.0	-1.0	0.0	0.0	0.9	-0.2	0.1	0.0	0.0*	0.0
Chemical products	1.6	-2.7	0.0	0.0	1.2	-2.3	-2.0*	0.4	-0.3*	0.1
Basic pharmaceuticals	0.7*	-3.7	0.0	0.0	2.6	-1.0	-2.3*	3.8	0.0*	0.0
Rubber and plastic	5.5	0.8	0.0	0.0	3.3	-1.0	0.0*	0.0	0.0*	0.0
Mineral products	4.0	0.1	0.0	0.0	2.9	-0.1	0.1	0.0	0.0*	0.0
Ferrous metals	7.6	1.3	0.1	0.0	3.5	-1.3	0.0	0.0	0.2*	0.1
Metals	6.8	-5.2	0.1	0.0	4.1	-4.2	0.0	-0.2	-0.1*	-0.3
Metal products	8.4	5.7	0.1	0.0	3.2	0.4	0.1	0.0	0.1*	0.0
Computer, electronics	1.2*	-0.8	0.0	0.0	0.3	-4.6	0.0	0.0	0.0*	0.1
Electrical equipment	1.4*	3.7	-0.7*	0.6	2.1	-4.8	0.0*	-0.2	-0.1*	0.2

Machinery, equipment	0.9*	–4.2	–0.1*	0.1	1.4	–4.4	0.0	–0.1	–0.9*	0.6
Motor vehicles and parts	–3.8*	39.2	0.0	0.0	–68.1*	43.3	0.0	0.0	0.0*	0.0
Transport equipment	–9.7	17.1	0.0	0.0	–44.3*	23.3	0.0	–0.1	–0.9*	3.3
Manufactures	5.3	–0.2	0.0	0.0	3.1	–2.8	0.0	0.0	0.0*	0.0
Transport	1.3–1.8	–0.7––0.1	0.0	0.0	1.3–2.1	0.1–3.6	0.0	0.0	–0.3–0.0	0.0–0.1
Communication	2.8	–0.3	0.0	0.0	1.5	–0.3	0.1	0.0	0.0	0.0
Utilities, construction	2.5–3.4	0.1–0.5	0.0	0.0	1.2–2.7	–0.5–0.0	0.0–0.1	0.0	–0.4–0.0	-0.1–0.3
Other service sectors	1.5–2.9	–0.6–0.2	0.0	0.0	1.0–2.0	-1.0–0.0	0.0–0.1	0.0	0.0	0.0–0.1

Note: The transport sector covers the three modes (air, land, and sea) and thus is reported as a range.

* Sectors facing a binding local content requirement.

Source: Model results.

Table 2.4 Argentina – Motor Vehicle Sector LCR, Detailed Effects on Automotive Production, Percentage Changes

(i) Motor vehicle sector

	Quantity					*Prices*			
	Total	*Use category*				*Use category*			
		Intermediate inputs	*Private consumption*	*Government consumption*	*Capital goods*	*Intermediate inputs*	*Private consumption*	*Government consumption*	*Capital goods*
Production	39%	101%	17%	66%	28%	-5%	-5%	-5%	-4%
Exports	51%	87%	31%	66%	38%	-7%	-3%	-5%	-4%
Domestic	23%	175%	12%	43%	13%	0%	-6%	-8%	-7%
Imports	-4%	3%	-12%	-2%	-16%	-1%	-2%	-1%	-2%
Total demand	7%	15%	5%	0%	0%		-5%	-2%	-5%

(ii) Transport equipment sector

	Quantity					*Prices*			
	Total	*Use category*				*Use category*			
		Intermediate inputs	*Private consumption*	*Government consumption*	*Capital goods*	*Intermediate inputs*	*Private consumption*	*Government consumption*	*Capital goods*
Production	17%	11%	19%	84%	28%	-4%	-4%	-4%	-4%
Exports	41%	32%	37%	84%	44%	-3%	-3%	-4%	-3%
Domestic	14%	11%	17%	54%	23%	-4%	-5%	-6%	-5%
Imports	-10%	-12%	-10%	-3%	-9%	-2%	-2%	-1%	-1%
Total demand	3%	6%	3%	0%			-3%	-1%	-3%

LCR = local content requirement.

Source: Model results.

Brazilian telecommunications industry

The measure is modeled as a requirement to source 70% of the inputs of electronic equipment and machinery and equipment to the communications sector from domestic sources. Prior to the policy implementation, these sectors had local content of around 30%. The telecommunications sector is part of the post and telecommunications sector in the METRO model. Telecommunications account for about 80% in the broader sector (IBGE, 2022). To the extent that postal services use electronic and machinery equipment as an input, the impact of the LCR will be overstated. The model assumes that employed technologies do not change. Finally, to the extent that firms decide not to comply and leave the market, the impact of the LCR is likely understated.

Results

Telecommunications account for 9% of GDP, and 8% of the sector's inputs are imported (Table 2.2). The LCR increases in domestic production in the targeted sectors are reported in Table 2.3 and Table 2.5. The model allows for the differentiation of domestic and export prices. This permits us to capture the ability of firms to engage in price discrimination, i.e., keeping their export prices low to protect or even increase market share overseas while raising domestic prices where, due to the LCR, competition is restricted. The electronic equipment sector benefits from increasing domestic demand due to the LCR exclusively from inputs into communications exports and production increasing 0.6% and 0.9%, respectively.

This LCR builds on existing restrictive policies in the Brazilian telecommunications sector (Stone, Messent, and Flaig, 2015). Thus, the costs of this policy are limited and have no noticeable additional effects on other sectors or on the aggregate level of output or labor income (Table 2.3). However, what the model does not capture to a sufficient degree are the costs imposed on the government to monitor and enforce the policy. If these could be accurately quantified, it is likely that overall welfare impacts would be negative.

Table 2.5 Brazil – LCR, Percentage Changes

(i) Electrical equipment sector

	Quantity					*Prices*			
	Total	*Use category*				*Use category*			
		Intermediate inputs	*Private consumption*	*Government consumption*	*Capital goods*	*Intermediate inputs*	*Private consumption*	*Government consumption*	*Capital goods*
Production	0.6%	3.1%	0.0%	–0.1%	0.0%	0.0%	0.0%	0.0%	0.0%
Exports	0.9%	2.0%	0.0%	–0.1%	0.0%	–0.1%	0.0%	0.0%	0.0%
Domestic	0.6%	3.6%	0.0%	–0.1%	0.0%	0.1%	0.0%	0.0%	0.0%
Imports	–0.7%	–1.3%	0.0%	0.0%	0.0%	–0.1%	0.0%	0.0%	0.0%
Total demand	0.0%	0.1%	0.0%	0.0%	0.0%		0.0%	0.0%	0.0%

(*Continued*)

Table 2.5 (Continued)

(ii) Machinery and equipment sector

	Quantity					*Prices*			
	Total	*Use category*				*Use category*			
		Intermediate inputs	*Private consumption*	*Government consumption*	*Capital goods*	*Intermediate inputs*	*Private consumption*	*Government consumption*	*Capital goods*
Production	0.1%	0.5%	0.0%	0.0%	0.0%	0.0%	0.0%	0.0%	0.0%
Exports	0.1%	0.3%	0.0%	−0.1%	0.0%	0.0%	0.0%	0.0%	0.0%
Domestic	0.1%	0.6%	0.0%	0.0%	0.0%	0.0%	0.0%	0.0%	0.0%
Imports	−0.1%	−0.2%	0.0%	0.0%	0.0%	0.0%	0.0%	0.0%	0.0%
Total demand	0.0%	0.0%	0.0%	0.0%	0.0%		0.0%	0.0%	0.0%

LCR = local content requirement.

Source: Model results.

Brazil: preferential margins on various products in public procurement processes

In 2013 and 2014, the government of Brazil decided to increase the preference margins for the public procurement of a variety of nationally produced goods. Preference margins are the maximum extent to which the price quoted by a local supplier may be above that of a competitor. The new margins range between 9% and 25% and include IT (15%), tractors with continuous tracks (20%), airplanes (9%–25%), various IT-related goods and services (15%–25%), capital goods (15%–20%), and toys (10%).

The price preference is implemented as a tax break on domestic products used in government procurement, introducing a price difference between domestic and imported commodities of 10% to 20%, depending on the sector. To determine the level of the price difference to implement the scenario, sales taxes and tariffs are adjusted simultaneously, keeping import prices constant. The LCR under review applies to government procurement, so this modeling approach, influencing government income and expenditure, is a reasonable choice. The results depend on the quality of the data representing government consumption in the database, whereby statistics on government consumption are generally rather critical. To the extent that the government use is understated in the database, the results will be larger. In addition, given that the tax break is implemented on average across the various sectors, the results for any specific supply sector will vary.

Results

Local content in Brazil's government consumption in the database is 5% for computers and electronic products, electrical equipment, and transport equipment and 26% for machinery. The policy doubles local content in these sectors. Local content is already high for motor vehicles (96%) and communication services (93%) and increases only marginally, to 97% and 95%, respectively. Government imports in the targeted sectors decrease between 5% and 25%.

However, government consumption in the targeted sectors accounts for a maximum 0.01% of consumption across all use categories, so the government sector is too small in this area to have a visible effect on the aggregate or sector level. Thus, these results provide a good example where, while identifiable and transparent, LCRs may not have a notable difference on economic outcomes.

Indonesia: LCR in the automotive industry

The LCR is modeled as a 100% LCR on motor vehicles, represented by two sectors – "motor vehicles and parts" and "transport equipment" – for final demand. Imported motor vehicles being used as intermediates into production in the automotive industry are not covered by the LCR, assuming these are parts going into assembly in Indonesia. Thus, the measure is well depicted in the database and relatively straightforward to model. However, the model implies that all current operators comply with the measure. To the extent that operators leave the sector as a result of the policy, the results are understated.

Results

The automotive industry in Indonesia accounts for 4% of GDP, and 32% of automobiles for intermediate and final demand are imported (Table 2.2). The LCR increases the local content of motor vehicles from 63% to 89% and local content of transport equipment from 75% to 87%. As a result, imports of motor vehicles and transport equipment drop strongly across uses, by 68% and 44%, respectively (Table 2.6). Imports of intermediates of these commodities decrease in most sectors, except in the automotive industry, which increases imports of parts to satisfy domestic demand. As a result of decreasing automotive imports, the exchange rate appreciates to balance the current account, and imports in other manufacturing sectors increase between 1% and 4% (Table 2.3). On the country level, imports and exports decrease by 2.3% and 2.5%, respectively, and the terms of trade improve by 0.7% (Table 2.2).

The policy increases demand for domestic motor vehicles strongly, and domestic production of motor vehicle and transport equipment increases 42% and 23%, respectively (Table 2.6). Increasing production leads to increasing demand for labor in the automotive industry, and workers reallocate to the automotive industries and wages increase 0.2%. Returns to capital increase 0.1%, so that sectors that are labor and capital intensive experience increasing production costs.

At the same time, import prices decrease. For inputs across other parts of the economy, import prices drop by 0.4% to 0.6% while, they decline 9%

Table 2.6 Indonesia – LCR in the Automotive Industry, Percentage Changes

(i) Motor vehicles sector

	Quantity					*Prices*			
	Total	*Use category*				*Use category*			
		Intermediate inputs	*Private consumption*	*Government consumption*	*Capital goods*	*Intermediate inputs*	*Private consumption*	*Government consumption*	*Capital goods*
Production	42%	110%	4%	-4%	43%	-1%	-1%	-1%	-1%
Exports	32%	57%	1%	-5%	24%	-6%	-1%	-1%	-3%
Domestic	45%	153%	5%	301%	47%	3%	0%	29%	0%
Imports	-68%	-62%	-56%	-16%	-91%	-9%	-8%	-3%	-20%
Total demand	3%	7%	1%	0%	0%		-1%	4%	0%

(ii) Transport equipment sector

	Quantity					*Prices*			
	Total	*Use category*				*Use category*			
		Intermediate inputs	*Private consumption*	*Government consumption*	*Capital goods*	*Intermediate inputs*	*Private consumption*	*Government consumption*	*Capital goods*
Production	23%	18%	4%	-1%	238%	0%	0%	0%	0%
Exports	28%	5%	-3%	-6%	109%	-1%	-1%	-1%	-5%
Domestic	22%	19%	5%	301%	311%	0%	0%	18%	2%
Imports	-44%	-3%	-58%	-16%	-87%	-1%	-6%	-2%	-12%
Total demand	6%	13%	0%	0%	0%		0%	2%	1%

LCR = local content requirement.

Source: Model results.

for motor vehicle parts (transport equipment – 1%) due to a policy-induced decrease in import demand. This price decrease benefits sectors with large import shares of intermediates such as petroleum, chemicals, computers and electrical equipment, electricity, and water and air transportation. Motor vehicle parts are a major input, so the effect is especially strong for motor vehicles.

Decreasing export competitiveness and increasing import competition, resulting from the currency appreciation, and increasing production costs in most other sectors, have a negative impact on production in non-targeted sectors (Table 2.3). Thus, on an aggregate level, production and GDP do not change.

Saudi Arabia: local content and government procurement measure on products in medicines and medical supplies

The measure is modeled as a 90% minimum requirement of domestic content for government procurement in the following sectors: textiles, wood products, paper products, chemicals, basic pharmaceuticals, rubber and plastic products, and electronic equipment. Allowing for products that are not subject to the measure, 10% of products in each sector are assumed exempt. As noted, accurate government procurement data are difficult to obtain. Thus, the model outcomes depend on the accuracy of Saudi Arabia's government procurement in the METRO database. To the extent that it is understated, the impact on government services, and indeed the total impact, will be understated.

Results

Government procurement of the targeted commodities, of which 20% are imported, accounts for 0.7% of Saudi Arabia's GDP (Table 2.2). On the commodity level, the LCR is binding for chemicals and pharmaceuticals, where local content increases from 66% and 40%, respectively, to 90%. Overall, government imports decrease 3.1%, while imports of all other uses increase slightly, leading to a total import decrease of 0.1% (Table 2.2). There is no noticeable effect on the exchange rate.

Table 2.7 shows the effects exemplarily for pharmaceuticals. Imports are substituted by domestic products in government procurement and trigger domestic production. Other uses are only slightly affected and show contrasting tendencies, increasing imports, and lowering demand for domestic goods as the government increases prices for domestic products. Government consumption is large enough to increase production in the sectors where the LCR is binding – 0.4% for chemicals and 3.8% for pharmaceuticals. Non-targeted sectors experience a small but negative effect (Table 2.3).

South Africa: new mining bill

The measure is modeled as an LCR on inputs to mining, abstracting from complex company ownership requirements. The model captures these measures by depicting the policies with respect to the domestic content requirement of 70% on goods and 80% on services. Once again, we assume that all current operators comply with the measure. To the extent that companies

Table 2.7 Saudi Arabia LCR – Pharmaceutical Sector, Percentage Changes

	Quantity					*Prices*			
	Total	*Use category*				*Use category*			
		Intermediate inputs	*Private consumption*	*Government consumption*	*Capital goods*	*Intermediate inputs*	*Private consumption*	*Government consumption*	*Capital goods*
Production	3.8%	–0.2%	0.0%	125.0%	-0.1%	0.0%	0.0%	0.0%	0.0%
Exports	0.5%	–0.2%	-0.1%	71.0%	-0.2%	0.0%	0.0%	-4.1%	0.0%
Domestic	4.2%	–0.1%	0.0%	127.1%	-0.1%	0.0%	0.0%	0.2%	0.0%
Imports	-2.3%	0.1%	0.1%	-83.4%	0.0%	0.0%	0.0%	-12.5%	0.0%
Total demand	0.0%	0.1%	0.0%	0.0%			0.0%	-1.0%	0.0%

LCR = local content requirement.

Source: Model results.

leave the market as a result of the policy, the impacts are understated. In addition, the extent to which the ownership structure impacts the degree of implementation will impact the results.

Results

Mining contributes 4% to South African GDP, and the sector imports 17% of its inputs (Table 2.2). The LCR is binding for most of the production inputs and increases domestic supply and production in sectors across the board, with the notable exceptions of metals and minerals (Table 2.3). The supply of mining products to the domestic market increases 2% (Table 2.8).

While there is no noticeable effect on input prices or production costs in mining, its output declines by 0.8%. This stems from a decline in export markets. Mining is an important export sector in South Africa – 97% of its total output is exported, and it accounts for 12% of the country's total exports. Exports decrease in response to relative exchange rate effects. As a consequence, mining exports decrease 0.9%, driving the decline in production.

US: Buy America bill enacted by various states

The US Buy America program is implemented through transportation grants across many US states. Thus, any public project funded by these grants must use some level of domestically produced iron, steel, and other manufactured goods. The amounts of both the grants and the LCR vary by state and by projects within states.

Table 2.8 South Africa LCR – Mining Sector, Percentage Changes

	Quantity					*Prices*			
	Total	*Use Category*				*Use Category*			
		Intermediate inputs	*Private consumption*	*Government consumption*	*Capital goods*	*Intermediate inputs*	*Private consumption*	*Government consumption*	*Capital goods*
Production	–0.8%	–0.8%	0.1%	0.1%	0.0%	0.0%	0.0%	0.0%	0.0%
Exports	–0.9%	–0.9%	0.1%	0.1%	0.0%	–0.1%	0.0%	0.0%	0.0%
Domestic	2.4%	2.4%	0.0%	0.1%	0.0%	1.8%	0.0%	0.0%	0.0%
Imports	–0.8%	–0.8%	0.0%	0.0%	0.0%	–0.2%	0.0%	0.0%	0.0%
Total demand	–0.1%	–0.1%	0.0%	0.0%			0.0%	0.0%	0.0%

LCR = local content requirement.

Source: Model results.

The model does not provide for measurement of individual grants at the subnational level. However, looking across hundreds of grants, accounting for the size of the grant and relative size of the transport budgets, this measure is modeled as an average increase in domestic content of 25 percentage points in total government spending on transport equipment and services. Thus, domestic content is raised from 61% in motor vehicles, 5% in transport equipment, and 55% in transport services, to 86%, 30%, and 80%, respectively. This is an average across hundreds of individual policies and grants and thus represents an average impact.

Results

Imports account for 49% of US government procurement spending in transport equipment and services (Table 2.2). The measure increases domestic demand in the targeted sectors and reduces imports. However, government procurement in this area accounts for only 0.002% of GDP, so the effect is not large enough to visibly impact on the sector level (Table 2.9 presents the example of motor vehicles). Again, while the measure is transparent and identifiable, it illustrates the case where large domestic markets can often afford to implement this policy with small measurable side effects. However, what the model fails to capture in this instance is the longer-term impacts this policy has on innovative behavior by firms. By having access to government contracts on a noncompetitive basis, firms have little incentive to invest in innovative or cost-cutting behavior. This reduces their competitive stance vis-à-vis firms that face contested markets.

Table 2.9 US LCR – Motor Vehicles Sector, Percentage Changes

	Quantity					*Prices*			
	Total	*Use category*				*Use category*			
		Intermediate inputs	*Private consumption*	*Government consumption*	*Capital goods*	*Intermediate inputs*	*Private consumption*	*Government consumption*	*Capital goods*
Production	0.0%	0.0%	0.0%	6.2%	0.0%	0.0%	0.0%	0.0%	0.0%
Exports	0.0%	0.0%	0.0%	4.0%	0.0%	0.0%	0.0%	-0.4%	0.0%
Domestic	0.0%	0.0%	0.0%	42.4%	0.0%	0.0%	0.0%	5.4%	0.0%
Imports	0.0%	0.0%	0.0%	-64.4%	0.0%	0.0%	0.0%	-8.6%	0.0%
Total demand	0.0%	0.0%	0.0%	0.0%	0.0%		0.0%	3.8%	0.0%

LCR = local content requirement, US = United States.

Source: Model results.

5 Concluding remarks

Policies that favor domestic industry at the expense of foreign competitors are growing in number, and the use of these measures has accelerated worldwide. While localization barriers have been traditionally used in the extractive sectors, they are now widely used across a variety of sectors, such as automobiles, IT, health care, and agriculture. The types of measures have also changed over time, with LCRs becoming more complex and less transparent. In the period right after the Global Financial Crisis, LCRs focused on ensuring that inputs and labor were sourced locally. However, the five years since 2014 saw a move toward incentivizing firms by offering tax breaks, preferential lending, or other perks tied to using local inputs or establishing local production. While the number of LCRs reported in the relevant databases has increased, counts of incidences across countries cannot be directly compared, as reported incidences vary by, if nothing else, sector coverage and the jurisdictional level at which they are imposed.

The overarching policy goal of an LCR is to stimulate the domestic economy. Given the complex nature of LCRs, several factors impact their ability to meet the stated policy objective. These are represented by four factors: market size and stability, policy design and coherence, the restrictiveness of the LCRs, and a sufficient domestic industrial base.

The modeling exercise focuses on a selection of measures that meet the following criteria: the sector or region of economic activity is clearly identified, the restriction itself is clearly identified, the sector or subnational region is large enough to be sufficiently captured in an economy-wide model, and the measure is enforceable and binding. The identified measures provide a good sample of the types of policies applied and the economies applying them. The economic effects of selected LCRs are analyzed using a CGE model. This model incorporates detailed trade by intermediate use category and relevant policy instruments, allowing the identification of economic impacts beyond the targeted sector.

The results show that the economic impact of LCRs is limited and generally negative. The policies tend to be focused on specific sectors and have little broader impact while undermining the long-run competitiveness of those sectors. By artificially increasing prices, these policies, in turn, artificially increase production, and the only way to maintain these production gains is through continued government intervention. This is not a long-term solution to employment or industry growth. A better solution with stronger domestic linkages would be to allow foreign firms to find competitive partners in the domestic economy on their own.

The model assumes the full employment of resources across sectors, so the LCRs applied to larger sectors highlight how an increase in the targeted inputs comes at the expense of the rest of the economy. This was illustrated in both the Argentine and Indonesian automotive LCRs. If there are large numbers of resources not employed, the subsequent price pressures would not be as large. However, if the LCR leads to competition between sectors for resources, an increase in domestic production leads to declines in other sectors as they were required to compete for resources with the now-supported sector domestically while losing competitiveness overseas. In addition, non-targeted industries substitute away from domestic production to imports to avoid increasing costs due to the LCR. As a result, total imports can increase, as shown, for example, by Argentina's LCR. So what is given to one sector can come at the expense of others across the economy – something picked up by a CGE model.

Finally, the results do not capture the resources needed to design, implement, monitor, and enforce LCR policies. These funds have opportunity costs associated with them: that is, the government and private-sector resources used to implement the LCR policy could, instead, be allocated to activities that lead to increased competitiveness and economic growth over the long run. Some of these policies include education and training, improved connectivity, and enhanced financial sector oversight and transparency.

Notes

1 Global Trade Alert (2022) monitors policy actions that could impact global trade. It documents a number of "state acts" across a variety of policy choices.

2 While work is underway to better capture these types of restrictions, the nature of data localization provisions and the data requirements necessary to measure these LCRs preclude their inclusion in this measurement exercise.

3 While many LCRs were implemented at the height of the coronavirus disease (COVID-19) crisis, most were subsequently withdrawn – making any empirical assessment of their impact problematic. Thus, we limited our analysis to one example of these measures.

4 For more information on the TiVA database, see OECD (n.d.).
5 The model derives from the GLOBE model developed by McDonald and Thierfelder (2013), which belongs to a family of models that derives from principles developed in the World Bank's 1–2–3 model (de Melo and Robinson, 1989; Devarajan, Lewis, and Robinson, 1990).

References

Ablo, A. D. 2017. The Micromechanisms of Power in Local Content Requirements and their Constraints on Ghanaian SMEs in the Oil and Gas Sector. *Norsk Geografisk Tidsskrift: Norwegian Journal of Geography*. 71 (2). pp. 67–78. https://doi.org/10.1080/00291951.2017.1299213

Aguiar, A., M. Chepeliev, E. L. Corong, R. McDougall, and D. van der Mensbrugghe. 2019. The GTAP Data Base: Version 10. *Journal of Global Economic Analysis*. 4 (1). pp. 1–27. https://doi.org/10.21642/JGEA.040101AF

Arriola, C., D. Flaig, S. Stone, and F. van Tongeren. 2020. *METRO Version 3 Model Documentation, TAD/TC/WP/RD(2020)1/FINAL*. Paris: Organisation for Economic Co-operation and Development, Trade and Agriculture Directorate, Trade Committee. www.oecd.org/officialdocuments/publicdisplaydocumentpdf/?cote=TAD/TC/WP/RD(2020)1/FINAL&docLanguage=En

Cimino-Isaacs, C., G. C. Hufbauer, and J. J. Schott. 2014. A Proposed Code to Discipline Local Content Requirements. *PIIE Policy Brief*. No. PB14–6. Washington, DC: Peterson Institute for International Economics. www.piie.com/publications/policy-briefs/proposed-code-discipline-local-content-requirements

de Melo, J., and S. Robinson. 1989. Product Differentiation and the Treatment of Foreign Trade in Computable General Equilibrium Models of Small Economies. *Journal of International Economics*. 27 (1–2). pp. 47–67.

Deringer, H., F. Erixon, P. Lamprecht, and E. van der Marel. 2018. The Economic Impact of Local Content Requirements: A Case Study of Heavy Vehicles. *ECIPE Occasional Paper Series*. No. 1/2018. Brussels: European Centre for International Political Economy. https://ecipe.org/publications/the-economic-impact-of-local-content-requirements/

Devarajan, S., J. D. Lewis, and S. Robinson. 1990. Policy Lessons from Trade-Focused, Two-Sector Models. *Journal of Policy Modeling*. 12 (4). pp. 625–657.

Dixon, P. B., M. T. Rimmer, and R. G. Waschik. 2018. Evaluating the Effects of Local Content Measures in a CGE Model: Eliminating the US Buy America(n) Programs. *Economic Modelling*. 68. pp. 155–166. https://doi.org/10.1016/j.econmod.2017.07.004

Ettmayr, C., and H. Lloyd. 2017. Local Content Requirements and the Impact on the South African Renewable Energy Sector: A Survey-Based Analysis. *South African Journal of Economic and Management Sciences*. 20 (1). pp. 1–11.

European Commission. 2022. *Market Access Database*. http://madb.europa.eu/ (accessed 1 December 2022).

Evenett, S. J., and J. Fritz. 2021. *Subsidies and Market Access: Towards an Inventory of Corporate Subsidies by China, the European Union and the United States: The 28th Global Trade Alert Report*. London: Centre for Economic Policy Research. www.globaltradealert.org/reports/gta-28-report

Ezell, S. J., R. Atkinson, and M. Wein. 2013. *Localization Barriers to Trade: Threat to the Global Innovation Economy*. Washington, DC: The Information Technology and Innovation Foundation. https://dx.doi.org/10.2139/ssrn.2370612

Fang, M. M. 2020. Local Content Measures and the WTO Regime: Addressing Contentions and Trade-offs. In D. S. Olawuyi, ed. *Local Content and Sustainable Development in Global Energy Markets* (Treaty Implementation for Sustainable Development). Cambridge, UK: Cambridge University Press. pp. 41–62.

Flaig, D., and S. F. Stone. 2017. Local Content Requirements Versus Tariff Equivalents: How We Measure Matters. *The World Economy.* 40 (5). pp. 931–948.

Global Trade Alert. 2022. www.globaltradealert.org (accessed 1 September 2022).

Grossman, G. 1981. The Theory of Domestic Content Protection and Content Preference. *The Quarterly Journal of Economics.* 96 (4). pp. 583–603.

Hufbauer, G. C., J. Schott, C. Cimino-Isaacs, M. Vieiro, and E. Wada. 2013. *Local Content Requirements: A Global Problem.* Washington, DC: Peterson Institute for International Economics. www.piie.com/bookstore/local-content-requirements-global-problem

IBGE. 2022. *Product: Input Matrix: Brazil, 2000–2005.* Rio de Janeiro: Instituto Brasileiro de Geografia e Estatística. www.ibge.gov.br/english/estatistica/economia/matrizinsumo_produto/default.shtm (accessed 1 September 2022).

Kaziboni, L., and M. Stern. 2021. The Impact of Local Content Policies on South Africa: Drawing Lessons from Foreign Investors' Experience of the PPPFA and REIP4. *Paper for the TIPS Forum 2021.* (accessed 2–3 August 2021).

Kingiri, A., and J. M. Okemwa. 2022. Local Content and Capabilities: Policy Processes and Stakeholders in Kenya. In R. Lema, M. H. Andersen, R. Hanlin, and C. Nzila, eds. *Building Innovation Capabilities for Sustainable Industrialisation: Renewable Electrification in Developing Economies.* Abingdon, UK: Routledge. https://doi.org/10.4324/9781003054665

Kolstad, I., and A. Kinyondo. 2017. Alternatives to Local Content Requirements in Resource-Rich Countries. *Oxford Development Studies.* 45 (4). pp. 409–423. https://doi.org/10.1080/13600818.2016.1262836

Kuntze, J. C., and T. Moerenhout. 2013. *Local Content Requirements and the Renewable Energy Industry: A Good Match?* Geneva: International Centre for Trade and Sustainable Development.

Lin, S. H., and Y. Weng. 2020. Can Strengthening the Local Content Requirements Meet a Government's Need to Raise Industrial Productivity and Production? *Journal of Applied Economics.* 23 (1). pp. 316–328. doi: 10.1080/15140326.2020.175346

López González, J., F. Casalini, and J. Porras. 2022. A Preliminary Mapping of Data Localisation Measures. *OECD Trade Policy Papers.* No. 262. Paris: Organisation for Economic Co-operation and Development. https://doi.org/10.1787/18166873

McDonald, S., and K. E. Thierfelder. 2013. Globe v1: A SAM Based Global CGE Model Using GTAP Data. *Model Documentation.* www.cgemod.org.uk/globe2.html

OECD. n.d. *Trade in Value Added.* www.oecd.org/sti/ind/measuring-trade-in-value-added.htm (accessed 1 September 2022).

OECD. 2020. Mapping Approaches to Data and Data Flows. *Report for the G20 Digital Economy Task Force, Saudi Arabia 2020.* Paris: Organisation for Economic Co-operation and Development. www.oecd.org/sti/mapping-approaches-to-data-and-data-flows.pdf

Ramdoo, I. 2015. Unpacking Local Content Requirements in the Extractive Sector: What Implications for the Global Trade and Investment Frameworks? *E15 Expert Group on Trade and Investment in Extractive Industries Think Piece.* Geneva: International Centre for Trade and Sustainable Development (ICTSD) and World Economic Forum. www.e15initiative.org/

Stephenson, S. 2013. *Addressing Local Content Requirements in a Sustainable Energy Trade Agreement.* Geneva: International Centre for Trade and Sustainable Development. www.files.ethz.ch/isn/166575/addressing-local-content-requirements_opt.pdf

Stone, S., J. Messent, and D. Flaig. 2015. Emerging Policy Issues: Localisation Barriers to Trade. *OECD Trade Policy Papers.* No. 180. Paris: Organisation for Economic Co-operation and Development. https://doi.org/10.1787/5js1m6v5qd5j-en

Tordo, S., M. Warner, M. Manzano, E. Osmel, and Y. Anouti. 2013. *Local Content in the Oil and Gas Sector.* Washington, DC: World Bank. https://openknowledge.worldbank.org/handle/10986/15930

Walmsley, T., A. Winters, and S. A. Ahmed. 2007. Measuring the Impact of the Movement of Labor Using a Model of Bilateral Migration Flows. *GTAP Technical Paper.* No. 28. West Lafayette, IN: Center for Global Trade Analysis, Department of Agricultural Economics, Purdue University.

Weiss, M. 2016. The Role of Local Content Policies in Manufacturing and Mining in Low-and Middle-Income Countries. *Department of Policy Research and Statistics Working Paper 19/2016*, UNIDO.

World Bank. 2022. *Temporary Trade Barriers Database.* www.worldbank.org/en/data/interactive/2021/03/02/temporary-trade-barriers-database (accessed 1 September 2022).

World Trade Organization. 2022. *Trade Monitoring Database.* https://tmdb.wto.org/en (accessed 1 September 2022).

Table 2A.1 Model Aggregation – Sectors, Regions and Factors of Production

Sectors		
Primary sector: • Agriculture • Food • Coal • Oil • Gas • Minerals	Manufacturing: • Textiles • Wood products • Paper products, publishing • Petroleum, coal products • Chemical products • Basic pharmaceutical products • Rubber and plastic products • Mineral products • Ferrous metals • Nonferrous metals • Metal products • Computer, electronic, and optical products • Electrical equipment • Machinery and equipment • Motor vehicles and parts • Transport equipment • Other manufacturing	Services: • Electricity • Gas manufacture, distribution • Water • Construction • Trade • Accommodation, food, and service activities • Land transport • Water transport • Air transport • Warehousing and support activities • Communication • Financial services • Insurance • Real estate activities • Business services • Recreational and other services • Public administration and defense • Education • Human health and social work • Dwellings
Regions		
Single countries: • Argentina • Brazil • Indonesia • Saudi Arabia • South Africa • United States	Aggregate regions: • Asia • Americas • Europe • Rest of the world	
Production factors		
Labor: • Tech/Associate professionals • Officials/managers/professionals • Clerks • Service/shop workers • Agricultural and other workers	Other production factors: • Capital • Land • Natural resources	

Source: Authors' compilation.

3 Local content policies in the mining sector

Jane Korinek and Paulo De Sa

Objectives of the chapter

Historically, the mining industry in resource-rich developing nations has operated as an enclave, extracting raw materials for export with few links with other sectors and little value added to the resource-rich country. This diminished the opportunity for direct economic and social benefits, causing many mining countries to endure undiversified economic structures, high unemployment rates, and macroeconomic frameworks vulnerable to commodity shocks.

Legal and fiscal frameworks adopted during the 1990s focused on the capacity of the mining sector to generate tax and royalty revenues whose benefits, it was assumed, would automatically trickle down to the rest of the economy (Bastida, 2014). However, this approach failed to appreciate that procurement of goods and services is the single largest in-country economic expenditure over the life of a mining project – sometimes larger than taxes, salaries, wages, and community investment combined.[1]

At present, global mining companies follow high procurement standards and tend to outsource their operational activities to globally competitive contractors. The move toward greater outsourcing has led to the emergence of global supply chains in the mining sector, enabled by falling transportation costs, lower trade barriers, improved information and communication technologies, and liberalized financial regulations (Östensson, 2017).

Since the procurement of goods and services is the single largest expense over the life of a mining project, local content requirements (LCRs) have become politically attractive, as they aim to respond to demands to create jobs and economic opportunities. Yet in practice, the design and implementation of policy frameworks for LCRs in mining that foster sustainable and competitive domestic suppliers has proven extremely difficult.

Many countries have introduced or amplified targets for locally supplied goods and services in legislative and regulatory instruments without surveying mining companies' procurement needs, establishing a baseline of local supply capabilities, or calculating the trade-offs from specific initiatives in terms of value created for the economy. Mining companies argue that such targets are often prescribed without due consideration of the complex operational

DOI: 10.4324/9781003415794-3

structures, strategies, and market conditions of the industry, and they have often responded with caution or sought to circumvent compliance with such targets. Notwithstanding, many companies have set up internal local content programs that also serve as risk-mitigation actions and have developed constructive engagement with governments and communities to reinforce their social license to operate.

This chapter draws on some observations regarding the effectiveness of LCRs' contribution to foster employment and economic diversification and increase government revenues in resource-rich countries. It addresses policy implications for countries that aim to maximize benefits from the mining sector while ensuring that their regulatory and business environments contribute to sustaining the sector's competitiveness in global markets.

The chapter begins with an introductory section that presents current definitions for LCRs and suggests a typology of local content policies that are used in the mining sector and some considerations when aiming to measure their impacts. The second section reviews local sourcing and domestic employment requirements, trade restrictions, and other local content measures that have been introduced in different countries to foster backward and forward linkages and analyses common pitfalls in their design and implementation.

The third section includes reflections on institutional frameworks relevant for countries that aim to deploy LCRs. It includes a brief discussion on the implications of World Trade Organization (WTO) rules and investment agreements on the use of such instruments.

The fourth section relies on a qualitative desk review of existing literature, research papers, and reports on LCR law and practice that aims to shed light on some of the potential economic impacts of the use of LCRs in resource-rich countries. It highlights difficulties in measuring the impacts of LCRs, due in part to a lack of data providing empirical evidence but also because the definition of LCRs varies from country to country, making comparisons difficult. Notwithstanding, empirical evidence suggests that LCRs seldom achieve their objectives of increasing the domestic value added in the supply of goods and services or developing sustainable linkages but have been somewhat successful in some cases in terms of job creation and skills transfer.

The last section presents a series of policy implications derived from the preceding analysis. It finds that LCRs, if implemented, must be aligned with what can be realistically achieved without threatening the long-term competitiveness of the industry. Therefore, they should be part of a broader set of public policies to leverage the sector's contribution to increase value addition throughout the economy, job creation, and economic diversification rather than the share of domestic procurement. Accordingly, many resource-rich countries have moved from prescribed local procurement requirements to creating the conditions to increase the export of mining-related services and integration in global supply chains.

Scope and content of LCRs

LCRs in the mining sector include all laws and regulations that prescribe measures to stimulate the use of locally sourced goods and services, create job opportunities, and generate broader spillover effects in the national and local economies of resource-rich countries. Their scope ranges from mandatory employment targets to tax exemptions on local procurement but also includes export restrictions to encourage downstream processing of domestic minerals, ownership requirements, the reservation of certain procurement from domestic firms, and demands that research and development (R&D) on mining-related technologies be conducted in the country where operations take place. An estimated 90% of resource-rich countries employ LCR, most of which are quantitative targets or requirements (McKinsey, 2013).

There is no commonly agreed definition of what constitutes "local content." The term "local" has been used in different ways (Korinek and Ramdoo, 2017; Intergovernmental Forum on Mining, Minerals, Metals and Sustainable Development [IGF], 2018c): it can refer to geographic proximity, such as the population living in the vicinity of a mining project, although local suppliers are often defined as businesses registered in the country at both the national and community levels. Similarly, local employment is generally associated with the nationality of the workforce and can target a wide range of job positions, including at the management level. In some countries, goods and services must be provided by firms with some percentage of domestic capital ownership. In others, mining companies may be requested to enter into partnerships with state-owned entities or local firms or to list a prescribed percentage of their shares on national stock exchanges.

The definition and scope of what constitutes "content" can vary from country to country but usually aims to accomplish one or more of the following: (i) upstream supplier development at the domestic and/or community level; (ii) skills enhancement at different stages of the value chain, including the creation of job opportunities and training of the local workforce; (iii) technological and knowledge transfer, in particular toward local small and medium-sized enterprises (SMEs) or government agencies, or investing in R&D activities in the country; (iv) shared ownership of assets; and/or (v) downstream value addition and beneficiation of locally produced raw materials (Korinek and Ramdoo, 2017).

Typology of main LCRs affecting the mining sector

LCRs are generally formulated in policy frameworks setting broad orientations – such as national development plans and policy statements – and are codified in legislative and regulatory instruments or as part of contract agreements negotiated with mining investors. There is a wide range of policies to promote local content, but in simple terms, they can be classified as either demand-side or supply-side policies. Demand-side policies focus on creating demand for locally procured goods and services. Supply-side policies emphasize skills development and building the capacity of local suppliers to bring them up to global standards of competitiveness on price, quality, and reliability. Measures range from mandatory or voluntary supplier development programs to stand-alone or public–private partnerships for skills development.

Measures can be further classified as mandatory ("requirement-based" approach) or rely on firms' voluntary programs or "best efforts" to grant preferences to local economic entities ("incentives-driven" approach). "Requirement-based" policies can be further classified into two categories. Some impose legally binding targets on firms, either in terms of *quantity* (e.g., the number of local staff to be employed or contracts to be awarded to local suppliers) or *value* (e.g., a percentage of total spending on local procurement). "Incentives-driven" requirements generally do not set specific targets but can also be binding. For example, companies may be requested to publish their procurement needs or report on the percentage of local employment, although the levels of local procurement and employment might not be prescribed. "Best efforts" provisions are usually embedded in legislation but do not subject the companies to any specific quantitative requirements.

LCRs can be further classified as aiming to foster greater linkages upstream of the mining sector, or downstream (Table 3.1). They contain measures aimed at developing job skills and the capacity of local suppliers, using the sector as the anchor client in the case of backward or upstream linkages or as the source of inputs in the case of forward or downstream linkages.

In the case of LCRs that aim to foster backward linkages or increase local procurement, local sourcing and domestic employment requirements are the most common examples of mandatory LCRs. The first often mandates the purchase of specific product categories or a prescribed volume or value of goods and services from local suppliers. They can also include tender preferences for local suppliers and are increasingly accompanied by the obligation to provide procurement plans, schedules, and implementation reports to local authorities (World Bank and Kaiser Economic Development Partners, 2015). Domestic employment requirements call for the hiring of specific percentages of local workers and for companies to reserve some categories of jobs exclusively for nationals (and, increasingly, for indigenous people, women, or disadvantaged groups). They can also limit the number of expatriates employed and mandate training programs for their replacement by local workers.

Governments can act as facilitators, providing incentives to firms to increase their local purchases. Supplier development programs (SDPs) are by far the most common government "incentives-driven" approach to increase upstream or backward linkages; other approaches include (i) tax reductions for firms that are part of mining supply chains, support workforce development, invest in innovation, or agree to transfer technology; (ii) grants and scholarships for students and employees willing to upgrade their skills or for training institutions that partner with industry to develop them; and (iii) support for

Table 3.1 Illustrative Examples of LCRs

Type	*Demand Side*	*Supply Side*
Policies that aim to increase upstream linkages		
Requirement based	Extractive firms are required to: • Meet numerical targets for local employment per type of jobs and/or level of competency or report on measures taken to hire locally • Extend preferences to local suppliers for procurement of goods and services	Extractive firms are required to: • Provide training to employees • Fund capacity development programs • Establish a "buddy system" whereby local staff are paired with expatriates for direct on-the-job training
Incentives driven	Extractive firms are required or encouraged to: • Publish job vacancies • Publish tenders on given websites and in the media • Set up or use existing networks of suppliers	Extractive firms are required or encouraged to: • Conduct training programs for potential suppliers to understand the needs and required standards of extractive firms • Conduct awareness campaigns about key procurement employment opportunities Governments and academic institutions: • Create engineering and technical curricula in conjunction with extractive firms' stated and future needs • Provide targeted training to enhance the skills of potential suppliers Governments or regulators: • Set up networks of suppliers and extractive firms • Provide forums for matchmaking between local suppliers and extractive firms to foster greater engagement
Policies that aim to increase downstream linkages		
Requirement based	Extractive firms are required to: • Sell a share of their raw materials in-country • Pay higher tax rates on exports of raw materials than processed products • Engage in downstream processing in order to obtain export licenses	Extractive firms are required to: • Invest in downstream processing facilities Concomitantly, governments or regulators may: • Provide tax concessions, concessional loans, and lower import duties on imported capital goods or subsidize energy, transport, or other infrastructure

Type	*Demand Side*	*Supply Side*
Incentives driven	• Extractive firms are given tax concessions if they favor in-country sale of raw materials • Extractive firms are required to divest a share of their equity if they do not process raw materials in-country	Extractive firms are required or encouraged to: • Collaborate with training institutions to ensure the necessary skills for processing industries Governments or regulators: • Provide tax or other concessions to processors to invest

LCR = local content requirement.

Source: Authors' conception; Korinek and Ramdoo (2017).

research, development, and innovation through dedicated funding to universities, research centers, and innovation incubators.

Notwithstanding, several countries have introduced prescriptive beneficiation requirements either in the form of across-the-board legislation or during negotiations of contracts with mining firms. These requirements are essentially of three types: (i) taxes on the export of unprocessed minerals; (ii) quantitative export restrictions on unprocessed minerals, either partial (quotas) or comprehensive bans; and (iii) export licensing requirements to control mineral exports (UNCTAD, 2017; Fung and Korinek, 2013). In other countries, governments have created or mandated existing state-owned enterprises to invest in the downstream sector. China is the most obvious example, with state entities owning and operating most copper processing facilities and supporting them with direct grants, low-interest loans, and tax incentives (Geipel, de Weerdt, and Alarcon, 2021).

Prescriptive beneficiation requirements are often accompanied by incentives to increase the rate of return of downstream investments such as tax reductions or exemptions, energy or water subsidies, and concessional loans or the provision of industry-specific infrastructure such as industrial parks. Governments may also offer protections for processing operations through customs tariffs and import restrictions on the products being processed (IGF, 2018c).

Measuring the impacts of LCRs

The economy-wide costs generated by local content measures should be measured and compared with the potential benefits they aim to provide. LCRs on intermediate inputs to the extractive industries may lead to an increase in production costs that will raise output prices, in the mining sector in the first instance.[2] The increased prices of raw materials raise costs for producers further down the value chain, reducing the competitiveness of downstream industries and ultimately hindering the development of the wider economy (Grossman, 1981) and economic diversification. The size of these efficiency losses will be proportional to the additional costs associated with purchasing required inputs domestically, due to the policy, compared with their cost on international markets (Stone, Messent and Flaig, 2015). In addition, such measures can reduce the amount of taxes collected by the government if they negatively affect the profitability of firms and hence shrink the tax base.

Using mandatory quantitative requirements to develop internationally competitive industries runs counter to the known positive spillovers from engaging in global value chains and the role trade plays in their development. Kimura and Obashi (2011), for example, argue that the success of global value chains in East Asia, especially compared with Latin America, relies heavily on such interlinkages between domestic and foreign markets.

Impacts on the investment climate of mandatory LCRs should also be measured. One of the central tenets to an attractive investment climate is nondiscrimination (OECD, 2015). Restrictions on foreign direct investment (FDI) and trade have been found to result in less FDI overall.

LCRs: some examples

Prescribed demand-side requirements that aim to create backward linkages have been used in many African countries recently; the cases of Ghana, South Africa, Tanzania, and Zambia are outlined here. Countries such as Australia, Canada, and Chile have preferred an incentives-based approach to develop competitive suppliers and strong linkages between mining and the domestic economy. Prescriptive requirements that aim to foster downstream minerals processing have been used in many countries; the cases of Indonesia and Botswana are discussed here at some length.

Demand-side requirement-based LCRs that aim to create backward linkages

First-generation local content legislation usually required "best efforts" from mining companies. More recently, especially after 2018, a growing number of African countries have adopted or revised mandatory LCRs in their mining laws – introducing mandated quantitative procurement targets, sometimes requiring foreign investors to open equity to local partners. This is the case of the Democratic Republic of Congo, Ghana, Namibia, South Africa, and Tanzania. Countries like Burkina Faso, Mali, Kenya, Mozambique, Nigeria, and Zambia are revising their mining and investment codes with the same purpose.

The efforts to promote demand-side, requirement-based LCRs in Africa through mining legislation provide valuable lessons. Firstly, they have created a complex landscape across the continent that is difficult to navigate. Moreover, many countries have prescribed levels of local procurement beyond what local suppliers are capable of meeting, and few efforts can be considered completely successful. Many of the quantitative targets are aspirational and have little chance of being successfully implemented without mechanisms to build the capacity of current and potential local suppliers (African Natural Resources Centre, 2021).

The following cases illustrate the challenges of designing and implementing LCRs in countries where, on many occasions, laws and regulations are frequently revised and retracted, creating complex regulatory frameworks and institutional ambiguity.

(i) The case of Ghana

Ghana's 2006 Minerals and Mining Law sought to facilitate production linkages, and the 2012 Minerals and Mining (General) Regulations set quotas and timelines for compliance applicable to both mining companies and suppliers regarding employment of the local workforce and procurement of locally produced goods and services. The regulations had five main features (IGF, 2018a):

- *Numerical employment targets* for the number of allowed expatriates, with restrictions for certain categories of positions reserved for local staff, and timeframes for compliance. Ghana's regulations require 100% local workers for administrative or labor positions. For more technical, specialist, or management roles, restrictions on how many foreign nationals can be employed are set on a case-by-case basis.
- *Mandatory procurement of locally produced goods and services* specified by a list published by the Minerals Commission. A first list, published in 2014, included eight products required to be sourced locally. In 2016, the number of products increased to 19, and currently 28 products are featured.
- *Compulsory reporting requirements* mandating mining companies to submit a five-year local procurement plan stating how much they will buy from local firms and report on it each year, including progress on the listed goods and services.
- *Use of a phased approach* with lead times to allow industrial capacity to meet the industry requirements for product cost, quality, and quantity.
- *Sanctions for noncompliance* with the LCRs, which is assessed annually.

The latest assessment indicates that local companies have managed to supply, on average, about half of the products specified in the Minerals Commission list, increasing local procurement from $148 million to $394 million between 2014 and 2018 (Atta-Quayson, 2022). However, these products are not necessarily produced locally since mining companies can meet LCRs for listed goods by purchasing from resellers. Regarding local employment, most companies have been able to meet the quotas set in the legislation for all professional categories listed (IGF, 2018d).[3]

(ii) The case of South Africa

South Africa has one of the world's most complex local content legislations. The 2000 Preferential Procurement Policy Framework enables the designation of specific sectors for preferential domestic manufacture (or "localization"), in line with national development and industrial policy goals. The 2011 Beneficiation Strategy for the Minerals Industry identified a range of crosscutting constraints to local beneficiation and proposed a series of policy, legal, and regulatory measures to increase value added in the mining sector and facilitate job creation, industrialization, and economic diversification.

The Broad-Based Socio-Economic Empowerment Charter for the Mining Industry (amended in 2010), commonly known as the Mining Charter, aimed to rectify the results of discrimination based on race, sex, and disability. It defined "Black Economically Empowered" (BEE) entities as those where historically disadvantaged persons hold a minimum of 25% plus one vote of capital. The charter requires the industry to procure from BEE entities according to set targets and to track procurement, employment, and other criteria in line with social transformation targets (de Weerdt and Geipel, 2020).

The Chamber of Mines established a Broad-Based Scorecard, which requires its members to comply with a procurement target from BEE entities of 70% and 80% for goods and services, respectively. Targets were then broken down into further subcategories with certain percentages devoted to different groups, including historically disadvantaged persons, BEE-compliant companies, and women- or youth-owned companies. Mining companies were given an implementation period of 5 years for goods, with interim targets leading to full implementation (Geipel, de Weerdt, and Alarcon, 2021).

While many of the 2010 charter's targets appear to have been met, they were essentially based on company ownership rather than the level of value addition generated by a specific business. Moreover, there was evidence that locally produced products for the mining sector at times were displaced by imports sold by businesses compliant with the targets (Korinek and Ramdoo, 2017).

As a result, the 2018 Mining Charter stipulated that 70% of all goods used in the mining industry must be manufactured in South Africa, within 5 years of the law's enactment, and not merely purchased from South African–registered suppliers. Yet mining companies have argued that the target was set too high and that there are not enough supply-side policies to support them. Overall, the disconnect between different definitions across various pieces of legislation, frameworks, and scorecards – and the lack of open dialogue and trust between government and industry – increased the uncertainty around the interpretation of the targets and the overall success of the policy (Moraka and van Rensburg, 2015; White, 2017).

It was determined that some of the complex ownership and participation requirements were not implemented in good faith, and a Code of Good Practice for the South African Mineral Industry was devised to set out administrative principles for the effective implementation of the mining legislation and the Broad-Based Socio-Economic Charter applicable to the mining industry. The code defines ethics of conduct to ensure the Mining Charter is implemented in good faith and to prevent abuses such as fronting practices and opportunistic behaviors that may divert potential benefits from the targeted stakeholders. For example, the Code of Good Practice defines practices considered fraudulent, such as situations in which local stakeholders may be appointed to a position but discouraged or inhibited from participating in core activities; economic diversion, in which economic benefits received do not flow back to the local stakeholder in the ratio specified in the legal document; and intermediaries leveraging their BEE status that have concluded agreements with mining companies (fronting operations) (Korinek and Ramdoo, 2017).

(iii) The cases of Tanzania and Zambia

In Tanzania, the 1997 Mineral Policy, the 2010 Mining Act and 2017 amendments – Written Laws (Miscellaneous Amendments) Act – emphasized the development of backward linkages but left implementation largely to voluntary compliance. In January 2018, the Minister for Minerals promulgated the Mining (Local Content) Regulations, introducing hard quotas for the procurement of goods and services from domestically owned providers, including in the banking, financial services, insurance, and legal sectors. Mining companies are now required to prepare an annual local content plan, including projections for procurement, employment, and training activities. The plan must be updated annually and submitted for approval to the Local Content Committee. It is also a requirement to prepare a revolving 3- to 5-year program for R&D, detailing planned activity expenditures and calls for proposals for their implementation. Licensees also need to publish a plan for technology transfer to the benefit of Tanzanian entities.

The regulations also stipulate that mining companies can only retain the services of Tanzanian financial entities and need approval of the Mining Commission to hire the services of foreign financial institutions. They must maintain a bank account and conduct business with a bank with majority Tanzanian shareholding and may only retain the services of Tanzanian legal practitioners whose principal office is in Tanzania (Herbert Smith Freehills, 2018). Difficulties in implementation led the government to pass in February 2019 the Mining (Local Content) (Amendment) Regulations of 2019, which amended the 2018 Regulations in a number of ways. Among other things, the amended regulations reduced ownership restrictions for financial institutions preference by removing the term "indigenous Tanzanian bank" and replacing it with "Tanzanian bank" – defined as a bank that is 100% Tanzanian or has not less than 20% of Tanzanian shareholding. Uncertainties remain regarding the practicality of the other aspects needed to ensure compliance with LCRs.

In Zambia, there is substantial scope to both forward and backward linkages in copper mining. In 2014, the Zambian Chamber of Mines, in partnership with the International Council on Mining and Metals, examined the nature of the industry's procurement spending on goods and services. The participating companies reported spending 80% of procurement for goods on local suppliers, but the study estimated that only $87 million out of $1.75 billion purchased (about 5%) went to locally manufactured goods (Geipel, de Weerdt, and Alarcon, 2021). Since 2015, firms are required to submit local procurement plans that detail how they will increase spending on national suppliers and to report annually on the progress achieved,[4] although there is little public information to suggest these plans are being meaningfully monitored or enforced.

In 2018, through a Statutory Instrument, Zambia also required that mining companies use domestic rail for 30% of all freight services. However, the capacity of the rail system could not provide the required volume of freight services for the companies, leading the government to provide waivers exempting companies from the requirement (African Natural Resources Centre, 2021).

Demand-side incentives-driven LCRs that aim to increase backward linkages

(a) The cases of Australia and Canada

Australia has developed a comparative advantage in the mining, equipment, technology, and services (METS)[5] sector based on close relationships between R&D organizations and mining firms. Although the drive for METS came from the mining sector, the Australian government provided strong support aimed at improving management and workforce skills, improving collaboration between research and industry, and facilitating access to global supply chains and promoting technologically advanced suppliers abroad (IGF, 2018a). Australia substantially increased the use of mining services, with almost all the growth being sourced domestically. Services currently account for about 26% of the value added of the Australian mining sector (Korinek, 2020).

In Canada, local content provisions focus on employment and procurement of goods and services, with no set quotas or timelines of enforcement. Mining firms are not required to enter employment or procurement contracts that are not competitive.

Notwithstanding, both Australia and Canada require mining companies to enter into formal agreements with local communities before the start of operations to define how those communities will benefit from each project. These agreements can range from statements of general principles in a memorandum of understanding to legally binding agreements that include grievance mechanisms and can be subject to dispute settlement. Many of these agreements contain different types of incentives-driven LCRs, including (i) education and training, (ii) local employment targets, (iii) provisions to guarantee that local suppliers benefit from business opportunities, and (iv) provisions to allocate financial benefits as compensation for the impact of projects on traditional lands (IGF, 2018c).

Australia's community development agreements, known as Indigenous Land Use Agreements, are three-way contracts between the government, a company, and an indigenous community in which clear guidelines for collaboration, local procurement, and economic development are established. Canada's Impact Benefit Agreements are negotiated between companies and indigenous communities, with government oversight.

(b) The case of Chile

Chile does not apply any mandated or prescriptive LCRs. A combination of stable legal and regulatory frameworks, a strong culture of partnerships with mining firms and research and training institutions, and a favorable environment for innovation have provided the basis for the development of local suppliers.

Chile is often considered the best example of successful SDPs because of its clear focus on upgrading the participation of local firms in global value chains. The first initiative was launched in 1998, when the state Production Development Corporation (CORFO) attempted to improve the competitiveness of SMEs and develop their linkages with large buyers.

In 2009, the World Class Suppliers program – launched by BHP with funding from the government, CODELCO (which joined in 2011), and participating mining firms and suppliers – aimed to develop 250 domestic suppliers into world-class global mining suppliers by 2020.[6] Mining firms provided technical, managerial, and financial support, training, technical assistance, and technological transfer to support local suppliers in the development of new technological solutions addressing critical aspects of the industry, such as water, energy, human capital, maintenance, and air quality. Mining companies also offered their operations as testing areas for the new technologies and assisted suppliers in accessing international markets (Columbia Center on Sustainable Investment, 2016). The program leveraged the proximity of Chilean suppliers to the mine sites, where they engaged in adapting technologies to the local conditions. As such, the program focused on adaptative rather than radical innovation and provided a niche for Chilean suppliers that global mining equipment manufacturers may be at a disadvantage to fill (Korinek, 2013).

In 2017, the program was restructured into two public–private initiatives: the Alta Ley National Mining Program, led by CORFO and the Ministry of

Mining, aiming to upgrade the number, export orientation, innovation capacity, and technological capabilities of mining suppliers; and Valor Minero, a public–private alliance promoting dialogue between different stakeholders to improve the sustainability of the mining sector.

Other initiatives involve collaboration between the government and the private sector in training and education projects. Since 2015, the Mining Skills Council (CCM), set up by Consejo Minero, a trade association, regularly updates three core products: (i) studies projecting demand, supply, and human-capital gaps based on data from every mining firm and industry education and training supplier; (ii) a qualification framework informing training requirements for different occupational profiles; and (iii) training packages (AfDB and Bill, and Melinda Gates Foundation, 2015).

CORFO and Fundación Chile, a public–private partnership, provide funding for innovation to an association of small local suppliers (Asociación de Proveedores Industriales de la Minería). Fundación Chile also identifies venture capitalists willing to invest in projects that promote technology transfer and new business models. Created in 2006, the Innovation for Competitiveness Fund is a state financing mechanism allocating a portion of copper tax revenues to other government agencies that promote innovation and competitiveness of local suppliers.

Another form of strategic public–private partnership is the creation of mining clusters[7] in key mining regions. Starting with the Antofagasta Region Mining Cluster (CMRA) in 2003, a series of clusters has been formed to promote investments and the competitiveness of goods, inputs, and services that supply the mining industry, such as human capital, skills, infrastructure, and access to finance.

Collaboration between the public and private sectors has facilitated the integration of many Chilean suppliers into global value chains, as the country moved from the promotion of local content to the export of goods, services, and knowledge. However, most Chilean suppliers still lag the world's leading METS industries of Australia, Canada, Japan, Finland, Sweden, and the United States (CSIRO, 2014). Studies suggest that horizontal cooperation relationships between suppliers, and with research institutions and academia, are weak; and the limited export capacity of Chilean suppliers reveals a lack of competitiveness and dependence on foreign technologies (Arías, Atienza, and Cademaroti, 2012).

Requirement-based LCRs that aim to increase forward linkages

Many resource-rich countries have the ambition to develop local manufacturing capabilities that add value to raw minerals by implementing LCRs to foster downstream or forward linkages with processing and manufacturing sectors. However, although geological factors largely determine where mining extraction takes place, not all countries with abundant mineral resources have a comparative advantage in moving into downstream processing. In the past, the export of processed minerals had an advantage derived from lower transportation costs on a volume basis over unprocessed ores. The fall in transportation costs gave an overall comparative advantage to locate processing facilities near consumer centers, providing processing firms with opportunities to build client relationships, react quickly to changing demand, reduce delivery times, and minimize the risk of potential import restrictions on finished products (Östensson and Löf, 2017).

Over the last 20 years, mining companies have increasingly been reluctant to integrate downstream because processing margins are smaller than the rents that can be earned in upstream extraction (Östensson, 2019). The mineral-processing industry is highly competitive and relies on processes that require significant economies of scale to reduce costs. Downstream processing plants must be built at minimum capacity levels and require an availability of inputs that does not always correspond to the domestic resource base.

The availability of low-cost inputs and the attractiveness of the investment regime also need to be considered when assessing the competitiveness of mineral processing. For example, the feasibility of energy-intensive downstream industries, such as aluminum smelters, depends on access to reliable and inexpensive energy sources. The availability of skilled labor, infrastructure, and financial services are also crucial, while macroeconomic stability and a currency that is not overvalued are critical for the viability of export-oriented industries.

Mineral-consuming countries have the power to influence location choices and have often managed to retain processing capacity, for example, by adopting higher import duties on semi-processed and finished products than on raw materials, to increase the effective rate of protection. When a country controls a substantial share of the demand for a given commodity, it can prevent efforts to develop forward linkages by raw mineral exporters. In the case of copper, for example, the market power of Chinese smelters and Chile's dependence on their demand restrained the construction of additional smelting and refining copper capacity in the South American country. Exporters of processed minerals without a domestic market capable of absorbing a large percentage of their output might be at a disadvantage compared with units located close to large consuming markets, which benefit from lower transportation costs and the proximity to a client base to generate higher margins.

These considerations notwithstanding, many countries have implemented LCRs that aim to increase mineral processing in-country. While few have accomplished their stated objectives (Fliess, Idsardi, and Rossouw, 2017), recent experiences in Indonesia and Botswana contribute to our collective understanding of the potential impacts of such measures.

(i) The case of Indonesia

Indonesia is an exceptional case, as an export ban introduced in 2014 with the aim of increasing mineral processing in-country – associated with requirements for foreign firms to divest[8] – had entirely distinct effects in the nickel and bauxite industries, largely because of differences in global market shares. The country's high-grade nickel ores required by Chinese customers[9] led to the construction of several new nickel smelters. Meanwhile, the export ban on bauxite failed in its objectives because the worldwide availability of bauxite allowed downstream firms, notably from China, to easily switch to other providers such as Australia and Malaysia, causing a loss of export mineral revenues that was not offset by new investments in domestic aluminum capacity. Indonesia's trade position in bauxite never recovered from the ban and continues to lag its 2013 export figures significantly (Lebdioui and Bilek, 2021).[10]

In 2009, Indonesia introduced the Mineral and Coal Mining Law (Law No. 4/2009), which laid the legal basis for a future export ban on several raw minerals by allowing the granting of export licenses only to firms that committed to process their ores domestically. Companies were given 5 years from the law's enactment date to invest in downstream facilities but expressed their concerns, arguing that it was not economically feasible for certain minerals to be processed in Indonesia and that the infrastructure was inadequate in many parts of the country to support downstream facilities (Warburton, 2017). Large mining companies initially failed to invest in mineral processing, believing the government would not enforce a hard ban and sacrifice substantial export revenues.

In January 2014, a comprehensive quantitative prohibition on the export of raw nickel and bauxite was introduced.[11] The regulations prescribed that only minerals at specified purity levels would be allowed to be exported and stipulated minimum levels of processing required to avoid the ban. Only ore with nickel content less than 1.7% was allowed to be exported without further processing.

Indonesia has 52% of the world's nickel reserves,[12,13] a metal that has been used primarily in stainless steel production but recently emerged as a key component in new battery technologies. Although before the ban, Indonesia was already the world's largest nickel ore producer, the country had only three nickel smelters. State-owned company PT Aneka Tambang (Antam) had an annual processing capacity of 20,000 tons of ferronickel, with Brazil's Vale processing 80,000 tons of nickel metal annually. PT Indoferro came a distant third, with an annual capacity of 3,000 tons (UNCTAD, 2017). The real targets of the ban were about 50 smaller mine operations on Sulawesi, which accounted for about 90% of nickel ore exports to China and were among the major causes of deforestation in the country (Lebdioui and Bilek, 2021). Falling commodity prices and global excess capacity exacerbated the impacts of the ban, with Indonesia's export value of unprocessed bauxite, copper, and nickel falling from $7 billion in 2013 to $2.9 billion in 2014. Nickel ore exports alone declined from 64.8 million tons to only 4.1 million tons in the same period (UNCTAD, 2017).

The export ban did not restrict which companies, foreign or domestic, could build smelters and thereby qualify for an export license and was accompanied by incentives for investors, including lower duties on imports of capital goods required for processing facilities and corporate tax breaks. Supported by increasing demand from China, three new smelters were operational at the beginning of 2016, adding 45,000 tons of nickel pig iron (NPI) for export to China.

The subsequent economic downturn and foregone revenues for regions dependent on raw mineral extraction proved to be too drastic for the ban to be politically feasible. In March 2017, the Ministry of Energy and Mineral Resources (MEMR) Regulation 5/2017 reversed the ban, allowing exports to resume under certain conditions for a period of 5 years, until January 2022. Following an increase in demand, this regulation was repealed by MEMR Regulation 11/2019, which banned the export of nickel ores as of 1 January 2020, 2 years earlier than scheduled. Only low-grade nickel ore with a content of less than 1.7% was allowed to be exported, under certain conditions and in the quantities approved by the MEMR.

Many foreign investors saw the reintroduction of the export ban as an inconsistency of policy, since the Indonesian government changed regulations three times in a decade (in 2014, 2017, and 2019). In January 2021, the European Union (EU) filed a WTO panel request against Indonesian export restrictions for raw materials used in the production of stainless steel – Dispute Settlement 592 – arguing that they unfairly limit the access of EU producers to raw materials for steel production. The EU is also challenging subsidies that encourage the use of local content by Indonesian producers and give preference to domestic over imported goods.

The complaint was initially filed in November 2019, followed by a period of consultations that ultimately failed to resolve the issue. The EU claimed that (i) the measures restricting the exports of certain raw materials, including those requiring domestic processing requirements, domestic market obligations, and export licensing requirements, appear to be inconsistent with Article XI:1 of the General Agreement on Tariffs and Trade (GATT) 1994; (ii) the subsidy scheme appears to be inconsistent with Article 3.1(b) of the Agreement on Subsidies and Countervailing Measures (SCM Agreement); and (iii) the failure to promptly publish the challenged measures appears to be inconsistent with Article X:1 of the GATT 1994. Indonesia claimed that the ban was introduced for the preservation of natural resources and to boost Indonesian participation in global value chains. In December 2019, the United States requested to join the consultations.

The production of processed nickel products surged from 24,000 metric tons in 2014 to 636,000 metric tons in 2020 (Huber, 2021). That year, Indonesia had 16 operating nickel smelters, the majority producing NPI and ferronickel. The five largest nickel smelters reached a combined annual capacity of 880,000 tons, with four Chinese companies leading the industry and Brazilian Vale occupying a distant fifth position with 70,000 tons annually. The number of smelters is expected to increase to 29 by 2025, according to the MEMR,[14] and Indonesia will likely be the source of almost all the growth in the supply of refined nickel for electric vehicle (EV) batteries over the next decade.[15] The nickel export ban increased downstream processing because Indonesia's exceptional resource endowment provided strong incentives for investments, mostly from Chinese companies (Lebdioui and Bilek, 2021). However, its standing among Western mining investors has fallen sharply: Indonesia is ranked the fourth worst mining jurisdiction globally (out of 78 jurisdictions), outranked only by Venezuela, the Chubut province of Argentina, and Tanzania, according to a survey of mining investors (Yunis and Aliakbari, 2020).

The Indonesian government is preparing a new nickel strategy, considering the possibility of levying an export tax on products with less than 70% nickel content, and limiting the construction of smelters for class 2 (lower-grade) products. This strategy is part of Indonesia's policy approach for the energy transition (Huber, 2021). The country aims to develop a fully integrated domestic supply chain for nickel, from ore extraction to battery production and EV assembling. The government has produced a road map for EV battery development and storage systems through 2026.

For example, in 2021, LG Energy Solution and Hyundai from the Republic of Korea (henceforth, Korea) jointly started building a $1.1 billion EV battery plant in West Java. In addition, the Chinese company Huayou is involved in several smelting projects on Sulawesi Island, including two projects with the Indonesian unit of Vale, estimated to cost around $6.3 billion. Ford Motor Company is negotiating its involvement in one of these projects. Huayou is also teaming up with Tsingshan and Volkswagen Group China, with the goal of supplying nickel and cobalt from Indonesia to support the production of batteries.[16]

Battery manufacturers are also investing. In April 2022, China's largest battery maker, Contemporary Amperex Technology Co., Limited (CATL), PT Aneka Tambang, and PT Industri Baterai Indonesia (IBC) signed an agreement to develop a project in Indonesia's North Maluku Province that will focus on nickel mining and processing, battery materials, and battery manufacturing, as well as battery recycling. CATL is investing in Indonesia through QMB New Energy Materials, a joint venture with Tsingshan and Chinese battery recycler GEM. Korean battery maker LG Energy Solution is separately partnering with IBC and Aneka Tambang to develop an end-to-end battery supply chain in Indonesia.

When these new foreign investments materialize, Indonesia will account for around half of the world's growth in nickel production between 2021 and 2025, according to the International Energy Agency, and could become a leading producer of nickel-based products, including EV batteries. The expectation in Indonesia is that large investments will increase the economies of scale and drive down costs, potentially making Indonesia a low-cost manufacturer, competitive in global markets.

(ii) The case of Botswana

Diamonds were first discovered in Botswana in 1966, shortly after independence, with large-scale production starting in 1971. Diamond mining became the greatest contributor to gross domestic product (GDP) (currently around 30%) and government tax revenues (currently around 60%) (Columbia Center on Sustainable Investment, 2016). In the early 1980s, the government of Botswana tried to promote the development of a diamond-cutting and -polishing industry. However, global mining company De Beers, which dominated production in Botswana and the sale and marketing of diamonds globally, did not support this ambition, arguing that cutting and polishing activities were not economically viable in Botswana. Three cutting and polishing factories were established between 1980 and 1990, but none of them ever reported a profit.

A second opportunity emerged in 2005, when De Beers' 25-year mining license was due for renewal. Botswana's negotiating leverage derived from De Beers' reliance on Debswana, a 50–50 joint venture with the government, which was responsible for about 60% of the company's global supply of rough diamonds. Botswana obtained a guarantee from De Beers that a percentage of the diamonds mined in the country would be allocated to national cutting and polishing companies and that all sorting and valuing operations would be undertaken in-country (UNIDO, 2012; Korinek, 2014). Subsequently, the government invited foreign cutting and polishing companies to set up operations in the country with the promise of a guaranteed long-term allocation of De Beers' diamonds at 20% to 30% below the market price, on the condition that they hire and train locals with cutting and polishing skills (IGF, 2018c; 2018d). Furthermore, a Diamond Academy was opened by the joint venture to train diamond sorters and valuation staff (Korinek, 2014).

In 2008, the Diamond Trading Company (DTC Botswana), a 50–50 joint venture between De Beers and the government, was established to sort and value Debswana's output and manage the supply of diamonds to the domestic cutting and polishing industry. De Beers also agreed to move its aggregation business – selecting and mixing the diamonds from De Beers mines for its customers – from London to Gaborone, in the hope of creating considerable spillovers to other industries such as hospitality, finance, and transportation, since diamond buyers would now have to go to Gaborone to buy De Beers' diamonds (Morris, Kaplinsky, and Kaplan, 2011).

Nonetheless, a remaining issue is the ability of Botswana's diamond-cutting and -polishing industry, which remains dependent on government incentives, to compete with low-cost factories in Asia, especially in India. Unless investments in support infrastructure decrease production costs substantially, Botswana's diamond-polishing sector may not survive in the longer term. Moreover, its diamond processing industry is built on access to raw diamonds, but domestic diamond reserves are expected to be exhausted in 30 to 40 years (Columbia Center on Sustainable Investment, 2016).

Institutional frameworks and coordination

High-quality institutions in charge of designing, governing, managing, enforcing, monitoring, and evaluating LCRs are vital to accomplish their objectives. Many regulatory entities do not have a deep knowledge of the mining supply chain and its potential to generate revenues, businesses opportunities, and employment. Many are understaffed or underfinanced and suffer from opaque decision-making processes.

The effectiveness of LCRs can be affected by gaps in the institutional framework and lack of coordination for the approval of cross-sector policies and regulations, responsibility for which is scattered across many ministries, which often operate in silos. Therefore, some countries have established dedicated local content entities to coordinate and monitor progress, drawing on the resources of all relevant government agencies. This is the case of the Local Content Committee in Tanzania and the Industry Participation National Framework Authority in Australia.

Reporting requirements are important tools to monitor LCRs, but their efficacy depends on the capacity of the entity in charge of enforcing them. Because many countries have yet to enact and enforce adequate reporting mechanisms, in practice, most existing LCRs enable noncompliance (White, 2017), as shown in some of the previous examples. To address this, governments are increasingly asking mining companies to submit local procurement plans as part of their yearly reporting requirements. Yet sometimes, these reports cover only the firms' local capacity-building activities and are not suitable to monitor progress toward achieving broader desired outcomes.

Insufficient collaboration between governments, the business community, and civil society can lead to situations in which procurement targets are set at unrealistic levels, causing enforcement difficulties or creating conditions that facilitate influence peddling or corruption of public officials. LCRs can provide preferential treatment to stakeholders with strong vested interests or that are politically affiliated and may engage in rent-seeking behavior; some examples of this effect are outlined above. Likewise, fear of competition may block cooperation among mining companies, leading to a duplication of uncoordinated initiatives that prevent local suppliers from achieving the scale needed to become competitive.

Partnerships between mining firms, governments, training institutions, and local stakeholders are important, in particular when implementing SDPs, as they tend to be more effective when they benefit from the participation of multiple institutional actors, including notably mining firms (African Natural Resources Centre, 2021). For example, some subnational governments offer technical assistance to SMEs in the procurement contract process or keep databases of local suppliers to reduce information gaps that diminish their chances of responding to tenders, thereby combining supply-side and demand-side policies.

WTO rules, investment agreements, and LCRs

LCRs and other measures to increase the use of domestic goods and services, such as trade restrictions, subsidies, tariffs, and tax incentives, can introduce distortions in favor of local producers and may therefore contravene a number of trade and investment agreement disciplines (see Annex Tables 3.A1 and 3.A2). The relevant WTO commitments that relate to LCRs (Columbia Center on Sustainable Investment, 2016; Korinek and Ramdoo, 2017; Korinek and Bartos, 2012) are:

- The National Treatment Obligation (Article III of the GATT) clause prevents governments from discriminating between like products from local industries and imports. This applies to policies such as those that force foreign companies to buy goods or services produced by locally owned companies or hire local service suppliers.
- The Agreement on Trade-Related Investment Measures (TRIMs) prohibits the use of most forms of performance requirements on goods, set out in an "illustrative list." These apply to domestic sourcing requirements, either in the form of lists of goods or quotas or percentages, as well as requirements to sell products domestically. However, developing countries have derogations to some of those commitments outlined in Article XVIII of the GATT.
- Article XI:1 of the GATT imposes a general ban on quantitative export restrictions, but Article XI:2 and Article XX offer broad-scope exemptions to the ban on export quotas. Notably, Article XX(g) allows for quantitative restrictions relating to the conservation of exhaustible natural resources on the condition that "such measures are made effective in conjunction with restrictions on domestic production or consumption."
- The SCM Agreement prevents governments from providing incentives and granting subsidies that are contingent on sourcing goods domestically. Common subsidies, such as targeted tax preferences, may also be actionable under WTO rules.
- The General Agreement on Trade in Services (GATS) regulates LCRs with regard to foreign investment and employment. Local equity requirements and employment quotas are generally prohibited, but these are only regulated to the extent that countries have taken specific commitments.

Despite clear rules prohibiting certain forms of LCRs, many countries maintain them or have introduced new ones in recent years. Countries that joined the WTO after 1995 have been subject to closer scrutiny and tighter obligations, and some of them, such as Kazakhstan, have agreed to remove many LCRs during their accession negotiations (Korinek and Ramdoo, 2017).

Measures imposing LCRs have been the subject of significant exemptions for developing countries within WTO rules, including to support infant industries and address balance-of-payments problems. Moreover, TRIMs apply to restrictions on goods; regarding services, they only apply to commitments contained in countries' GATS schedules.

Few complaints regarding LCRs in the extractive industries have been brought to the WTO, although some have been filed regarding export restrictions (see claims regarding Indonesia and the case against China described earlier). Disputes regarding the enforcement of LCRs go through the WTO's settlement system, which is usually a costly and long process (African Natural Resources Centre, 2021); moreover, the WTO dispute settlement system has been effectively halted in recent periods.

International and bilateral investment treaties often go beyond WTO restrictions, e.g., by including restrictions on performance requirements for technology-transfer and R&D programs to be conducted in-country. They can also contain fair and equitable treatment obligations preventing governments from interfering with foreign investors' "expectations" for their operations. Most treaties do not include these provisions but, when included, the obligations tend to be implemented more frequently, since these agreements usually use investor-state arbitration rather than the WTO's state-to-state arbitration system, which increases the likelihood of complaints being filed (Columbia Center on Sustainable Investment, 2016).

Some reflections regarding the economic impacts of LCRs

Many LCRs lack a broader policy framework, such as overall political economy objectives, policy statements, and national development plans, to support them. Many countries have adopted stringent targets in regulatory instruments that lack detail and clarity and have a narrow scope of objectives. Before introducing them, governments must ascertain where the mining sector fits in relation to national development objectives, including its potential contribution to foster employment, government revenues, and economic diversification.

Demand-side, requirement-based LCRs often aim for high percentages of local content without developing a detailed view of procurement spending, establishing a baseline of local suppliers' capabilities, and quantifying the trade-offs from specific initiatives in terms of value added created (Elborai et al., 2019).

Inaccurate understanding of mining firms' procurement needs and of the absorptive capacity of local suppliers have led to the prescription of unrealistic targets, set beyond levels that local firms can meet, especially in countries with a weak industrial base and a private sector that is small, informal, and with low productivity. This can be a deterrent to the mining industry, especially without supporting government-sponsored supply-side measures. This was one of the issues confronted by Ghana's many LCRs applied to the mining sector.

While a broad definition of local content provides more flexibility for firms to meet targets and objectives, it is difficult to assess to what extent LCRs create local value-added and spillover effects for the rest of the economy. Ownership requirements do not always yield the best outcome in terms of domestic value added (ACET, 2017). Local ownership is not a relevant factor as long as companies create economic opportunities, and employment, and improve local labor skills (Esteves et al., 2014). Foreign-owned but locally based businesses can add value to the local economy, whereas local sourcing of imported goods usually does not. Duty-free imports of inputs by domestically owned firms place potential local producers and suppliers of such inputs at a disadvantage. For example, in less developed countries with a weak industrial base, many mining firms may report a relatively high percentage of local sourcing while, in reality, a large proportion of purchases originate from imports by local firms or representatives of foreign suppliers. This was found in Kazakhstan before it removed many of its LCRs; correspondingly, when the LCRs were removed, few local jobs were lost or displaced.

Ownership requirements can also create an environment conducive to lack of transparency, corruption, and favoritism, where benefits may be captured by local elites embracing rent-seeking behaviors and failing to encourage entrepreneurial development. They tend to be ineffective, as foreign companies may bypass limits imposed on dividend distribution and exert effective control of joint ventures through shareholders' agreements. Experience with such practices in South Africa prompted the authorities to institute a Code of Good Practice for the South African Mineral Industry to define ethics of conduct and prevent abuses such as fronting practices (Korinek and Ramdoo, 2017).

Prescriptive beneficiation (downstream processing) requirements have often failed because there is little guarantee that domestic processing industries can become competitive in the longer term. For example, in late 2019, Zambia was forced to end a 15% export tax on raw gemstones because the tax was decreasing investments in the sector, and overall production had fallen. Another high-profile case was Tanzania's ban on exports of raw gold, silver, copper, and other metallic minerals starting in March 2017. The ban did not achieve its goal of having mining companies invest in processing facilities, and raw mined gold stockpiled in the country until the ban was lifted (Geipel, de Weerdt, and Alarcon, 2021). Another illustration among many is the Indonesian bauxite sector, which has not recovered its exports since the export ban on bauxite was instituted in 2014.

The examples of Indonesian nickel and Botswanan diamonds show, however, that governments have more leverage in negotiations with foreign investors regarding prescriptive beneficiation requirements when the country possesses an exceptional resource endowment. In the case of Indonesian nickel, the draw of a substantial share of global reserves of high-quality ore, high projected demand for the mineral for batteries, and continued dependence on access to the mineral by China forced investments in downstream smelters. In Botswana, the favorable conditions guaranteeing access to cheaper rough diamonds granted to downstream cutting and processing firms incentivized investors to open facilities. However, even these examples call into question the longer-term sustainability of the downstream processing operations – in Indonesia for reasons of investment climate and in Botswana due to falling diamond reserves and lower productivity among diamond-cutting and -polishing operations compared with international competitors. Moreover, the global market for the specific mineral must present very favorable trends, with high projected future demand threatening a potential situation of scarcity, for such policies to be feasible even in the medium term.

Governments are more likely to achieve their aims if they are bargaining from a favorable position either because they have strong negotiating capacity or because the mining company needs to renew the terms of its license or concession in a mine that is an essential component of its profitability. Botswana has expanded its reach through the value chain of diamond valuation, aggregation, and sorting in a step-by-step fashion, in the context of subsequent license and permit negotiations (Korinek, 2014). This gradual approach helped to ensure the industry partner was supportive of the policies and that responses were found to supply-side constraints, such as the opening of a Diamond Academy to train potential employees for diamond sorting, valuing, and aggregation jobs.

Although empirical evidence suggests that "best efforts" clauses do not have much impact on their own (Geipel, de Weerdt, and Alarcon, 2021), the reality on the ground suggests that mandatory quantitative LCRs have yet to generate significant amounts of locally sourced inputs or strengthened inter-sector linkages. Local employment and some training of the local workforce appear to have been their most successful outcomes (Ellis and McMillan, 2020; White, 2017).

Supply-side initiatives appear to work better than prescriptive targets when they focus on building workforce skills – through both targeted training and skills-transfer activities, including in business management skills – and the capacity of local businesses to supply goods and services competitively and integrate in global supply chains (McCulloch et al., 2017). Some of the most interesting examples come from public–private partnerships that combine mining firms' SDPs with government-sponsored skills transfer and training initiatives developed in close collaboration with universities and technical centers. These exist in many countries; one example covered above comes from Chile's copper sector.

More generally, it appears that countries applying more inclusive approaches have been more successful than those following more protectionist methods focused on short-term goals and narrow targets. Policies that fail to consider long-term economic diversification objectives, focusing instead on narrow targets for the local sourcing of goods and services and the employment of the local workforce, are likely to generate businesses and skills that are dependent on the mining sector or even on a specific project (Weldegiorgis, Dietsche, and Franks, 2021; Lebdioui, 2019). Value added, created exclusively within the mining industry, perpetuates the vulnerability to commodity price fluctuations and macroeconomic shocks (Marcel et al., 2016; ACET, 2017). This is the case in particular of the downstream linkage policies implemented in Botswana.

LCRs tend, incorrectly, to be considered fiscally neutral, not presenting any financial implications for the government. In fact, they can create fiscal shortcomings if they negatively affect the profitability of the mining sector, reducing the amount of taxes and royalties collected by the government. LCRs can be costly to implement due to the incentives granted to promote the use of local inputs and develop competitive local supplier businesses. Governments often face a trade-off between maximizing tax revenues and developing local content, but the extra cost of adopting LCRs can be justified only if it expands the tax base over the long term (Marcel et al., 2016).

This will fail to materialize when LCRs reduce the industry's competitiveness. Protectionist measures can lead to the prevalence of uncompetitive suppliers for long periods, raising production costs and having a detrimental effect on sectors using mining products as inputs (McCulloch et al., 2017). On the other hand, imported intermediate goods and services are an important channel to increase productivity and the adoption of new technologies and can play a significant role in integration in global value chains. By increasing the specialization in the production of specific inputs, they can generate economies of scale that maximize productivity and provide opportunities to move into higher value activities over time through upgrading (Korinek and Ramdoo, 2017).

Finally, LCRs can cause disruption in global markets, in particular when they target minerals considered "critical" for certain key industrial sectors, inflicting supply risks, and affecting the sustainability of industries in resource-dependent countries. In a few instances in which LCRs are not WTO-compatible, this has led to costly disputes. For example, beginning in 2006, China imposed several restrictions on the export of rare earth metals and quotas on the export of unprocessed ores. This contributed to a steep increase in prices starting in 2010. In 2012, the United States initiated a dispute at the WTO against these restrictions, which the EU, Japan, and Canada joined as complainants. In 2014, the WTO Appellate Body decided in favor of the complainants, and China was required to remove its export restrictions.

Policy implications: from local value added to integrating global supply chains

Economy-wide impacts must be taken into account when considering implementing LCRs. If used, LCRs should be part of broader public policies, institutional arrangements, and partnerships that public authorities put in place to leverage the sector's contribution to broader economic diversification (Dietsche, 2017). In particular, it should be kept in mind that supporting sectors that are dependent on mineral extraction may not increase economic diversification, may increase the impacts of resource price cycles, and may have substantial environmental consequences.

More generally, governments can adopt a broad set of horizontal measures to remove constraints to business development throughout the economy, with an aim to promote macroeconomic stability; provide regulatory clarity and stability; support SMEs; and improve infrastructure in areas like energy, transport, communications, information technology, and finance. A supportive environment can be created for the mining industry and its suppliers by removing overly burdensome regulatory requirements, improving business infrastructure, promoting skills development, strengthening institutional coordination and collaboration among local suppliers, and supporting increased access to finance, in particular for SMEs often ill-equipped to access global supply chains (AfDB and Bill and Melinda Gates Foundation, 2015). LCRs that are more likely to deliver on their expectations are (i) guided by a comprehensive understanding of firms' procurement needs, strategies, and capabilities; (ii) based on a thorough understanding of the local capacities and bottlenecks to their enhancement; and (iii) cognizant of the factors that may impact policy effectiveness and the potential unintended consequences of such measures.

If prescriptive LCRs are to be introduced, they should be based on forecasts of the mining industry's future needs, spending projections for specific goods and services in existing and future mining projects, and assessments of the capacity of local firms to supply goods and services of sufficient quality at competitive prices. An evaluation of the skills and competencies required by the industry, as well as the timing and quantity of labor force requirements, should be used to inform potential policy reforms in education and training in order to strengthen and upgrade skills (IGF, 2018a, 2018c).

LCRs must be aligned with what can be realistically implemented, given the capacity of local suppliers, to ensure the long-term competitiveness of the mining industry. Before the decision is made to introduce them, a detailed analysis of the procurement needs of mining firms should be undertaken, ideally in close conjunction with the firms, as was done by Canada and Australia. The analysis should assess the type of procurement opportunities that are available in major projects for each phase in their life cycle, as well as the capacity of domestic suppliers and the workforce to respond to the needs of these projects, leading to the identification of the gaps that need to be filled to enable them to take advantage of existing and potential opportunities.

If demand-side policies are implemented, they tend to work better when pursued in conjunction with supply-side policies. For example, governments can complement regulation establishing minimum targets or quotas for local employees by implementing measures to promote training and skills development of the workforce. Although the form and content of training plans can be a voluntary component of a company's human resources program, some countries have mandated training requirements or support for the development of training facilities (IGF, 2018e).

Prescriptive LCRs entail long time frames between their announcement and effective implementation. As such, they are vulnerable to changes in market prices and in political commitment (ACET, 2017). If countries nonetheless want to implement them, they should be introduced gradually, in a phased approach, along with capacity-building efforts to allow domestic suppliers to adjust to them. Governments should periodically assess progress against objectives, adjusting them as local capacity increases and knowledge about future supply and demand improves. Any protection provided to local suppliers should be temporary and disbanded gradually. Sunset clauses, which prescribe that a regulation shall cease to have effect after a specified date, are good practice in local content policies (African Natural Resources Centre, 2021).

Mining companies might be required or voluntarily take the initiative to design and implement SDPs. Larger companies are better placed to develop and implement such programs, but cooperation among firms, coordinated, for instance, by a Chamber of Mines, can facilitate the participation of smaller companies. Examples of successful supplier development programs include Anglo American's Zimele Enterprise Program in South Africa and the joint Newmont–International Finance Corporation's Ahafo Linkages program in Ghana.

In some cases, mining companies support local suppliers by implementing measures other than LCRs, such as (i) breaking large contracts into smaller ones (unbundling) so that local firms may provide a smaller portion of the total contract tendered; (ii) posting all contracts, tender opportunities, and instructions for bidding processes on local supplier portals; (iii) sole-sourcing arrangements with local suppliers or firms from disadvantaged groups; (iv) stipulating requirements for outside suppliers to subcontract or enter into joint ventures with local firms; (v) assigning higher preference weightings to local businesses in competitive bidding processes or providing them with longer time frames for bidding; (vi) price-matching, allowing local suppliers to match the price of other suppliers; (vii) supporting local suppliers to obtain the certifications necessary to respond to tenders or compete for contracts; and (viii) using procurement methods in which bids are awarded to local suppliers when their price is within a certain percentage of the best offer – e.g., 2% in Ghana, 10% in Tanzania, or within 20% of the lowest foreign bid price in Kazakhstan (Esteves et al., 2014).

Monitoring and reporting of policy outcomes, potentially with in-built sanctions for noncompliance, is key to increasing understanding about policy design and implementation. Governments and industry should publicly report on procurement processes, contracted suppliers, spending, and tax implications to improve oversight and accountability (Pitman and Toroskainen, 2020). Monitoring of LCRs has, in many cases, shown them to be ineffective. However, Australia and Ghana have implemented strong reporting mechanisms with sanctions if firms do not report on their local content objectives.

Mining companies are highly dependent on contractors and suppliers as a source of technological innovation. Empirical evidence shows that local suppliers that thrive are generally incumbent firms whose experience in the market has allowed them to develop close relationships with large mining companies and benefit from their support. Their most important market niches seem to be in areas where there is less foreign competition because of their specific context (e.g., ore characteristics, harsh natural environments, or water scarcity). Investing in R&D can help enable local firms to move up the value chain and increase their competitive capacity. Moreover, strong innovation systems seem to be strongly correlated with robust performance in the export of mining services (Molina, Olivari and Pietrobelli, 2016).

Governments in mineral-rich countries should ultimately seek to maximize value addition throughout their economy rather than the share of domestic content in the minerals sector – thereby increasing the potential for integration in and benefit from global supply chains. Many resource-rich countries have been moving from prescribed domestic procurement requirements to creating conditions that facilitate the export of services and the integration of suppliers in global supply chains.

There are many situations in which a single country's mining operations do not provide sufficient demand to achieve the economies of scale required for suppliers to be competitive. In these cases, a regional approach would be desirable. To date, however, no regional SDPs have been put in place.

Disclaimer

This contribution builds on the publication Korinek, J. and I. Ramdoo (2017), "Local content policies in mineral-exporting countries", OECD Trade Policy Papers, No. 209, OECD Publishing, Paris, https://doi.org/10.1787/4b9b2617-en. The additional opinions expressed and arguments employed herein are those of the authors and do not necessarily reflect the official views of the OECD or of its member countries.

Notes

1 Mining procurement on goods and services typically represents more than 40% of total spending, while taxes and royalties are typically 10% to 20% (Geipel, de Weerdt, and Alarcon, 2021). The mining project life cycle is composed of four main stages – exploration, construction, production, and closure – with firms spending 75% to 90% of their total expenditures during the production stage (McKinsey, 2013).
2 A review of mandatory quantitative LCRs found that in all but one case, the price of products in the affected sectors increased (Stone, Messent, and Flaig, 2015. p. 8).
3 See also IGF's detailed case study on Ghana (IGF, 2018b).
4 This type of requirement is also mandatory in Tanzania since 2018.
5 The METS sector includes equipment manufacturers; contractors; engineering, purchasing, and construction management companies; small and medium-sized software companies; consultancies; and technology and support services.
6 BHP defines world-class suppliers as those that sell more than 30% of their product internationally, have standards equal to the industry leader, and add a high level of value to their customers.

7 A cluster is defined as the geographic concentration of a combination of related industries and associated and supporting institutions (companies, specialized and service providers, among others), which have various links in common such as knowledge, skills, inputs, and demand, among others (Labó Fossa, 2021).

8 Divestment obligations require foreign mining companies to sell shares to Indonesian parties, either government or private business entities. The price of the divested shares is stipulated at fair market value, without considering the mineral reserves at the time of divestment. Smelter companies are 100% open for foreign ownership, with no share divestment requirement.

9 Indonesia's high nickel grade and high iron content made it ideal for China's stainless steel production. Higher-grade nickel ores require less energy to process, which significantly lowers smelting costs.

10 A third mineral that was subject to export bans of unprocessed ore was copper. In the case of copper, the government of Indonesia engaged in negotiations with Freeport-McMoRan over divestment obligations linked to the conversion of the contract of work of the Grasberg copper mine into a special mining business license, ultimately leading the company to yield a 51% share in the project to the government. In October 2021, in observation of the 2017 regulations, Freeport-McMoRan started construction of a $3 billion copper smelter in the Gresik special economic zone, East Java, with annual capacity of 600,000 tons of copper cathode, and a $200 million precious metal refinery with annual output capacity of 54 tons (*The Jakarta Post*, 2021).

11 The ban distinguishes between two types of minerals: type 1 minerals (bauxite, nickel, tin, chromium, gold, and silver) must be fully processed before being exported; type 2 minerals (copper, iron, lead, manganese, ilmenite, tantalum, and zinc) could be exported as concentrates without further refining until January 2028 provided that the industry (i) develops smelting facilities individually or collectively; and (ii) pays export duties that vary depending on the degree of concentration (IGF, 2018c).

12 See United States Geological Survey (n.d.).

13 Indonesian nickel is sold in the form of unprocessed ore; nickel pig iron (NPI) and ferronickel, lower-grade intermediates used in stainless steel (called Class 2 products); and nickel matte, a high-grade intermediate used to make nickel metal or chemicals (Class 1 nickel). The country is rich in laterite ores, which are a good feed for Class 2 products used in steel making, but lacks sulphide ores, primarily used to produce battery cathode products that contain a minimum of 99.8% nickel. Still, recent technological developments have allowed the use of laterites to make intermediate products like mixed hydroxide precipitate (MHP) via hydrometallurgical processes such as high-pressure acid leach (HPAL) and be further refined to Class 1 nickel (Huber, 2021).

14 See Christina (2021).

15 See Lennon (n.d.).

16 In a related development, PT ChengTok Lithium Indonesia, a joint venture between China's Shenzhen Chengxin Lithium Group Co. Ltd. and a subsidiary of the Tsingshan Group, will invest $350 million in a lithium project for the EV battery sector, located in Sulawesi's Morowali Industrial Park, where Tsingshan already operates an NPI smelter.

References

ACET. 2017. *Comparative Study on Local Content and Value Addition in Mineral, Oil and Gas Sectors: Policies, Legal and Institutional Frameworks: Trends and Responses in Selected African Countries*. Ghana: African Center for Economic Transformation. www.acetforafrica.org

AfDB and Bill, and Melinda Gates Foundation. 2015. Creating Local Content for Human Development in Africa's New Natural Resource-Rich Countries. *Flagship Report Paper Series.* No. 6. African Development Bank and Bill & Melinda Gates Foundation. www.NaturalResourcesForHumanDev.org

African Natural Resources Centre. 2021. *Assessment of Supplier Development Programmes in the Extractive Sector in Africa: Strengths, Weaknesses, Opportunities and Critical Success Factors.* Abidjan, Côte d'Ivoire: African Development Bank. www.afdb.org/en/documents/assessment-supplier-development-programmes-extractive-sector-africa-strengths-weaknesses-opportunities-and-critical-success-factors

Arías, M., M. Atienza, and J. Cademaroti. 2012. Large Mining Enterprises and Regional Development: Between the Enclave and Cluster. *Serie de Documentos de Trabajo en Economía y Ciencia Regional.* 15. Antofagasta, Chile: Universidad Católica del Norte. https://sites.google.com/a/ucn.cl/wpeconomia/

Atta-Quayson, A. 2022. Local Procurement in the Mining Sector: Is Ghana Swimming with the Tide? *Journal of the Southern African Institute of Mining and Metallurgy.* 122 (2). pp. 59–72. http://dx.doi.org/10.17159/2411–9717/1586/2022

Bastida, A.E. 2014. From Extractive to Transformative Industries: Pathways to Linkages and Diversification in a Resource-Driven Model. *Mineral Economics.* 27 (2–3). pp. 73–87. doi: 10.1007/s13563-014-0062-8. www.researchgate.net/publication/268741388_From_Extractive_to_Transformative_Industries_Pathways_to_Linkages_and_Diversification_in_a_Resource-Driven_Model

Christina, B. 2021. Indonesia Drawing Plans to Restrict Nickel Pig Iron, Ferronickel Smelters. *Reuters.* 24 June. www.reuters.com/article/us-indonesia-nickel/indonesia-drawing-plans-to-restrict-nickel-pig-iron-ferronickel-smelters-idUSKCN2E00IG

Columbia Center on Sustainable Investment. 2016. *Linkages to the Resource Sector: The Role of Companies, Governments, and International Development Cooperation.* New York, NY: Columbia Center on Sustainable Investment. https://scholarship.law.columbia.edu/cgi/viewcontent.cgi?article=1017&context=sustainable_investment_staffpubs

CSIRO. 2014. *The Future of Mining in Chile.* Santiago, Chile.

de Weerdt, K., and J. Geipel. 2020. Local Procurement Regulations for Extractive Industries in the SADC Region. *Policy Insights.* No. 90. Cape Town: South African Institute of International Affairs. https://saiia.org.za/research/local-procurement-regulations-for-extractive-industries-in-the-sadc-region/

Dietsche, E. 2017. New Industrial Policy and the Extractive Industries. *WIDER Working Paper.* No. 2017/161. Helsinki: United Nations University World Institute for Development Economics Research (UNU-WIDER). www.wider.unu.edu/publication/new-industrial-policy-and-extractive-industries

Elborai, S., R. Kombargi, Y. Anouti, and A. Yammine. 2019. Three Biases that Impede Local Content Development: Seeing Through the Illusions. *Strategy&.* www.strategyand.pwc.com/m1/en/reports/three-biases-that-impede-local-content-development.pdf

Ellis, M., and M. McMillan. 2020. "Local Content: Are There Benefits for Tanzania?" In J. Page, and F. Tarp (eds.) *Mining for Change: Natural Resources and Industry in Africa.* Oxford: United Nations University World Institute for Development Economics Research (UNU-WIDER). pp. 282–303. https://doi.org/10.1093/oso/9780198851172.003.0013

Esteves, A.M., V. Ogorodnikova, C. Putz, and B. Coyne. 2014. *Increasing Domestic Procurement by the Mining Industry in Central Asia*. Washington, DC: World Bank. https://openknowledge.worldbank.org/handle/10986/18950

Fliess, B., E. Idsardi, and R. Rossouw. 2017. Export Controls and Competitiveness in African Mining and Minerals Processing Industries. *OECD Trade Policy Papers*. No. 204. Paris: Organisation for Economic Co-operation and Development. http://dx.doi.org/10.1787/1fddd828-en

Fung, K., and J. Korinek. 2013. Economics of Export Restrictions as Applied to Industrial Raw Materials. *OECD Trade Policy Papers*. No. 155. Paris: Organisation for Economic Co-operation and Development. http://dx.doi.org/10.1787/5k46j0r5xvhd-en

Geipel, J., K. de Weerdt, and T. Alarcon. 2021. Overview of the Local Content in the Mining Sector in Southern Africa. *Southern Africa Resource Watch Resource Insight*. Issue No. 24. Johannesburg: Southern Africa Resource Watch. www.sarwatch.co.za/publication/overview-of-the-local-content-in-the-mining-sector-in-southern-africa/

Greenaway, D. 1992. Trade Related Investment Measures and Development Strategy. *Kyklos*. 45. pp. 139–159.

Grossman, G.M. 1981. The Theory of Domestic Content Protection and Content Preference. *Quarterly Journal of Economics*. 96 (4). pp. 583–603.

Herbert Smith Freehills. 2018. Tanzania's New Integrity Pledge for Mining Companies: Does it Meet International Best Practice? 13 September 2018. www.herbertsmithfreehills.com/latest-thinking/tanzanias-new-integrity-pledge-for-mining-companies-does-it-meet-international-best

Huber, I. 2021. *Indonesia's Nickel Industrial Strategy*. 8 December. Washington, DC: Center for Strategic and International Studies. www.csis.org/analysis/indonesias-nickel-industrial-strategy

IGF. 2018a. *Designing Local Content Policies in Mineral-Rich Countries*. Winnipeg: International Institute for Sustainable Development. www.iisd.org/system/files/publications/local-content-policies-mineral-rich-countries.pdf

IGF. 2018b. *Ghana: Direct Employment-Comparing Local Content Frameworks in Mining and Oil and Gas Industries*. Winnipeg: International Institute for Sustainable Development. www.iisd.org/sites/default/files/publications/case-study-ghana-direct-employment.pdf

IGF. 2018c. *IGF Guidance for Governments: Local Content Policies*. Winnipeg: International Institute for Sustainable Development. www.iisd.org/system/files/publications/igf-guidance-for-governments-local-content.pdf

IGF. 2018d. *Local Content Policies in the Mining Sector: Fostering Downstream Linkages*. Winnipeg: International Institute for Sustainable Development. www.iisd.org/system/files/publications/local-content-policies-mining-downstream-linkages.pdf

IGF. 2018e. *Local Content Policies in the Mining Sector: Stimulating Direct Local Employment*. Winnipeg: International Institute for Sustainable Development. www.iisd.org/system/files/publications/local-content-policies-mining-direct-local-employment.pdf

The Jakarta Post. 2021. *Freeport Breaks Ground on $3 Billion Copper Smelter in Gresik*. 14 October. www.thejakartapost.com/paper/2021/10/13/freeport-breaks-ground-on-3-billion-copper-smelter-in-gresik.html

Kimura, F., and A. Obashi. 2011. Production Networks in East Asia: What We Know So Far. *ADBI Working Paper Series*. No. 320. Tokyo: Asian Development Bank Institute. www.adb.org/sites/default/files/publication/156175/adbi-wp320.pdf

Korinek, J. 2013. Mineral Resource Trade in Chile: Contribution to Development and Policy Implications. *OECD Trade Policy Papers.* No. 145. Paris: Organisation for Economic Co-operation and Development. http://dx.doi.org/10.1787/5k4bw6twpf24-en

Korinek, J. 2014. Export Restrictions on Raw Materials: Experience with Alternative Policies in Botswana. *OECD Trade Policy Papers.* No. 163. Paris: Organisation for Economic Co-operation and Development. http://dx.doi.org/10.1787/5jzb6v86kz32-en

Korinek, J. 2020. The Mining Global Value Chain. *OECD Trade Policy Papers.* No. 235. Paris: Organisation for Economic Co-operation and Development. http://dx.doi.org/10.1787/2827283e-en

Korinek, J., and J. Bartos. 2012. Multilateralising Regionalism: Disciplines on Export Restrictions in Regional Trade Agreements. *OECD Trade Policy Papers.* No. 139. Paris: Organisation for Economic Co-operation and Development. http://dx.doi.org/10.1787/5k962hf7hfnr-en

Korinek, J., and I. Ramdoo. 2017. Local Content Policies in Mineral-Exporting Countries. *OECD Trade Policy Papers.* No. 209. Paris: Organisation for Economic Co-operation and Development. http://dx.doi.org/10.1787/4b9b2617-en

Labó Fossa, R. 2021. Hacia un Clúster Minero en el Sur del Perú. *Documento de Política.* Lima, Peru: Consorcio de Investigación Económica y Social. https://cies.org.pe/investigacion/hacia-un-cluster-minero-en-el-sur-del-peru/

Lebdioui, A.A. 2019. *Economic Diversification and Development in Resource-dependent Economies: Lessons from Chile and Malaysia.* Doctoral thesis. Cambridge, UK: University of Cambridge, Centre of Development Studies. https://doi.org/10.17863/CAM.46517

Lebdioui, A.A., and P. Bilek. 2021. Do Forward Linkages Reduce or Worsen Dependency in the Extractive Sector? *Background Paper.* Natural Resource Governance Institute. https://resourcegovernance.org/sites/default/files/documents/do-forward-linkages-reduce-or-worsen-dependency-in-the-extractive-sector.pdf

Lennon, J. n.d. *Blog.* LinkedIn. www.linkedin.com/posts/jim-lennon-3a2b9216_here-are-my-thoughts-on-battery-material-activity-6879506091382763521-W_WH

Marcel, V., R. Tissot, A. Paul, and E. Omonbude. 2016. *A Local Content Decision Tree for Emerging Producers Energy.* London: Chatham House, Environment and Resources Department. www.chathamhouse.org/sites/default/files/publications/research/2016-07-13-local-content-decision-tree-marcel-tissot-paul-omonbude.pdf

McCulloch, N., N. Balchin, M. Mendez-Parra, and K. Onyeka. 2017. Local Content Policies and Backward integration in Nigeria. *SET Briefing Paper.* London: Overseas Development Institute. https://set.odi.org/wp-content/uploads/2017/10/SET-Nigeria_Backward-Integration_Final-Brief.pdf

McCulloch, N., A. Winters, and X. Cirera. 2001. *Trade Liberalization and Poverty: A Handbook.* London: Centre for Economic Policy Research.

McKinsey Global Institute. 2013. *Reversing the Curse: Maximizing the Potential of Resource-Driven Economies.* December. www.mckinsey.com/industries/metals-and-mining/our-insights/reverse-the-curse-maximizing-the-potential-of-resource-driven-economies

Molina, O., J. Olivari, and C. Pietrobelli. 2016. Global Value Chains in the Peruvian Mining Sector. *IDB Technical Note.* No. IDB-TN-1114. Washington,

DC: Inter-American Development Bank. https://publications.iadb.org/en/global-value-chains-peruvian-mining-sector
Moraka, N.V., and M. J. van Rensburg. 2015. Transformation in the South African Mining Industry-Looking Beyond the Employment Equity Scorecard. *Journal of the Southern African Institute of Mining and Metallurgy*. 115 (8). pp. 669–678. www.scielo.org.za/scielo.php?script=sci_abstract&pid=S2225-62532015000800005
Morris, M., R. Kaplinsky, and D. Kaplan. 2011. "One Thing Leads to Another" – Commodities, Linkages and Industrial Development: A Conceptual Overview. *MMCP Discussion Paper*. No. 12 (Revised). The Open University. www.researchgate.net/publication/279475209_One_thing_leads_to_anothercommodities_-_linkages_and_industrial_development_a_conceptual_overview
OECD. 2015. *Policy Framework for Investment, 2015 Edition*. Paris: Organisation for Economic Co-operation and Development. https://doi.org/10.1787/9789264208667-en
Östensson, O. 2017. Local Content, Supply Chains, and Shared Infrastructure. *WIDER Working Paper*. No. 2017/96. Helsinki: United Nations University World Institute for Development Economics Research. www.wider.unu.edu/publication/local-content-supply-chains-and-shared-infrastructure
Östensson, O. 2019. Promoting Downstream Processing: Resource Nationalism or Industrial Policy? *Mineral Economics*. 32 (2). pp. 205–212. https://doi.org/10.1007/s13563-019-00170-x. www.researchgate.net/publication/331099414_Promoting_downstream_processing_resource_nationalism_or_industrial_policy
Östensson, O., and A. Löf. 2017. Downstream Activities: The Possibilities and the Realities. *WIDER Working Paper*. No. 2017/113. Helsinki: United Nations University World Institute for Development Economics Research. www.wider.unu.edu/publication/downstream-activities
Pitman, R., and K. Toroskainen. 2020. *Beneath the Surface: The Case for Oversight of Extractive Industry Suppliers*. National Resource Governance Institute. https://resourcegovernance.org/sites/default/files/documents/beneath_the_surface.pdf
Stone, S., J. Messent, and D. Flaig. 2015. Emerging Policy Issues: Localisation Barriers to Trade. *OECD Trade Policy Papers*. No. 180. Paris: Organisation for Economic Co-operation and Development. http://dx.doi.org/10.1787/5js1m6v5qd5j-en
UNCTAD. 2017. *Using Trade Policy to Drive Value Addition: Lessons from Indonesia's Ban on Nickel Exports*. Geneva: United Nations Conference on Trade and Development. https://unctad.org/system/files/non-official-document/suc2017d8_en.pdf
UNIDO. 2012. *Promoting Industrial Diversification in Resource Intensive Economies: The Experiences of Sub-Saharan Africa and Central Asia Regions*. Vienna: United Nations Industrial Development Organization. https://open.unido.org/api/documents/4811549/download/Promoting%20Industrial%20Diversification%20in%20Resource%20Intensive%20Economies%20-%20The%20Experiences%20of%20Sub-Saharan%20Africa%20and%20Central%20Asia%20Regions
United States Geological Survey. n.d. *Nickel Statistics and Information*. www.usgs.gov/centers/national-minerals-information-center/nickel-statistics-and-information
Warburton, E. 2017. The Life and Death of Indonesia's Mineral Export Ban. *Inside Indonesia*. Edition 130. www.insideindonesia.org/the-life-and-death-of-indonesia-s-mineral-export-ban
Weldegiorgis, F.S., E. Dietsche, and D.M. Franks. 2021. Building Mining's Economic Linkages: A Critical Review of Local Content Policy Theory. *Resources Policy*. 74.

p. 102312 www.sciencedirect.com/science/article/abs/pii/S0301420721003226?via%3Dihub

White, S. 2017. Regulating for Local Content: Limitations of Legal and Regulatory Instruments in Promoting Small Scale Suppliers in Extractive Industries in Developing Economies. *The Extractive Industries and Society*. 4 (2). pp. 260–266. https://researchrepository.murdoch.edu.au/id/eprint/34791/

World Bank, and Kaiser Economic Development Partners. 2015. *A Practical Guide to Increasing Mining Local Procurement in West Africa*. Washington, DC: World Bank. https://openknowledge.worldbank.org/handle/10986/21489

Yunis, J., and E. Aliakbari. 2020. *Fraser Institute Annual Survey of Mining Companies 2020*. Vancouver: Fraser Institute. www.fraserinstitute.org/sites/default/files/annual-survey-of-mining-companies-2020.pdf

Annex. Consistency with WTO rules

Table 3.A1 Consistency of Local Content Policies with WTO Provisions

Measures		*Relevant WTO Provisions*	*Consistency with WTO*
Measures affecting sourcing of inputs			
Local procurement requirements			
Quota related to local sourcing	A percentage of value added or specific volume of intermediate inputs to be purchased locally	TRIMs illustrative list para. 1 (a)	Quotas or specific percentages prohibited
Trade balancing requirements	Imports of one product linked to export performance of other products	TRIMs illustrative list 1(b) for internal measures; 2 (a) for border measures	Prohibited
Manufacturing requirements	Certain products are required to be manufactured locally	TRIMs illustrative list	Prohibited
Limitations on imports	Amount of goods and services that can be imported for the production process is limited	GATT Art. III.5; GATT Art. XI.1; TRIMs illustrative list, para. 2(a)	Prohibited
Foreign exchange restrictions	Restrict the inflow of foreign exchange attributable to an investor to constrain the amount of imported intermediate goods	TRIMs illustrative list, para 2 (b)	Prohibited Exception for developing countries GATT Arts. XII and XVIII:B

(*Continued*)

Table 3.A1 (Continued)

Measures		*Relevant WTO Provisions*	*Consistency with WTO*
Preference for local substitutes	Investors to purchase local substitutes for imports if "like product" is manufactured locally	GATT Article III.4 (national treatment) if (i) imported products are accorded less favorable treatment compared to local suppliers; (ii) imported goods and the domestic products are considered like products; and (iii) measures are inscribed in laws, regulations, and requirements.	Prohibited
Ownership requirements			
Local equity participation	Some proportion of equity must be held locally	GATS Art. XVI for market access restrictions and Art. XVII for national treatment, in schedule of commitments	Prohibited only if countries have taken commitments in their services schedules; otherwise not disciplined
Employment requirements			
Local employment targets	Specified employment targets must be met	GATS Art. XVI for market access restrictions and Art. XVII for national treatment, provided in schedule of commitments	Prohibited only if countries have taken commitments in their services schedules; otherwise not disciplined

Measures		*Relevant WTO Provisions*	*Consistency with WTO*
Quotas for foreign employment	A maximum number of expatriate staff is specified		Prohibited only if countries have taken commitments in their services schedules; otherwise not disciplined
National participation in management	Certain staff must be nationals or a schedule for "indigenization" of management must be set		Prohibited only if countries have taken commitments in their services schedules; otherwise not disciplined
Technology transfer requirements			
R&D requirements	Investors should commit to invest in R&D locally	GATS Art. IV; TRIPS Arts. 3, 7, and 8; SCM Agreement Arts. 2 and 8	Prohibited
Technology transfer	Specified foreign technology be used locally		Not disciplined
Measures affecting production			
Minimum export requirements	Certain percentage of production must be exported	GATT Art. III.5; GATT Art. XI.1; TRIMs illustrative list, para. 2(a)	Prohibited
Trade balancing requirements	Imports must be a certain proportion of locally produced exports, either in terms of volume or in terms of value	TRIMs illustrative list 1(b) for internal measures; 2 (a) for border measures	Prohibited
Domestic sales requirements	Certain product may not be exported	GATT Art. III.5; GATT Art. XI: 1; TRIMs illustrative list 2(c)	Prohibited
Market reserve policy	Some markets are reserved for local production	GATT Art. III.4	Prohibited

(*Continued*)

Table 3.A1 (Continued)

Measures		*Relevant WTO Provisions*	*Consistency with WTO*
Product mandating requirements	Some products to be exported by the hosting country only	GATT Art. III.5; GATT Art. XI: 1; TRIMs illustrative list 2(c)	Prohibited
Licensing requirements	Investors to obtain license for production in the host country	GATT Art. XI.1	Prohibited
Technology transfers	Investors are committed to a specified embodied technology	TRIPS Arts. 3, 7, and 8; SCM Agreement Arts. 2 and 8	Disciplined
Other measures relevant to LCPs			
State trading enterprises	Foreign firms to enter into joint venture with SOEs	Article XVII of GATT, applicable when SOEs enter commercial operations	Provision does not regulate obligations of foreign firms to enter into joint venture with SOEs
Subsidies to support local suppliers	Governments give financial incentives to local suppliers to favor local products over imports	SCM Art. 3.1(b)	Actionable if specific; otherwise non-actionable
Subsidies to R&D and innovation	Government policies support R&D and innovation	SCM Art. 8.2	Actionable if specific; otherwise non-actionable

Art. = Article, GATS = General Agreement on Trade in Services, GATT = General Agreement on Tariffs and Trade, LCP = local content policy, R&D = research and development, SCM = Agreement on Subsidies and Countervailing Measures, SOE = state-owned enterprise, TRIMs = Trade-Related Investment Measures, TRIPS = Agreement on Trade-Related Aspects of Intellectual Property Rights, WTO = World Trade Organization.

Note: Exceptions for developing countries – developing countries are permitted to retain TRIMs that constitute a violation of GATT Art. III or XI, provided the measures meet the conditions of GATT Art. XVIII, which allows specified derogation from the GATT provisions for the economic development needs of developing countries.

Source: Korinek and Ramdoo (2017), adapted from Greenaway (1992); McCulloch et al. (2001).

Table 3.A2 Measures Not Prohibited by WTO Rules

Measures	*Remarks*
Measures affecting imports	
Tariff measures	WTO does not prohibit tariffs. Countries must bind their tariffs and can modify their tariff rates within the range if bound tariffs are different to applied tariffs.
Nontariff measures (of a quantitative nature)	Generally prohibited (QRs, licensing, etc.) but with the exception for imposition of import quotas for BOP purposes (Art. XVIII:B). This is temporary in nature.
Measures to support enterprises	
Exchange rates	No WTO agreement deals expressly with exchange rates, although GATT Art. XV concerns exchange arrangements.
Government procurement	Permitted, except if a country is member of the GPA.
Export finance/ insurance/guarantees	Allowed but may be considered an export subsidy if they are granted at premium rates insufficient to cover long-term operating costs and losses.
Production subsidies	Allowed if nonspecific*
Trade finance	Not prohibited
Measures to promote technology	
Technology-related requirements for FDI (e.g., technological transfer)	Not prohibited
Support to R&D/ innovation	Unless specific, otherwise permitted
Human capital development	Not prohibited
Employment of local labor	Not prohibited
Regional assistance	Not prohibited
Investment incentives	
Export performance requirement as a condition for investment	Not prohibited
Equity requirement by FDI	Not prohibited
Measures subject to disciplines under specific circumstances	
Credit subsidies	Not prohibited, provided they are not product or sector specific

(*Continued*)

Table 3.A1 (Continued)

Measures	*Remarks*
Tax subsidies/holidays	Not prohibited, provided they are not product or sector specific
Clusters/EPZ/SEZ	Not specially regulated by a particular WTO Agreement** but may be subject to disciplines when measures contravene other WTO disciplines (e.g., subsidies, etc.). Fiscal facilitation provided in SEZ is not prohibited.
Contingency measures	
Safeguard measures **Anti-dumping measures** **Countervailing measures**	These measures allow countries to apply import restrictions in particular circumstances, provided they can prove their economy/economic actors are affected by (i) a surge in imports (safeguard); (ii) a product that is being sold below its normal price on the domestic market by an exporting country (dumping); and (iii) a distorting effect of a subsidy by a foreign government.

Art. = Article, BOP = balance of payments, FDI = foreign direct investment, GATT = General Agreement on Tariffs and Trade, GPA = Government Procurement Agreement, QR = quantitative restrictions, R&D = research and development, SCM = Agreement on Subsidies and Countervailing Measures, SEZ = Special Export Zone, WTO = World Trade Organization.

* The WTO Agreement on Subsidies and Countervailing Measures disciplines the use of subsidies. The disciplines only apply to "specific subsidies," that is, to subsidies available only to an enterprise, industry, group of enterprises, or group of industries in the country that gives the subsidies. They can refer to domestic or export subsidies.

** SEZ is mentioned in a footnote to GATT Art. XVI and in the SCM, excluding from the definition of a subsidy one of the fiscal facilitation measures provided to SEZs – an exemption from import duties and taxes on goods exported from SEZs.

Source: Korinek and Ramdoo (2017).

4 The unintended consequences of high regional content requirements

Keith Head, Thierry Mayer, and Marc Melitz

1 Introduction

When the Trump administration launched its revision of the treaty governing trade between the US and its neighbors, the US negotiators emphasized the need for stricter rules of origin. The US Trade Representative, Robert Lighthizer, reportedly asked his counterparts to raise the regional content requirement (RCR) to 85%, a large increase from the level set in 1993 (62.5%).[1] Canada and Mexico balked at such a high rate, and the three parties finally settled on an increase to 75%, bolstered with additional binding requirements. The political appeal of stricter origin rules lies in the hope that they will increase domestic employment in the parts industry. Lighthizer (2020) acknowledged this intent, writing "The USMCA rebalances the NAFTA to promote increased production in the United States and North America."

From an economic standpoint it is hard to justify onerous restrictions on sourcing. If the goal is merely to limit imports of parts, then tariffs on parts would be a more efficient tool. While trade agreements that lack a common external tariff need some rule of origin to prevent back-door entry to the high-tariff market via the low-tariff country, this issue was not relevant in the USMCA negotiation for two reasons. First, because the actual differences in tariffs were small, so much smaller content restrictions would be sufficient to prevent this tariff-hopping.[2] Second, it was the lower-tariff member, the US, that was asking for the stricter rules.

Going back to the work of Grossman (1981), economists have investigated whether, even as protectionist devices, strict rules of origin could fail to achieve their goals. Grossman's Proposition 3 (p. 591) states that small increases in local content requirements have ambiguous effects on industry value added, defined as the sum of value added in components and in final goods.

> Whereas the content protection policy causes an increase in the output of domestic components, it will normally result in a concomitant contraction of final good production. Which effect will dominate depends on how sensitive intermediate good production is to changes in its output price, and how sensitive final good production is to changes in the price of its intermediate input.

DOI: 10.4324/9781003415794-4

In this chapter, we extend the Grossman approach to take into account the very large number of diverse parts that go into modern manufactured goods such as automobiles. For each part, the firm decides whether to source it from inside the region (where there is a free trade agreement) or from outside countries. The core trade-off the firm faces is that within-region sourcing helps it comply with rules of origin (RoO), but necessitates forgoing opportunities to obtain cheaper parts elsewhere. In section 4, we give an overview of the theoretical model developed in Head et al. (2022) that analyzes these trade-offs. We show that RoOs generate competing incentives for part sourcing within a Regional Trade Area (RTA). Even though the rules are intended to relocate production of parts within the RTA, they can have the opposite effect when they are overly restrictive. This main result does not work via declines in final goods production, as in Grossman (1981). However, we also quantify the negative impact of higher costs induced by the RoOs for part production. This quantification exercise predicts how *any* given RoO would affect market share changes and the associated production and employment changes across all vehicle plans selling in the region. Drawing on the attractive aggregation properties of our model, we derive average price, market share, production, and part employment changes across groups of carlines – including the group of all carlines assembled within the region.

This chapter is organized as follows. Section 2 provides an overview of recent changes in rules of origin that impacted the auto industry in North America and Europe. The following section presents empirical patterns of sourcing in North America that inform the model and the way we quantify it. Section 4 summarizes the key mechanisms of the model developed in Head et al. (2022). We then estimate the model to fit the pattern of sourcing observed at the level of individual car models prior to the 2020 changes in RCRs. Section 5 describes how we use that fitted model to evaluate the impact of counterfactual RoOs. Section 6 reports the effects of changing those rules for both NAFTA and the EU-UK trade agreement.

2 Changing rules of origin in North America and Europe

Rules of origin in the auto industry were first introduced in the 1965 Auto Pact between Canada and the United States. To avoid non-US companies setting up sales enterprises in Canada to serve the US market, it was agreed that only cars with 50% content from the US and Canada would benefit from the new tariff-free regime.[3] In the negotiation of the North American Free Trade Agreement in 1991, the American side sought a more restrictive rule. Irwin (2017) describes the initial negotiating positions and how they reached the peculiar regional content requirement of 62.5%:

> Rules of origin were particularly important in the case of automobiles. The US auto industry wanted high North American content rules to ensure that Mexico did not become an export platform for Japanese

> or other foreign producers who would simply send parts to Mexico for assembly and then ship the vehicles into the United States. . . . For NAFTA, the United Auto Workers pushed for an 80 percent rule, Ford and Chrysler 70 percent, and General Motors 60 percent. Mexico and Canada wanted to keep the 50 percent requirement in the US-Canada FTA, but reluctantly accepted 60 percent. US negotiators had promised auto producers a number higher than 60 percent to prevent their opposition. While they were able to persuade Mexico to go to 65 percent, Canada remained firm at 60 percent and so the negotiators split the difference and arrived at a 62.5 percent rule.

Irwin goes on to describe how the US compromise led to an apoplectic call to the US trade negotiator from Ford's CEO, who felt betrayed by the failure to obtain the promised 65%. The case points to the central importance assigned to rules of origin as well as the presumption that US producers would benefit from a stricter rule of origin than the one the US had settled on for NAFTA.

When President Trump's negotiators set out to replace NAFTA, one of their focal points was stricter rules of origin for the auto industry. Eventually, Canada, the US, and Mexico agreed in 2019 to replace the 1994–2020 NAFTA with a new agreement called the USMCA (in the United States). Lighthizer (2020) offered the following justification for stricter rules of origin:

> The USMCA rebalances the NAFTA to promote increased production in the United States and North America and to ensure that non-parties do not gain unwarranted benefits through the agreement. The USMCA features innovative rules of origin for automobiles and automobile parts that, once fully implemented, will create strong incentives to invest and manufacture in the United States and North America.

The new agreement devoted 39 pages in an appendix to the new rules, so we cannot do full justice to their complexity here. The following were the main ways in which the requirements for qualifying for tariff-free treatment became more difficult for the auto sector:

1. The minimum North American regional content requirement (RCR) was increased to 75% (from 62.5%).
2. A new labor value content (LVC) rule requires that 40% to 45% of auto content be made by workers earning at least $16 per hour.
3. Seventy percent of both the steel and the aluminum going into each car must originate in North America.
4. Six "super-core" parts – including engines and transmissions – must themselves comply with the 75% RCR.

The new requirements are clearly intended to discourage firms from sourcing parts from outside North America: if the vehicles currently assembled in the USMCA area with non-USMCA parts do not satisfy the new higher requirements, they will no longer qualify for duty-free imports within the USMCA area. The $16 hourly wage minimum also tilts sourcing preferences against Mexico in favor of Canada or the US. This is because either factory wages must quadruple from about $4 per hour, or the cars made with Mexican parts become non-compliant and have to pay tariffs. While this Mexico-specific feature of the USMCA RoO is important, it does not fit well within our modelling structure, so we leave further quantification of its consequences to future work. However, our model does say something about the qualitative effects of the labor-value requirement. The policy appears to be designed to lower the attractiveness of Mexico as a supplier. However, a less competitive Mexican supply sector also raises the expected costs of cars assembled elsewhere in North America. Thus, it could bring additional unintended consequences beyond those that we quantify in this chapter.

Table 4.1 provides some early evidence on how the car industry is responding to the phasing in of the USMCA's stricter rules of origin. We see that in 2019, compliance with the agreement was very high, at least for those cars and light trucks shipped across the borders within North America. By 2021, the RCR had risen to 69%. The striking outcome is large drops in preference utilization for cars shipped from Mexico into the US and even larger drop for imports into Canada. RoO compliance for exported Mexican trucks remains higher, in line with the much higher penalty for non-compliant trucks imported into the US: a 25% tariff.

The other major regional trade agreement, the European Union, had no need for rules of origin since it is a customs union with a common external tariff. This came to an end in 2020 with the conclusion of the negotiations creating the European Union and United Kingdom Trade and Cooperation Act (TCA). While the status of fisheries and Northern

Table 4.1 Use of Preferential Tariffs by US and Canada

Year:	*2019*	*2020*	*2021*	*2019*	*2020*	*2021*
RCR:	*62.5%*	*66%*	*69%*	*62.5%*	*66%*	*69%*
Importer: USA			*Origin:*			
Product		*Canada*			*Mexico*	
8703 (Cars)	99.2	97.9	97.7	99.4	95.2	86.8
8704 (Trucks)	97.8	93.7	94.2	100.0	99.8	99.8
Importer: Canada			*Origin:*			
Product		*USA*			*Mexico*	
8703 (Cars)	97.3	97.6	86.3	99.2	96.5	81.5
8704 (Trucks)	96.8	97.7	96.7	99.1	98.5	98.9

Ireland garnered more press attention, debates over rules of origin again proved to be a sticking point. A "Swiss-style" agreement would have retained better access to the EU market, but the UK government demanded that its negotiators "Give us Canada."[4]

The inevitable consequence of a Canada-style deal would be rules of origin. Predictably, based on Canada's history of negotiations with its larger trade partner, the EU wanted stricter rules than the UK. Michel Barnier, the chief EU negotiator, gave a speech in the summer of 2020 arguing, "Do we really want to take a risk with rules of origin that would allow the UK to become a manufacturing hub for the EU, by allowing it to assemble materials and goods sourced all over the world, and export them to the single market as British goods: tariff-and-quota-free?"[5] The final version of the TCA specified that motor vehicles would satisfy the RoO provided that the Maximum value of Non-Originating Materials (MaxNOM) was kept below 45%. The minimum RCR for regionally sourced parts is therefore 100 – 45 = 55%, more lenient than NAFTA – even before the 2020 rule changes.

Section 6 quantifies the consequences for consumers and producers of these recent changes in RoOs in North America and Europe. We also consider counterfactuals of stricter RoOs that might have been enacted. Before those numerical exercises, we need to introduce our model. To ground the model, we first describe data on sourcing of automotive parts in North America.

3 Regional parts use in NAFTA: key patterns

We use two data sources on regional parts use in North America. The first is extremely detailed data on sourcing of engines and transmissions, two of the highest-value components of internal combustion engine (ICE) vehicles. The second source is data from the American Automobile Labelling Act, which examines sourcing of all components aggregated together.

3.1 Sourcing of engines and transmissions (IHS data)

Figure 4.1 displays the 2018 production shares of all the main powertrain sourcing configurations, which we define as a pair of countries where the first provides the engine and the second supplies the transmission. The source of the data is the automotive consultancy IHS Markit. They provide the number of units manufactured in each plant for all firms, detailed by engine and transmission source. The fill color of squares shows where the engine was produced whereas circles do the same for transmissions. Even with all non-NAFTA source countries aggregated into a single rest-of-the-world (RoW) group, there are a large number of possibilities. To keep the figure readable, we only show configurations that account for at least 1% of local production.

The main takeaway from Figure 4.1 is the heterogeneity in sourcing patterns, even when considering just two components. The most common configurations differ across the three countries. When assembly takes place in

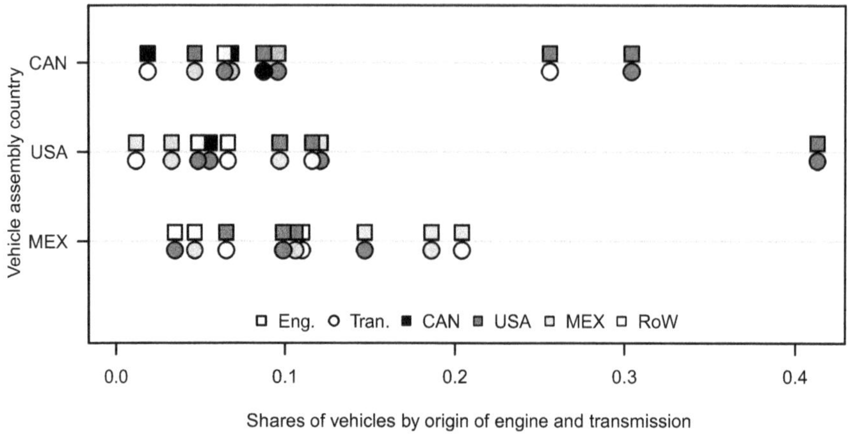

Figure 4.1 Heterogeneity in Engine and Transmission Sourcing Configurations for North American Vehicles

Note: The horizontal axis shows, for each assembly country (or group), the share of cars assembled in that area using various engine (squares) and transmission (circles) sourcing configurations. The assembly countries depicted on the vertical axis are Canada (CAN), the United States (USA), and Mexico (MEX). Configurations are included if they account for 1% of cars in each country.

Canada, vehicles with both engines and transmissions from the US are the most common configuration, accounting for over 30% of the cars assembled there. US factories use domestic engines and transmissions for over 40% of vehicles. In Mexico, USA-USA accounts for about 10% of assembly.[6] Canadian parts are often included in the powertrain for cars assembled in Canada but much less so in the US. Outside those two countries, Canadian engines and transmissions have negligible use.

The diversity of configurations observed for just two parts establishes the importance of allowing for heterogeneity *within* countries. This features prominently in the model described in the next section. One of the key ideas in the model is that some parts are likely to be sourced domestically even with rather lenient rules of origin. Firms would be more reluctant to bring sourcing of other parts into the region and would do so only when compelled by a stricter RoO. One factor underlying this asymmetry could be differences in the part-specific cost of remote sourcing.

Figure 4.2, also based on the IHS Markit data, provides compelling evidence that remote sourcing of engines is relatively rare throughout the global vehicle industry. On the other hand, long-distance sourcing seems less costly for transmissions. Thus, in the context of our model, engines are examples of parts that firms source locally even without pressure from RoOs, whereas transmissions are the marginal part that would be added only to avoid incurring tariffs when rules are strict.

Figure 4.2 plots the cumulative distribution functions (CDF) of distances for engines and transmissions.[7] For every distance between an engine or

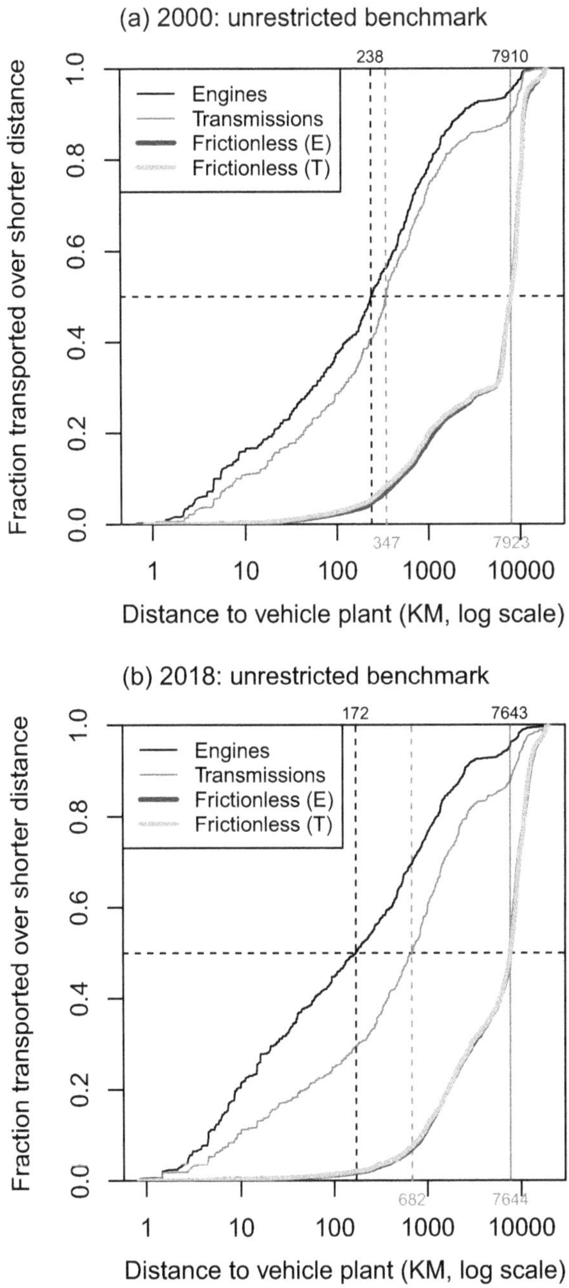

Figure 4.2 The Distribution of Sourcing Distances

Note: Each line graphs the fraction of engines (darker) or transmissions (lighter) transported by less than or equal distance from their point of manufacture to the final assembly location. The thick lines are benchmarks expected under frictionless (random) sourcing. The benchmarks in figures (a) and (b) treat engines and transmissions as homogeneously usable by any vehicle. Figures (c) and (d) respect distinctions in the HS code of each vehicle and the vertical relationships between the core parts and assemblers.

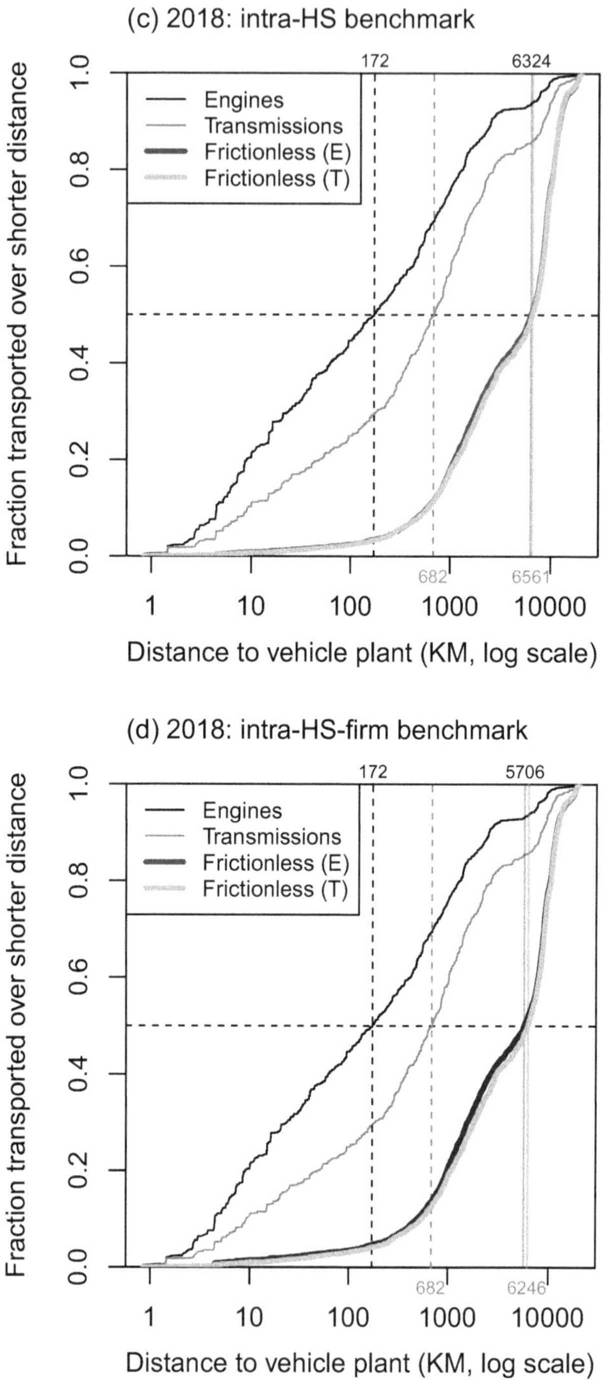

Figure 4.2 (Continued)

transmission factory and an assembly factory, we calculate the share of all vehicles made from engines or transmissions transported less than that distance. The thinner lines in Figure 4.2 depict these CDFs for engines and transmissions, respectively. In 2000, we see that over half of all cars are built using engines that travelled less than 238 kilometers (347 km for transmissions). Nearly 20 years later, the median distance that a transmission was shipped had almost doubled to 682 km. In contrast, the median engine was transported an even shorter distance than before.

To what extent do these observed distances simply reflect geographic clustering of plants? To answer this, we compute a benchmark CDF based on plant locations under a null hypothesis of random sourcing. That is, in this hypothetical data-generating process for distances, each engine is equally likely to end up in every car. Thus, the fraction of engines from plant A travelling *d* km to plant B would be equal to plant B's share of world vehicle production. The thicker lines in panels (a) and (b) graph these CDFs in 2000 and 2018. We see that median distances under the null are vastly larger – about 7,900 km in 2000 and 7,640 km in 2018. In other words, if distance did not matter, we should see much higher shares of engines and transmissions crossing oceans.

The null benchmark of panels (a) and (b) ignore some simple constraints. Automatic transmissions made in Japan will not be transported to factories in Europe to equip manual-transmission cars. The relatively high displacement engines made for pickup trucks in North America will not end up in cars assembled in Japan. Panel (c) takes into account these product-compatibility constraints by re-calculating the benchmark CDFs. This lowers the median benchmark distance by about 1,000 km but obviously cannot explain the much shorter actual distances. Panel (d) constructs a benchmark that obeys additional data constraints. It takes into account that if a factory builds an engine that in reality goes to a Mazda factory, then even in the random benchmark, it must still end up in a Mazda factory (albeit not the same one). This rules out, among other things, that it ends up in India, where Mazda has no factories. This additional element of realism in the benchmark only drives down the median by an additional 300 km (transmissions) or 600 km (engines). Evidently, the bias towards proximate sources is not something that can be eliminated by simple benchmark corrections.

Shipping heavy car parts and coordinating with distant assembly plants is costly. This implies that many parts would be sourced regionally even in the absence of rules of origin. The unconstrained regional sourcing is an important part of our model. The point to note is that these benefits of local sourcing differ, even within components of the powertrain. A more extreme contrast between parts would be between car seats and electronics: The former are almost always assembled locally while the latter almost all come from Asia. We now turn to broader evidence on the sourcing of all car parts going into cars sold in Canada and the US.

3.2 *North American input cost shares (AALA data)*

Our source of data regarding variation in regional cost shares is based on annual reports mandated by the American Automobile Labeling Act (AALA) of 1992. The law requires that "A label with the US/Canada content percentage and related additional information must be displayed on these vehicles up to the time of first retail sale." According to AALA, each new passenger motor vehicle must be labeled with the following information:

1 The percentage of US/Canadian equipment (parts) content
2 The name and percentage content for any countries other than the US and Canada that individually contributes 15% or more of the equipment content (with a maximum of two countries)
3 The countries of final assembly, engine manufacture, and transmission manufacture.

The data are available in PDF form on the AALA website.[8] Information on component suppliers other than the US and Canada begins in 2011. The cost share data is reported by AALA at the carline level, which usually corresponds to a brand-model assembled at a specific factory. AALA often provides more detail for carlines, with information such as engine size.

We represent the model-level AALA data as a collection of cumulative densities in Figure 4.3. These are plotted with the original data pooled over the 2011–2020 period. We plot the CDFs separately for the cars that are the most

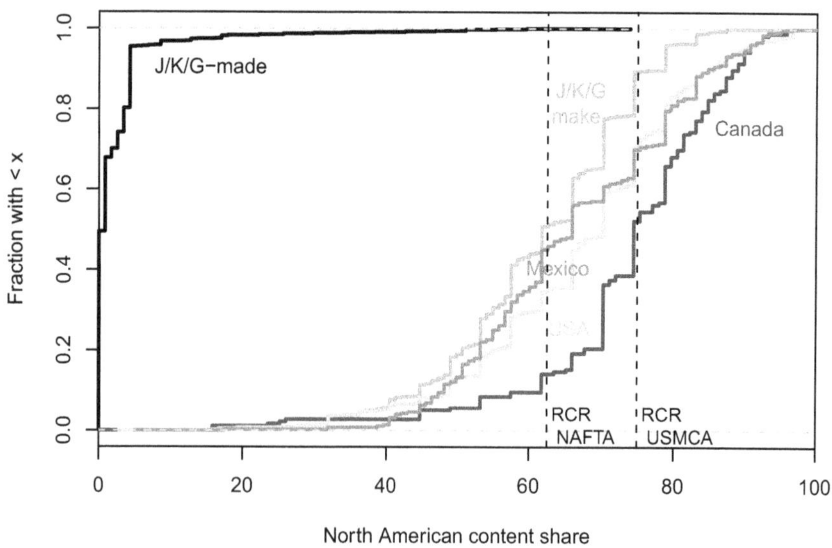

Figure 4.3 NAFTA Regional Cost Share by Location of Production (CDFs)

potentially affected by the RoO, i.e., those produced in Canada, Mexico, and the US. We also present separate densities for the Japanese, Korean, and German brands that are produced in NAFTA (J/K/G *make*). Finally, we also plot a density for the models sold in the US but assembled in Japan, Korea, or Germany (J/K/G *made*).

The AALA reports give estimates of the share of parts costs, not accounting for assembly costs. In order to compare those numbers to the RCR, we therefore need to add on the regional costs attributable to assembly. Figure 4.3 computes the overall regional cost share under the assumption that final assembly amounts to 15% of the total production cost of each regionally made car.

Four main findings emerge. The majority of carlines in each NAFTA country have cost shares that indicate compliance with the 62.5% RCR prescribed by the original NAFTA. Second, compliance is highest in Canada, lowest in Mexico, and intermediate in the US. Car brands headquartered in the three major car-producing countries outside NAFTA have lower NAFTA input shares even when producing in NAFTA. Finally, North American cost shares for cars assembled outside North America tend to be very small.

4 A theoretical model of parts sourcing

As we previously discussed, rules of origin (RoO) can generate competing incentives for the location of part production within a regional trade area (RTA). Those rules are intended to relocate the production of parts within the RTA; but when they are overly restrictive, the impact on regional sourcing will be reversed and part sourcing will be relocated outside the region. We now sketch a simple model based on our companion paper Head et al. (2022) that illustrates why RoOs will induce such a hump-shaped response for that regional part share. In order to focus on the sourcing decision for parts and the intuition for this hump-shaped response – which we call the Laffer curve for RoOs – we keep the location of assembly fixed. Our companion paper shows how RoOs will also impact that assembly location choice and how overly restrictive RoOs will not only lead to lower regional part sourcing but also induce final good producers to relocate assembly outside the region.

4.1 Model structure

The potential for the downward-sloping segment of the RoO Laffer curve, where stricter RoOs lead to reductions in the regional part share, arises when final good firms (a carline producer in our data) make sourcing decisions for many parts. Although we would technically only need a minimum of two parts to highlight this effect, we develop a model with a continuum of parts due to its analytical tractability. And it also fits well with our empirical application in which car producers make sourcing decisions on a very large number of parts.

Each car part can be sourced from either within the region at one cost or outside the region, denoted Foreign, at a different cost. Each part cost for regional and Foreign production is modeled as a stochastic draw from a Weibull distribution with parameter $\theta \geq 1$.[9] We normalize the mean cost for regional production to 1. The mean cost of the Foreign-sourced parts is $\delta > 0$. This parameter varies across firms. Firms with $\delta > 1$ have a lower regional production cost for parts *on average*. As we mentioned earlier, we ignore the assembly location choice in order to focus on the part-sourcing decision (regional or Foreign); and we therefore do not model the associated assembly costs until the quantification in section 6.

Free Trade (No Rules or Origin) When there are no RoOs, a firm δ decides whether to source each part from either within or outside the region based on whichever cost is lower. This is the firm's unrestricted part-sourcing choice, which we denote with a subscript U. The resulting share of regionally sourced parts is given by the probability that the regional cost for a given part is lower than the Foreign cost. Given our distributional assumptions for the Weibull cost draws, that probability and resulting share is:

$$\chi_U(\delta) = \left(1 + \delta^{-\theta}\right)^{-1} \tag{1}$$

Firms with higher δs have a comparative advantage in regional part production and hence source a higher share of their parts domestically. This sourcing decision then leads to a total parts cost (aggregating over both the regional and Foreign parts) of $C_U(\delta) = \chi_U(\delta)^{1/\theta}$.

As we will see, these cost differences will be inconsequential for a firm's response to a RoO, because that will only depend on how a RoO *increases* the firm's cost above this benchmark $C_U(\delta)$.

Rules of Origin A RoO mandates that firms source a minimum fraction of their parts χ_R regionally, or else it will face a Most Favored Nation (MFN) tariff rate on the final good exported within the RTA. We model this additional cost as an average tariff $\tau > 1$ incurred across all final good units produced. In the quantification in section 5, we will construct this average tariff rate based on the share of a carline's within-RTA exports relative to all its other sales. If a firm chooses to comply with the RoO and avoid the tariff, it sources progressively more expensive parts regionally (relative to foreign-sourced) until the minimum threshold is met. In our companion paper, we show how the sourcing choices to comply with a RoO χ_R are equivalent to the ones the firm would make if a tariff were imposed on foreign parts (with the tariff revenue subsequently rebated back to the firm). We also describe the connections between a RoO specified as a regional part χ_R and a RoO specified as a regional cost share λ_R: a mandated minimum cost-share for regionally produced parts. Both types of RoOs have qualitatively identical effects on regional part sourcing because there is a monotonic relationship between χ_R and λ_R. This connection is important in the quantification because RoOs for cars in NAFTA and the EU-UK TCA are specified as cost shares.

When a binding RoO $\chi_R > \chi_U(\delta)$ is mandated, the firm's total part cost increases from $C_U(\delta)$ to:

$$C(\chi_R,\delta) = \chi_R^{\frac{1+\theta}{\theta}} + (1-\chi_R)^{\frac{1+\theta}{\theta}}\delta \tag{2}$$

This represents an increase in the firm's total part cost relative to its unrestricted (lower bound) cost $C_U(\delta)$ given by the ratio

$$\tilde{C}(\chi_R,\delta) = C(\chi_R,\delta)/C_U(\delta) > 1$$

This cost ratio captures the compliance cost penalty associated with the RoO χ_R. It is represented in the top panel of Figure 4.4 as a function of the RoO χ_R for three different firms. Anticipating our empirical application, we use our fitted distribution for δs across NAFTA-assembled carlines. Firm 2 has $\delta_2 = 0.12$, which is the median δ (representing a 12% average cost advantage for NAFTA-produced parts).[10] We then show two other firms (δ_1 and δ_3) that are, respectively, at the 5% and 95% percentile for that empirical distribution. For any given firm – a given δ – there is a range in which its unrestricted sourcing choice $\chi_U(\delta)$ is above χ_R and therefore complies with the RoO. There is no cost associated with compliance, so $\tilde{C}(\chi_R, \delta)$ is at its lower-bound of 1. We denote this case compliant-unconstrained. As the RoO χ_R rises above $\chi_U(\delta)$, compliance with the RoO entails a cost compliance penalty $\tilde{C}(\chi_R, \delta) > 1$. As anticipated, this cost penalty then increases monotonically with the RoO χ_R: compliance becomes increasingly costly as the RoO becomes more restrictive. Looking across firms, we see that, as expected, the compliance cost with a given RoO χ_R is always higher for firms with lower δ whenever they are not unconstrained: those firms have a comparative advantage in Foreign-sourced parts, so complying with a given RoO is more expensive.

4.2 Compliance

As we mentioned, a firm δ can choose not to satisfy the RoO χ_R and instead pay the average tariff τ. It will do so whenever the compliance cost is greater than the tariff penalty: $\tilde{C}(\chi_R, \delta) \geq \tau$. In this case, we label the firm as *non-compliant*, and it then reverts to its unconstrained part sourcing with regional share $\chi_U(\delta)$ and associated cost $C_U(\delta) = \chi_U(\delta)^{1/\theta}$. The horizontal line in the top panel of Figure 4.4 shows the example of a 6.2% tariff penalty. Continuing with our anticipated empirical application, this represents the non-compliance tariff that would be paid on average across all vehicles assembled in Mexico based on the empirical proportion of Mexican-assembled vehicles that are exported to

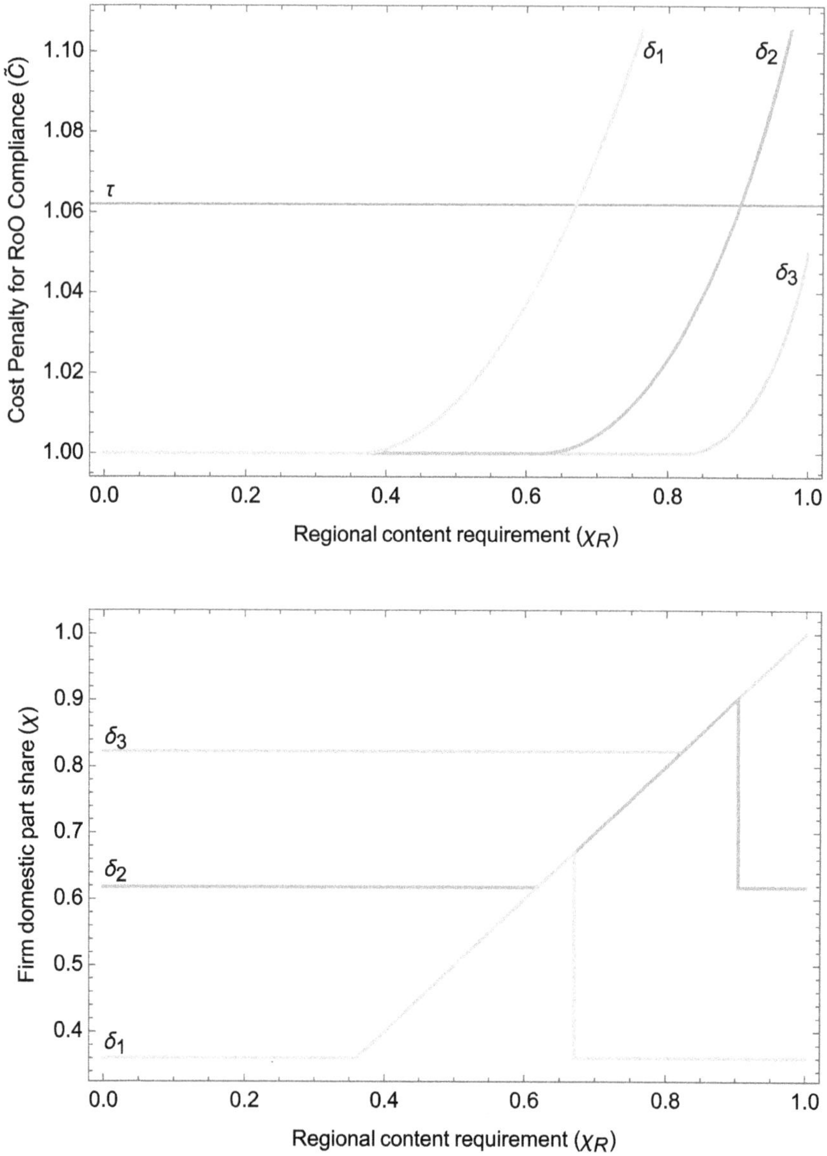

Figure 4.4 Compliance Cost and Sourcing Decision for 3 Firms

its NAFTA partners, the United States and Canada, and their associated MFN tariffs.

The bottom panel of Figure 4.4 shows the regional part share chosen by the three firms, given their compliance decision. When the RoO χ_R is low enough, all three firms are *compliant-unconstrained* and choose their unrestricted part share $\chi_U(\delta)$. This corresponds to the case of no compliance cost penalty, $\tilde{C}(\chi_R, \delta) = 1$, in the top panel. As the RoO χ_R increases, firm 1, followed by firm 2 and then firm 3 become *compliant-constrained*: The compliance cost penalty $\tilde{C}(\chi_R, \delta)$ rises above 1 but remains below the tariff penalty τ. In this case, the firms choose the regional share χ_R to comply with the RoO. This is captured by the 45-degree increasing line in the bottom panel: a chosen regional share equal to the RoO. As the RoO χ_R further increases, firm 1 and then firm 2 choose non-compliance: the cost penalty is higher than the tariff penalty. In those cases, their chosen regional part-shares drop back to their initial unrestricted levels $\chi_U(\delta)$. Note that firm 3 will never choose to be non-compliant: Complying with even the most restrictive RoO of 100% is still less costly than the tariff penalty. We label firms of this type as *always-compliers*.

4.3 *Laffer curve for rules of origin*

Setting aside those firms that are always-compliers, we see in Figure 4.4 that increasing a RoO from 0% to 100% will initially induce firms to increase their regional part-share – when they are compliant-constrained – but will then induce those firms to sharply reduce their part-share once the RoO rises above a threshold where the firms choose non-compliance. In our companion paper, we show that this non-monotonic response, in this individual firm case an inverted-V, requires a firm-sourcing decision over multiple parts. When there is a single part, that non-monotonic sourcing response disappears: Increasing the RoO can never induce a firm to *reduce* its regional part-share. And we also show that as we smooth that inverted-V sourcing response at the firm level over a set of firms with heterogeneous δ, then the average regional sourcing share becomes a smooth inverted-U Laffer curve. So long as we exclude the always-compliers, then the average regional part-share returns to its initial ($\chi_R = 0$) level as the RoO increases to its 100% upward bound. When we consider the full set of firms including always-compliers, then the average regional part-share remains above its initial level as the RoO increases to its upward bound.[11]

5 Simulating policy changes in the model

The model delineated in the previous section provides key qualitative insights. Most importantly, it demonstrates the unintended consequences of an overly strict set of rules of origin. When the cost of compliance is higher than the penalty for non-compliance, firms will opt into non-compliance, cutting regional input use down to their unconstrained levels. The key unanswered questions are whether recent policy changes put North America into this range of counter-productive rules. Answering this question requires us to calibrate several different dimensions of heterogeneity. We do this by finding parameter values that induce the best fit between our simulated data and the observed data for the pre-USCMCA period, when the RCR was 62.5%.

When taking the model to the data, we have to take a stand on the level at which the content decision is made. While the model refers to "firms," the AALA reports show that different carlines owned by the same firm use very different shares of North American inputs. For example, the made-in-Mexico Ford Fiesta uses 80% North American parts, whereas the US-assembled Ford Mustang has 46% of its parts originating in North America. The Volkswagen Golf R, made in Germany, has only 1% of North American parts, but the Golf GTI assembled in Mexico has 42%. The US-assembled VW Passat has 61% for the version with a 2.0-liter engine (made in Mexico) and just 30% for the 3.6-liter version (engine imported from Germany).[12] Thus, the data suggest that the content decision is taken in response to variation in relative costs (δ in the model) at the level of specific carlines. The actual decision-maker could be a plant manager or global headquarters. In the model, it does not matter whether the decision is centralized, because profit maximization implies that costs should be minimized for each carline. There is a single compliance decision for all the vehicles that come out of the same production line, regardless of their final destination. This assumption comes from observation in the IHS Markit data that it is extremely rare for the same carline to source a given engine or transmission from more than one country. Also, the AALA data provide single NAFTA shares for each carline.

It is important to simulate the model at the carline level because the tariff penalty for non-compliance (τ in the model) varies greatly across carlines because of their different sales destinations. For example, the Ford Mustang has 2018 sales of 76,000 units in the US. These cars will not pay any tariff penalties for non-compliance with USMCA rules, nor will the roughly 12,000 units headed to Australia and China.[13] Only the 7,600 Mustangs sold in Canada and the 1,900 sold in Mexico will face MFN tariffs as a penalty for non-compliance with the USMCA RoO. The situation of the Ford Fiesta made in Mexico is very different. The company sends the lion's share of its total production (66,000 cars) to its USMCA partners: to the US (52,000 cars) and Canada (1,200 cars). Meanwhile, only 4,500 Fiestas stay in Mexico. The overwhelming dominance of export sales to NAFTA partners gives the Fiesta plant very strong compliance incentives, as compared to the Mustang. We capture this important source of heterogeneity by using the IHS Markit data to compute tariff penalties for every carline.

The tariff penalty tends to be much lower than the MFN tariffs because large shares of output in the regional plants of a carmaker tend to stay within the country of production or go to markets outside the region (as in the Mustang example). Table 4.2 provides more granular information for the 20 largest tariff penalties.

We use a simulation of our model to estimate the underlying heterogeneity parameters. The idea is that carlines receive their comparative advantage "draws" according to a particular "guess" for the mean and standard deviation of δ. At the same time, they draw a parameter determining the importance of assembly costs for that carline. Then the simulated carlines each decide

Table 4.2 Top Tariff Penalties for USMCA Carlines in 2018

Brand	*Model*	*Assembly country*	*Tariff penalty*	*sh. rest of RTA*
Chevrolet	Silverado	Mexico	1.23	0.96
Toyota	Tacoma	Mexico	1.22	0.97
Nissan	NV200	Mexico	1.22	0.99
Ram	2500/3500	Mexico	1.21	0.94
Ram	ProMaster	Mexico	1.20	0.92
GMC	Sierra	Mexico	1.20	0.99
Ram	1500	Mexico	1.19	0.96
GMC	Sierra	Canada	1.18	0.80
Mercedes-Benz	Sprinter	United States	1.09	0.73
Chevrolet	Silverado	Canada	1.05	0.29
Volkswagen	Golf SportWagen	Mexico	1.03	0.96
Chevrolet	Cruze	Mexico	1.03	0.93
Nissan	Note	Mexico	1.03	0.86
Volkswagen	Golf	Mexico	1.03	0.81
GMC	Terrain	Mexico	1.03	0.98
Toyota	Corolla	Canada	1.03	0.85
Infiniti	QX50	Mexico	1.03	0.93
Buick	Regal	Canada	1.03	0.97
Dodge	Journey	Mexico	1.03	0.94
Dodge	Charger	Canada	1.03	0.89

Note: Head et al. (2022) provides the formula used to compute the carline-level tariff penalty in a way that takes into account market share changes in response to tariff changes.

whether to comply with a content requirement of 62.5%. Depending on the assembly cost share, this RCR converts to a particular parts costs share (λ_R in the model), which in turn converts to an implied share of regional parts (χ_R in the model). If compliance is too costly relative to the tariff penalty, then the carline selects its unconstrained cost, minimizing North American parts share. The result is a vector of parts costs shares emerging from the simulated model. Recognizing that the model is an approximation, and the data reporting in AALA is far from perfect, the simulation builds in random measurement error.[14] The result is a simulation-based distribution of North American parts shares, which we compare to the actual distribution from the AALA reports. We quantify the discrepancy in terms of the sum of squared deviations between model and data. The algorithm then repeats the procedure for a large grid of different guesses for the parameters, selecting the ones that achieve the best fit between simulation and observation. Head et al. (2022) provides a more formal description of this procedure for estimating the model parameters.

The estimated parameters allow the distribution of the simulated carlines to tightly fit the distribution of North American content reported by AALA. To provide external validation for the quantified version of the model, we follow the common practice of considering a feature in the data that was not part of the original moment-matching exercise. For this purpose, we compare the implied RoO compliance rates (also referred to as preference utilization rates) for auto trade (HS 8703) to those that emerge from the simulation based on the calibration described earlier. As shown in Table 4.1, the true rate of preference utilization for US-made cars entering Canada was 97% in 2019 (before the change in the regional content requirement in 2020). The calibrated model obtains a rate of 92%. Thus, our model is able to closely mirror the distribution of North American content rates at the carline level and also match reasonably well the RoO satisfaction rates observed for aggregate trade flows within North America.

After obtaining the best-fit values, we can solve the model for *any* potential RCR. This requires computing how each individual carline will respond to a stricter RCR. Depending on their parameter draws, they might increase regional parts shares just enough to match the new requirement, or they might opt into non-compliance. Based on this decision, the change in costs (from increasing regional content in response to a stricter rule) or the tariff penalties (from opting not to comply with a stricter rule) will reallocate market share towards foreign carlines, as well as those domestic carlines that were not complying before the stricter rule. In computing the changes in this step, we take advantage of the aggregation properties of the constant elasticity of substitution (CES) demand system. This provides an exact aggregation for the resulting changes in the price index and employment in the next section.

6 Quantification of the impact of RoO changes

In this section, we use our model, with parameters chosen to fit the distribution of regional content by North American carlines, to quantify the effects of two recent changes in RoOs. The first is the tightening of RoOs for North American vehicle trade, which was one of the most salient features of the USMCA. The second is the application of rules of origin to UK–EU trade, required by Britain's exit from the customs union in the final Brexit deal.

We evaluate changes in the strictness of the RoO, as measured by changes in the RCR for the enacted policies. We also consider alternative RCR levels that *might* have been chosen. For each policy change, we report outcomes for groups of carlines based on their compliance decisions before and after the RoO changes. For example, the first group in each table is the one for carlines that comply exactly with the old RoO but then decline to comply with the new RoO. The first numerical column shows the share of carlines in each group (in percent). The last four columns report the simulated changes induced by the change in the RCR. These outcome variables comprise the percentage changes in the price index, the group's market share, the weighted average regional parts share, and employment.

6.1 USMCA

Table 4.3 describes the simulated outcomes for the USMCA increase in the RCR from 62.5% to 75%. According to the calibrated model, just over a third of carlines switch from complying unconstrained to complying at the

Table 4.3 Increase in RCR from NAFTA (62.5%) to USMCA (75%)

Compliance status under:		*Percent changes in*				
NAFTA (RCR = 62.5%)	*USMCA (RCR = 75%)*	*Share of carlines*	*Price*	*Mkt share*	*Parts share*	*Parts Emp.*
Comply-constrained	Non-compliant	16.90	0.57	-1.05	-10.40	-11.85
Comply-unconstrained	Non-compliant	7.10	0.27	-0.16	0.02	-0.40
Comply-constrained	Comply-constrained	7.30	1.32	-3.23	20.97	15.53
Comply-unconstrained	Comply-constrained	34.50	0.21	0.00	8.26	8.03
Non-compliant	Non-compliant	8.30	0.00	0.65	0.00	0.65
Comply-unconstrained	Comply-unconstrained	25.80	0.00	0.65	0.00	0.65
All	All	100.00	0.28	-0.20	2.80	2.30

Notes: "Share of carlines" refers to the percentage of all domestic carlines in the corresponding status tuple. "Parts share" is a quantity-weighted average of the shares of parts from NAFTA origins across regionally assembled carlines. "Parts Emp." is employment in parts manufacture for domestically assembled vehicles.

minimum required level of 75%. These carlines will increase their regional parts shares by about 8%. The increase in average costs for the group is just one fifth of a percent. There is no discernible reduction in market share for this group, and its employment rises by almost the same amount as its average parts shares. Greater employment gains are recorded by the 7.3% of carlines that were just complying at 62.5% and raise their regional content up to 75%. These carlines increase their parts shares (X) by 21%, slightly more than the overall cost change of 0.75/0.625 – 1 = 20%. The implied rise in employment is just under 16%. The dampening comes from the 3% market share reduction for this group, which itself follows from their 1.32% rise in their average price.

The increase in employment for the constrained compliers is mostly offset by a reduction in employment by carlines that stop complying once faced with the 75% RCR. The overall employment gain is just 2.3%, much lower than the naive expectation of 20% (0.75/0.625 = 1.2) that would follow from assuming that all carlines mechanically comply with the RoO. While the employment gains are modest, so are the price increases faced by consumers: the price index for regionally assembled cars rises by just 0.28%. As predicted by the convex cost curves shown in Figure 4.4, there will be a higher cost of further rises in the RCR.

Table 4.4 reports the results of a counterfactual rise in the RCR from 75% to 85% (the original US ask during the USMCA negotiations). The last row of the rightmost column gives an interesting message for policy. It shows that had the US succeeded in negotiating an 85% RCR, this would have *reduced*

Table 4.4 Increase in RCR from USMCA (75%) to US Negotiating Point (85%)

Compliance status under:		*Percent changes in*				
USMCA (RCR = 75%)	*US ask (RCR = 85%)*	*Share of carlines*	*Price*	*Mkt. share*	*Parts share*	*Parts Emp.*
Comply-constrained	Non-compliant	28.90	0.54	-0.75	-10.69	-11.84
Comply-unconstrained	Non-compliant	4.30	0.24	0.13	0.01	-0.10
Comply-constrained	Comply-constrained	12.90	1.38	-3.19	14.50	9.34
Comply-unconstrained	Comply-constrained	18.00	0.25	0.13	7.15	7.02
Non-compliant	Non-compliant	32.40	0.00	0.86	0.00	0.86
Comply-unconstrained	Comply-unconstrained	3.40	0.00	0.86	0.00	0.86
All	All	100.00	0.39	-0.29	0.07	-0.60

Notes: "Share of carlines" refers to the percentage of all domestic carlines in the corresponding status tuple. "Parts share" is a quantity-weighted average of the shares of parts from NAFTA origins across regionally assembled carlines. "Parts Emp." is employment in parts manufacture for domestically assembled vehicles.

employment in the parts industry. 85% is on the wrong side of the Laffer curve for employment, although it is approximately the peak for the regional parts share. Compared to the move from 62.5% to 75%, the further 10-percentage-point (ppt) increase in the RCR causes the share of carlines dropping out of compliance to rise to 29%. Those carlines, whose average tariff penalty is just 1.2%, reduce their regional parts by nearly 11%. By contrast, only 13% of carlines decide to remain compliant with the 85% RCR. Those mainly consist of light trucks (as we see in Table 4.2), which face a much larger average tariff penalty of 7.8%.

The negative result of the 85% RCR for employment in the parts sector, as opposed to the slight positive change for the parts share, comes from the demand side. The carlines that are constrained compliant with the RoO at both levels see their market shares fall by 3.2%. This means that even though their sourcing pattern is using 14.5% more regional parts, substitution away from the more expensive compliant cars limits employment gains to just 9.3%. Consumer price increases from the stricter RoOs remain modest at 0.4%.

The Inflation Reduction Act (IRA) of 2022 included a $7,500 subsidy to consumers who purchase electric vehicles (EV). It also required that by 2029, in order to receive the subsidy, the EV would need a battery whose components were 100% made in North America (or other trade agreement partners). It was reported that no EV currently on the market uses batteries that comply with that requirement.[15] This extreme content rule motivated us to consider an equally extreme revision to NAFTA: going to a 100% RCR (from the current USMCA level). Our parameter estimates imply that only

Table 4.5 Increase in RCR from 75% to 100% Regional Content

Compliance status under:		*Percent changes in*				
USMCA (RCR = 75%)	*RCR = 100%*	*Share of carlines*	*Price*	*Mkt. share*	*Parts share*	*Parts Emp.*
Comply-constrained	Non-compliant	38.90	1.06	−0.97	-9.80	-11.61
Comply-unconstrained	Non-compliant	24.40	0.90	−0.47	−0.01	-1.37
Comply-constrained	Comply-constrained	3.00	11.09	−25.44	45.55	−2.31
Comply-unconstrained	Comply-constrained	1.40	5.79	−13.65	32.24	7.94
Non-compliant	Non-compliant	32.40	0.00	2.22	0.00	2.22
All	All	100.00	0.98	−0.72	−3.04	−4.67

Notes: "Share of carlines" refers to the percentage of all domestic carlines in the corresponding status tuple. "Parts share" is a quantity-weighted average of the shares of parts from NAFTA origins across regionally assembled carlines. "Parts Emp." is employment in parts manufacture for domestically assembled vehicles.

4.4% of carlines would comply with this policy, and their prices would rise by 11% if already constrained at the 75% level or by 6% if newly constrained. For the other 95% of carlines that would stop complying with the RoO, prices would rise by about 1% (except for one-third that were already non-compliant). The bottom line number is that a policy feature, ostensibly designed to be pro-employment, would actually reduce employment by almost 5% in the parts industry.

The phase-in of the 100% content rule for batteries is a feature of the IRA that we highlight because it relates to our model. The Senate actually voted down a motion (by a Republican who opposed the overall legislation) to implement the 100% rule immediately rather than start in 2024 with a 40% requirement. This suggests that a goal of the policy is to induce relocation of the production of battery inputs to North America over the next five years. Currently, China's share of world refining for minerals used in batteries is 59% (lithium) and 75% (cobalt).[16] Our model does not consider plant location decisions by components suppliers. In principle, this might bolster the case for stricter RoOs. However, opening up the possibility of plant relocation can also dramatically worsen the employment effects of stricter RoOs, as we show in a model extension developed in Head et al. (2022). Knowing that they will not comply with the RoO erodes the firm's rationale for local assembly. Firms that decide to relocate outside the region not only reduce assembly jobs; due to high trade costs on intermediate inputs, they sharply reduce their use of inputs from the region they exited. Recall that Figure 4.3 shows that Japanese and German makers use far lower shares of North American inputs in their cars assembled outside North America.

Table 4.6 Changes Due to Imposing the NAFTA Content Requirement

Compliance status under:		*Percent changes in*				
No RoO (RCR = 0%)	*NAFTA (RCR = 62.5%)*	*Share of carlines*	*Price*	*Mkt share*	*Parts share*	*Parts Emp.*
Comply-unconstrained	Non-compliant	8.30	0.51	−1.27	0.15	−1.62
Comply-unconstrained	Comply-constrained	24.30	0.25	−0.52	10.62	9.76
Comply-unconstrained	Comply-unconstrained	67.40	0.00	0.23	0.00	0.23
All	All	100.00	0.10	−0.08	2.21	2.03

Notes: "Share of carlines" refers to the percentage of all domestic carlines in the corresponding status tuple. "Parts share" is a quantity-weighted average of the shares of parts from NAFTA origins across regionally assembled carlines. "Parts Emp." is employment in parts manufacture for domestically assembled vehicles.

Table 4.6 compares the old NAFTA RoO to a hypothetical situation without any RoO. This could be interpreted as a North American customs union. This case presents the most straightforward set of outcomes, since all carlines are initially unconstrained. Roughly two-thirds remain unconstrained with the 62.5% RoO, reflecting the inherent desirability of local sourcing (to avoid transport costs). Moving from no content requirement to 62.5% leads to a 2% increase in employment, whereas prices and market shares hardly change. The rise in employment comes almost entirely from a quarter of the carlines moving from unconstrained choices to using higher North American content as a result of the 62.5% rule becoming binding. Those carlines collectively increase production (and hence jobs) by 10% with very little in terms of offsetting effects, since only 8% of carlines begin to pay tariffs.

6.2 *Brexit and the UK-EU TCA*

We now apply the parameters estimated for the North American data to consider the impact of the new rules of origin brought in by the post-Brexit trading arrangement between the UK and the remaining 27 EU members. The reason we do not re-estimate the parameters is that the AALA data contains only those cars sold in the US and therefore omits many of the mass-market cars in Europe.[17] Also, the coverage of country-level costs outside Canada and the US has many omissions due to the 15% reporting threshold. The parameters estimated for North American carlines are still relevant for counterfactuals in Europe. This is because the mean δ reflects high transport costs for parts seen worldwide (see Figure 4.2). Moreover, the standard deviation of δ reflects cost heterogeneity across carlines based on access to regional or third-country parts suppliers. Thus, in North America, there are substantial differences in the geographic structure of supply chains for the "Big 3" US and the Japanese producers on one hand – which have developed their North American supply chains over decades – and the German producers on the other hand, which have only recently entered the North American market. Similar differences are at work in Europe.

There are two notable differences between our post-Brexit simulations and those we conduct for the USMCA. First, the TCA imposes a RoO of just 55%, compared to the USMCA's 75%. Going in the other direction, the EU and UK tariffs on non-compliant cars are 10%, 4 times the 2.5% charged in the US. However, the tariff penalty does not just depend on the MFN tariff but also on the destination of export sales. As seen in Figure 4.5, the shipment-weighted tariff penalty has a mode that is *much* lower than 10%. Reflecting its smaller market size, cars assembled in the UK face a longer, thicker tail of high tariff penalties than cars assembled in the EU27. Eight of the top 10 tariff penalties shown in Table 4.7 are for UK-made carlines, with two Toyota models so strongly oriented toward the continent that their effective tariff penalties of 8% are very close to the MFN tariff.

Table 4.8 considers the impact of moving from a customs union with regional content requirement to a free trade agreement with an RCR of 55%.[18] The first striking point is that 85% of carlines in the UK and EU27 remain unconstrained under the RCR of 55%. This is because the fraction of comply-unconstrained depends only on the RCR and the carline-specific parameters, which are drawn from the same distribution for both economies. What differs in the UK/EU simulation are the tariff penalties, but they only influence the decision of whether to just comply (constrained) or not comply. Recall that the tariff penalty is generally higher in the UK. Hence, we see that the EU27 assembles more than twice the UK fraction of non-compliant carlines. In both

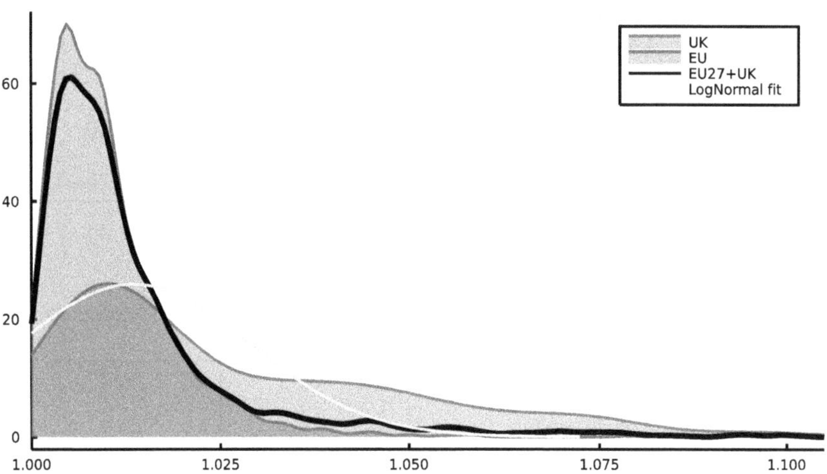

Figure 4.5 The Distribution of the Tariff Penalty for the UK/EU TCA

Table 4.7 Top Tariff Penalty Indexes for UK/EU TCA in 2018

Brand	*Model*	*Assembly country*	*tariff penalty*	*sh. rest of TCA*
Toyota	Avensis	United Kingdom	1.08	0.86
Toyota	Auris	United Kingdom	1.08	0.81
Opel	Astra	United Kingdom	1.08	0.81
Opel	Vivaro	United Kingdom	1.08	0.63
Nissan	Qashqai	United Kingdom	1.06	0.61
Honda	CR-V	United Kingdom	1.05	0.59
Volkswagen	Scirocco	Portugal	1.05	0.56
Nissan	Juke	United Kingdom	1.05	0.56
Nissan	Leaf	United Kingdom	1.05	0.54
Audi	A1	Spain	1.05	0.51
Opel	Mokka	Spain	1.04	0.49
Mini	Clubman	United Kingdom	1.04	0.41
Mini	Mini	United Kingdom	1.03	0.38
Land Rover	Range Rover Evoque	United Kingdom	1.03	0.36
Nissan	Navara	Spain	1.03	0.26
Ford	Fiesta	Germany	1.03	0.33
Opel	Corsa	Germany	1.03	0.32
Audi	TT	Hungary	1.03	0.29
Jaguar	F-Type	United Kingdom	1.02	0.27
Jaguar	E-PACE	Austria	1.02	0.27

Notes: Head et al. (2022) provides the formula used to compute the carline-level tariff penalty. The share rest of TCA is EU 27 sales divided by total sales for UK-assembled cars and UK sales divided by total sales for EU-assembled cars.

Table 4.8 UK/EU TCA Adopts a 55% RCR, Replacing Customs Union

Compliance status under:		*Percent changes in*				
No RoO (RCR = 0%)	*TCA (RCR = 55%)*	*Share of carlines*	*Price*	*Mkt. share*	*Parts share*	*Parts Emp.*
United Kingdom:						
Comply-unconstrained	Non-compliant	0.90	0.77	−2.17	0.30	−2.63
Comply-unconstrained	Comply-constrained	14.10	0.28	−0.73	12.70	11.56
Comply-unconstrained	Comply-unconstrained	85.00	0.00	0.10	0.00	0.10
All	All	100.00	0.05	−0.03	1.30	1.22
European Union at 27:						
Comply-unconstrained	Non-compliant	2.40	0.55	−1.56	0.17	−1.93
Comply-unconstrained	Comply-constrained	12.60	0.20	−0.52	10.72	9.92
Comply-unconstrained	Comply-unconstrained	85.00	0.00	0.09	−0.00	0.09
All	All	100.00	0.04	−0.03	1.01	0.94

Notes: Same parameters as NAFTA counterfactuals but different distribution of the tariff penalty.

countries, the cost increases from non-compliance are high enough that they more than offset the increase in parts share and thus lead to falling employment. Nevertheless, employment gains among the 13% (EU27) or 14% (UK) of carlines that comply at the 55% level are large enough to produce a 1% increase in parts employment.

The results in Table 4.9 indicate that further employment gains were available if that had been the object of the TCA negotiators. Although roughly 10% of the carlines that were constrained at 55% would opt into paying MFN duties at an RCR of 75%, their employment losses would not be severe enough to offset the rising employment of carlines that become or stay exactly compliant. With its larger tariff penalty, the UK sees the biggest gains (7%), while the EU27 has gains of just over 3%. It is worth emphasizing that the naive calculation based upon the ratio of RCRs (0.75/0.55) would imply a 36% increase.

Table 4.9 Changes Due to UK/EU TCA Moving to a USMCA 75% RCR

Compliance status under:		*Percent changes in*				
TCA (RCR = 55%)	*Alt. TCA (RCR = 75%)*	*Share of carlines*	*Price*	*Mkt. share*	*Parts share*	*Parts Emp.*
United Kingdom:						
Comply-constrained	Non-compliant	8.40	1.47	−3.06	−13.29	−17.16
Comply-unconstrained	Non-compliant	6.40	0.64	−0.62	0.08	-1.17
Comply-constrained	Comply-constrained	5.80	2.73	−6.58	38.14	25.62
Comply-unconstrained	Comply-constrained	52.90	0.49	−0.18	13.18	12.43
Non-compliant	Non-compliant	0.90	0.00	1.29	0.00	1.29
Comply-unconstrained	Comply-unconstrained	25.70	0.00	1.29	−0.00	1.29
All	All	100.00	0.57	−0.42	7.91	6.84
European Union at 27:						
Comply-constrained	Non-compliant	12.00	0.87	−1.78	−9.89	−12.26
Comply-unconstrained	Non-compliant	17.70	0.53	−0.77	0.06	-1.23
Comply-constrained	Comply-constrained	0.70	2.38	−6.04	36.52	25.29
Comply-unconstrained	Comply-constrained	41.70	0.35	−0.23	10.57	9.94
Non-compliant	Non-compliant	2.40	0.00	0.81	0.00	0.81
Comply-unconstrained	Comply-unconstrained	25.60	0.00	0.81	0.00	0.81
All	All	100.00	0.36	−0.26	3.89	3.26

Notes: Same parameters as NAFTA counterfactuals but different distribution of the tariff penalty.

7 Policy implications and discussion

The USMCA was welcomed by the chief lobbyist for Canadian auto parts manufacturers, Flavio Volpe. In an interview, he contended, "That deal [USMCA] . . . is the best single positive hit for supplier business across North America in the history of the auto business. We think there's going to be 25% more in absolute volume bought from local suppliers." In addition, the head of the Mexican auto parts industry association predicted a ten percent increase in production in Mexico's part sector.[19] In contrast, the calibrated version of our model implies a much smaller effect of 2.3% (Table 4.3, bottom row).

What is it about our model that implies much lower employment gains from RoO increases than naive calculations? The key point is that complying with a strict rule of origin is a choice. The benefit is preferential tariff access to the other North American markets. However, so long as the US maintains its 2.5% MFN tariff on finished cars, this is not a huge penalty. Moreover, some German factories in the US may care far more about their sales in other markets – such as China, for example – than they do about losing sales in Mexico or Canada. If bringing transmission sourcing to North America will add to the costs and make the vehicle non-competitive in China, the firm might prefer not to comply on sales to Mexico or Canada and then source engines from Europe as well if the only reason it had only sourced locally was to comply with the old NAFTA rules.

The results from our quantification suggest that the old NAFTA rule and the current TCA rule are both under the parts employment-maximizing levels. However, the original Trump administration demand of 85% would have been counter-productive even from a purely protectionist standpoint. Our results also suggest the 100% content requirements for batteries for EVs are likely to lower employment while significantly raising the costs of EV adoption.

Notes

1 Husisian et al. (2018) note the 85% proposal in their overview of the USMCA.
2 Felbermayr et al. (2019) present evidence that this argument applies to most rules of origin.
3 Anastakis (2005) provides a book-length treatment of this pioneering regional agreement.
4 "Inside the Brexit deal: the agreement and the aftermath" George Parker, Peter Foster, Sam Fleming and Jim Brunsden, *Financial Times* January 21, 2021.
5 "What's driving the EU on rules of origin?" Jim Brunsden, *Financial Times* October 29, 2020.
6 By contrast in the main manufacturing countries outside North America – Japan, Korea, and Germany – the USA-USA pairing is used for just 1% of cars.
7 Figure 4.2 applies the great circle formula to calculate the distance between engine (or transmission) factories and the final vehicle assembly factory. Since engines and transmissions are too heavy and bulky for air shipment, road, rail, or sea distances would be more accurate. Past work finds high correlations between great circle and actual road distances within countries. For intercontinental trade, air routes diverge in a more severe way from sea routes. Thus, we should expect that any

measurement error is larger for long distances, but we see relatively little trade at distances over 2,000 km.

8 www.nhtsa.gov/part-583-american-automobile-labeling-act-reports
9 The parameter θ governs the variance of the cost draws. As θ increases, the variance decreases. In the limit, as θ goes to infinity, the variance goes to zero, and there is no variation in the cost draws around their mean.
10 We also set $\theta = 4$.
11 Hypothetically, if the distribution of δs is such that it is dominated by always-compliers, then it is possible for the average regional part-share to monotonically increase with the RoO. However, we show that this is not the case for NAFTA.
12 All these percentages are cost shares from the 2019 AALA report.
13 The tariffs China imposes on US exports do not depend on their North American content.
14 Among the sources of error are the AALA exemption for reporting Mexico content if it is below 15%. Additional measurement error comes from rounding, which the law permits to the nearest 5%. We also intend for the error to capture deviations from the continuum assumption in the model. Since many parts have non-negligible cost shares, a firm that intends to "just comply" will in fact be observed to over-comply depending on the share of the last part.
15 *The Verge*, August 8, 2022
16 *Business Insider* August 10, 2022
17 Renault, Peugeot, Seat, and Skoda are examples of popular brands in Europe that are not offered in the US.
18 There are some complexities in the UK-EU TCA as regards electric vehicles.
19 Reuters, October 1, 2018.

References

Anastakis, D. (2005). *Auto Pact: Creating a Borderless North American Auto Industry 1960–1971*. Toronto: University of Toronto Press.

Felbermayr, G., F. Teti, and E. Yalcin (2019). Rules of origin and the profitability of trade deflection. *Journal of International Economics 121*, 1032–1048.

Grossman, G. M. (1981). The theory of domestic content protection and content preference. *The Quarterly Journal of Economics 96*(4), 583–603.

Head, K., T. Mayer, and M. Melitz (2022). The Laffer curve for rules of origin. Manuscript.

Husisian, G., A. Gomez-Strozzi, and A. Alvarez (2018). International trade: A new dawn for North American trade. Technical report, Foley LLP.

Irwin, D. A. (2017). *Clashing Over Commerce*. Chicago: University of Chicago Press.

Lighthizer, R. E. (2020). *2020 Trade Policy Agenda and 2019 Annual Report*. Washington, DC: Office of the US Trade Representative.

5 LCR Policies in China and their impacts on domestic value added in exports

Kun Cai and Zhi Wang

1 Introduction

Due to the rapid development of global value chains (GVCs) over the last three decades, the "Made in" label typically applied to manufactured goods, attributing them to a specific economy, has become an archaic symbol, as most manufactured products are now "Made in the World" (they are produced at stages in several countries, with value added at each stage). The rise of GVCs has significantly changed the nature and structure of international trade and investment and brought considerable benefits to China and is the major driver behind China's rapid industrialization.

However, the growth of GVCs has slowed since 2012, after a quick recovery following the Global Financial Crisis (World Trade Organization, 2019). Bakas (2019) points to this decline as suggesting that the world has entered a period of "slobalization." The GVC participation rate in China has plateaued since 2007 and was below the world average in 2019 (Asian Development Bank, 2021). The trade war between the US and China in 2018 further worsened China's international environment. The US government first attempted to reduce US imports from China through higher tariffs, then proceeded to impose strict export controls to cut off key high-tech components supply to Chinese high-tech firms such as the ban of semiconductor sales to Huawei. For some hawkish members of the US Congress, undoing 40 years of ever-closer economic relations with China and rolling back US reliance on Chinese factories was always one of their political objectives. An "Economic Prosperity Network" of like-minded countries, a concept initially proposed by the Trump administration and inherited and strengthened by the Biden administration, aims to convince Western firms to extricate themselves from China and instead partner with firms headquartered within member countries of the network based on the common goal of reducing economic dependence on Beijing ("friend shoring"). Economic nationalism and various protective measures are on the rise.

China has made strategic moves to prepare itself for this less favorable international economic environment. Beijing has announced a dual-circulation economic strategy that emphasizes domestic consumption as the major vehicle for economic development. Since Beijing launched a campaign to develop

DOI: 10.4324/9781003415794-5

more advanced technologies at home and rely less on the United States and other Western suppliers in 2012, it has been pursuing its own form of "made in China" for more than a decade. Achieving technological independence from the West, especially the United States, has been a stated goal of the Chinese government and reaffirmed by the current leader.[1] Beijing is pursuing two key objectives: (1) eliminating its dependence on foreign countries for critical technologies and products and (2) encouraging domestic indigenous firms to bolster their own capacity for innovation in order to become leaders in advanced technologies. To achieve such key objectives, various government agencies at different levels in China proposed and implemented a series of industrial policies, including some implicit local content requirements (LCRs), to encourage domestic production and innovation.

This chapter reviews these policies and measures the changing trend of domestic content in China's exports from 2007 to 2017 based on detailed trade statistics from the China Custom administration and the most recent national input-output tables (IOTs) published by National Bureau of Statistics (NBS). We also seek to assess the implications of various implicit LCR measures proposed in China on domestic content in Chinese exports. The chapter is organized as follows. Section 2 reviews the major industrial policies and implicit LCR measures in recent years proposed by Chinese central and local governments and by major manufacturing industries. Following Koopman et al. (2012), Section 3 outlines the conceptual framework for estimating domestic value added (DVA) in a country's exports when processing exports are important. We extend their methodology to decompose production activities into pure domestic, traditional trade and GVC activities at the country/sector level based on national IOTs. Section 4 presents the major empirical results and uses them to evaluate the impact of China's LCR measures on domestic content in Chinese exports. We find no empirical evidence that those policy measures implemented by the Chinese government in recent years have played any significant role in promoting domestic content in its exports, at least at the aggregate level. Section 5 concludes.

2 Recent local content requirement policy development in China[2]

A local content requirement is a measure that supports the use of local inputs in the production of goods or services as a precondition for gaining market access or obtaining financial incentives. Countries that have taken these measures hope to compel foreign companies to source from local firms to promote the development of their own industries. This support of local inputs incentivizes firms to select their suppliers based on their nationality rather than quality and cost.

The scope of LCR measures is not clearly defined. Hestermeyer and Nielsen (2014) classified LCR policies into three categories: licensing, government procurement and financial incentives. Hufbauer et al. (2013) believe LCRs can take many forms, including price preferences awarded to domestic firms that bid on government procurement contracts, mandatory minimum percentages required for domestic goods and services used in production, import licensing procedures designed to discourage foreign suppliers and discretionary guidelines that both encourage domestic firms and discourage foreign firms. They identified 117 LCR measures implemented across the world since the 2008 financial crisis and pointed out the distinctive characteristics that LCRs have compared with other trade policies. Following their work, Stone et al. (2015) provide a quantitative analysis of the localization barriers to trade. They group various LCR measures in two dimensions, which are the targeted market and identified benefits. The targeted markets include inputs, ownership, labor, government procurement and data. The benefits include market access, price preference, tax policies, government funds and domestic branding schemes. The OECD had deemed recent "Made in XX" or "Buy XX" programs initiated by some countries as localization barriers to trade.[3]

The LCR measures applied by China before its WTO accession were explicit. For instance, preferential tariff and tax incentives were provided based on the percentage of local inputs, and foreign enterprises were forced to follow the mandatory technology transfer requirements. After 2001, explicit LCR percentages for goods or services were gradually lifted. However, implicit localization trade barriers ingrained in the implementation of industrial policies emerged. These implicit LCRs aim to promote the innovative capacity of China and to cultivate indigenous domestic companies. On the surface, these policies treat producers equally regardless of nationality, while in practice, foreign producers may be encouraged to conduct localization strategies voluntarily, or it may be the case that only indigenous firms truly benefit from these preferential policies. Due to their opacity and covertness, these LCRs can be difficult to identify.

The heterogeneity of localization policies is prominent across sectors. A sector-by-sector approach is taken to present the localization policies in China, which take the forms of market access, subsidies, licensing and government procurement. We focus on the automobile, integrated circuits (IC), telecommunications, pharmaceutical and medical equipment industries because they are of vital importance to China's industrial system, and for that in Made in China 2025, specific targets of the localization rate or market share are set forth for many critical materials, products and processing equipment in these industries. By looking at the LCR policies in these sectors, we hope to shed some light on the roles they played in production activities and their effect on the changing trend of domestic contents in Chinese exports.

2.1 Auto industry

The auto industry is one of the pillar industries in the Chinese economy. The value added of auto vehicle and auto parts production accounts for approximately 2% of China's GDP.[4] In 2021, both the domestic sales and production of cars in China reached 26 million, which means that approximately 32.5% of total world auto production is conducted in China and 31.8% of global automobile sales are conducted in China, making China the largest car manufacturing and consumption country.

Auto manufacturing in China relies heavily on locally made components. Figure 5.1 presents the value of the imported auto parts per vehicle and

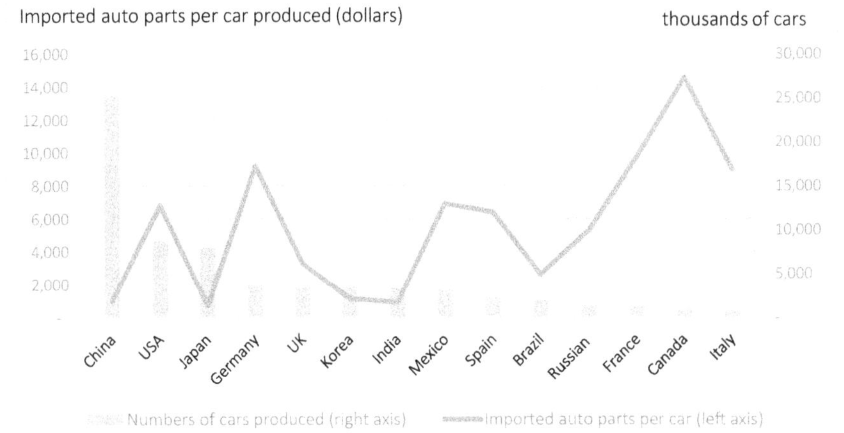

Figure 5.1 Imported Automobile Parts and Automobile Production of Major Producing Countries in 2020

Notes: Auto production includes both commercial and passenger vehicles. Imported auto parts per car are calculated as total imported auto parts divided by the number of cars produced in a country.

Sources: Authors' calculation based on production statistics from the International Organization of Motor Vehicle Manufacturers (OICA). https://www.oica.net/production-statistics/. UN Comtrade Database. https://comtrade.un.org/data/.

Table 5.1 MNEs and Their Joint Ventures in China

MNEs	*Country*	*Joint ventures in China*	*Year of establishment*	*Shareholdings*
Volkswagen	Germany	SAIC Volkswagen	1984	50% by Shanghai Auto Industry Co. (SAIC), 40% by Volkswagen, 10% by Volkswagen China
		FAW Volkswagen	1991	60% by China FAW Group Co., (FAW), 20% by Volkswagen, 10% by Audi AG, 10% by VW China
		JAC Volkswagen	2017	50% by Volkswagen, 50% by JAC Group (JAC) In 2020, VW brought in 50% stakes of JAC Group and increased the share in JAC VW to75%.
Daimler		Beijing Benz	1983	51% by Beijing Automobile Co., LTD (BAIC), 49% by Daimler
		Foton Daimler	2011	50% by Beijing Foton, 50% by Daimler

(*Continued*)

Table 5.1 (Continued)

MNEs	*Country*	*Joint ventures in China*	*Year of establishment*	*Shareholdings*
		Fujian Daimler	2007	35% by Beijing Auto, 15% by Fujian Auto, 50% by Daimler
BMW		BMW	2003	50% by BMW, 50% by Brilliance Auto. In 2022, BMW increased stakes to 75%.
Hyundai	Korea	Beijing Hyundai	2002	50% by Beijing Auto, 50% by Hyundai
Toyota	Japan	FAW Toyota	2003	35% by FAW, 50% by Toyota, 15% by Tianjin FAW Xiali Co. LTD The current ratio is 38% by FAW, 32% by Toyota, 30% by Tianjin FAW Toyota (TFTM).
		GAC Toyota	2004	50% by Guangzhou Automobile Group Co. LTD (GAC), 30.5% by Toyota, 19.5% by Toyota China
Honda		Guangqi Honda	1998	50% by GAC, 40% by Honda, 10% by Honda Technical Research Industry (China) Investment
		Dongfeng Honda	2003	50% by Dongfeng Motor Group Co. LTD (DFG), 40% by Honda, 10% by Honda China
Nissan		Dongfeng	2003	50% by DFG, 50% by Nissan Group of China
GM	US	SAIC GM	1997	50% by SAIC, 50% by GM
		SAIC-GM-Wuling	2002	50.1% by SAIC, 44% by GM, 5.9% by Guangxi Auto (formerly called Wuling)
		SGM Norsom	2004	25% by SAIC, 25% by GM China, 50% by Shanghai GM
Ford		Changan Ford	2001	50% by Changan, 35% by Ford Asia Pacific Motor Holdings LTD, 15% by Ford China
		JMC Ford	1997	41% by Nanchang Jiangling Investment Co., LTD, 32% by Ford, others by public shareholders
Tesla		–	2018	100% by Tesla

Source: Collected from official websites of the companies in the table and the enterprises big data platform operated by Baidu, https://aiqicha.baidu.com/.

the number of cars produced in major car-manufacturing countries. Each car produced in China used approximately $1,021 of imported components, far less than Canada ($14,564), France ($9,792), Germany ($9,200) and the US ($6,806). Other emerging economies, such as Mexico ($6,901), Russia ($5,330) and Brazil ($2,615), also use a higher value of imported parts than China. Among the top 15 auto-manufacturing countries, Japan has the lowest value sourced from overseas, approximately $778. The imported value per car in Korea ($1,154) and India ($961) is roughly the same as that in China.

One reason that auto components and parts remain largely locally sourced is related to the auto market access policy in China. In 1994, the Automotive Industrial Policy was published, which requires foreign carmakers to form a joint venture (JV) to gain access to the Chinese market. An equity cap of 50% is also set for foreign shareholders. Table 5.1 lists the joint ventures and the shareholding of multinational enterprises (MNEs) in China. The requirements of JVs and the equity caps have gradually relaxed in recent years. BMW raised its equity share to 75%, becoming the first foreign company to have a majority share in auto JVs in China. In 2019, Tesla became the first foreign automobile company with a wholly owned Gigafactory in China, as shown in Table 5.1.

In recent years, fiscal subsidies have been provided to new-energy vehicle (NEV) producers, which is another one of China's efforts to promote domestic auto production. The subsidies are not exclusively provided to indigenous manufacturers, but domestic producers seem to have benefitted the most. Table 5.2 shows the top 20 companies that received the most fiscal subsidies from 2017 to 2020. Each year, they collectively account for approximately 90% of total subsidies to NEVs.

In 2021, China published *the Provisions on the Security Regulation of Automobile Data*, laying down the rules that all important data must be stored within the geographic boundaries of China. The so-called important data include data of pedestrian flow, traffic stream, data of electric automobile charging networks, videos and images of car plates and drivers' faces. Any cross-border transfer of such data must be examined by local authorities. Complying with the regulations on auto data, many MNEs, such as Tesla, have set up data centers[5] in China to facilitate the localization of data storage and processing.

2.2 *Integrated circuit (IC) industry*

The goal of IC-promoting schemes in China is to cultivate comprehensive and mature domestic IC supply chains, covering all production stages and achieving chip self-sufficiency. Statistics show that the global production share of China's IC industry was only approximately 5% in 2020, far behind that of the US (47%), Korea (20%), Japan (10%) and Europe (10%). Additionally, China is more concentrated on relatively capital-intensive activities, including materials, wafer fabrication, assembly, packing and testing. The value added captured by China accounts for approximately 9% of the total semiconductor value chains.[6]

Table 5.2 Top 20 NEV Subsidies Beneficiaries, 2017–2020

2020		*2019*		*2018*		*2017*	
Company	*Subsidies (CNY, million)*	*Company*	*Subsidies (CNY, million)*	*Company*	*Subsidies (CNY, million)*	*Company*	*Subsidies (CNY, million)*
Tesla Shanghai	2123.37	BYD Auto	1134.74	DFAC	696.06	BAIC Motor	1448.91
BYD Auto	2046.87	Geely Auto	966.35	BAIC Motor	636.35	DFAC	776.33
GAC Motor	951.32	Yutong Bus	890.39	Geely Auto	468.71	Geely Auto	549.93
Great Wall Motor	830.56	BAIC Motor	801.73	BYD Auto	465.22	Chery Motor	496.38
Chery Motor	550.41	DFAC	783.86	JMC Motor	369.93	Zhongtong Bus	275.74
JAC Motor	539.57	Golden Dragon Bus	741.16	Chery Motor	341.56	Dayun Auto	232.18
SAIC Motor	410.86	Zhongtong Bus	599.59	SAIC Motor	340.52	Guangtong Manufacture	190.75
Yutong Bus	379.02	Changan Auto	343.26	Changan Auto	253.3	Changan Auto	187.98
Geely Auto	338.97	SAIC Motor	315.32	Jiangnan Auto	245.46	BYD Auto	170.9
BAIC Motor	303.97	Great Wall Motor	275.76	Guangtong Manufacture	227.23	Sunlong Bus	136.93
SGMW Auto	300.87	CRRC Times EV	267.54	JAC Motor	220.93	Golden Dragon Bus	135.53
Xiaopeng	248.74	Chery Motor	266.12	Golden Dragon Bus	215.56	SAIC Motor	122.72
WM Motor	238.44	Sunlong Bus	175.32	Winnerway Motors	187.71	Jiangnan Auto	118.87
Haima Motor	195.62	SAIC-VW	166.04	Sunlong Bus	152.81	CRRC Times EV	105.32
GAC-Toyota	166.74	Foton Auto	161.01	BMW	112.98	Yaxing Bue	100.47
Golden Dragon Bus	150.89	BMW	159.81	CRRC Times EV	109.16	Shuchi Bus	82.22
Hozonauto	110.42	Anhui Ankai Auto	142.51	Yutong Bus	92.38	Joylong Auto	79.06
Zhongtong Bus	105.16	Winnerway Motors	128.95	Great Wall Motor	91.32	Foton Auto	75.06
DFAC	80.59	GAC Motor	121.79	Zhongtong Bus	83.63	Victory Auto	68.46
Lixiang Auto	66.6	Yaxing Bus	91.06	Foton Auto	63.57	Xinchufeng Auto	63.56
Total	10537.17	Total	9578.99	Total	6075.8	Total	5890.34

Source: Based on data from the Ministry of Industry and Information Technology. https://wap.miit.gov.cn/zwgk/wjgs/art/2021/art_99ac13aa81d04a358e0443700fe100ce.html

Table 5.3 Invested Firms and the Shareholdings of National IC Fund Phase I (accessed on April 24, 2022)

Segmented production	*Firms*	*Shareholdings of ICF*	*Subscribed capital (CNY million)*
Wafer fabrication	Semiconductor Manufacturing North China (Beijing) Corporation (SMNC)	32.00	10291.20*
	Semiconductor Manufacturing South China Corporation (SMSC)	14.56	6341.55*
	Huahong Wuxi	29.00	3698.40*
	Yangtze Memory	24.09	13558.42
	Shanghai Huali Integrated Circuit Corporation	39.19	11600
	Ningbo Semiconductor International Corporation (NSI)	13.55	60
	Beijing Yan Dong Microelectronic Technology Co., Ltd. (YDME)	18.84	113
	Silex MiroSystems	30.00	600
Compound semiconductor	Sanan Optoelectronics	6.47	-
	Beijing Century Golden Light Semiconductor Co., Ltd. (CENGOL)	9.61	29.57
Packing and testing	JCET	13.31	-
	Tongfu Microelectronics Co., Ltd. (TFME)	15.13	-
	JCET Shaoxing	26.00	1300
Specialized equipment and key components	NAURA Technology Group Co., Ltd. (NAURA)	7.48	-
	Hangzhou Changchuan Tech (CCTECH)	6.76	-
	Shanghai Precision Measurement Semiconductor Technology, Inc. (PMISH)	7.30	100
	RSIC scientific instrument (Shanghai) Co., Ltd.	8.78	37.58
	Sky Technology Development Co., Ltd. Chinese Academy of Sciences (SKY)	19.73	-
	National Silicon Industry Group (NSIG)	20.84	-
Materials	Jiangsu Xinhua Semiconductor Material Technology (Xinhua Semiconductor)	23.56	306.29
	BDStar Navigation	8.57	-
Chip design	Unisoc (Shanghai) Technologies (Unisoc)	13.96	705.88
	Shanghai AisinoChip Electronics Technology Co., Ltd. (AisinoChip)	21.06	13.5
	Empyrean Technology	11.1	48.19
	Telink Microelectromics Shanghai (Telink)	11.94	21.49

Note: * indicates the original figures are in USD and the numbers are converted using the foreign exchange rate of 6.70 RMB/USD.

— indicates data not available.

Source: Based on the financial statement of public companies; the enterprise big data platform operated by Baidu, https://aiqicha.baidu.com/.

Table 5.4 Invested Firms and the Shareholdings of National IC Fund Phase II (accessed on April 24, 2022)

Segmented production tasks	*Firms*	*Shareholdings of ICF*	*Subscribed capital (CNY million)*
Wafer fabrication	Semiconductor Manufacturing International Corporation (SMIC)	1.61	–
	Yangtze Memory	30.00	18000.00
	Semiconductor Manufacturing Beijing Corporation (SMBC)	24.49	8204.15*
	Semiconductor Manufacturing South China Corporation (SMSC)	23.08	3559.71*
	Semiconductor Manufacturing East China Corporation (SMEC)	16.76	6177.4*
	Xiamen Silan Microchip Manufacturing	14.66	560.99
	UniVsta	13.95	330.00
	Ruili Semiconductor	9.80	4760.45
	Hefei Payton Storage Technology Co., Ltd.	31.05	950.00
Packing and testing	NAURA Technology Group Co., Ltd. (NAURA)	0.94	–
Specialized equipment and key components	Hangzhou Changchuan Intelligent Manufacturing Co., Ltd.	33.33	300.00
	Peric Special Gases	1.41	63.50
	New Ray Musk	21.28	500.00
Materials	National Silicon Industry Group (NSIG)	2.65	–
	Unisoc (Shanghai) Technologies (Unisoc)	3.74	189.00
Chip design	ChangXin Memory Technologies, Inc. (CXMT)	28.00	12546.91
	Apex Microelectronics	7.89	6.51
	Beijing Smartchip Microelectronics Technology Co., Ltd.	7.19	461.16
	SmartSens Technology	8.21	29.54
	FA software (Shanghai) Co., Ltd	14.56	11.64

Note: * indicates the original figures are in USD and the numbers are converted using the foreign exchange rate of 6.70 RMB/USD.

— indicates data not available.

Source: Based on the financial statement of public companies; the enterprise big data platform operated by Baidu, https://aiqicha.baidu.com/

Made in China 2025 specifies the target of localization rate in IC testing and packing equipment and materials by the end of 2030 to be 100%, that is, to achieve full self-sufficiency. A large scale of funds is put in to build fabs and to bolster domestic chip manufacturing. In 2014, the National IC Investment Fund (ICF) was established, which raised CNY 98.72 billion and invested in promising corporations such as SMIC, UNIS and JCET Group in the forms of public-private consortiums and equity ejection. Founding members of the ICF include the Ministry of Finance (36%), CDB Capital (22%), China Tobacco (11%), Beijing E-town Capital (10%) and others. Table 5.3 presents some of the companies in which the National IC Fund has ejected equity and the current share held by the Fund. In 2019, the fundraising of the National IC Industry Investment Fund (Phase II) was completed with a pool of more than 204.15 billion RMB. Table 5.4 presents some of the investments it has made thus far.

2.3 *Communications industry*

The Provisions on the Administration of Foreign-Funded Telecommunications Enterprises were enforced in 2002, opening the industry to foreign investors with restrictive conditions of forming joint ventures with a less-than-50% equity share cap and of a minimum registered capital. The telecommunication industry has been on the restricted list of the Catalogs for Guidance of Industries for Foreign Investment ever since. In the 2019 version of the Negative List for Foreign Investment, the restrictions on three kinds of value-added telecommunications services were lifted, namely, domestic multiparty communication services, store and forward services and calling centers, while restrictions on other value-added services and basic services are still maintained. Moreover, a licensing system was set up at the beginning of 2001 in *Telecommunication Regulations* promulgated by the State Council. MIIT is responsible for issuing licenses and assigning frequency spectra, and they can exclude the use of foreign standards and technology.

There are many forms of subsidies provided for communications enterprises, aiming to speed up theoretical research and promote the commercialization of new technology, such as grants for the establishment of innovation platforms and funding R&D activities in scientific research institutions and enterprises, mainly SOEs. Table 5.5 presents the subsidies received by some public companies in the communication industry during the period of 2017 to 2020. Among the listed companies, ZTC and China Unicom are the main subsidy beneficiaries.

2.4 *Pharmaceutical and medical equipment industry*

In 2019, China initiated a centralized drug-procurement program, and after several rounds of government procurement, the average price of medicines

Table 5.5 Government Subsidies Received by Public Firms, Selected Telecommunication Companies, 2017–2020

Production segmentation	*Company name*	*Stock symbols*	*Received government subsidies (CNY, million)*			
			2017	*2018*	*2019*	*2020*
Communication system solution supplier	Hangzhou Prevail Optoelectronic Equipment Co., Ltd.	300710	13.82	13.69	15.92	15.24
	Qingdao Topscomm Communication Inc.	603421		86.68	119.88	63.18
	Hytera Communications Corporation Limited	002583	159.64	169.20	230.45	206.68
Communications equipment manufacturing	Sichuan Tianyi Comheart Telecom Co., Ltd.	300504	4.93	4.08	9.88	20.68
	Shenzhen Zhongxing Telecom Co., Ltd	000063	3019.14	2081.46	1695.88	1572.67
	GHT Co. Ltd	002130	24.72	43.90	46.89	57.15
Ethernet switches	Kylan Technology Co., Ltd.	300353	34.87	25.49	34.49	28.96
	3onedata Co., Ltd	688618				13.14
IoT communications equipment	Fibocom Wireless Inc.	300638	5.07	17.20	30.05	37.21
	Shenzhen Neoway Technology Co., Ltd	688159			10.54	13.70
Optical communications	Tongding Interconnection Information Co., Ltd.	300004	4.35	6.69	3.28	3.58
	Suzhou TFC Optical Communication Co., Ltd.	300394	3.97	2.83	3.75	9.15
	Eoptolink Technology Inc., Ltd	300502	7.80	8.11	6.49	13.02
	Broadex Technologies Co., Ltd.	300548	5.55	7.45	9.16	15.24
	T&S Communications Co., Ltd.	300570	1.64	6.02	15.54	14.69
	Jiangsu Hengtong Photoelectric stock Co., Ltd.	600487	298.38	280.83	270.75	325.02
	Fiberhome Telecommunication Technologies	600498		325.32	284.48	281.33
	Zhongtian Technology Submarine Cable Co., Ltd.	600522		211.62	364.76	174.50
	Yangtze Optical Fiber and Cable Joint Stock Limited Company	601869		27.86	203.94	127.39
	Tianjin Futong Information Science & Technology Co., Ltd.	000836	36.53	6.73	15.47	17.11
	Accelink technologies Co., Ltd.	002281	56.04	62.04	39.42	44.15
Quantum communications	Kaile Science and Technology	600260	53.41	32.59	41.66	14.05
	QuantumCTek Co., Ltd.	688027				65.60
Telecommunication operation service	China Unicom	600050	196.40	185.21	776.36	1909.20

Source: Annual reports and financial statements published by the listed companies.

Table 5.6 Selected Regulations and Policies Regarding the Procurement of Drugs, Medical Devices and Equipment Published by Chinese Central and Local Governments

Local/central government	*Date of issue*	*Regulations and policies*	*Content*
Central	2021.5	Government Procurement of Imported Products Audit Guidance Standards (2021)	Government institutions are required to purchase 100% domestic equipment for 137 kinds of medical devices, out of all 178 medical devices and equipment.
Central	2021.2	Opinions of The General Office of the State Council on Promoting the regular and institutionalized Development of Centralized Drug Procurement with Quantity	Establish the rules and principle in the normalization of a centralized drug-procurement system and provide guidance on improving the operation mechanism and supporting measures.
Central	2017.10	Opinions on deepening the reform of the review and approval system and on encouraging the innovation of drugs and medical devices	Call for strict enforcement of the government procurement law to ensure that government funds give priority to the purchase of domestic medical equipment.
Anhui	2022.5	Notice on Matters Concerning the Regulation of Government Procurement of Imported Products by Public Medical Institutions	The purchase of imported medical products must go through an online examination and approval procedure by the financial departments at or above the municipal level.
Zhejiang	2020.5	Suggestions on promoting the high-quality development of pharmaceutical industry in Zhejiang Province	Medical institutions, including private medical institutions, are encouraged to purchase domestic medical equipment.
Zhejiang	2018.7	Notice on the Unified Demonstration List of imported Products (medical equipment) purchased by the provincial government in 2018–2019	A total of 232 kinds of medical equipment are allowed to be imported after verification, and the rest of the medical equipment is required to be domestically produced.
Sichuan	2018	List of imported products for government procurement in 2018–2019	The number of medical equipment allowed to be purchased from imported products has been reduced from 93 to 39, with 15 types of medical equipment all requiring domestic products should be used for clinical work.
Guangdong	2019.7	Technical evaluation standards for Class B large medical Equipment, 2018–2020 (trial)	Public medical device users are encouraged to give priority to the allocation of domestic brand Class B large medical equipment, and gradually improve the allocation level of domestic medical equipment.
Guangdong	2017.7	Class B large medical equipment approved in 2017	List 50 hospitals that must purchase domestic equipment.

Source: Collected from official websites of the central and local government of China.

declined by approximately 50%.[7] High-value medical consumables and other medical devices and equipment are also included in the program. Public hospitals are encouraged to favor domestically manufactured medical instruments and equipment in the program to promote indigenous innovation of domestic medical and pharmaceutical enterprises, trying to change a longstanding practice in which foreign medicines and medical equipment are given preferences.

Table 5.6 lists some of the policies published by the central and provincial government regarding the procurement of domestic medicines and medical equipment, showing that China will continue to encourage the substitution of domestic pharmaceuticals and medical equipment for imported ones.

3 Domestic content[8] in production – conceptual framework

As discussed, China has initiated various implicit LCR measures as part of its industrial policy in recent years. What are the effects of these policy initiatives on domestic content in its production? Did the LCR measures discussed earlier increase domestic content in China's exports? Such empirical questions need to be addressed by a quantitative method supported by real-world data. If we can find empirical evidence that there is a dramatic increase in domestic contents in China's production and exports, then a further econometric analysis of the major driving factors behind such an increase may be in order.

To measure domestic content in production and exports, recent literature heavily relies on the gross trade accounting framework proposed by Koopman et al. (2014) and extended by Wang et al. (2013) and Borin and Mancini (2019), which is based on inter-country input-output (ICIO) tables. However, available ICIO tables are usually very aggregate, with only limited industry and country coverage and significant time delays due to the tremendous data requests in compiling such tables, which significantly reduce the analytical power of the gross trade accounting method. Fortunately, national Supply and Use Tables (SUTs) and/or IOTs are more widely available and usually with higher sector details and shorter time frequencies. Simplified decomposition methods based on national IOTs that can preserve most of the features of the gross trade accounting framework will increase its analytical power and empirical applications. In this section, we first outline such a simplified method in a standard noncomparative IO framework, in which imported and domestically produced intermediate inputs are accounted for separately, and then extend it to the situation when processing trade can be taken into account.

3.1 Domestic content in production – standard noncompetitive national IO tables

The noncompetitive IO tables[9] can be specified as follows:

$$A^D X + Y^D = X \quad (1)$$

$$A^M X + Y^M = M \quad (2)$$

where $A^D = [a^d_{kj}]$ is a matrix of direct input coefficients of domestic products; $A^M = [a^m_{kj}]$ is a matrix of direct inputs of imported goods and services; Υ^D and Υ^M are $n \times 1$ vectors of final demands for domestically produced and imported products, respectively, including usage in gross capital formation, private and public final consumption and gross exports (re-exports); X is a $n \times 1$ vector of gross output; M is a $n \times 1$ vector of imports; subscripts k and j indicate sectors; and superscripts D and M represent domestically produced and imported products, respectively.

Equations (1) and (2) define two horizontal balance conditions for domestically produced and imported products, respectively. A typical Row k in Equation (1) specifies that the total domestic production of product k should be equal to the sum of the sales of product k to all intermediate and final users in the economy (the final sales include domestic consumption and capital formation, plus exports of product k). A typical Row k in Equation (2) specifies that the total imports of product k should be equal to the sum of the sales of product k to all users in the economy, including intermediate inputs for all sectors, plus final domestic consumption, capital formation and re-exports.

From Equation (1), we have

$$X = (I - A^D)^{-1} \Upsilon^D \qquad (3)$$

$(I - A^D)^{-1}$ is the well-known Leontief inverse, a matrix of coefficients for the total domestic product requirement. Defining a vector of domestic content, or domestic value added, as DVA, GDP by industry can be computed as

$$DVA = GDP = A_v (I - A^D)^{-1} \Upsilon^D \qquad (4)$$

where $A_v = [av_j]$ is a $1 \times n$ vector of each sector j's ratio of value added to gross output. If we further split Υ^D into three vectors, domestic final demand Υ^f, exports of final products Υ^{ef} and exports of intermediate products Υ^{ei}, then $\Upsilon^D = \Upsilon^f + \Upsilon^{ef} + \Upsilon^{ei}$ by definition.[10] Inserting it into Equation 5 and rearranging, we can obtain the decomposition of each industry's domestic value added, or GDP, into three parts:

$$DVA = GDP = A_v (I - A^D)^{-1} \Upsilon^f + A_v (I - A^D)^{-1} \Upsilon^{ef} + A_v (I - A^D)^{-1} \Upsilon^{ei} \qquad (5)$$

The first part is value added domestically produced and consumed. This part does not involve cross-border exchanges. An example is a haircut and these can be defined as pure domestic production activities.[11] The second part is value added embodied in final product exports. This embodied domestic factor content crosses national borders for consumption only. An example is the classical case of "Portuguese wine in exchange for English cloth." The whole production process is also completed domestically and can be defined as production activities of traditional trade. The last part is value added embodied in exports of intermediate goods and services, which will be used in production activities in other countries and involves cross-country production sharing, so it can be defined as GVC activities. It includes both the simple GVC (DVA crosses borders only once) and complex GVC (DVA crosses borders multiple times) activities defined in Wang et al. (2017).

The DVA decomposition results from Equation (5) will be the same based on a national IO table as using a global ICIO table if there is no need to separate the part of DVA that is first exported but eventually returns home. It is also straightforward and computes domestic contents in a country's gross exports as the sum of the second and the third part of Equation (5).

It is important to note that this method is limited because it relies on national IOTs. Although it can decompose production into pure domestic, traditional trade and GVC activities and compute DVA in exports, including direct and indirect value-added exports via upstream or downstream sectors, it cannot estimate DVA first exported but returned home via imports, indirect exports of DVA via third countries, distinguish simple and complex GVC activities, decompose bilateral trade flows, measure double counting due to intermediate goods trade and trace foreign value added and/or vertical specialization by country sources. These quantitative measures must be obtained from ICIO tables.

3.2 *Domestic content in exports – when processing exports*[12] *are important*

The production of processing exports often has a very different intensity in the use of imported inputs than that in domestic final sales and normal exports. To reflect such heterogeneity, one needs to keep track separately of the IO coefficients of the processing exports and those of domestic final sales and normal exports. The extended IO table with a separate account for processing exports is represented by Table 5.7.

In such an extended IO table, domestic production has been separated into two parts: (1) production for domestic final demand and normal exports represented by superscript D and (2) production of processing exports represented by superscript P. Mathematically, the model can be specified as Equations (6) and (7),

$$\begin{bmatrix} I - A^{DD} & -A^{DP} \\ 0 & I \end{bmatrix} \begin{bmatrix} X - E^{P} \\ E^{P} \end{bmatrix} = \begin{bmatrix} \Upsilon^{D} - E^{P} \\ E^{P} \end{bmatrix} \tag{6}$$

$$A^{MD}\left(X - E^{P}\right) + A^{MP}E^{P} + \Upsilon^{M} = M \tag{7}$$

where $A^{DD} = Z^{DD}(X - E^{P})^{-1}$ and $A^{DP} = Z^{DP}(E^{P})^{-1}$ denote the input coefficient matrix for the production of domestic use and normal exports and the input coefficient matrix for the production of processing exports, respectively.

Table 5.7 Input-Output Table with Separate Production Accounts for Processing Trade

			Intermediate use			
			Production for domestic use & normal exports	*Production of processing exports*	*Final use (C + I + G + E)*	*Gross output or imports*
		DIM	*1,2, . . ., N*	*1,2, . . ., N*	*1*	*1*
Domestic intermediate inputs	Production for domestic use & normal exports (D)	1 . . . N	Z^{DD}	Z^{DP}	$\Upsilon^D - E^P$	$X - E^P$
	Processing exports (P)	1 . . . N	0	0	E^P	E^P
Intermediate inputs from imports		1 . . . N	Z^{MD}	Z^{MP}	Υ^M	M
Value added		1	V^D	V^P		
Gross output		1	$X - E^P$	E^P		

Source: Adopted from Koopman et al. (2012).

The analytical solution of this extended IO model is

$$\begin{bmatrix} X - E^P \\ E^P \end{bmatrix} = \begin{bmatrix} I - A^{DD} & -A^{DP} \\ 0 & I \end{bmatrix}^{-1} \begin{bmatrix} \Upsilon^D - E^P \\ E^P \end{bmatrix} \tag{8}$$

Its Leontief inverse can be computed as follows:

$$L = \begin{bmatrix} I - A^{DD} & -A^{DP} \\ 0 & I \end{bmatrix}^{-1} = \begin{bmatrix} L^{DD} & L^{DP} \\ L^{PD} & L^{PP} \end{bmatrix} \tag{9}$$

$$= \begin{bmatrix} \left(I - A^{DD}\right)^{-1} & \left(I - A^{DD}\right)^{-1} A^{DP} \\ 0 & I \end{bmatrix}$$

Substituting Equation (9) into Equation (8), we have:

$$X - E^P = (I - A^{DD})^{-1}\left(Y^D - E^P\right) + (1 - A^{DD})^{-1} A^{DP} E^p \tag{10}$$

Substituting Equation (10) into Equation (7), the total demand for imported intermediate inputs can be computed as

$$\begin{aligned} M - Y^M &= A^{MD}(I - A^{DD})^{-1}\left(Y^D - E^P\right) \\ &\quad + A^{MD}(1 - A^{DD})^{-1} A^{DP} E^P + A^{MP} E^p \end{aligned} \tag{11}$$

It has three components: the first term is total imported content in final domestic sales and normal exports, and the second and the third terms are indirect and direct imported content in processing exports, respectively.

DVA (GDP) at the industry level can be computed as:

$$\begin{aligned} \begin{vmatrix} DVA^D \\ DVA^P \end{vmatrix}^T &= \left(A_V^D \quad A_V^P\right)\begin{bmatrix} \left(I - A^{DD}\right)^{-1} & \left(I - A^{DD}\right)^{-1} A^{DP} \\ 0 & I \end{bmatrix} \\ &= \begin{vmatrix} A_V^D\left(I - A^{DD}\right)^{-1} \\ A_V^D\left(I - A^{DD}\right)^{-1} A^{DP} + A_V^P \end{vmatrix}^T \begin{bmatrix} Y^D - E^P \\ E^P \end{bmatrix} \end{aligned} \tag{12}$$

where A_v^D and A_v^P are n × 1 vectors that denote the direct value-added coefficient vectors for domestic sale/normal exports and processing exports, respectively. Equation (12) can be rewritten as:

$$\begin{aligned} DVA = GDP &= A_V^D(I - A^{DD})^{-1}\left(Y^D - E^P\right) \\ &\quad + A_V^D(1 - A^{DD})^{-1} A^{DP} E^P + A_V^P E^P \end{aligned} \tag{13}$$

It also has three components: the first term is DVA in final domestic sale and normal exports, and the second and the third terms are indirect and direct DVA in processing exports, respectively. Notice that $Y^D = Y^f + Y^{ef} + Y^{ei}$; if we insert it into Equation (13) and rearrange, we can decompose each industry's domestic value added, or GDP, into the following four parts:

$$\begin{aligned} DVA = GDP &= A_V^D(I - A^D)^{-1} Y^f + A_V^D\left(I - A^D\right)^{-1}(Y^{ef} - E^{Pf}) \\ &+ A_V^D(I - A^D)^{-1}\left(Y^{ei} - E^{Pi}\right) + (A_V^D\left(1 - A^{DD}\right)^{-1} A^{DP} + A_V^P\right) E^P \end{aligned} \tag{14}$$

where E^{Pf} and E^{Pi} are processing exports for final and intermediate products, respectively, and $E^{Pf} + E^{Pi} = E^{P}$ by definition. Equation (14) is an extension of the GDP decomposition Equation (5) with an additional fourth term that is generated from processing export production.

4 Data sources and estimation results

To estimate the extended IO table that accounts for processing exports separately, we closely follow the Quadratic Programing procedures described in Section 2.3 of Koopman et al. (2012).[13] The purpose of these procedures is to minimize a quadratic penalty function subject to a series of accounting identities and adding-up constraints based on official statistics. Standard national IOTs are used to determine sector-level production and trade, and information from trade statistics is used to determine the relative proportion of processing and normal exports within each sector; thus, all available data are used to split the national economy into processing and non-processing blocks, each with its own IO structure.

After describing the data sources, we report the estimation results for China's share of domestic content in its production and gross exports at the aggregate level, by firm ownership, by major destination countries and by manufacturing industries.

4.1 Data

Inter-industry transaction and direct value-added data are from China's 2007, 2012, and 2017 benchmark IOTs published by the NBS of China, while detailed trade data from 2007 to 2017 are from the General Customs Administration of China. The trade statistics are first aggregated from the 8-digit HS level to China's IO industries. We partition both imports and exports in a given commodity classification into different parts based on the distinction between processing and normal trade in the trade statistics and on the UN BEC classification. A summary of such partitions as a percentage of China's total exports and imports along with the share of processing exports during 2007–2017 is reported in Table 5.8 and Table 5.9. The UNBEC classifies each HS 6-digit product into one of three categories: intermediate inputs, capital goods and consumption products. In Table 5.8, we further decompose the first two categories into two subcategories: processing imports used for the production of processing exports that cannot be sold to domestic users by regulation and non-processing imports used for domestic sale and normal exports. Columns (1) to (5) in Table 5.8 sum to 100%; Columns (1) to (3) and (4) to (6) in Table 5.9 sum to 100%.[14] These data are important parameters in our optimization model and the key information to understand our estimates of domestic and imported content shares in Chinese exports, especially their cross-sector heterogeneities and changing trends over time.

4.2 Domestic contents in aggregate exports

Table 5.10 presents the results for the decomposition of aggregate foreign and domestic value-added shares in 2007, 2012 and 2017. The estimated aggregate DVA share in China's total gross exports was 64.2% in 2007, 65.2% in 2012 and 69.8% in 2017. Such numbers for merchandise exports

Table 5.8 Major Imports Share Parameters Used in Domestic Content Estimation, 2007–2017

Year	*Imported intermediates %*		*Imported capital goods %*		*Imported final consumption %*	*Processing exports as % of total exports*
	For processing exports	*For normal use*	*For processing exports*	*For normal use*		
	(1)	*(2)*	*(3)*	*(4)*	*(5)*	*(6)*
2007	37.8	47.3	8.3	4.0	2.6	51.6
2008	32.3	53.4	8.1	3.3	2.9	48.1
2009	30.8	53.9	9.8	2.1	3.4	49.8
2010	29.0	55.1	10.4	1.8	3.7	48.0
2011	25.6	58.4	10.3	1.6	4.1	45.2
2012	24.9	59.4	9.7	1.4	4.6	44.1
2013	24.9	59.7	9.6	0.9	4.9	41.6
2014	26.5	57.1	10.0	0.9	5.6	39.6
2015	27.1	55.6	9.9	0.9	6.5	36.8
2016	25.3	56.2	10.1	0.7	7.7	35.7
2017	23.6	58.5	9.6	0.7	7.6	35.1

Source: Authors' calculations based on China Custom trade statistics and United Nations Broad Economic Categories (UNBEC) classification scheme.

Table 5.9 Major Exports Share Parameters Used in Production Decomposition 2007–2017

Year	*Normal exports %*			*Processing exports %*		
	Share of intermediates	*Share of capital goods*	*Share of consumption goods*	*Share of intermediates*	*Share of capital goods*	*Share of consumption goods*
	(1)	*(2)*	*(3)*	*(4)*	*(5)*	*(6)*
2007	49.92	13.39	36.69	33.28	34.26	32.46
2008	53.06	14.28	32.66	32.68	35.12	32.21
2009	46.80	15.23	37.97	31.20	36.34	32.46
2010	48.39	14.78	36.83	31.92	37.21	30.87
2011	49.38	15.01	35.61	31.82	37.34	30.84
2012	47.72	15.86	36.42	30.45	38.19	31.36
2013	46.95	15.86	37.19	31.75	36.57	31.67
2014	47.27	16.27	36.46	31.63	34.93	33.44
2015	46.87	16.87	36.26	32.77	36.37	30.86
2016	46.72	16.74	36.54	33.59	36.01	30.40
2017	47.86	16.59	35.54	33.85	35.86	30.29

Source: Authors' calculations based on China Custom trade statistics and United Nations Broad Economic Categories (UNBEC) classification scheme.

were 60.1%, 59.5% and 64.4%, respectively. For manufacturing products only, these estimated shares are lower from 59.2% in 2007 to 63.5% in 2017. In general, the estimated direct domestic value-added shares are less than one-third of the total domestic value-added shares. However, the difference between the direct foreign value-added share and the estimated indirect foreign value-added share was relatively small, indicating that most of the foreign content comes directly from imported foreign inputs and generates much less indirect value added compared to domestic value added.

It is interesting that the DVA shares in normal and processing exports trend in opposite directions: the DVA share in China's normal manufacturing exports increased from 82.9% in 2007 to 84.7% in 2017, but this share declined in processing exports from 36.6% in 2007 to 27.7% in 2017, which is completely different from the previous decades (more domestically produced inputs were used in China's processing exports between 1997 and 2007, the DVA "share increased from 20.7% in 1997 to 37.0% in 2007, up by more than 16 percentage points" (Koopman et al., 2012)). This indicates that the increase in the DVA share between 2007 and 2017 in China's total exports (approximately 5.3 percentage points increase) was mainly driven by the decline in processing exports in China's total merchandise exports (decreased from 51.6% in 2007 to 35.1% in 2017) and

Table 5.10 Domestic and Foreign Values Added: Processing vs Normal Exports (in Percent of Total Exports)

	Normal exports			*Processing exports*			*Weighted sum*		
	2007	*2012*	*2017*	*2007*	*2012*	*2017*	*2007*	*2012*	*2017*
Total exports (including service sectors)									
Total foreign value added	15.3	14.6	12.7	63.0	70.0	71.9	35.8	34.8	30.3
Direct foreign value added	4.9	4.7	4.8	58.0	66.4	69.5	27.7	27.2	24.0
Total domestic value added	84.7	85.4	87.3	37.0	30.1	28.1	64.2	65.2	69.8
Direct domestic value added	28.6	30.4	30.4	9.5	8.9	9.3	20.4	22.5	24.1
All merchandise									
Total foreign value added	16.7	16.6	14.9	63.0	70.0	72.0	39.9	40.5	35.6
Direct foreign value added	5.6	5.6	5.9	58.1	66.5	69.7	31.9	32.8	29.0
Total domestic value added	83.3	83.4	85.1	37.0	30.0	28.0	60.1	59.5	64.4
Direct domestic value added	23.4	22.1	22.3	9.4	8.9	9.2	16.4	16.2	17.6
Manufacturing goods (food processing sectors are excluded)									
Total foreign value added	17.1	17.1	15.3	63.4	70.3	72.3	40.8	41.4	36.5
Direct foreign value added	5.7	5.8	6.1	58.4	66.8	69.6	32.7	33.7	29.8
Total domestic value added	82.9	82.9	84.7	36.6	29.7	27.7	59.2	58.6	63.5
Direct domestic value added	22.5	21.4	21.6	9.4	8.9	9.2	15.8	15.7	17.0

Source: Authors' estimates based on China's 2007, 2012, 2017 benchmark input-output table published by the Bureau of National Statistics and Official China trade statistics from China Customs.

the increase in exports in services (increased from 14.4% in 2007 to 19% in 2017). The increase in the DVA share in China's normal merchandise exports only played a relatively minor role (increased only approximately 1.1 percentage point from 84% in 2007 to 85.1% in 2017). This empirical finding may indicate that the various industrial policies and implicit LCR measures proposed in China during recent decades played no significant role in promoting DVA in China's total exports, at least at the aggregate level during 2007–2017.

4.3 Domestic content in exports by firm ownership

There is a significant change in export structure by firm ownership between 2007 and 2017. The share of private firms increased dramatically, from 21.3% in 2007 to 44.2% in 2017, more than doubling within 10 years. At the same time, the share of both state-owned and foreign-invested enterprises (SOEs and FIEs) declined from 18.9% to 9.1% and 56.3% to 45.3%, respectively. Both private firms and FIEs are the major players in China's export success, and one may be interested in the DVA share in their exports. However, since there is no information on separate input-output coefficients by firm ownership, we cannot meaningfully distinguish foreign versus local firms within a sector. Instead, we provide an estimate of the DVA share of aggregate merchandise exports by firm ownership. By construction, the differences across firms of different ownerships are driven entirely by different degrees of their reliance on processing exports within a sector and the difference in the sector composition of their total exports (both are observed directly from the customs trade statistics).

Estimates of the DVA shares by firm ownership for China's merchandise exports are presented in Table 5.11. The results show that exports by wholly foreign-owned enterprises exhibit the lowest share of DVA, followed by Sino-foreign joint-venture companies (decreased from 44.2% and 56.7% in 2007 to 43% and 52.7% in 2017, respectively). Exports from Chinese private enterprises embodied the highest DVA shares (80.7% in 2007, 77.8% in 2012 and 81.1% in 2017), while those from state-owned firms were in the middle (approximately 70% in the three years). It is also interesting to observe that the variation of DVA share in normal exports is relatively small by different firm ownerships and over the three benchmark years (between 82% and 85%). The weights of processing exports are the decisive factor behind the difference in DVA share between private firms and FIEs (private firms only have approximately 10% of their exports as processing exports, while approximately two-thirds of exports from FIEs are processing exports). Note that these are estimations based on the currently available information; better estimates can be derived once information on I/O coefficients by firm ownership becomes available.

Compared to Table 5.11 of Koopman et al. (2012), the most noticeable feature of this table is the relatively stable DVA share in exports produced by FIEs from 2007 to 2017 (it slightly declines). From 2002 to 2007, the DVA share increased by more than 10 percentage points. It seems that FIE exporters did not source more of their intermediate inputs within China after 2007. This finding provides further evidence that the implicit LCR measures we described in Section 2 did not affect most FIEs' decision to source their production inputs outside China at the aggregate level. Their use of imported inputs increased during this period.

4.4 Domestic content in Chinese exports by trading partners

By assuming that DVA shares within a given sector and export regime (normal/processing) are the same for all destination countries, we can further estimate the DVA share in China's exports to each of its major trading partners. However, the variation by destination is driven solely by China's export structure (share of processing exports and sector composition) to each of its trading partners. The results for China's total merchandise exports to each of its major trading partners are reported in Table 5.12 in increasing order of the estimated weighted DVA share in 2017.

Hong Kong, Singapore, Japan, the United States and Korea are the top five in both 2012 and 2017, with less than 60% of China's DVA embodied in its imports from China. China's exports to all emerging economies and developing countries embodied much higher DVA than its exports to OECD countries. The difference is more than 10 percentage points.

Interestingly, the DVA share uniformly increased in China's non-processing exports to all its major trading partners from 2012 to 2017, while it uniformly declined for processing exports to all countries. This information suggests that the LCR policies we discussed in Section 2 did not reduce exporting firms' sources of raw materials, parts and components around the world, at least in China's production of processing exports.

4.5 Domestic content in Chinese exports by industries

To see if there are interesting patterns at the sector level, Table 5.13 reports, in ascending order of the weighted DVA share of 2012, the value-added decomposition in Chinese manufacturing exports by industry in 2012 and 2017, respectively, together with the shares of processing trade and foreign invested firms in each sector's exports and the sector's share in China's total merchandise exports. Because the sector classifications are more consistent between 2012 and 2017 than those in 2007 due to a new version of industrial classification in China (CSIC, 2002 to CSIC, 2011[15]), we present the results of each sector for the years 2012 and 2017 only.

Thirteen out of the 68 manufacturing industries reported in Table 5.13 had a share of DVA in their exports of less than 51% in 2012, collectively accounting for 34% of China's total exports. It is worth noting that more than half of these industries are relatively sophisticated and high-tech, such as

Table 5.11 Share of Domestic Value Added in Total Merchandise Exports by Firm Ownership (%), 2007, 2012 and 2017

	Share of processing exports in total exports	*None-processing*		*Processing*		*Weighted sum*		*Share of exports by firm ownership in China's total exports*
		Direct domestic value added	*Total domestic value added*	*Direct domestic value added*	*Total domestic value added*	*Direct domestic value added*	*Total domestic value added*	
2017								
Wholly foreign owned	73.5	22.0	84.8	9.0	28.0	12.5	43.0	32.1
Joint venture firms	57.8	22.5	84.8	9.6	29.2	15.1	52.7	12.4
State owned firms	18.7	23.2	84.2	9.2	22.4	20.6	72.7	9.1
Collectively owned firms	9.9	21.2	83.5	9.4	32.5	20.1	78.5	2.1
Private firms	8.0	22.3	85.6	9.5	30.2	21.3	81.1	44.2
All firms	36.2	22.3	85.2	9.2	28.2	17.6	64.5	100.0
2012								
Wholly foreign owned	79.2	21.8	82.6	8.7	30.0	11.4	40.9	36.5
Joint venture firms	57.5	21.8	82.5	8.8	31.2	14.3	53.0	15.0
State owned firms	22.3	21.8	81.7	10.3	28.4	19.2	69.8	12.4
Collectively owned firms	16.9	21.9	82.3	9.4	33.9	19.8	74.1	2.5
Private firms	12.0	22.3	84.3	9.6	29.8	20.8	77.8	33.6
All firms	44.7	22.1	83.4	8.9	30.1	16.2	59.6	100.0
2007								
Wholly foreign owned	83.0	23.8	83.8	11.4	36.1	13.5	44.2	38.0
Joint venture firms	59.7	22.9	83.6	10.3	38.5	15.4	56.7	17.8
State owned firms	25.9	23.4	83.4	10.0	39.4	19.9	72.0	18.9
Collectively owned firms	24.3	22.4	83.1	8.8	41.8	19.1	73.1	4.0
Private firms	9.7	23.5	84.9	9.8	42.2	22.2	80.7	21.3
All firms	50.1	23.5	83.4	9.5	37.1	16.5	60.2	100.0

Source: Authors' estimates based on China's 2007, 2012, 2017 benchmark input-output table published by the Bureau of National Statistics and Official China trade statistics from China Customs.

Table 5.12 Domestic Value Added Share in Chinese Gross Merchandise Exports to its Major Trading Partners, as Percentages, 2012 and 2017

Region description	*% of processing exports*		*Non processing*		*Processing*		*Weighted sum*		*% of exports to the world*	
Year	*2012*	*2017*	*2012*	*2017*	*2012*	*2017*	*2012*	*2017*	*2012*	*2017*
Hong Kong	75.2	59.2	81.7	83.8	28.8	28.8	41.9	51.3	14.0	11.3
Singapore	57.7	51.0	82.2	83.0	27.4	24.7	50.6	53.3	2.0	2.0
Japan	54.1	50.4	85.3	86.8	32.3	29.8	56.6	58.1	7.6	6.1
United States	54.6	46.3	84.1	85.6	29.9	28.1	54.5	59.0	17.6	19.1
Korea Rep	54.4	46.9	82.0	85.3	31.8	29.3	54.7	59.1	4.3	4.5
Taiwan province	51.1	44.6	81.6	85.2	32.7	28.0	56.6	59.7	1.7	1.8
Mexico	45.3	36.8	82.4	84.5	30.1	28.0	58.7	63.7	1.3	1.6
East EU12	44.0	36.7	82.8	84.5	29.6	27.8	59.4	63.7	2.0	2.2
West EU15	44.3	36.8	83.9	85.5	29.9	28.1	60.0	64.4	14.8	14.3
Australia/NZ	36.8	31.8	83.5	85.6	31.8	27.1	64.5	67.0	2.1	2.1
Rest of OECD	37.8	31.3	84.1	85.8	31.3	27.6	64.1	67.6	1.7	1.7
Rest of Southeast Asia	30.3	29.3	83.9	85.2	32.8	27.8	68.4	68.4	1.8	1.9
Thailand	32.9	24.9	82.3	85.1	33.7	29.6	66.3	71.3	1.6	1.7
Brazil	28.6	19.0	82.6	84.5	32.6	28.9	68.4	74.0	1.6	1.3
Indonesia	23.9	14.6	82.6	85.0	28.2	27.2	69.6	76.6	1.7	1.6
Rest of Latin Amer/Caribbean	22.6	17.0	82.1	84.7	29.7	26.7	70.3	74.8	3.8	3.0
India	21.1	16.9	81.7	83.9	32.1	29.1	71.2	74.6	2.4	3.1
Philippines	22.1	14.8	82.8	85.3	31.6	25.3	71.5	76.4	0.8	1.5
RUS	20.7	18.8	84.5	85.9	30.1	28.3	73.2	75.1	2.2	1.9
Middle East/North Africa	17.8	14.2	83.7	85.3	30.4	27.8	74.2	77.1	5.5	5.6
Sub-Saharan Africa	15.3	9.3	83.3	85.4	30.8	27.3	75.2	79.9	3.2	3.2
Rest of South Asia	16.8	16.7	83.9	85.7	33.5	29.6	75.5	76.3	3.9	6.1
Eastern Europe/Central Asia	15.8	13.3	84.0	85.4	33.4	29.7	76.0	78.0	2.5	2.3
Total	44.7	36.3	83.4	85.2	30.2	28.3	59.6	64.6	100.0	100.0

Source: Authors' estimates based on China's 2012 and 2017 benchmark input-output table published by the Bureau of National Statistics and Official China trade statistics from China Customs.

computers, communication equipment and electronic components, and they are also those sectors in which foreign invested enterprises play a leading role, with a higher share of processing exports of approximately 70%. In 2017, the number of industries that have a DVA less than –51% in exports declined to 10, and the sum of their share in total exports declined to approximately 27%.

The number of sectors with shares of DVA in the range of 51% to 75% was 23; they contributed 20% of China's total exports in 2012. The sectors in this group are typically capital intensive, such as the manufacturing of basic chemicals, iron and steel, lifting and handling equipment and pumps, generators and batteries. The number of sectors with a middle-level DVA share was 21 in 2017, with a slight difference in sector composition; they collectively accounted for 22% of China's total exports.

There are 32 industries with shares of DVA above 75%; as a group, they account for approximately 25% of China's total exports in 2012. Most labor-intensive sectors are among this group, such as textiles, apparel, footwear, leather, fur and furniture. However, the manufacturing of auto and auto parts were also in this group, with shares of DVA of 79.7% and 76.2% in 2012, respectively. In 2017, 37 industries had shares of DVA greater than 75%. The weights of high-DVA sectors in China's total exports increase to 30%.

Between 2012 and 2017, the average increase in the DVA share in manufacturing exports was 4.94%. Among the 68 manufacturing sector exports reported, 15 sectors have an increase of over 5%, and 4 of them increased over 9%. Those sectors are fabricated metal products, sports goods, games and toys, audiovisual apparatus, wire and cable. These sectors also feature the largest declines in the share of their processing exports and/or FIE exports. For the four sectors with an approximately 10% increase in the DVA share, the share of processing exports declined by 14% to 21% during the 5-year period. Twenty-three sectors have increased their DVA share in exports, ranging from 2% to 5%, and those sectors are most with low- or middle-level DVA shares in 2012. Ten sectors experienced a decline in their DVA share in the same period. Examples of these sectors are motor vehicles, nonferrous metal rolling products and lifting and handling equipment. The share of processing and FIE exports increased in the auto sectors by 9.2% and 8.1%, respectively, which was the main driver of the over 5% decline in the DVA share in exports during this period.

With respect to the change in the absolute value of DVA, communication equipment, fabricated metal products and textile and wearing apparels are the three sectors with an increase in DVA of more than 10 million USD. The communication equipment has the largest increase in DVA of more than 27 million USD. The auto parts and other related sectors, such as batteries, have experienced a moderate-level increase in the DVA level, but the DVA in the whole auto sector has declined. Therefore, the correlation between localization policies and the change in domestic content needs further investigation. One may argue that the localization policies discussed in Section 2 may have played some roles in boosting DVA in these sectors. A formal econometric

Table 5.13 Domestic Value-Added Share in Manufacturing Exports by Sector, 2012 and 2017

Code	Sector label	2012						2017					
		Value-added decomposition %			% of processing exports	% of FIE exports	% of total exports	Value-added decomposition %			% of processing exports	% of FIE exports	% of total exports
		Non-processing	Processing	Weighted sum				Non-processing	Processing	Weighted sum			
88	AV Apparatus	77.5	15.4	25.0	84.5	72.0	1.2	73.1	15.2	35.4	65.1	57.6	1.0
85	Computer	80.9	23.8	26.5	95.2	95.3	8.0	78.4	25.0	30.6	89.5	88.0	6.5
77	Boats	85.3	24.1	30.3	89.9	35.9	1.7	85.2	21.5	32.3	83.0	29.4	0.9
68	OfficeEquip.	73.5	31.8	35.5	91.0	92.5	1.1	70.2	35.7	41.7	82.5	86.2	0.6
50	Rubber	82.3	23.7	36.9	77.5	43.7	0.9	84.7	22.3	44.8	63.9	36.1	0.7
39	Refined oil	57.8	10.6	41.5	34.5	24.9	0.8	67.3	2.5	42.9	37.7	21.5	0.7
86	CommuEquip	78.6	32.3	43.7	75.3	81.0	6.0	81.2	30.9	47.7	66.6	67.9	8.1
89	Elect Parts	82.0	29.5	43.9	72.4	81.0	5.5	84.6	29.3	50.2	62.2	74.6	5.2
91	Measuring	77.0	32.8	43.9	74.7	77.3	1.3	79.8	33.0	50.0	63.7	69.1	1.4
83	Electrical	81.3	19.7	49.0	52.4	57.4	1.8	84.3	14.8	57.6	38.4	47.4	1.9
87	Tele Equip	72.1	33.6	49.1	59.8	64.3	1.3	69.2	34.9	46.5	66.2	66.1	1.6
38	Toys	86.0	18.5	49.3	54.4	42.9	3.6	84.3	28.5	61.8	40.4	39.9	3.3
45	Synthetic	77.8	29.8	50.6	56.9	61.6	0.5	83.8	28.5	56.6	49.2	51.2	0.6
80	Power Equip	80.3	34.3	54.0	57.2	67.6	2.3	83.5	14.1	52.8	44.2	61.5	2.2
61	NFMetal	76.6	27.2	55.5	42.6	30.2	0.4	81.0	27.3	55.6	47.3	19.9	0.3
81	Wire&Cable	80.5	32.8	56.0	51.4	61.9	0.8	83.8	27.2	65.6	32.1	47.8	0.9
84	Batteries	74.1	31.3	60.8	31.0	43.2	1.8	74.8	41.9	67.6	21.9	31.1	2.0
49	Chem. Fibers	77.1	49.2	61.8	55.1	45.4	0.3	80.4	26.1	62.0	33.9	35.2	0.2
82	Houseapp	72.9	45.8	62.0	40.0	58.8	0.4	77.7	34.3	65.1	29.0	38.5	0.5
76	RailEquip	79.1	52.4	62.2	63.1	10.8	0.2	80.8	8.5	58.4	31.0	12.6	0.1
63	FabMetal	82.9	25.2	63.0	34.4	34.0	3.1	86.3	26.9	78.5	13.3	30.5	3.2
73	SP Mach.	81.2	42.4	63.6	45.4	60.0	1.4	84.2	24.5	64.5	32.9	47.4	1.6
78	Trans Equip.	77.1	35.4	64.9	29.2	44.3	0.7	78.6	22.2	65.5	23.2	38.9	0.8

(*Continued*)

Table 5.13 (Continued)

Code	*Sector label*	*2012*						*2017*					
		Value-added decomposition %			*% of processing exports*	*% of FIE exports*	*% of total exports*	*Value-added decomposition %*			*% of processing exports*	*% of FIE exports*	*% of total exports*
		Non-processing	*Processing*	*Weighted sum*				*Non-processing*	*Processing*	*Weighted sum*			
79	Generators	78.5	41.7	65.0	36.7	51.0	0.7	81.5	33.4	67.1	30.0	50.6	0.7
66	Lifting Equip.	81.3	36.1	66.5	32.8	53.5	0.5	82.2	13.1	61.8	29.6	53.5	0.5
51	Plastic	83.8	35.6	67.7	33.5	39.2	1.5	86.6	24.2	73.0	21.8	30.3	1.9
46	SpecialChem.	81.3	30.2	68.3	25.4	48.9	0.6	85.0	28.3	76.2	15.6	39.6	0.6
36	Paper	83.3	50.8	69.4	42.9	46.1	0.4	87.9	32.8	67.7	36.8	39.6	0.5
62	NFMtetal roll	79.4	43.0	70.4	24.6	40.1	0.7	82.6	7.7	64.8	23.7	30.1	0.6
69	GP Mach.	82.4	39.6	71.5	25.5	45.3	1.8	84.5	24.6	70.5	23.4	42.4	2.0
43	Pesticides	72.3	50.5	72.3	0.0	27.6	0.1	77.7	7.5	77.4	0.4	24.1	0.2
47	Daily Chem.	81.5	41.7	73.0	21.4	39.1	0.2	85.1	38.3	76.9	17.6	34.3	0.3
59	Iron&Steel	73.1	51.8	73.0	0.5	21.1	0.2	4.6	0.0	72.6	0.3	21.7	0.1
92	Other Manu	78.4	56.6	74.2	19.5	34.7	0.4	80.5	43.3	75.3	13.9	19.6	0.5
72	FFAF Mach	79.8	56.0	74.3	23.1	38.1	0.2	81.5	52.8	74.7	23.4	37.8	0.2
67	Pump	80.4	49.5	74.5	18.9	46.9	1.0	83.9	36.3	76.3	15.9	44.4	1.1
70	Mine Mach.	82.0	41.0	75.1	17.0	34.2	0.8	85.1	45.2	78.6	16.4	36.2	0.6
60	Steel roll.	77.1	49.2	75.4	6.2	22.8	2.0	80.5	40.9	78.5	5.1	15.1	1.9
55	Glass	81.1	41.5	75.7	13.8	26.1	0.7	85.0	11.6	78.6	8.6	24.9	0.5
41	BasicChem	80.2	42.8	75.8	11.8	26.6	1.7	84.5	38.1	78.3	13.3	25.9	1.5
64	Boiler	81.2	41.4	76.1	12.8	32.1	0.5	85.0	50.3	79.7	15.2	39.2	0.4
75	Auto parts	83.2	48.5	76.2	20.1	57.1	0.9	86.6	37.9	79.8	13.9	49.7	1.1
44	Paints	77.5	51.1	77.4	0.3	36.7	0.2	80.7	8.2	80.2	0.7	25.3	0.3
65	Metal Mach.	79.7	56.5	77.4	9.9	35.1	0.2	82.3	39.5	78.6	8.7	29.6	0.2
33	Footwear	88.6	40.8	78.3	21.4	27.4	1.6	88.1	31.2	79.4	15.4	20.3	1.5
71	Chem Mach	81.4	56.7	78.5	11.7	39.9	0.3	83.9	48.9	79.9	11.3	33.0	0.4
56	Porcelain	79.7	55.1	79.3	1.7	20.3	0.4	85.1	13.5	84.4	1.0	9.0	0.6

74	Auto	85.3	49.2	79.7	15.5	30.1	0.8	88.8	29.0	74.0	24.7	38.1	0.7
37	Printing	86.9	59.4	79.8	25.6	37.5	0.1	89.7	60.7	84.5	18.1	29.2	0.1
42	Fertilizers	79.8	0.0	79.8	0.0	5.2	0.3	83.5	0.0	83.5	0.0	3.4	0.2
48	Pharmacy	87.9	34.0	80.4	13.8	32.1	0.9	90.0	35.4	82.5	13.7	31.0	0.9
27	Wool	89.6	59.8	80.5	30.6	44.8	0.1	89.9	60.0	81.1	29.5	42.9	0.1
53	Cement prod.	85.1	53.8	80.9	13.5	22.9	0.1	89.8	15.4	81.7	11.0	13.9	0.1
58	Graphite	82.6	55.5	81.2	5.3	24.9	0.2	85.7	9.1	82.4	4.4	16.9	0.2
29	KC Fabrics	88.2	58.6	81.4	23.2	36.3	0.5	88.3	49.0	82.9	13.7	26.1	0.6
31	Apparel	90.8	29.8	81.7	14.9	25.9	5.1	91.0	22.9	84.0	10.2	18.5	4.9
35	Furniture	87.1	47.1	81.7	13.5	30.7	2.1	88.8	31.2	82.2	11.4	28.4	2.4
57	Refractory	83.1	57.4	82.7	1.7	51.7	0.1	84.2	16.8	83.2	1.4	44.7	0.1
28	Silk	84.1	56.5	82.9	4.4	13.6	0.1	84.1	9.9	81.7	3.2	15.1	0.1
34	Timber	86.7	57.3	83.0	12.6	26.2	0.6	89.3	44.0	84.8	9.9	17.7	0.5
32	Leather	91.4	40.4	83.0	16.6	26.8	1.3	91.0	33.4	84.9	10.5	19.6	1.1
54	Brick	84.2	55.3	83.5	2.7	10.2	0.5	88.4	10.0	87.3	1.5	8.2	0.2
26	Cotton	90.0	46.2	83.6	14.6	19.4	1.5	90.8	47.1	87.7	7.0	14.0	1.5
30	Made Text	89.2	58.9	85.3	12.8	27.0	1.6	88.4	64.2	86.3	8.4	21.9	1.5
52	Cement	86.8	0.0	86.8	0.0	18.1	0.0	91.1	0.0	91.1	0.0	26.8	0.0
40	Coal Prod.	90.4	0.0	90.4	0.0	18.4	0.0	93.0	0.0	93.0	0.0	5.7	0.1
93	Waste	92.4	48.9	92.0	0.9	17.0	0.0	95.2	30.0	95.0	0.3	18.5	0.1
25	Tobacco	94.7	52.8	94.6	0.3	0.3	0.0	95.6	43.6	95.5	0.2	0.2	0.0
	Total manu	82.9	29.7	58.6	45.8	52.1	78.5	84.7	27.7	63.5	37.2	45.4	78.2
	Total goods	83.4	30.0	59.5	44.7	51.4	81.4	85.1	28.0	64.4	36.2	44.5	81.4
	TOT	85.4	30.1	65.2	36.5	51.5	100.0	87.3	28.1	69.8	29.7	36.3	100.0

Data source: Author's estimates. China's 2012 and 2017 I/O tables have 95 and 97 goods producing sectors, respectively, and they both coincide with China's 4-digit classification of economic activities (GB/T 4754–2007). This enables us to aggregate each year's estimates to 93 consistent merchandise industries. After excluding food processing industries and the sectors that do not export, there are 68 manufacturing industries, as reported in this table.

analysis is needed to confirm or reject such a hypothesis, but it is beyond the scope of this chapter.

5 Concluding remarks

This chapter describes China's LCR measures as part of its industrial policy to promote domestic industries in recent years and proposes a quantitative method to estimate domestic content in production and exports based on national IOTs. Applying the proposed methodology to the most recent IOTs published by the NBS of China, we find that the various implicit LCR policy measures proposed by the Chinese government in recent years seem to have played no significant role in promoting domestic content in China's exports during the 2007–2017 period, at least at the aggregate level. Further checking China's exports by firm ownership also indicates that those LCR measures did not affect most FIEs' decisions to source their production inputs outside China at the aggregate level. Their use of imported inputs increased during this period. China's exports to the major destination market also indicate that those LCR measures did not reduce exporting firms' sourcing their raw materials, parts, and components around the world, especially in China's production of processing exports, and its DVA share declined during the 10-year period. The pattern of changing DVA shares in exports is mixed at the sector level, and those localization policies may play some roles in promoting domestic content in production in certain sectors; however, without a formal econometric analysis, one cannot confirm or reject such hypotheses. While this chapter does not perform formal hypothesis testing, the decomposition and estimation results provide necessary inputs for future work to carry out such tests.

Notes

1 See Bloomberg report, "Xi Mobilizes China for Tech Revolution to Cut Dependence on West," March 2, 2021.

2 To abide by WTO disciplines, China undertook a revision of laws and regulations to eliminate any discriminatory policies against foreign goods, services and enterprises. The explicit LCRs, such as a percentage of local content required as a condition to access a local market, get administrative approvals or benefit from preferential policies are eliminated in the public documents of both central and subcentral governments as implementation of China's WTO accession commitment. However, implicit LCRs could exist in the practices of industrial policies in China. For example, a subsidy conditional on domestic content will be challenged by other WTO members and prohibited under WTO nondiscrimination rules. A facially neutral subsidy provided to all firms equally could favor local manufacturers in implementation. The subcentral governments of China may have played critical roles in shaping local production networks. The problem of lacking transparency, as well as inconsistent law enforcement, has been fully discussed in literature, such as Hufbauer et al. (2013), Stone et al. (2015) and OECD (2019). For such reasons, we take an indirect approach in this section, by identifying four industries in which targets of localization rate are set in Made in China 2025 program and by identifying related localization policies enacted and resources allocated to domestic and foreign firms by China to achieve that goal.

3 See OCED website, www.oecd.org/trade/topics/local-content-requirements/.

4 Authors' calculation based on Chinese input-output table in 2018 provided by the National Bureau of Statistics.
5 See CNN report. "Tesla sets up data center in China amid spying concerns", on May 26, 2021.
6 See 2021 Report published by Semiconductor Industry Association (SIA). Available at www.semiconductors.org/wp-content/uploads/2021/09/2021-SIA-State-of-the-Industry-Report.pdf
7 See on https://english.www.gov.cn/statecouncil/ministries/202011/21/content_WS5fb86defc6d0f7257694042b.html
8 We use the terms "domestic value added" and "domestic content" interchangeably. It is an objective measure that quantifies domestic factor content embodied in a country's production and exports. It is welfare neutral. If a country tries to increase its DVA share by artificially replacing key imported inputs with inferior domestic versions, the result is likely to make the country's exports less competitive in the international market thus adversely affecting the welfare in the society. See Chapter 7, "Should high domestic value added in exports be an objective of policy?" in *Global Value Chain Development Report 2019* for a detailed discussion on this topic. www.wto.org/english/res_e/booksp_e/gvc_dev_report_2019_e_prelims.pdf
9 Such IO tables account for imported and domestically produced intermediate inputs separately, and thus they are different from standard IO tables.
10 In practice, we separate Y^{ef} and Y^{ei} in export statistics by UN BEC classification.
11 In today's world, it is difficult to find a product that does not contain any imported content. However, domestic and import IO coefficient matrices in IOTs provide key information that allow us to distinguish domestic and foreign-factor content in various production activities analytically.
12 China officially reports processing and normal exports at the 8-digit HS level based on customs records. Processing exports are defined by China Customs, which include trade regime "Process & assembling" and "Process with imported materials" in China Customs statistics. These statistics are relatively accurate because they involve duty exemption and value-added tax rebates, which are under intensive Customs monitoring.
13 The procedure belongs to a class of mathematical methods called constraint matrix balancing.
14 Detailed trade share parameters used in estimation for each I/O industry in the three-benchmark year are listed in online Appendix Tables A–C.
15 China's Industrial Classification standard GB/T 4754 was updated in both 2002 and 2011. For example, in 2002, the industrial category "Weapons and ammunition manufacturing" was merged into "Special equipment manufacturing" in 2011.

References

Asian Development Bank (ADB) (2021), Global value chain development report 2021: Beyond production, Manila: ADB. http://dx.doi.org/10.22617/TCS210400-2

Bakas A. (2019), The Economist, 19 January 2019: 17. www.economist.com/briefing/2019/01/24/globalisation-has-faltered, 21 March 2019.

Borin A, Mancini M. (2019), Measuring what matters in global value chains and value-added trade[J]. World Bank policy research working paper (8804).

Hestermeyer, H P, Nielsen L. (2014), The legality of local content measures under WTO law. *Journal of World Trade*, 48(3): 553–591.

Hufbauer G C, Schott J, Cimino, C, Vieiro, M, Wada E. (2013), Local content requirements: A global problem, Peterson Institute for International Economics.

Koopman R, Wang Z, Wei S J. (2012), Estimating domestic content in exports when processing trade is pervasive[J]. *Journal of Development Economics*, 99(1): 178–189.
Koopman R, Wang Z, Wei S J. (2014). Tracing value-added and double counting in gross exports[J]. *American Economic Review*, 104(2): 459–494.
OECD (2019), Measuring distortions in international markets: The semiconductor value chain, OECD Trade Policy Papers, No. 234, Paris: OECD Publishing, https://doi.org/10.1787/8fe4491d-en.
Stone S, Messent J, Flaig D. (2015), Emerging policy issues: Localisation barriers to trade, OECD Trade Policy Papers, No. 180, Paris: OECD Publishing, https://doi.org/10.1787/5js1m6v5qd5j-en.
Wang Z, Wei S-J, Yu X, Zhu K. (2017), Measures of participation in global value chains and global business cycles, No. 23222, NBER Working Papers, National Bureau of Economic Research, Inc.
Wang Z, Wei S-J, Zhu K (2013), Quantifying international production sharing at the bilateral and sector levels. No. w19677. National Bureau of Economic Research.
World Trade Organization (WTO) (2019), Global value chain development report 2019: Technological innovation, supply chain trade, and workers in a globalized world, Geneva: WTO. www.wto.org/english/res_e/publications_e/gvcd_report_19_e.htm

6 Conformity of Indonesia's LCRs with its trade and investment commitments

Michelle Limenta, Lili Yan Ing, Junianto James Losari, and Oscar Fernando

1 Introduction

International agreements restrict countries' ability to use tariffs for protectionist purposes. In the face of these commitments, governments sometimes resort to non-tariff measures such as local content requirements (LCRs) to protect domestic industry (Stone and Flaig, 2015). The main aspect of LCRs is the requirement for firms to procure a minimum percentage of value added or intermediate inputs domestically (OECD, 2019). Many governments believe that implementing LCRs is a way to promote domestic industry, create employment, and even encourage domestic innovation (Johnson, 2021).

LCRs regained popularity, particularly after the Global Financial Crisis of 2007–2008. The Organisation for Economic Co-operation and Development (OECD) identified 146 new LCR measures implemented worldwide from 2008 to 2015. Another policy that frequently comes with LCRs is the export restraint measure, which aims to ensure that domestic needs are satisfied. In 2020, 257 export restraint measures were recorded, a sevenfold increase from the previous four-year average (Global Trade Alert, 2020).

Indonesia is one of the countries that uses LCR measures as a strategy for increasing domestic value added and creating local jobs. The use of LCRs in Indonesia can be traced to several initiatives, e.g., the Benteng Program in 1950–1957, the Deletion Program in 1974–1993, and the National Car Program in 1996 (Negara, 2016). In 2009, Indonesia reinvigorated its local content strategy by implementing the Increased Use of Domestic Production (*Peningkatan Penggunaan Produksi Dalam Negeri* or P3DN) program through the signing of Presidential Instruction No. 2 of 2009 concerning Utilization of Domestic Products in Government Procurement of Goods and/or Services.[1] The P3DN program has been incorporated into subsequent laws and regulations, including Law No. 3 of 2014 concerning Industrial Affairs and Government Regulation No. 29 of 2018 concerning Industrial Empowerment, which mandate the use of local content in public procurement. The Industrial Empowerment Regulation regulates public procurement at both the planning and implementation stages by stipulating a minimum level of domestic components (i.e., the use of domestic components in goods, services, or

DOI: 10.4324/9781003415794-6

a combination thereof). Furthermore, the use of LCRs is encouraged in the Ministry of Industry's Strategic Plan for 2020–2024, which outlines seven development agendas, one of which is to increase domestic economic value added (Ministry of Industry, 2020).

In recent years, specifically between 2009 and 2022, several members of the Trade-Related Investment Measures (TRIMs) Committee of the WTO have expressed concerns over Indonesia's LCR measures, particularly in the energy, telecommunications, pharmaceutical, and modern retail sectors. However, despite these concerns, Indonesia (and many other governments worldwide) continue to use LCRs as incentives for industries they consider strategic, such as manufacturing, automotive, pharmaceuticals, telecommunications, and electric vehicles, to promote domestic value added.

This chapter aims to assess whether Indonesian regulations concerning LCRs in specific sectors are consistent with its international commitments. Section 2 reviews Indonesia's LCR policy and its implementation in specific sectors. Section 3 examines Indonesia's international obligations relating to LCRs under the WTO agreements, free trade agreements (FTAs), and international investment agreements (IIAs). Section 4 explores LCRs adopted by other countries and lessons learned for Indonesia. Section 5 concludes.

2 Indonesia's trade and industrial policies on LCRs

Over the years, several WTO members have expressed concerns over Indonesia's measures prioritizing the use of domestic products in multiple areas – raising the issue of the inconsistency of such measures with WTO commitments (WTO, 2020). For instance, the United States (US) and the European Union (EU) pointed out that Indonesia's adoption and implementation of LCRs for 4G Long-Term Evolution (LTE) mobile devices and base stations as a longstanding issue that WTO members had questioned for several years (Committee on TRIMs, 2020).

The EU has also raised concerns regarding the imposition of LCRs for pharmaceutical products, which they argue is problematic because Indonesia imports more than 95% of its active pharmaceutical ingredients. Japan and Australia have also expressed similar concerns, particularly in relation to LCRs for 4G LTE mobile devices, local processing requirements in the energy sector, and LCRs in the retail sector. Indonesia has defended its measures, stating that they were implemented to facilitate foreign investment, which has shown positive results and is on an upward trajectory. Indonesia also maintains that most of the LCRs adopted are voluntary and applied only to government procurement, as part of its policy to ensure inclusive economic development (Committee on TRIMs, 2019).

Export bans and domestic processing requirements on nickel ore are other examples of Indonesia's industrial policies containing LCRs. These measures were challenged in the WTO dispute settlement body. In November 2022, the WTO Panel found that the measures breached WTO obligations regarding the prohibition of quantitative restrictions. It is noteworthy that the main claims raised by the EU against Indonesia were related to the country's export ban and subsidy schemes rather than the local-content aspect of the measures.

The following subsection describes Indonesia's LCRs, particularly in sectors deemed important by Indonesia: the energy, telecommunications, pharmaceutical, and modern retail sectors. The discussion concludes that Indonesian laws and regulations containing LCRs can be categorized into four groups: (i) those dealing only with government procurement;[2] (ii) those voluntary LCRs that do not mandate the use of domestic products to conduct business or place sanctions on a failure to do so;[3] (iii) those providing the methodology to calculate the local content for certain products, without requiring the use of local content;[4] and (iv) those requiring the use of local content or domestic products to conduct business or providing benefits or incentives if local content or domestic products are used.

2.1 Energy sector: electricity, oil and gas, and crude oil

To increase the use of domestic goods and services in the electricity power sector, the Minister of Industry (MOI) issued Regulation No. 54/M-IND/PER/3/2012 concerning Guidelines for the Utilization of Domestic Products for the Development of Electric Power Infrastructure (MOI Regulation No. 54/2012) and its amendment (MOI Regulation No. 05/M-IND/PER/2/2017). The minimum level of local content under MOI Regulation No. 54/2012 and its amendment is determined based on (i) the power sources (e.g., steam, hydro, geothermal, gas, and solar); and (ii) power plant capacity (in megawatts or per block), with more flexibility provided for business entities undertaking larger-capacity projects. The regulation also specifies the local components of goods and services for each type of power plant.

Moreover, Minister of Energy and Mineral Resources (MEMR) Regulation No. 4 of 2020 concerning Second Amendment to MEMR Regulation No. 50 of 2017 concerning Utilization of Renewable Energy Resources for the Supply of Electricity states that in selecting a power plant developer (i.e., power supply business entity cooperating with Indonesia's state-owned electricity enterprise, PT Perusahaan Listrik Negara (PLN) under a power grid sale and purchase agreement), PT PLN, must prioritize the developer that satisfies the required level of local content value.

In the oil and gas sector, MEMR Regulation No. 15 of 2013 concerning Utilization of Domestic Products in the Upstream Oil and Gas Business Activities (MEMR Regulation No. 15/2013) Article 4 requires every contractor, local producer, and supplier of goods and services that procures goods and services in the upstream oil and gas operations to use, optimize, and empower the use of domestic goods and services. The local component targets for goods (e.g., pumping unit, machinery, and equipment) and services (e.g., survey, seismic, and geological studies) are specified in Appendix I of the regulation.

Under MEMR Regulation No. 15/2013, the Upstream Oil and Gas Regulatory Special Task Force (SKK Migas) must set a local content target in each work and budget plan and/or in the list of the procurement plan, which the contractors must refer to in procuring goods and services. The contractors must ensure that domestic producers and suppliers of goods and services meet the local-content-level commitment stipulated in the procurement contract. The government also offers price preference in government procurement as an incentive, provided that the local content level reaches at least 25% for goods and 30% for services. An additional 2.5% in price preference is also added to business entities that retain the status of "local" company. Contractors are subject to sanctions for failure to comply from SKK Migas for noncompliance with their local component obligations. Also, producers and suppliers face administrative sanctions from the Head of MEMR's Directorate General of Oil and Gas.

In the crude oil sector, MEMR Regulation 18 of 2021 concerning Priorities for the Utilization of Crude Oil to Meet Domestic Needs (MEMR Regulation No. 18/2021) mandates state-owned oil and gas company, Pertamina, and crude oil-processing license holders, to prioritize the use of domestic crude oil supplied by domestic contractors before imports.

2.2 *Telecommunication devices*

Minister of Communication and Informatics (MCI) Regulation No. 27 of 2015 concerning the Technical Requirements for LTE Technology Standard Based Telecommunication Tool and Equipment provides for LCRs for the base station (i.e., instruments providing connectivity to the subscriber station, such as the network and antenna) and subscriber station (i.e., any communication devices on the consumer side, such as smartphones, modems, laptops, and tablets). The local content threshold was set at 30% for the base station and 20% for the subscriber station in 2015; it was increased to 40% for the base station and 30% for the subscriber station in 2017. The local component threshold for the 4G and 5G subscriber stations is set to increase again from 30% to 35% through the issuance of MCI Regulation No. 13 of 2021 on 12 October 2021.

Specific calculation methods to determine the local content value (TKDN) for LTE-based telecommunication devices are found in various regulations issued by the MOI. Examples include MOI Regulation No. 29/M-IND/PER/7/2017 concerning Provisions and Procedures to Calculate Domestic Component Levels for Mobile Phones, Handheld Devices, and Tablet Computers; and MOI Regulation No. 22 of 2020 concerning Provisions and Procedures for Calculations of Domestic Component Level Values for Electronic and Telematics Products.

2.3 Pharmaceutical products

Presidential Directive No. 6 of 2016 concerning the Acceleration of the Development of the Pharmaceutical and Medical Equipment Industry (PD No. 6/2016) mandated the Minister of Health to prioritize domestic pharmaceutical products and medical devices through e-tendering and e-purchasing and the MOI to monitor and evaluate the implementation of local content value in the field of pharmaceutical and medical devices.

To align with PD No. 6/2016, the MOI issued Regulation No. 16 of 2020 concerning Provisions and Procedures for the Calculation of Local Component Level for Pharmaceutical Products (MOI Regulation No. 16/2020) on 29 May 2020. The regulation thereof provides for specific calculation methods of local content for pharmaceutical products based on their raw materials (50%), research and development (30%), manufacturing (15%), and packaging (5%).

It is worth noting that MOI Regulation No. 16/2020 does not stipulate any sanctions for failure to obtain the TKDN certificate. The requirements of the local content value calculation and certificate are currently linked to benefits obtained in the government procurement process.

2.4 Modern retail

Minister of Trade (MOT) Regulation No. 70/M-DAG/PER/12/2013 concerning Guidelines for Organizing and Developing Traditional Markets, Shopping Centers, and Modern Stores (MOT Regulation No. 70/2013) mandates that modern stores prioritize the supply of local goods produced by micro, small, and medium-sized enterprises (MSMEs). Moreover, shopping centers and modern stores must ensure that 80% of the sale or inventory products (i.e., the store's entire stock-keeping unit) are domestically produced products. A waiver of the local sourcing requirement is available under certain circumstances. Under MOT Regulation No. 56/M-DAG/PER/9/2014 concerning the Amendment to MOT Regulation No. 70/M-DAG/PER/12/2013 (MOT Regulation No. 56/2014), self-service stores such as stand-alone brand and specialty stores qualify for the waiver as long as they satisfy the following requirements: (i) the goods require uniformity of production and are part of the global supply chain, (ii) the goods carry a globally renowned brand or mark (premium products) and have no production base in Indonesia, and (iii) the goods come from certain countries to meet the demands of citizens of those countries residing in Indonesia.

In the latest development, the requirement of 80% local product inventory is not stated anymore in MOT Regulation No. 23 of 2021 that revokes MOT Regulation No. 56/2014 and MOT Regulation No. 70/2013. The most recent MOT Regulation No. 23 of 2021 only requires supermarket to prioritize the supply of local goods produced by MSMEs.

3 Conformity of Indonesia's LCRs with its trade and investment agreements

This section sets out Indonesia's international legal obligations applicable to LCRs. These may be found in trade agreements as well as investment agreements and are discussed along with the consistency of Indonesia's LCRs with these obligations.

3.1 Conformity of Indonesia's LCRs with its multilateral trade agreements

As a member of the WTO, Indonesia is bound by the WTO agreements. LCRs fall under the discipline of four WTO agreements – the TRIMs Agreement, the General Agreement on Tariffs and Trade (GATT), the General Agreement on Trade in Services (GATS), and the Agreement on Subsidies and Countervailing Measures (SCM Agreement). Other trade agreements that bind Indonesia and may deal with LCRs are Indonesia's FTAs, which are explained in greater detail in Section 3.2. Given that most of the trade rules in these FTAs follow the WTO agreements, this section will not analyze the trade rules in the FTAs but rather focus on the rules found in the four WTO agreements mentioned, while discussion on the FTAs will focus on the investment rules contained therein. Table 6.1 outlines relevant disputes and provisions in WTO Agreements dealing with LCRs.

a Trade-Related Investment Measures

In principle, the TRIMs Agreement prohibits any investment measures related to trade in goods that is inconsistent with the obligation of national treatment (non-discrimination) and the prohibition on quantitative restrictions obligation under GATT Articles III:4 and XI:1, respectively. Therefore, any investment measures or requirements imposed on foreign investors fall within the purview of GATT Articles III and XI. Moreover, if such investment measures fall within the coverage of the illustrative list of violations annexed to the TRIMs Agreement, they are automatically inconsistent with GATT Articles III:4 and XI:1 (Hestermeyer and Nielsen, 2014). Para. 1(a) of the illustrative list covers "local content" TRIMs, requiring the purchase or use by an enterprise of products of domestic origin or source. Para. 1(b) covers "trade-balancing" TRIMs, limiting an enterprise's purchases or use of imported products to an amount related to the volume or value of local products it exports.

The panel in the Indonesia-Auto case explained that the wording of the illustrative list makes it clear that a simple advantage that is conditional on the use of domestic goods is inconsistent with the TRIMs Agreement, particularly Article 2, even if the LCR is not binding. These provisions and practices suggest that if Indonesia's local content policy in 4G LTE-based telecommunication

Table 6.1 Selected LCR Disputes and WTO Agreements

No.	*WTO Agreement*	*Relevant provisions and disputes pertaining to LCRs*
1	TRIMs Agreement	• Article 2.1 of the TRIMs Agreement prohibits WTO members from imposing any investment measures related to trade in goods (TRIMs) inconsistent with Articles III and XI of the GATT. • Article 2.2 of the TRIMs Agreement refers to an illustrative list of violations of Articles III:4 and XI:1 of the GATT annexed to it. Related WTO disputes: *Canada – Renewable Energy* (WTO, 2012)/*Feed-in Tariff Program*; *India – Solar Cells* (WTO, 2016); *Indonesia – Autos* (WTO, 1998)
2	GATT	Paragraphs under GATT Article III (national treatment) that are relevant to LCRs: • Article III:4 provides a nondiscrimination principle that imported products shall be accorded no less favorable treatment than domestic products. • Article III:5 specifically prohibits WTO members from maintaining any internal quantitative regulations (i.e., requirements to source domestically a portion of the product that will be used in mixture with other components, in processing, or by itself), as they hamper the competitive process in the market. • Article III:8(a) suggests that government procurement is not subject to the obligations under Article III. Paragraph under GATT Article XI (quantitative restrictions) that is relevant to LCRs: • Article XI:1 prohibits quantitative restrictions on the importation or exportation of any product. Related WTO disputes: *China – Measures Affecting the Imports of Automobile Parts*; *Turkey – Rice* (WTO, 2007); *US – Section 337* (WTO, 1989), *Canada – Renewable Energy*
3	GATS	GATS Article XVI:2 (Market Access) particularly prohibits LCRs on foreign investors seeking to gain market access through (i) restriction or requirement of certain types of legal entities or joint ventures, or (ii) limitation of foreign capital participation. In addition, certain LCRs can also breach GATS Article XVII (national treatment). Related WTO disputes: *China – Audiovisual*
4	SCM Agreement	Pursuant to Article 3 of the SCM Agreement, there are two types of prohibited subsidies: export subsidies and import-substitution subsidies. • Article 3.1(a) prohibits subsidies contingent on export performance, such as direct export subsidies and export retention schemes, which involve a bonus on exports. • Article 3.1(b) prohibits import-substitution subsidies, defined as those contingent on domestic use over imported products. Related WTO dispute: *Canada – Autos* (WTO, 2000a), *US – Tax Incentives*.

GATS = General Agreement on Trade in Services, GATT = General Agreement on Tariffs and Trade, LCR = local content requirement, SCM = Subsidies and Countervailing Measures, TRIMs = Trade-Related Investment Measures, US = United States, WTO = World Trade Organization.

Source: Authors' compilation.

devices is challenged in a WTO dispute settlement, it is likely to be found inconsistent with the TRIMs Agreement, as the country's LCR element falls within the coverage of paragraph 1(a) of the illustrative list.

b General Agreement on Tariffs and Trade

GATT Article III prescribes the national treatment principle, one of the central non-discrimination principles of the WTO system. According to this principle, imported products should not be treated less favorably than like domestic products once the imported products have entered the domestic market, i.e., once customs have cleared them. As LCR policies essentially facilitate a preference for domestic products over imported products, they are often inconsistent with Article III, as they constitute origin-based discrimination (Hestermeyer and Nielsen, 2014).

For a measure to be found consistent with GATT Article III:4, the following elements must be demonstrated: (i) the measure at issue must be an internal regulation, (ii) the imported and domestic products are like products, and (iii) the like imported products are not accorded "less favorable" treatment than like domestic products (WTO, 2000b: para. 133). Thus, if a complainant can demonstrate that an LCR measure of Indonesia grants an advantage based on the use of local goods, and such measure negatively affects and modifies competitive opportunities of like imported goods, the LCR measure in question would be found inconsistent with GATT Article III:4.

Although most LCR measures can be challenged under Article III:4, the wording of Article III:8(a) suggests that government procurement is not subject to the obligations under Article III. Further, the WTO panel in the *Canada – Renewable Energy* dispute found that Article III:8(a) derogation is also "applicable to measures that fall within the scope of Article 2.2 of the TRIMs Agreement and the Illustrative List annexed thereto" (WTO, 2013: para. 5.33).

Indonesia's preference for domestic products in government procurement projects would arguably be excluded from the scope of national treatment under Article III (also the TRIMs Agreement) by virtue of the operation of Article III:8(a), provided that these LCR measures in government procurement meet the requirements set out in the provision as explained further in what follows (Limenta and Ing, 2022).

For a measure to fall within the scope of Article III:8(a), (i) there must be a connection between the challenged measure (i.e., the law, regulation, or requirement) and the procurement; (ii) the measure must involve "procurement by a governmental agency"; and (iii) the "products purchased" must be procured for "governmental purposes" and "may not be procured with a view to commercial resale or with a view to use in the production of goods for commercial sale" (WTO, 2013: para. 5.39).

The first prong is significant and relevant to Indonesia's LCRs in the energy sector (electricity infrastructure and upstream oil and gas). In the *Canada – Renewable Energy* dispute, the Appellate Body found that the domestic content requirement at issue is renewable energy generation equipment, which is "completely disconnected" from the product purchased by the government, which is electricity, neither of which are in the competitive relationship (WTO, 2013: para. 5.80). Consequently, if a complainant against Indonesia's LCRs in the energy sector can demonstrate that the product subject to the LCRs is generation equipment (e.g., power plant, pumping unit, or machinery) while the product procured is electricity or oil and gas, and the "product purchased" and the "product of foreign origin discriminated against" do not compete, Indonesia would find it hard to rely on the derogation of Article III:8(a).

Moreover, the purchase of local components by a power plant developer or contractor (private entity) to enjoy the benefits offered by a government agency in the procurement process (i.e., PLN or SKK Migas) will not satisfy the second prong of Article III:8(a), which will therefore not apply (Hestermeyer and Nielsen, 2014).

c General Agreement on Trade in Services

While the TRIMs Agreement regulates investment measures affecting trade in goods, the GATS covers trade in services (Mode 3 on the commercial presence of foreign direct investment). Although Indonesian LCRs have not been challenged under the GATS, the panel found in *China – Measures Affecting Trading Rights and Distribution Services for Certain Publications and Audiovisual Entertainment Products* that it is possible to have an LCR in the service sector, and the LCR may be subject to the discipline of the GATS. The panel found that China had made commitments in audiovisual home entertainment (AVHE) distribution without any reservation regarding the level of foreign equity participation for contractual joint ventures. Since the relevant measure provided that the Chinese joint venture partner should hold no less than 51% of any equity in a contractual joint venture engaging in the distribution of AVHE products, the panel found that the measure was inconsistent with GATS Article XVI:2(f) (WTO, 2009 [DS 363]).

d Agreement on Subsidies and Countervailing Measures

Considering that some LCR regulations provide certain types of benefits to firms that comply with them, these could also be considered subsidies. Such LCRs could be problematic under the SCM Agreement. To be challenged under the SCM Agreement, a measure must constitute a subsidy. Article 1.1 of the SCM Agreement defines "subsidy" as containing three main elements: (i) a financial contribution, (ii) by a government or any public body within the territory of a WTO member, (iii) which confers a benefit to its recipient. Moreover, only "specific" subsidies are subject to the SCM Agreement disciplines, which include (i) enterprise specificity; (ii) industry specificity; (iii) regional specificity; and (iv) prohibited subsidy, i.e., a government's subsidy targeting export goods or goods using domestic inputs.

Indonesia's LCRs to support the local pharmaceutical industry to manufacture exported pharmaceutical products could be problematic under the SCM Agreement. Similarly, LCR measures to reduce the import dependence on pharmaceutical raw materials and promote the domestic upstream pharmaceutical industry can be characterized as an import-substitution subsidy.

Article 3.1(a) prohibits subsidies contingent on export performance, such as direct export subsidies and export retention schemes, which involve a bonus on exports.[5] Put differently, subsidies requiring recipients to meet certain export targets or to use domestic goods are prohibited, as they are likely to negatively affect other countries' trade. As an illustration, the WTO Appellate Body in *Canada – Autos* concluded that an import duty exemption that is available only to a manufacturer that exports motor vehicles is contrary to Article 3.1(a) of the SCM Agreement, as the exemption is conditional on the exportation of products (WTO, 2004: para. 104). If the government of Indonesia issues a price preference, bonus, or any tax incentives (benefits) that are only available when the producers meet LCRs for exports, this might conflict with Article 3.1(a) of the SCM Agreement.

Moreover, import-substitution subsidies are prohibited under Article 3.1(b) of the SCM Agreement, which defines import-substitution subsidies as those contingent on domestic use over imported products. Often, such schemes take the form of LCRs. The Appellate Body in *US – Tax Incentives* noted that the term "over" in Article 3.1(b) refers to "the use of domestic goods in preference to, or instead of, imported goods" (WTO, 2017: para. 5.11). If the provision of a price preference for government procurement (benefit) is contingent on the fulfillment of certain local content value, including the use of domestic products instead of imported ones, potential legal issues with Article 3.1(b) of the SCM Agreement could arise.

The SCM provisions in Indonesia's FTAs are merely a reaffirmation of the rights and obligations of the contracting parties under the WTO's SCM Agreement. Some FTAs do not even have provisions on SCM. Chapter 7 of the Regional Comprehensive Economic Partnership (RCEP) Agreement has several procedural provisions related to the investigation of anti-dumping and countervailing duties but has no substantive provisions related to LCRs. Additionally, Article 7.16 of the RCEP Agreement explicitly excludes the applicability of the dispute settlement mechanism for Section B of Chapter 7 (Fernando and Ing, 2022). Hence, no party has any recourse to dispute settlement under the RCEP Agreement for any matter arising under Section B of Chapter 7 of the RCEP Agreement.

3.2 Conformity of Indonesia's LCRs with its international investment agreements

In international investment law, LCRs are regulated under performance requirements provisions (similar to the regulation under the TRIMs Agreement, as elaborated earlier) and national treatment provisions. However, to bring a national treatment claim, the investor must demonstrate that it is, or its investments are, in "like circumstances" (Algazzar, 2021) to other investors who or investments that receive more favorable treatment (Ing and Losari, 2022). In this section, we assess the performance requirements and national treatment commitments in Indonesia's IIAs – bilateral investment treaties (BITs), investment chapters in FTAs, regional investment agreements (RIAs), or comprehensive economic partnership agreements (CEPAs).

a BITs

As of the time of writing, Indonesia has 27 BITs in force (UNCTAD, 2022). Of the 25 BITs reviewed by this study, none contains any provisions concerning performance requirements, but eight contain national treatment provisions.[6] Notably, any breach of the national treatment provision can be brought directly by an investor against the state to the investor–state dispute settlement (ISDS) mechanism, and if found in breach of the provision, the state must pay for any damages incurred due to losses suffered by the investor.

b Investment chapters in FTAs and CEPAs and regional investment agreements

Investment chapters in FTAs and CEPAs, as well as regional investment agreements (RIAs), usually have both performance requirements and national treatment provisions. Currently, Indonesia has 16 RIAs, FTAs, and CEPAs. As a member of the Association of Southeast Asian Nations (ASEAN), all ASEAN FTAs also bind Indonesia. Table 6.2 summarizes the types of legal obligations under these agreements that are applicable to LCRs.

The performance requirements provision in the ASEAN–Korea investment agreement incorporates provisions of the TRIMs Agreement, *mutatis mutandis.* Meanwhile, the ASEAN–Australia–New Zealand Free Trade Area (AANZFTA) Agreement prohibits the parties from applying any measure that is inconsistent with the TRIMs Agreement in connection with the establishment, acquisition, expansion, management, conduct, operation, or sale or disposition of an investment of an investor of a party in its territory. However, the provisions in some of Indonesia's FTAs are different from the provisions in the TRIMs Agreement. For example, the provisions in the RCEP Agreement are more detailed in specifying the requirements that parties shall not impose, such as the transfer of a particular technology and restrictions on selling the goods produced by the

Table 6.2 Indonesia's International Investment Commitments Related to LCRs Under the RIA, FTAs, and CEPAs

No.	*Agreement*	*National treatment*	*Prohibition of performance requirements*
1	ASEAN Comprehensive Investment Agreement	Article 6	Article 7, as amended by 4th Protocol of ACIA
2	Agreement establishing the ASEAN – Australia – New Zealand Free Trade Area	Article 4 of Chapter 11	Article 5 of Chapter 11
3	Investment Agreement of the ASEAN – Hong Kong, China	Article 3	N/A
4	Investment Agreement of the ASEAN – China Free Trade Area	Article 4	N/A
5	Investment Agreement of the ASEAN – India Free Trade Area	Article 3	N/A
6	ASEAN – Japan CEP (investment chapter is incorporated by the First Protocol Amendment)	Article 51.3	Article 51.5
7	ASEAN – Korea Investment Agreement	Article 3	Article 6
8	Indonesia – Australia CEPA	Article 14.4	Article 14.6
9	Indonesia – Chile CEPA (no investment chapter)	N/A	N/A
10	Indonesia – Pakistan Preferential Trade Agreement (no investment chapter)	N/A	N/A
11	Preferential Tariff Arrangement – Group of Eight Developing Countries (no investment chapter)	N/A	N/A
12	Indonesia – Japan Economic Partnership Agreement	Article 59	Article 63
13	Indonesia – EFTA FTA	Article 4.4	N/A
14	Indonesia – Mozambique Preferential Trade Agreement (no investment chapter)	N/A	N/A
15	Indonesia – Korea CEPA	Article 7.4	Article 7.8
16	RCEP Agreement	Article 10.3	Article 10.6

ACIA = ASEAN Comprehensive Investment Agreement, ASEAN = Association of Southeast Asian Nations, CEPA = comprehensive economic partnership agreement, EFTA = European Free Trade Association, FTA = free trade agreement, LCR = local content requirement, N/A = not applicable, RCEP = Regional Comprehensive Economic Partnership, RIA = regional investment agreement.

Source: Authors' compilation.

investment domestically in relation to the volume or value of its exports or foreign exchange earnings.

The performance requirements provisions in the investment chapters are mostly subject to state-to-state dispute settlement (SSDS), except the agreements with Japan that also provide for the ISDS mechanism. This means

Japanese investors subject to Indonesia's LCRs that allegedly breach the provisions may directly bring a claim for damages against the Indonesian government, and if the tribunal finds such a breach, the government must compensate the investor for damages caused by the LCR to the investor or its investment. Table 6.3 sets out the dispute settlement mechanisms (DSMs) applicable to the provisions of Indonesia's RIAs, FTAs, and CEPAs.

Table 6.3 DSMs in Indonesian RIAs, FTAs, and CEPAs for Performance Requirements Provisions

No.	*Indonesia's RIAs, FTAs and CEPAs*	*Performance requirements provision*	*DSM*
1	RCEP Agreement	Chapter 10, Article 10.6	SSDS
2	ASEAN Comprehensive Investment Agreement	Article 7 as amended by the 4th Protocol of ACIA	SSDS
3	ASEAN – Japan CEP (investment chapter is incorporated by the First Protocol Amendment)	Article 51.5	ISDS and SSDS
4	Agreement establishing the ASEAN – Australia – New Zealand Free Trade Area	Chapter 11, Article 5	SSDS
5	ASEAN – Korea Investment Agreement	Article 6	SSDS
6	Indonesia – Australia CEPA	Article 14.6	SSDS
7	Indonesia – Japan Economic Partnership Agreement	Article 63	ISDS and SSDS
8.	Indonesia – Korea CEPA	Article 7.8	SSDS

ACIA = ASEAN Comprehensive Investment Agreement, ASEAN = Association of Southeast Asian Nations, CEPA = comprehensive economic partnership agreement, DSM = dispute settlement mechanism, FTA = free trade agreement, ISDS = investor – state dispute settlement, LCR = local content requirement, RCEP = Regional Comprehensive Economic Partnership, RIA = regional investment agreement, SSDS = state-to-state dispute settlement.

Source: Authors' compilation.

Notes: All RIAs, FTAs, and CEPAs are in effect.

Our research uncovered no case law on national treatment or performance requirements initiated under these 16 RIAs, FTAs, and CEPAs to date. It remains to be seen how the national treatment and performance requirements provisions in these agreements would be interpreted in the case of a dispute. However, given that the discipline of national treatment in these agreements is a reaffirmation of rights and obligations under the GATT 1994 or incorporation of Article III of the GATT, previous WTO cases would be a useful reference in assessing the consistency of Indonesia's LCR measures.

c Lessons learned regarding Indonesia's LCRs based on ISDS cases

Indonesia has never been sued in any Investor-State Dispute Settlement (ISDS) cases, nor raised any concerns over other countries, in relation to LCR measures, particularly regarding breaches of performance requirements and national treatment provisions. Therefore, it is useful to explore the experiences of other countries to draw lessons that may guide Indonesia in designing its policies.

I PROVISIONS RELATING TO LCRS IN IIAS MAY PROVIDE AN ALTERNATIVE DISPUTE SETTLEMENT FORUM FOR FOREIGN INVESTORS

Unlike trade agreements, which require states to bring a case against another state, e.g., through the WTO dispute settlement mechanisms, some IIAs allow foreign investors who suffer damages from a host government's LCR measures to bring a claim directly against the government to ISDS as mentioned above and demonstrated in the cases discussed in what follows.

II PERFORMANCE REQUIREMENTS PROVISIONS IN IIAS COVER BOTH GOODS AND SERVICES

Unlike the TRIMs Agreement, which only covers measures relating to goods, and the GATS, which only covers measures relating to services, IIA performance requirements provisions and national treatment provisions cover LCRs applicable to both goods and services. For example, in *Mobil Investments Canada Inc. and Murphy Oil Corporation v. Canada*,[7] the Canadian Newfoundland and Labrador Offshore Petroleum Board enforced guidelines on research and expenditure. The investors claimed that the guidelines breached the performance requirements provision in the North American Free Trade Agreement (NAFTA) Article 1106(1). The guidelines required investors to spend a fixed percentage of project revenues on research and development (R&D) and education and training (E&T) in Newfoundland. The tribunal found that the R&D and E&T requirements constituted "services" covered under Article 1106 and that the guidelines were "designed to be applied as a matter of legal obligation by means of Benefits Plans" with the purpose of introducing "an obligatory expenditure requirement."[8]

Canada argued that the requirement to carry out R&D or E&T in NL did not compel the investors to purchase, use, or accord a preference to any domestic goods or services, and there were alternative ways to comply. However, the tribunal was not convinced because the implementation of the guidelines would require local expenditures, and certain actions could not be implemented without according a preference for services provided in NL, e.g., endowing a university chair, furnishing a classroom, providing scholarships, and establishing an in-house research facility. Such actions would require according a preference to local goods and services to undertake its construction and operation.[9] Accordingly, the guidelines were in breach of Article 1106.

III PERFORMANCE REQUIREMENTS PROVISIONS IN IIAS CAN ALSO APPLY TO DE FACTO MEASURES

Governments may design their LCRs in such a way that they do not expressly compel investors to consume domestic goods or services, but such measures may still breach the performance requirements provision in an IIA if the measures de facto or by their design in practice require or compel such consumption.

As shown in *Mobil v. Canada*, even though the guidelines did not compel the investors to use domestic goods and services, there was no way for the investors to comply with the guidelines without doing so. Thus, the tribunal found that the measure breached the performance requirements provision.

Similarly, in *Archer Daniels Midland Company (ADM) v. Mexico*[10] and *Cargill, Inc. v. Mexico*,[11] the tribunals found that Mexico violating the performance requirements provision in NAFTA Article 1106(3) by imposing a 20% tax on beverages and other products that contained sweeteners other than cane sugar, i.e., high fructose corn syrup (HFCS). These cases were brought by foreign investors who distributed HFCS in Mexico. At the time, HFCS was either produced outside Mexico or by primarily foreign-owned firms in Mexico, while cane sugar was produced by Mexican-owned companies in Mexico.[12] The tribunal in *ADM* found that the tax conferred advantages on the sugar industry in Mexico and had a detrimental effect on ADM's investments. Further, the tribunals in *ADM* and *Cargill* found that the advantage given to cane sugar (which the tribunal considered essentially domestic) discriminated against the HFCS industry and thus was inconsistent with NAFTA Article 1106(3).[13]

Nevertheless, despite being faced with a similar factual circumstance as in *ADM* and *Cargill*, the tribunal in *Corn Products International, Inc. (CPI) v. Mexico*[14] found that the imposition of tax on soft drinks using HFCS did not require any local procurement of sugar in Mexico. Further, the tribunal opined that the tax that reduced the use of CPI's HFCS, if considered performance requirements, was placed on the soft drink manufacturers and was not mandatory.[15] The finding of the tribunal in *CPI* was rather surprising because it seemed to limit the applicability of the performance requirements provision to investors who produced the final products (in that case, the soft drink bottlers) rather than the manufacturers of the intermediate goods (i.e., HFCS), while nothing in NAFTA Article 1106 suggested such limitation. It was also unexpected that the tribunal found that the tax was not mandatory while the fulfillment of the requirement was necessary to obtain such an advantage, i.e., not being taxed 20%.

Most of the tribunal members in *S.D. Myers v. Canada*[16] took the same approach as the tribunal in *Cargill* regarding a de facto LCR. In this case, the investor carried out polychlorinated biphenyl (PCB) waste treatment by exporting the PCB waste from Canada to the US, where the treatment was done. The investor alleged a breach of the performance requirements provision (NAFTA Article 1106), but the tribunal, by majority, found that based on the substance and effect of the export ban, no "requirements" as defined in Article 1106 were imposed on the investor; hence, there was no breach. Nevertheless, this finding is rather curious because most of the tribunal did not see the measure's effect or analyze the de facto measure, unlike the tribunal in *Mobil v. Canada*. In fact, one of the tribunal members dissented and considered that the effect of the export ban was to require S.D. Myers, Inc. to undertake all its operations in Canada, in breach of subparagraph (b) of Article 1106.[17] He said, "[t]he practical effect of the export ban was contrary to Article 1106(b); S.D. Myers [the investor] and its affiliate Myers Canada were effectively required to carry out a major step in the remediation process, the physical disposal of the waste, in Canada."[18]

Cargill and *S.D. Myers v. Canada* highlight the possibility of diverging interpretations in investment treaty arbitration because precedents (past decisions) are not binding on any future tribunals.

IV LCRS MAY BREACH NATIONAL TREATMENT PROVISIONS IN IIAS

Similar to the national treatment provisions in the GATT and the GATS, the national treatment provisions in IIAs can also be used to claim against LCRs. For example, in *ADM, Cargill*, and *CPI*, the tribunals found that the additional tax on HFCS amounted to a breach of the national treatment provision under NAFTA, as the HFCS suppliers were "in like circumstances" as the domestic sugar suppliers to the soft drink industry.[19]

Similarly, in *S.D. Myers v. Canada*, the US investor alleged a breach of the national treatment provision (NAFTA Article 1102) because of Canada's export ban on PCB waste as explained in Section 3.2.c.III. According to the investor, it (along with its subsidiary) was treated discriminatorily compared with Canadian operators, which also carried out PCB waste remediation services, as the export ban effectively required the investor to carry out a major part of its proposed business in Canada; hence, it was required to consume goods and services in Canada.[20] The tribunal found that the investor and its Canadian subsidiary were "in like circumstances" with domestic Canadian operators, as they engaged in providing PCB waste remediation services,[21] and that while Canada had a legitimate goal, it could have achieved it through a number of legitimate ways rather than the export ban. Accordingly, the tribunal found that the export ban was in breach of the national treatment provision.[22]

Nevertheless, it is noteworthy that establishing "like circumstances" is not always straightforward. In *Merrill & Ring Forestry LP v. Canada*,[23] the investor claimed that Canada breached the national treatment provision by implementing an export regime for logs that imposes harvesting requirements, the surplus test, and other rules for properties located in remote areas. In assessing "like circumstances," the tribunal took investors in identical circumstances as the comparator of those operating on lands under the same federal jurisdiction instead of investors in other federal states of Canada.[24] Given that investors in British Colombia were identically treated as the investor, the tribunal found no breach of the national treatment provision.

4 Lessons for Indonesia from WTO disputes and ISDS involving other countries

This section distills some key lessons learned from WTO and ISDS cases, which were faced by several countries, as summarized further in Table 6.4.

US – Renewable Energy

The *US – Renewable Energy* dispute was brought by India in September 2016 against 11 measures concerning LCRs and subsidies given to promote renewable energy instituted by the governments of seven US states. In June 2019, the panel found that all the measures at issue violating GATT Article III:4 obligations as they provide an advantage for the use of domestic products, which amount to less favorable treatment for like imported products. The panel exercised judicial economy regarding all India's claims on the TRIMs and SCM Agreements violation. The US and India notified the WTO in July 2023 that they finally reached a mutually agreed solution.

China – Auto Parts

The *China – Auto Parts* dispute, brought by the EU, the US, and Canada to the WTO dispute settlement body in 2006, concerns a set of regulations imposed by China on imported automobile parts used in the manufacture of mobile vehicles. The measures establish thresholds related to the type or value of imported auto parts used to assemble specific vehicle models in China. If the imported parts exceed the thresholds, these parts are considered a "complete vehicle" and therefore are subject to a 25% charge (equal to the tariff on complete vehicles). Canada argued that the measures impose different charges, depending on the domestic content of the auto parts used in the manufacture, thus the local manufacturers acquire an advantage if they use local parts. The panel, upheld by the Appellate Body, found that the measures at issue, favoring the use of domestic auto parts over imported parts, are inconsistent with GATT Article III:4.

China – Audiovisual

In this case, besides claiming a breach of national treatment under GATS Article XVI, the US argued that China's limitation on the participation of foreign capital in contractual joint ventures engaging in the distribution of AVHE products was inconsistent with GATS Article XVI:2(f). The panel found that China had made commitments in this sector without any reservation regarding the level of foreign equity participation for contractual joint ventures. Since the relevant measure provided that the Chinese joint venture partner should hold no less than 51% of any equity in a contractual joint venture engaging in the distribution of AVHE products, the panel found that the measure was inconsistent with GATS Article XVI:2(f). This measure demonstrates that LCR measures affecting the services sector, e.g., market access for foreign direct investment, may be subject to the discipline of the GATS.

ADF Group Inc. v. United States of America

ADF Group Inc. (ADF) is a Canadian company that invested in the US. It challenged the US measures requiring steel materials to be 100% produced and fabricated in the US if they were to be used in constructing a highway interchange in northern Virginia. The investor argued that the measures breached NAFTA Article 1102 (national treatment) and NAFTA Article 1106 (performance requirements).

As regards the alleged breach of national treatment, the tribunal found no breach because the investor could not prove that the measures constituted less favorable treatment to the investor or to its steel vis-à-vis other similarly situated US steel fabricators or their manufactured steel. Although the measures constituted an LCR under NAFTA Article 1106(1)(b) and a requirement to accord preference to goods produced or services provided in the US, the US argued that NAFTA Article 1108 provided an exemption to Article 1106 in cases of "procurement by a Party." The tribunal interpreted further whether "a Party" only covers the federal government or both the federal and state governments. The tribunal accepted the US's argument and found that the construction project of the highway interchange constituted or involved government procurement covered under Article 1108 even if it was procured by the state government (Commonwealth of Virginia); hence, there was no breach of Article 1106. This case is an example of a *de jure* LCR policy that expressly obliged investors to use domestic products, but it did not amount to a breach given the existing exception.

All the cases mentioned demonstrate that LCR measures are likely to result in a breach of at least the "national treatment" obligation of a state, either under a trade agreement or an investment agreement. While an exception typically exists for breaches of measures taken for government procurement purposes, the exception must be expressly provided in the relevant agreement, and the relevant criteria in the exception clause must be met. Considering this potential breach, governments must be mindful of the possible consequences when adopting LCR measures.

Table 6.4 WTO DSB and ISDS Cases on LCR Measures of China, the Republic of Korea, Japan, and the US

6.4a WTO Disputes on LCRs

DS No.	*Title of the dispute*	*Finding*
Cases involving US' LCR measures		
DS510 (India)	*US – Certain Measures Relating to Renewable Energy* (WTO, 2019)	Breach of GATT Article III:4, but exercised judicial economy on the TRIMs Agreement claim
Cases involving China's LCR measures		
DS342 (Canada) DS340 (US) DS339 (EC)	*China – Measures Affecting Imports of Automobile Parts* (WTO, 2008)	Breach of GATT Article III:4, but exercised judicial economy on the TRIMs Agreement claim
DS 363	*China – Measures Affecting Trading Rights and Distribution Services for Certain Publications and Audiovisual Entertainment Products*	Breach of GATS Article XVI
Cases involving the Republic of Korea's LCR measures		
None	None	None
Cases involving Japan's LCR measures		
None	None	None

6.4b Investor – State Arbitration Disputes on LCRs

Case No.	*Title of the Dispute*	*Finding*
Cases involving US' LCR measures		
ICSID Case No. ARB (AF)/00/1	*ADF Group Inc. v. United States of America*	No, because the LCR was done for the purpose of government procurement, hence exempted under NAFTA
Cases involving China's LCR measures		
None	None	None
Cases involving the Republic of Korea's LCR measures		
None	None	None
Cases involving Japan's LCR measures		
None	None	None

DSB = Dispute Settlement Body, EC = European Community, GATS = General Agreement on Trade in Services, GATT = General Agreement on Tariffs and Trade, ICSID = International Centre for Settlement of Investment Disputes, ISDS = investor – state dispute settlement, LCR = local content requirement, NAFTA = North America Free Trade Agreement, TRIMs = Trade-Related Investment Measures, US = United States, WTO = World Trade Organization.

Source: Authors' compilation.

5 Conclusions

Indonesia has signed and ratified various binding international legal instruments, including WTO agreements, FTAs/CEPAs, and IIAs, that discipline the use of LCRs. Any LCR that breaches the relevant provisions in these agreements may lead to disputes brought to the relevant dispute settlement forum. Therefore, it is crucial for Indonesia to ensure compliance with these obligations and to design and implement its laws and regulations prudently.

It has been reported that Indonesia has increased its use of LCR measures, particularly in sectors that the government considers "strategic," such as pharmaceuticals, energy, telecommunications, and modern retail. The broader objectives of adopting LCRs are to increase domestic value added and to rebalance the trade deficit. However, our assessment indicates that Indonesia's LCRs in these strategic sectors are questionable and may potentially violate Indonesia's commitments in the WTO and/or its CEPAs/FTAs and IIAs. An advantage that is conditioned on the use of domestic goods, which has a negative effect on and modifies competitive opportunities of similar imported goods, is inconsistent with the TRIMs Agreement and the GATT, especially the national treatment principle. This remains true even if the measures are presented in a voluntary manner.

Our assessment found that various of Indonesia's LCR measures are being applied for government procurement purposes. While government procurement is excluded from the national treatment obligation, the assessment by the panel and the Appellate Body in *Canada – Renewable Energy* narrowed the scope of what can be considered "government procurement" that is eligible for Article III:8(a) derogation. Therefore, unless certain elements or criteria are demonstrated, it would be difficult for Indonesia to protect the LCRs required in government procurement from the national treatment obligation by invoking Article III:8(a). Even if LCR measures governing government procurement qualify for Article III:8(a) derogation, the measures can be challenged under the SCM Agreement if the government offers a price preference, bonus, or any tax incentives to beneficiaries that meet the LCRs in the production of export-oriented products.

The use of LCR measures may also result in violations of provisions in IIAs. While some governments attempt to design measures that do not explicitly appear as LCR measures, if the measures have the same effect as LCR measures prohibited under the national treatment or performance requirements provision of an IIA, they may still be considered breaches. This has been observed in cases such as *Mobil v. Canada*, *ADM v. Mexico*, *Cargill v. Mexico*, and *S.D. Myers v. Canada*. In the case of Indonesia, alleged breaches of the performance requirements provisions in most of its FTAs can only be brought to SSDS. However, there are exceptions, such as alleged breaches of the performance requirements provisions in the investment chapters of the Indonesia–Japan

Economic Partnership Agreement and the ASEAN–Japan FTA, which can be brought to ISDS. Breaches of the national treatment provisions in Indonesia's IIAs can be brought to either ISDS or SSDS.

The Indonesian government should consider alternative policy tools that are consistent with its trade and investment commitments to achieve the objective of promoting and developing local industries. A comprehensive mix of policies is necessary, including investments in education and healthcare, science, technology, engineering, and mathematics (STEM); incentives for training, research, and innovation; infrastructure development, including digital connectivity; public services in utilities; and creating a business-friendly environment for trade and investment. These policies are a first-order priority to improve the quality of human capital and infrastructure, nurture domestic industries, create more jobs, and enhance competitiveness in a sustainable manner. Additionally, providing legal certainty will improve the confidence of business players in conducting trade and investment with and in Indonesia.

Notes

1 The program urges the relevant government institutions and agencies to use domestic goods and services in government procurement projects. LCRs in Indonesia are also known as the domestic component level (TKDN). We limit our discussion to LCRs defined in the General Agreement on Tariffs and Trade (GATT), Article III on national treatment, and do not include domestic processing requirements, as there is no differential treatment between imported products and locally produced products in the domestic processing requirements.

2 These regulations include (i) Law No. 3 of 2014 on Industry; (ii) Presidential Decree No. 16 of 2018, which is amended by Presidential Decree No. 12 of 2021 on Government Procurement for Goods and Services; (iii) Minister of Industry (MOI) Regulation No. 48 of 2010 on Guidelines on Utilization of Domestic Products in Development of Electricity Infrastructure; (iv) MOI Regulation No. 16 of 2020 on Provisions and Procedures of Local Content Calculation for Pharmaceutical Products; and (v) Government Regulation No. 29 of 2018 on Industry Empowerment.

3 These regulations include (i) Presidential Decree No. 146 of 2015 on Construction and Development of Oil Refinery, which encourages this sector to prioritize domestic products; and (ii) Minister of Trade (MOT) Regulation No. 71 of 2019 on Operation of Franchises, which encourages franchise businesses to prioritize domestic products.

4 These regulations include (i) MOI Regulation No. 29 of 2017 on Procedures to Calculate Local Content of Cell Phones, Laptops, and Tablet Computers; (ii) MOI Regulation No. 22 of 2020 on Procedures to Calculate Local Content on Electronics and Telematics Products; and (iii) MOI Regulation No. 27 of 2020 on Specification, Roadmap for Development, and Calculation of Local Content for Battery Electric Vehicles.

5 The Illustrative List of Export Subsidies is in Annex I of the SCM Agreement.

6 These are the BITs between Indonesia and Finland, the Republic of Korea, the Russian Federation, Sri Lanka, Singapore, Denmark, Saudi Arabia, and Tunisia.

7 *Mobil Investments Canada Inc. and Murphy Oil Corporation v. Canada*, International Centre for Settlement of Investment Disputes (ICSID) Case No.

ARB/07/4, Decision on Liability and on Principles of Quantum, 22 May 2012 (*Mobil v. Canada*).
8 *Mobil v. Canada*, para. 234.
9 *Mobil v. Canada*, para. 237.
10 *Archer Daniels Midland Company (ADM) v. Mexico*, ICSID Case No. ARB(AF)/04/05, Award, 21 November 2007 (*ADM*).
11 *Cargill, Inc. v. Mexico*, ICSID Case No. ARB(AF)/05/2, Award, 18 September 2009 (*Cargill*).
12 *Cargill*, paras. 105–106.
13 *ADM*, paras. 226–227; see also *Cargill*, paras. 317–319.
14 *Corn Products International, Inc. (CPI) v Mexico*, ICSID Case No. ARB (AF)/04/1, Decision on Responsibility, 15 January 2008 (*CPI*).
15 *CPI*, para. 80.
16 *S.D. Myers, Inc. v. Canada*, Partial Award, 13 November 2000 (*S.D. Myers v. Canada*).
17 *S.D. Myers v. Canada*, para. 277.
18 *S.D. Myers Inc. v. Canada*, Separate Opinion by Bryan Schwartz, concurring except with respect to performance requirements, in the partial award of the tribunal, 12 November 2020 (*S.D. Myers v. Canada*, Separate Opinion), para. 193.
19 *ADM*, paras. 197–213; *Cargill*, paras. 190–223; *CPI*, paras. 109–143.
20 *S.D. Myers*, para. 270.
21 *S.D. Myers*, para. 251.
22 *S.D. Myers*, para. 255.
23 *Merrill & Ring Forestry LP v. Canada*, ICSID Case No. UNCT/07/1, Award, 31 March 2010 (*Merrill & Ring*).
24 *Merrill & Ring*, para. 90.

References

Algazzar, A. 2021. Similarity/In Like Circumstances. *Jus Mundi*. https://jusmundi.com/en/document/wiki/en-similarity-in-like-circumstances#:~:text=comparator(s).-,III.,fact%20and%20context%2Dsensitive%20inquiry

Committee on TRIMs. 2019. Minutes of the Meeting Held on 6 June 2019. G/TRIMS/M/46. 20 September.

Committee on TRIMs. 2020. Minutes of the Meeting Held on 15 September 2020. G/TRIMS/M/48. 30 October.

Fernando, O. and L. Y. Ing. 2022. Indonesia's Local Content Requirements: An Assessment on Consistency with Free Trade Agreement Commitments. *ERIA Discussion Paper Series*, No. 420. Jakarta: Economic Research Institute for ASEAN and East Asia.

Global Trade Alert. 2020. Export Restrictions Data. www.globaltradealert.org/

Hestermeyer, H. P. and L. Nielsen. 2014. The Legality of Local Content Measures under WTO Law. *Journal of World Trade*, 48 (3), pp. 553–591.

Ing, L. Y. and J. J. Losari. 2022. Local Content Requirements: Assessment from Investment Law. *ERIA Discussion Paper Series*, No. 416. Jakarta: Economic Research Institute for ASEAN and East Asia.

Johnson, L. 2021. Space for Local Content Policies and Strategies: A Crucial Time to Revisit an Old Debate. Bonn: Deutsche Gesellschaft für Internationale Zusammenarbeit (GIZ). https://scholarship.law.columbia.edu/sustainable_investment_staffpubs/16

Limenta, M. and L. Y. Ing. 2022. Indonesia's Local Content Requirements: Assessment with WTO Rules. *ERIA Discussion Paper Series*, No. 414. Jakarta: Economic Research Institute for ASEAN and East Asia.

Ministry of Industry. 2020. *Strategic Plan of Ministry of Industry 2020–2024*. Jakarta: Kementerian Perindustrian. https://kemenperin.go.id/download/24297/Rencana-Strategis-Kementerian-Perindustrian-2020-2024

Munadi, E., L. Y. Ing, D. Christian, and D. Sanotona. 2022. The List of Indonesia's Laws and Regulations Containing LCRs and their Affected Products, from January 2009 to March 2022. Unpublished.

Negara, S. D. 2016. The Impact of Local Content Requirements on the Indonesian Manufacturing Industry. *ISEAS Economics Working Paper*, No. 2016–4. Singapore: ISEAS – Yusof Ishak Institute.

OECD. 2019. Local Content Requirements. *Trade Policy Brief*. February. Paris: Organisation for Economic Co-operation and Development.

Stone, S., J. Messent, and D. Flaig. 2015. Emerging Policy Issues: Localisation Barriers to Trade. *OECD Trade Policy Papers*, No. 180. Paris: Organisation for Economic Co-operation and Development.

UNCTAD. 2022. Investment Policy Hub: International Investment Agreements Navigator. https://investmentpolicy.unctad.org/international-investment-agreements. (The texts of the Indonesia – UAE BIT and Indonesia-Venezuela BIT are not publicly available.)

WTO. 1989. *United States – Section 337 of the Tariff Act of 1930. Report of the Panel.* L/6439–36S/345. 16 January.

WTO. 1998. *Indonesia – Certain Measures Affecting the Automobile Industry. Report of the Panel.* WT/DS54/R; WT/DS55/R; WT/DS59/R; WT/DS64/R. 2 July.

WTO. 2000a. *Canada – Certain Measures Affecting the Automotive Industry. Report of the Appellate Body.* WT/DS139/AB/R; WT/DS142/AB/R. 31 May.

WTO. 2000b. *Korea – Measures Affecting Imports of Fresh, Chilled and Frozen Beef. Report of the Appellate Body.* WT/DS161/AB/R; WT/DS169/AB/R. 11 December.

WTO. 2004. *Canada – Certain Measures Affecting the Automotive Industry. Report of the Appellate Body.* WT/DS139/AB/R; WT/DS142/AB/R. 31 May.

WTO. 2007. *Turkey – Measures Affecting the Importation of Rice. Report of the Panel.* WT/DS334/R. 21 September.

WTO. 2008. *China – Measures Affecting Imports of Automobile Parts. Report of the Appellate Body.* WT/DS339/AB/R; WT/DS340/AB/R; WT/DS342/AB/R, 15 December.

WTO. 2009. *China – Measures Affecting Trading Rights and Distribution Services for Certain Publications and Audiovisual Entertainment Products. Report of the Panel.* WT/DS363/R. 12 August.

WTO. 2012. *Canada – Certain Measures Affecting the Renewable Energy Generation Sector. Report of the Panel.* WT/DS412/R. 19 December.

WTO. 2013. *Canada – Certain Measures Affecting the Renewable Energy Generation Sector. Report of the Appellate Body.* WT/DS412/AB/R. 6 May.

WTO. 2016. *India – Certain Measures Relating to Solar Cells and Solar Modules. Report of the Panel.* WT/DS456/R. 24 February.

WTO. 2017. *United States – Conditional Tax Incentives for Large Civil Aircraft. Report of the Appellate Body.* WT/DS487/AB/R. 4 September.

WTO. 2019. *United States – Certain Measures Relating to the Renewable Energy Sector. Report of the Panel.* WT/DS510/R. 27 June.

WTO. 2020. *Members Probe Indonesia's and Russia's Local Content Measures in Investment Committee.* WTO News. 15 September. www.wto.org/english/news_e/news20_e/trim_15sep20_e.htm

Appendix

Table 6.A1 Local Content Requirement Regulations in Indonesia

No.	*Regulation*	*Affected sector*
1	Minister of Industry Regulation No. 4 of 2009 concerning the Guidelines for Utilization of Domestic Products for Electricity Infrastructure Development	Energy
2	Minister of Energy and Natural Resources Regulation No. 15 of 2013 concerning the Use of Domestic Products in Upstream Oil and Gas Businesses	Energy
3	Minister of Industry Regulation No. 54 of 2012 on Guidelines on Utilizing Domestic Products for Construction of Infrastructure on Electricity	Energy
4	Minister of Industry Regulation No. 15 of 2016 on Technical and Price Standards for Domestic Transmission Tower and Conductor in Relation to Acceleration of Development of Infrastructure on Electricity	Energy
5	Minister of Energy and Mineral Resources Regulation No. 4 of 2020 on Second Amendment to Minister of Energy and Mineral Resources Regulation No. 50 of 2017 concerning Utilization of Renewable Energy Resources for the Supply of Electricity	Energy
6	Minister of Industry Regulation No. 4 of 2017 concerning the Stipulations and Assessment of Local Content in Solar Power Plants	Energy
7	Minister of Energy and Mineral Resources Regulation No. 18 of 2021 concerning Priorities for the Utilization of Crude Oil to Meet Domestic Needs	Energy
8	Minister of Communication and Information Regulation No. 7 of 2009 concerning Radio Frequency Band Setup for Wireless Broadband Services	Telecommunications

No.	*Regulation*	*Affected sector*
9	Minister of Communication and Information Regulation No. 30 of 2009 concerning Provisions of Internet Protocol Television Services (IPTV) in Indonesia	Telecommunications
10	Minister of Communication and Information Regulation No. 11 of 2010 concerning the Delivery of Internet Protocol Television (IPTV) Services	Telecommunications
11	Minister of Communication and Information Regulation No. 26 of 2013 concerning the Technical Requirement for Internet Protocol Set Top Box	Telecommunications
12	Minister of Communication and Information Regulation No. 32 of 2013 concerning Operation of Digital Television and Multiplexing Broadcasting through the Terrestrial System	Telecommunication
13	Minister of Communication and Information Regulation No. 9 of 2014 concerning the Technical Requirement for Digital Broadcasting Television Tools and Equipment Based on Terrestrial (Second Generation) Digital Video Broadcasting Standards	Telecommunications
14	Minister of Communication and Information Regulation No. 27 of 2015 on Technical Requirements for Telecommunication Devices with LTE Technology	Telecommunications
15	Minister of Industry Regulation No. 65 of 2016 concerning Provisions and Procedures of the Calculation of the Value of Domestic Component Level (TKDN) of Cell Phones, Handheld, Computers, and Tablet Computers	Telecommunications
16	Minister of Communication and Information Regulation No. 6 of 2017 concerning Operation of Internet Protocol Television Services	Telecommunications
17	Minister of Industry Regulation No. 29 of 2017 concerning Provisions and Procedures to Calculate Domestic Component Levels for Mobile Phones, Handheld Devices, and Tablet Computers	Telecommunications
18	Minister of Communication and Information Regulation No. 4 of 2019 on Technical Requirements for Telecommunication Devices for Television and Radio Broadcasting	Telecommunications
19	Minister of Communication and Information Regulation No. 12 of 2019 concerning Procedure for Assessing Achievement of Domestic Component in Capital and Operational Expenditure of Telecommunications Operator	Telecommunications

(*Continued*)

Table 6.A1 (Continued)

No.	*Regulation*	*Affected sector*
20	Minister of Communication and Information Regulation No. 13 of 2021 on Amendment of Minister of Communication and Informatics Regulation No. 27 of 2015 concerning the Technical Requirements for Long-Term Evolution Technology Standard Based Telecommunication Tool and Equipment	Telecommunications
21	Presidential Directive No. 6 of 2016 concerning the Acceleration of the Development of the Pharmaceutical and Medical Equipment Industry	Pharmaceutical
22	Minister of Health Regulation No. 17 of 2017 concerning Action Plan for the Development of the Pharmaceutical and Medical Equipment Industry	Pharmaceutical and medical
23	Minister of Industry Regulation No. 16 of 2020 concerning Provisions and Procedures for the Calculation of Local Component Level for Pharmaceutical Products	Pharmaceutical
24	Minister of Industry Regulation No. 80 of 2014 concerning the Motor Vehicles Industry, amended by Ministry of Industry Regulation No. 34 of 2015 concerning the Industry of Motor Vehicles with Four Wheels or More and Motorcycle Industry	Automotive
25	Minister of Industry Regulation No. 34 of 2017 on 4-Wheeled or more Automotive Industry, as amended by Minister of Industry Regulation No. 5 of 2018 concerning 4-Wheeled or more Automotive Industry, and as replaced by Minister of Industry Regulation No. 23 of 2021 concerning 4-Wheeled or more Automotive Industry	Automotive
26	Presidential Regulation No. 55 of 2019 on Acceleration of Battery Electric Vehicle for Road Transportation Program	Electric vehicles
27	Head of Investment Coordinating Board Regulation No. 6 of 2018 on Guidelines regarding Investment Approval and Facilitation	Investment
28	Minister of Trade Regulation No. 23 of 2021 on the Amendment of the Minister of Trade Regulation No. 70/M-DAG/PER/12/2013 concerning Guidelines for Organizing and Developing Traditional Markets, Shopping Centers, and Modern Stores	Modern retail
29	Minister of Industry Regulation No. 61 of 2009 concerning the Official Price of 3-kg LPG Steel Tube, Its Accessories, and Single Burner Gas Stove for Micro Businesses in Relation to the Conversion Program from Kerosene to LPG	Household appliances

No.	*Regulation*	*Affected sector*
30	Minister of Trade Regulation No. 70 of 2013 concerning the Guidelines for the Arrangement and Development of Traditional Markets, Shopping Centers, and Modern Stores	Modern retail
31	Minister of Trade Regulation No. 53 of 2012 concerning Franchising	Franchise business
32	Minister of Trade Regulation No. 68 of 2012 concerning Franchising of Modern Stores	Franchise business
33	Minister of Trade Regulation No. 7 of 2013 concerning Development of Partnership for Food and Beverages Franchises	Food and beverage (franchise business)

kg = kilogram, LCR = local content requirement, LPG = liquefied petroleum gas, TKDN = *tingkat komponen dalam negeri* (domestic component level), TRIMs = Trade-Related Investment Measures, WTO = World Trade Organization.

Source: Munadi, E., L. Y. Ing, D. Christian, and D. Sanotona 2022.

Notes: The List of Indonesia's Laws and Regulations contains LCRs and their affected products, from January 2009 to March 2022. The list includes Indonesia's LCRs in selected sectors, raised by members at the WTO TRIMs Committee as trade concerns from October 2009 to March 2022. The list does not include domestic processing requirements.

Table 6.A2 Trade Concerns Raised at the WTO TRIMs Committee Meeting Regarding Indonesia, October 2009–March 2022

TRIMs Committee meeting	*Trade agenda items and countries raising concerns*
23 March 2022 12 October 2021 23 March 2021 15 September 2020 13 November 2019 6 June 2019	*Indonesia – Comprehensive Review of Localization Measures:* • US: Indonesia's broad and expanding use of LCRs across the telecommunications, mobile technology, energy, retail, and franchising sectors • EU: LCRs in the pharmaceutical and energy sectors, including mining, oil and gas, electricity, and renewables • Japan: 4G and 5G LTE mobile devices, TVs, retailers, and franchise businesses • Australia: supported the statements by the US, the EU, and Japan on Indonesia's localization requirements
17 October 2018 1 June 2018	*Indonesia – Local Content Requirements for 4G LTE Mobile Devices:* • US, EU, Japan, Australia, and Chinese Taipei *Indonesia – Certain Local Content Provisions in the Energy Sector (Mining, Oil, and Gas):* • Japan, EU, US, and Australia

(*Continued*)

Table 6.A2 (Continued)

TRIMs Committee meeting	*Trade agenda items and countries raising concerns*
6 November 2017	*Indonesia – Local Content Requirements for 4G LTE Mobile Devices:* • US, EU, Australia, and Chinese Taipei *Indonesia – Certain Local Content Provisions in the Energy Sector (Mining, Oil, and Gas):* • Japan, EU, US, Canada, and Australia *Indonesia – Minimum Local Product Requirement for Modern Retail Sector:* • Japan, EU, US, New Zealand, and Australia *Indonesia – Certain Measures Addressing Local Content in Investment in the Telecommunication Sector:* • Japan, EU, and US *Indonesia – Local Content Requirements for Dairy Importation and Distribution:* • Japan, EU, US, and New Zealand
12 May 2017 17 October 2016 13 June 2016 5 October 2015	*Indonesia – Local Content Requirements for 4G LTE Mobile Devices:* • US, EU, Australia, and Chinese Taipei *Indonesia – Certain Local Content Provisions in the Energy Sector (Mining, Oil, and Gas):* • Japan, EU, US, Canada, and Australia *Indonesia – Minimum Local Product Requirement for Modern Retail Sector:* • Japan, EU, US, New Zealand, and Australia *Indonesia – Certain Measures Addressing Local Content in Investment in the Telecommunication Sector:* • Japan, EU, and US
16 April 2015	*Indonesia – Local Content Requirements for 4G LTE Mobile Devices:* • US, EU, Australia, and Chinese Taipei *Indonesia – Certain Local Content Provisions in the Energy Sector (Mining, Oil, and Gas):* • Japan, EU, US, Canada, and Australia *Indonesia – Minimum Local Product Requirement for Modern Retail Sector:* • Japan, EU, US, New Zealand, and Australia
6 October 2014 20 June 2014	*Indonesia – Certain Measures Addressing Local Content in Investment in the Telecommunications Sector:* • EU, US, and Japan *Indonesia – Certain Local Content Provisions in the Energy Sector (Mining, Oil, and Gas):* • EU, US, and Japan *Indonesia – Minimum Local Product Requirement for Modern Retail Sector:* • EU, US, and Japan

TRIMs Committee meeting	*Trade agenda items and countries raising concerns*
4 October 2013 30 April 2013	*Indonesia – Certain Measures Addressing Local Content in Investment in the Telecommunications Sector:* • EU, US, Japan, and Canada *Indonesia – Certain Local Content Provisions in the Energy Sector (Mining, Oil, and Gas) Sector:* • EU, US, Japan, Canada, and Australia
1 October 2012	*Indonesia – Certain Local Content Provisions in the Energy Sector (Mining, Oil, and Gas):* • EU, US, and Japan
4 May 2012	*Indonesia – Certain Local Content Provisions in the Energy Sector (Mining, Oil, and Gas):* • Canada, EU, US, and Japan
3 October 2011	*Certain Measures by Indonesia Addressing Local Content in Investment in the Telecommunications Sector:* • EU, US, and Japan
1 October 2010 16 October 2009	*Certain Measures by Indonesia Addressing Local Content in Investment in the Telecommunications Sector:* • EU and US *Certain Indonesia Laws and Draft Implementing Regulations on Mineral and Coal Mining:* • US

EU = European Union, LCR = local content requirement, TRIMs = Trade-Related Investment Measures, US = United States, WTO = World Trade Organization.

Source: Authors' compilation.

7 The effects of local content requirements on trade

The case of Indonesia

Yessi Vadila and David Christian

1 Introduction

Many countries employ local content requirements (LCRs) to promote local input use and support domestic industry growth. LCRs can encompass a diverse range of policy instruments, ranging from minimum shares of locally sourced goods or services, stipulations on technology transfers, or research and development to domestic equity and ownership. The scope of LCRs also varies, ranging from one narrow subsector involving a few specific products to entire industries. The rationale for LCRs usually lies within the context of industrial development, such as the infant industry argument and strengthening certain industries. Proponents of LCRs argue that LCRs lead to job creation and learning spillovers as well as the fostering of nascent industries (Weiss, 2016). However, Deringer et al. (2018) note that LCRs can have detrimental effects on three types of economic agents: downstream firms, internationally operating firms, and consumers.

Weiss (2016) notes that since the 2008 financial crisis, the use of local content policies has increased. In addition, they are widespread across developed and developing countries and amount to over 100 new measures just in Australia, Canada, the United States, Argentina, Brazil, China, India, Indonesia, and Kazakhstan. There were also 72 new measures in Brazil, Russia, India, China, and South Africa (BRICS) alone until 2018 (Deringer et al., 2018). Indonesia is no exception to the rising trend in LCRs. Global Trade Alert reports that Indonesia had the sixth-highest incidence of LCRs in the world from 2008 to 2021 (Flaig and Stone, 2023). Among the BRICS countries, Indonesia had the highest number of LCRs imposed since the 2008 Global Financial Crisis (Araújo and Flaig, 2017; Hufbauer et al., 2013).

Indonesia's LCRs policy dates back to 1950, with the Benteng program.[1] The policy continued with initiatives such as the Deletion program (1974–1993) and National Car program (1996). In the aftermath of the 1997–98 Asian financial crisis, Indonesia undertook major economic reforms, including trade liberalization, that lowered trade barriers. Since then, local content policies have been less frequently employed but were not completely abandoned. In 2009, the government of Indonesia began revisiting localization strategies to

DOI: 10.4324/9781003415794-7

increase domestic investment in local supporting industries, particularly the parts and components industry, as exemplified by Minister of Finance Regulation 176/PMK.011/2009, which provides a duty exemption on machines, goods, and materials imports, on the condition that at least 30 percent of the total value of machines used were purchased locally. This legislation was intended to encourage the use of domestically built machinery and to foster the expansion of the domestic parts and components sector (Negara, 2016).

Despite concerns that the LCRs policy runs counter to the World Trade Organization (WTO) commitment, this policy remains appealing to Indonesian policymakers due to the ongoing emphasis on domestic value added, including in exports, when formulating industrial and trade policies (Athukorala and Patunru, 2022). The government of Indonesia has been aiming to maximize domestic value added in several identified priority industries. To achieve this goal, it has adopted various policy instruments, including downstreaming (*hilirisasi*), trade prohibitions and restrictions (*lartas*), and LCRs. Over the years, many public projects in Indonesia have focused on developing domestic industries for advanced, technology-intensive goods. In the last two decades, LCRs policy in Indonesia has been widely recognized under the abbreviation TKDN, which stands for *Tingkat Komponen Dalam Negeri* (value of domestic component level).

With the growing use of LCRs, it has become increasingly crucial to assess their potential impact on Indonesia's trade flow patterns and domestic industry dynamics. Despite their potential importance, few studies have explored the effects of LCRs in Indonesia, particularly on trade outcomes. Therefore, it remains unclear what effects the LCR policy has had on Indonesia's trade flows and patterns. Our study aims to address this research gap.

In this study, we investigate the impact of LCRs on Indonesia's trade outcomes between 2004 and 2020. Specifically, we evaluate whether imposing an LCR on a given product significantly affects its imports and exports, considering other relevant factors. To achieve this, we compile a comprehensive dataset of the LCRs that were implemented (or are still in effect) in Indonesia from 2004 to 2020.

We employ the difference-in-differences (DID) estimator developed by de Chaisemartin and D'Haultfœuille (2022a) to assess the impact of LCRs on Indonesia's trade. Our findings indicate minimal and somewhat negative effects of LCRs on trade. Specifically, we observe a weak association between a product's exposure to an LCR and increased imports within 5 years of its implementation. Notably, the positive effects of LCRs on imports were more pronounced for high-tech products. On the other hand, we observe a decline in the export volume and value of products subject to LCRs within 5 years after their implementation. This decline was particularly evident among manufacturing and input products that are closely linked to other industries with LCRs (i.e., product groups with high links to LCR sectors). These results suggest an indication of a competitiveness loss in the export market arising from LCRs.

This chapter is organized as follows. Section 2 reviews recent studies on local content requirements (LCRs) and summarizes their findings on the impact of LCRs on trade. Section 3 outlines our data and variables, including the LCR dataset. Section 4 explains an empirical methodology. Section 5 presents main findings. Section 6 includes robustness checks. Section 7 concludes.

2 Literature review

Essentially, local content protection (or LCR, interchangeably) mandates that a certain proportion of value added in the production of the products on which it is imposed comes from domestic sources. Such a policy is typically employed to protect or foster domestic industries, particularly intermediate goods. In addition to tariffs, economists have long been interested in estimating the impact of local content protection.

In a seminal paper, Grossman (1981) developed a model with intermediate and final good producers to investigate the effect of local content protection on domestic resource allocation. He finds that LCRs affect the producers of intermediate and final goods differently. On final goods producers, his model shows that LCRs generate negative output effects and cause higher retail (final goods) prices due to the increased costliness of sourcing inputs domestically in the aftermath of the policy. However, the output and price effects on domestic intermediate goods producers are ambiguous as two forces work in opposite directions. While LCRs could shift demand toward domestic intermediate goods, they might also depress demand for domestic intermediate goods due to their negative effects on final goods production. The overall impact of domestic content requirements on output is, as a result, ambiguous and depends on the specific circumstances of the market and the production process, such as market structure, the elasticity of demand, the elasticity of substitution, the degree of product differentiation, and access to the foreign market.

Many economists have extended Grossman's model or built new ones to study the impact of LCRs on various economic outcomes under different market structures. With some exceptions, the literature generally points to the tendency of LCRs to increase the prices of domestic intermediate goods,[2] which corresponds to higher input prices for the producers of final goods. This is then typically followed by higher prices and decreased production of domestic final goods at the expense of consumers and downstream firms. Findings in the literature most often point to the ambiguous net effects of LCRs on the outputs of the targeted domestic input producers.[3] Meanwhile, there is no strong evidence that LCRs improve the productivity of targeted or protected firms (i.e., typically intermediates or input producers), in contrast to some evidence of LCRs' productivity penalty for exposed firms (i.e., typically final goods producers) (Hayakawa and Ito, 2019; Korinek and Ramdoo, 2017; Deringer et al., 2018).

Concerning the effects of LCRs on trade outcomes in particular, the literature tends to find that LCRs[4] suppress trade flows. For example, Hufbauer et al. (2013) estimate that the worldwide proliferation of LCRs reduced global trade by USD 200 billion to 300 billion, of which 80% (Stone et al., 2015) was trade in intermediate goods. The direct requirements of the LCRs, along with their negative effects on final goods production, will likely reduce the demand for and imports of intermediate goods. This is consistent with findings from the current literature, which suggest mostly negative effects of LCRs on imported intermediate goods. Furthermore, the higher input costs (at possibly lower quality) and the resulting loss in competitiveness due to LCRs tend to reduce the gains from exports, especially those of final goods (Deringer et al., 2018; Araújo and Flaig, 2017; Athukorala and Patunru, 2022). LCRs artificially inflate domestic production in the targeted sectors, which draws resources away from other sectors, thereby limiting the export potential of these other sectors (Deringer et al., 2018; OECD, 2016).

LCRs have a well-established impact on domestic output and exports. However, their impact on imported final goods is more ambiguous. On the one hand, a stricter LCR could potentially depress domestic final goods output and lead to a surge in imports of those final goods, as some studies have shown (Madan, 1998). On the other hand, studies have shown that the negative impact of a stricter LCR on trade can be equivalent to a specific rate of ad-valorem import tariff, which could reduce imports of those final goods (Deringer et al., 2018). Moreover, in the regional context, studies have shown that rules of origin (RoOs) may have trade-diverting effects, reducing trade with non-FTA (free trade agreement) partners relative to that with FTA partners (Augier et al., 2005; Conconi et al., 2018; Sytsma, 2019). These findings suggest that the impact of LCRs on imported final goods depends on various factors, such as the specific industry, trade partners, and regional context.

As excellently summarized by Negara (2016), the literature on LCRs presents some mixed findings, which typically fall under three broad groups. First, some studies point to the largely negative effects of LCRs on economic outcomes (Deringer et al., 2018; Hufbauer et al., 2013; Korinek and Ramdoo, 2017). Second, some other studies claim that the effects of LCRs can be ambiguous but also show that LCRs can promote favorable outcomes under certain conditions (Grossman, 1981; Lin and Weng, 2020; Scheifele et al., 2022). Third, some studies even go so far as to show that LCRs can be designed to achieve a particular objective given the current economic structure (Qiu and Tao, 2001; Veloso, 2006).

Despite the numerous studies discussed here, the number of existing empirical studies that examine the impact of LCRs on trade flows using observational data is limited. Studies on the effects of LCRs are typically based on either parametric, general equilibrium-based models of heterogeneous firms or cross-country, input-output-based models (e.g., ICIO, GTAP, OECD Metro). However, the effects of LCRs produced by model predictions or simulation results may not always be reflected in the observed trade flow data. To the best of our knowledge, there are currently only a few empirical studies investigating the impact of LCRs on trade flows using regression methods on observational data. This is the gap in the literature that we seek to fill through our study.

3 Data and variables

3.1 LCR dataset and variables

We conduct a thorough analysis of all Indonesian government legislation between 2004 and 2020 and identify those that include local content requirements (LCRs) for particular sectors or goods. We collect both the mandatory regulations and the non-mandatory ones[5] that only call for the prioritization (or equivalent words) of the use of domestic inputs without any specific level of requirement. However, we exclude regulatory documents that only contain information on how firms are to self-assess the level of domestic content in their production and find out whether they have fulfilled the LCRs. Furthermore, we exclude from our dataset the local content-promoting regulations that may provide incentives for using locally sourced materials. Finally, we also exclude LCR regulations that are exclusively related to government procurement as their general stipulations often imply coverage for all products across the board, which then rules out the possibility of making the necessary distinction between LCR and non-LCR products for our analysis.

We then examine the relevant regulatory documents to assign affected product codes to each LCR and note their implementation and revocation dates. This process enables us to identify which products at the 8-digit Harmonized System (HS) code level were affected by each of the LCRs. We use an HS concordance to harmonize our dataset into HS 2012 nomenclature. Our master LCR dataset includes information on the presence (or absence) of LCRs for each of the 9,342 products annually from 2004 to 2020. The result is a comprehensive annual dataset from which we can identify whether at least one LCR exists for each product at any given year and, ultimately, which products belong to the treatment group and which do not. Note, however, that our dataset measures LCRs as counts, regardless of their severity levels.[6]

Our study focuses primarily on LCRs with backward consequences. To illustrate, consider a hypothetical example where a product A is produced using inputs B, C, and D, and a 30% LCR is imposed on product A. In this case, we would classify this LCR as backward-affecting product A. Thus, product A would be coded as being affected by a backward LCR. This study concentrates on studying the impact of backward LCRs, as most LCRs are typically imposed on downstream, final products. By this definition, every LCR considered in this study is of the backward type.

We have identified 16 sets of regulatory documents that contain LCRs, as presented in Table 7.A1. There is a large variation in the coverage of LCRs with respect to the number of affected HS codes. The earliest LCR we identified was officially in effect as of January 2004, while the most recent was implemented in September 2020. Industries exposed to LCRs also vary, ranging

Table 7.1 Date of First Exposure to LCRs, by Number of Products

Year	*# HS codes*	*Percent*
2004	66	8.9
2009	85	11.5
2012	37	5.0
2013	82	11.1
2015	279	37.7
2016	191	25.8
Never exposed to LCR	8,602	-

Source: Authors' compilation

Notes: Percent is calculated relative to the number of products that were imposed by at least one LCR in our period of analysis (i.e., 740).

from upstream oil and gas to electronics and telecommunications equipment, electricity infrastructure projects, and automotive.

Within our analysis period, approximately 8% of all products were exposed to at least one LCR. The remaining 92% of products were never subject to any LCRs during this period. Table 7.1 reports the distribution of products based on when they received the first LCR treatment. It shows that exposure to LCRs began at different points in time, underscoring the importance of using an estimator that can accommodate variation in treatment timing.

3.2 *Trade-related indicators*

To construct our trade outcome variables, we collect annual information on Indonesia's export and import volume and value, both aggregated and by trade partner, for the years 2004–2020 from the Ministry of Trade. We utilize an HS concordance to harmonize the trade data into 8-digit HS 2012 nomenclature. We then merge these trade outcome variables with the annual LCRs dataset we described earlier. Our unit of observation is product-by-year.

To generate the covariates in our regression models, we gather information on each product's MFN and average applied tariff rates, which include tariffs imposed by Indonesia on imports from other countries and tariffs imposed by other countries on exports from Indonesia. Additionally, we specifically identify the top three trading partners (i.e., import origin and export destination) for each product-by-year and then acquired information on the indicators (real GDP and its growth rate; GDP per capita; population; domestic demand; exports and imports of goods and services) of those sets of countries to proxy for their demand for Indonesian products. Specifically, we take the average of those indicators[7] for each set of three top trading partners for each product i at year t to proxy for demand for traded goods. We also include various indicators from those sets of countries that might affect trade flows with Indonesia, such as the logistics performance index, the real effective exchange rate, and tariff rates. The complete list of control variables used in our study is presented in Table 7.A2.

4 Empirical strategy

Our study aims to examine both the contemporaneous and dynamic effects of LCR imposition on Indonesia's trade flows. To achieve this, we utilize a binary variable in our dataset that represents the LCR policy treatment. This variable takes a value of 1 if a product is subject to any LCRs in a given year and 0 if it is not. A commonly used method that researchers utilize to estimate the impact of a policy treatment on trade outcomes is linear regressions with both time and product fixed effects. This method is often referred to in the literature as a two-way fixed effects (TWFE) regression. However, given that LCRs may have delayed effects on trade flows, we use an event-study framework to gain a better understanding of how the trajectory of future trade flows is affected by current LCRs. Therefore, one can construct a dynamic[8] TWFE regression that captures both the contemporaneous and dynamic effects of LCRs with the following specification:

$$Y_{it} = \sum_{e=-E}^{Z} \beta_e 1\{t - F_i = e\} + \theta \boldsymbol{X}_{it} + \alpha_i + \gamma_t + v_{it} \quad (1)$$

where Y_{it} is the log of trade outcome variable of product i in year t. Four trade outcome variables are examined in this study: export volume, import volume, export value, and import value. Next, $1\{t - F_i = e\}$ is a set of relative time indicator variables, which are event study dummies equal to 1 if a product i is e years away at year t from its initial LCR treatment[9] or equal to 0 otherwise. F_i represents the first year the product i was exposed to any LCRs in our analysis period. These indicator variables are always equal to zero for products that were never exposed to any LCRs.

The main parameters of interest are β_e, which represents the LCR treatment effects on trade outcomes e years after its initial implementation. If $e = 0$, β_e measures the contemporaneous effect of LCR on product i's trade outcome in the same year that it was first implemented. We include event study dummies for $e < 0$ to check for any pre-trends and to ensure the parallel trend assumption is satisfied.[10] Additionally, X_{it} is a vector of time-varying control variables for product i in year t that includes all the variables described in Section 3.2 and listed in Table 7.A2. The product fixed-effect, α_i, and the year fixed-effect, γ_t, capture the time-invariant characteristics of each product as well as any sector-specific or nationwide shocks that may influence trade flows. We also incorporate a variable, $\omega_s t$, in some specifications, which captures sector-specific linear trends at a more aggregated 2-digit HS level to account for shocks that occur in specific industries at certain years,[11] following Angrist and Pischke (2009). Lastly, v_{it} is the idiosyncratic error term, and standard errors are clustered by HS 2-digit industry to account for the potential correlation of error terms within an industry, given that LCR imposition tends to be industry-based rather than product-based.

Ordinary least squares (OLS) regressions with product and time fixed effects can be utilized to estimate (1). Given the binary policy variable, this setup bears some similarities to a difference-in-differences (DID) approach. The use of DID is appropriate for the context of our study since LCR policy treatment only applies to certain products, and we seek to compare the differences in the trade outcome trajectories between the treated and non-treated products. However, some recent works in the econometric literature on DID, such as Sun and Abraham (2021), Callaway and Sant'Anna (2021), de Chaisemartin and D'Haultfœuille (2020, 2022a), and Goodman-Bacon (2021), have demonstrated that OLS TWFE estimators are unbiased only if *both* the parallel trends and constant effect assumptions hold. The constant effect assumption requires the treatment effects to be homogeneous across groups of products and over time for OLS estimators to be unbiased (de Chaisemartin and D'Haultfœuille, 2022a).

The constant effect assumption is potentially violated in the context of this study because the effects of LCRs may vary across different industries or lengths of exposure to the policy. If the treatment effects of the policy are heterogeneous, estimating (1) with OLS would yield a biased and inconsistent set of estimators β_e with questionable causal interpretability. Thus, we need an alternative DID estimator that can accommodate variation in the timing of policy treatment and is robust to heterogeneous treatment effects.

To address these challenges, we propose to employ a DID estimator developed by de Chaisemartin and D'Haultfœuille (2022a) (hereafter, DCDH22) to estimate (1). This estimator is specifically designed to address the source of bias in standard OLS TWFE estimators. We provide a detailed explanation of the construction of the DCDH22 DID estimator in Appendix Section 1. Like any DID estimator, the validity of the DCDH22 estimator also hinges on the parallel trend assumption, which stipulates that without the treatment, both the LCR-treated and control products would have experienced the same evolution of trade outcomes. This assumption also requires that no significant pre-trends exist between treated products and control products.

It is worth noting that the LCR policy could be endogenous, which might stem from selection bias and the non-random assignment of LCRs. This means that some products are more likely to enjoy trade protection than others (Trefler, 1993). Nevertheless, the DCDH22 estimator can still be utilized for estimating the effects of an endogenous treatment, as one of the identifying assumptions underlying their method is that in the absence of treatments, all products would have experienced a similar evolution of their trade outcome. Thus, to the extent that these identifying assumptions are satisfied, we do not expect the potential endogeneity of LCR treatments to be a significant issue for our analysis.

To sum up, we will utilize DCDH22 to estimate (1) for each of the four trade flows separately. We expect the DCDH22 estimators to be more robust to the heterogeneous treatment effects of LCRs and provide more reliable estimates of the true, unbiased effects of LCRs. We will first conduct regressions on the full sample containing all products, followed by separate regressions on different subsamples to better understand which product groups drive the overall results or show a noticeable deviation in estimated LCR effects from the entire group of products.

5 Findings

The section discusses the estimated impacts of LCRs on imports and exports, and it proceeds by analyzing the overall effects across all products and specific product groups to explore heterogeneity in treatment effects. The section concludes by presenting the results of both the static model and an alternative definition of LCRs. To maintain conciseness, the section mainly focuses on reporting the effects of LCRs on trade volume.

5.1 Overall effects on imports

Table 7.2 presents the estimated post-treatment dynamic effects, up to 5 years,[12] of LCR imposition on Indonesia's import volume. Columns 1 and 2 report the coefficients β_e when regressions are performed on the full sample containing all products. Columns 3 and 4 present the coefficients β_e from regressions on manufacturing products only. Columns 2 and 4 report the results of our preferred specifications, as both incorporate control variables and sector-specific linear trends. Table 7.2 also shows that LCRs have not had significant effects on imports. There is no discernible pattern of effects, as demonstrated by the frequently alternating signs of the coefficients across different years following the introduction of LCRs. Similarly, there are no significant and systematic effects observed among manufacturing products. In both manufacturing and all products, and in the fourth year for all products following the LCR implementation, the average effects suggest positive but statistically insignificant effects of LCRs on imports. However, joint-significance tests of treatment effects in specifications 2 and 4 reveal that the contemporaneous and all the dynamic treatment effects, taken together, differ statistically from zero at a 5% significance level. These results suggest that the imposition of LCRs might be weakly linked to higher imports of the goods subject to them. These findings are consistent with Negara's (2016) study, which fails to find any indication that the LCR policy has effectively reduced firms' dependence on imported inputs in the long term.

Figure 7.1 presents an event-study plot that displays the results reported in Table 7.2, Column 4, specifically the estimated effects of LCRs on manufacturing imports following their implementation in the manufacturing sector. The plot shows that while there are statistically significant spikes in manufacturing

Table 7.2 Dynamic Effects of LCRs on Imports

	(1)	*(2)*	*(3)*	*(4)*
0 Years after	–0.103	–0.095	–0.074	–0.089
	(0.129)	(0.129)	(0.129)	(0.137)
1 Year after	0.192	0.272	0.069	0.148
	(0.308)	(0.314)	(0.115)	(0.138)
2 Years after	0.059	0.063	–0.047	–0.019
	(0.340)	(0.321)	(0.172)	(0.176)
3 Years after	0.572	0.623*	0.574*	0.624**
	(0.368)	(0.371)	(0.306)	(0.304)
4 Years after	0.267	0.314*	0.201	0.233
	(0.190)	(0.189)	(0.198)	(0.195)
5 Years after	–0.455	–0.431	–0.187	–0.157
	(0.425)	(0.384)	(0.163)	(0.183)
Average Effects	0.153	0.193	0.119	0.156
	(0.207)	(0.208)	(0.117)	(0.123)
Control variables	Yes	Yes	Yes	Yes
2-digit HS linear trend	No	Yes	No	Yes
Manufacturing only	No	No	Yes	Yes
Number of observations	158,814	158,814	138,907	138,907
Effects jointly significant at 5%	No	Yes	Yes	Yes
Pre-trend significant at 5%	No	No	No	No

Source: Authors' calculation.

Notes: This table reports the estimated coefficients β_ℓ from DCDH22 DID regressions. They represent the effects of being exposed to the first LCR up until 5 years after the LCR's starting implementation date under various specifications. The dependent variable is log of (Indonesia's import volume in kg + 1). Inferring the magnitude of the effects requires taking exponential over the estimated coefficients in this table. Standard errors are estimated using 100 bootstrap replications clustered at the 2-digit HS code level and reported in parentheses. To check for pre-trends at a 5% significance level, the results from joint-significance tests of all placebo estimators up until 3 years before the LCR implementation are summarized in the last row of the table. Average Effects reports the estimated average total effects of the treatment, i.e., the average of all the instantaneous and dynamic LCR effects across treated products. The results of joint-significance tests, which verify whether the contemporaneous and all dynamic treatment effects are jointly different from zero statistically at a 5% significance level, are provided in the table.

imports in the third and fourth years after the imposition of LCRs, the overall effects of LCRs on imports are minimal and mostly hover around zero. This finding is consistent with the results in Table 7.2, which suggest that the choice of trade flow is not a significant issue because the effects of LCRs on both import volume and import value are relatively similar.

To investigate whether specific product groups are driving the overall results, we estimate equation (1) separately for different subsamples corresponding to specific product groups. We then compare the point estimates with the baseline results obtained from regressions on all products or manufacturing products only. Table 7.3 shows that the largely insignificant effects of LCRs on imports are consistent across almost all product groups. Almost none of the product groups exhibit statistically significant average effects or

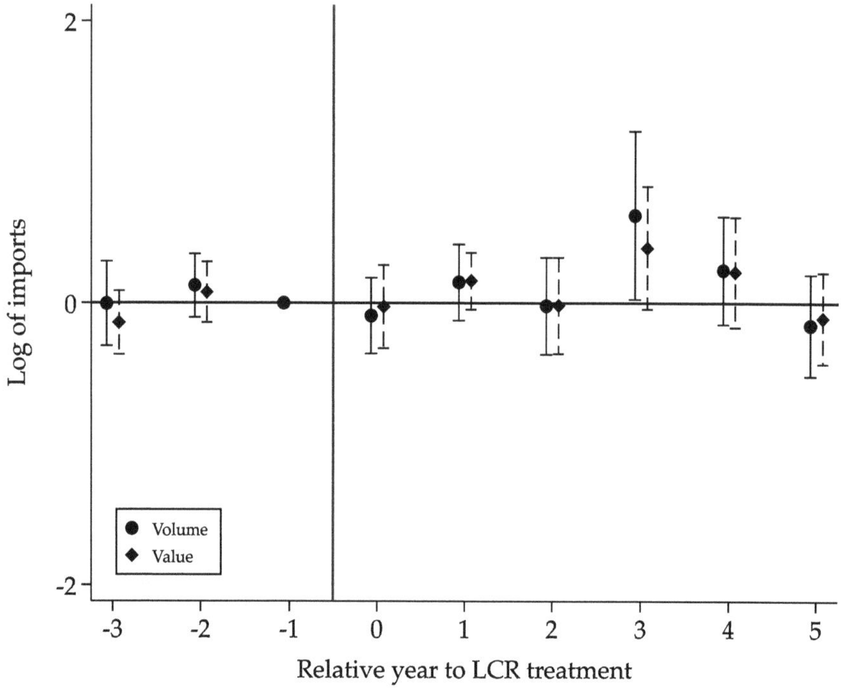

Figure 7.1 Effects of LCRs on Manufacturing Imports

Source: Authors' estimation.

Notes: This figure presents the dynamic effects of being exposed to an LCR on log of import volume and import value of manufacturing products based on DCDH22 DID estimators. The reported specifications include control variables and 2-digit HS linear trends. Standard errors are estimated using 100 bootstrap replications clustered at 2-digit HS code level. 95% confidence intervals are displayed for each year.

systematic patterns of effects over time. However, joint-significance tests of treatment effects in Table 7.3 confirm that the combined instantaneous and dynamic effects of LCRs on import volume differ statistically from zero at a 5% significance level for most product groups.

Interestingly, Table 7.3 Columns 7 and 8 exhibit opposing signs in the estimated effects of LCRs for product groups with high and low links to other sectors with LCRs, as reflected by their average effects. A feature of our LCR dataset is that it contains information on the input-output (IO) table sectoral code of the broader industry to which every product belongs. Using this information and the last four editions of Indonesia's IO tables, we construct a time-varying annual variable called *LinktoLCRsectors*, which measures the share of the output of each product flowing as an input for other industries with LCRs in every year from 2004–2020. We then calculate the 2004–20 average value of this variable for each product and rank the products. We consider a product to have a high link to LCR sectors if

Table 7.3 Dynamic Effects of LCRs on Imports, by Product Group

	(1) *All products*	(2) *Manufacturing*	(3) *Capital goods*	(4) *Consumer goods*	(5) *Intermediate goods*	(6) *Down-stream*	(7) *High link to LCR sectors*	(8) *Low link to LCR sectors*	(9) *High-tech products*	(10) *Medium-tech products*
0 Years after	−0.095	−0.089	−0.178	0.054	−0.061	−0.074	−0.256	0.029	0.332***	−0.212
	(0.129)	(0.137)	(0.281)	(0.260)	(0.180)	(0.237)	(0.169)	(0.208)	(0.123)	(0.314)
1 Year after	0.272	0.148	0.209	−0.022	0.512	0.327*	−0.389	0.234	0.680*	0.228
	(0.314)	(0.138)	(0.191)	(0.179)	(0.862)	(0.178)	(0.285)	(0.203)	(0.386)	(0.161)
2 Years after	0.063	−0.019	−0.029	−0.169	0.477	−0.024	−0.653*	0.233	0.466	−0.102
	(0.321)	(0.176)	(0.194)	(0.282)	(0.920)	(0.307)	(0.393)	(0.284)	(0.315)	(0.165)
3 Years after	0.623*	0.624**	0.426	0.473	1.188	1.029	−0.363	1.873**	1.541***	0.224
	(0.371)	(0.304)	(0.292)	(0.498)	(0.969)	(0.645)	(0.372)	(0.865)	(0.235)	(0.488)
4 Years after	0.314*	0.233	0.097	0.080	0.880	0.244	0.106	0.264	0.630***	0.359
	(0.189)	(0.195)	(0.244)	(0.262)	(0.425)	(0.272)	(0.427)	(0.292)	(0.179)	(0.425)
5 Years after	0.431	−0.157	−0.099	−0.582	−0.852	0.085	−0.652	0.516	0.557	−0.276**
	(0.384)	(0.183)	(0.440)	(0.809)	(1.553)	(0.323)	(0.649)	(0.425)	(1.194)	(0.136)
Average Effects	0.193	0.156	0.103	0.036	0.497	0.320	−0.381	0.582**	0.712***	0.080
	(0.208)	(0.123)	(0.206)	(0.201)	(0.499)	(0.253)	(0.268)	(0.288)	(0.158)	(0.159)
Number of products	9,342	8,171	2,381	2,774	4,213	3,788	3,827	3,874	677	2,118
Products with LCRs (%)	7.9	8.0	11.2	11.4	5.3	10.4	13.0	4.5	6.8	12.1
Number of observations	158,814	138,907	40,477	47,158	71,621	64,396	65,059	65,858	11,509	36,006
Effects jointly significant at 5%	Yes	Yes	No	Yes	Yes	Yes	No	No	Yes	No
Pre-trend significant at 5%	No	No	No	No	No	No	No	No	Yes	No

Source: Authors' calculation.

Notes: This table reports the DCDH22 DID estimators of the effects of being exposed to the first LCR up until 5 years after the LCR's starting implementation date for separate product groups. Detailed definitions of the product groups are available in Table 7.A3. The dependent variable is log of (Indonesia's import volume in kg + 1). Inferring the magnitude of the effects requires taking exponential over the estimated coefficients in this table. Standard errors are estimated using 100 bootstrap replications clustered at the 2-digit HS code level and reported in parentheses. To check for pre-trends at a 5% significance level, the results from joint-significance tests of all placebo estimators up until 3 years before the LCR implementation are summarized in the last row of the table. Average Effects reports the estimated average total effects of the treatment, i.e., the average of all the instantaneous and dynamic LCR effects across treated products. The results of joint-significance tests, which verify whether the contemporaneous and all dynamic treatment effects are jointly different from zero statistically at a 5% significance level, are provided in the table.

its value lies at the 60th percentile or above and a low link if it is at the 40th percentile or below.

The findings in Table 7.3 Column 7 suggest that the introduction of LCRs is negatively associated with imports of products with high links to LCR sectors. In contrast, the results in Column 8 indicate that the imposition of LCR is positively correlated with imports of products with low links to LCR sectors. This divergence is more visually apparent in the event-study plot provided in Figure 7.A1. In other words, if a product is exposed to a new LCR and happens to be an essential input for another sector that is also exposed to another LCR, then its imports are likely to fall following the introduction of that new LCR. This is likely due to the increased demand generated by the existence of other LCRs in other sectors that are highly linked to the product. As local producers expand their production volumes to meet this increased demand, there will be less need for imports of the product. It is important to note, however, that the average effects for the product group with a high link to LCR sectors are statistically insignificant.

On the other hand, if a product had a low link to other LCR sectors, the implementation of the new LCR would likely have resulted in an increase in its imports. Table 7.3 Columns 7 and 8 indicate that the average effects of LCRs on imports of product groups with a low link to LCRs are positive and statistically significant, although this interpretation requires caution due to the joint insignificance of the contemporaneous and dynamic effects. Products with low links to LCR sectors have minor contributions as inputs for other sectors that are currently affected by LCRs. Therefore, such products would not have experienced greater demand due to the LCRs in other industries, and there would be no immediate need for local producers to increase their production. Combined with the necessary adjustment and potentially higher costs to comply with the LCRs for its production in the first place, local production of goods may not be able to catch up quickly enough. Ultimately, this supply gap will likely be filled with increased imports, as suggested by the estimates in Table 7.3 Column 8.

Another interesting finding is apparent in Table 7.3. Column 9 suggests that the imposition of LCRs on high-tech products is strongly associated with an increase in imports. However, Column 10 shows that the effects of LCRs on medium-tech products are less certain. This result is not surprising given that Indonesia's current comparative advantage lies in low- to medium-tech products. Local producers are more likely to comply with LCRs if the products they manufacture align with Indonesia's level of technological ability and comparative advantage. As such, the results in Table 7.3 Columns 9 and 10 imply that imports of high-tech products are likely to remain substantial in the near future, despite the introduction of LCRs. This finding suggests that it may take a considerable amount of time for technological advancement to occur to the extent that it becomes possible and competitive to produce high-tech products locally. However, we should be cautious when interpreting the estimates in Table 7.3 Column 9, as we detect a significant pre-trend at a 5% level.

5.2 *Overall effects on exports*

Table 7.4 presents the estimated effects of LCRs on exports. The overall findings suggest that LCRs do not have statistically significant effects on the pattern and quantity of exports. Joint-significance tests of treatment effects support this conclusion, except for the export volume of manufacturing products. Although the average effects of LCRs on the export volume of all products are negative, they are statistically insignificant. The results from our preferred specifications are presented in Columns 2 and 4 for all products and manufacturing products, respectively. These specifications incorporate control variables and sector-specific linear trends. While the estimates lack statistical significance, except for the first year after the implementation of LCR, five out of six year-by-year estimates reveal negative effects of LCRs. Although our findings indicate some statistically significant spikes in imports by about 21%

Table 7.4 Dynamic Effects of LCRs on Exports

	(1)	*(2)*	*(3)*	*(4)*
0 Years after	–0.148	–0.117	–0.166	–0.139
	(0.097)	(0.115)	(0.106)	(0.116)
1 Year after	–0.211	–0.235*	–0.212	–0.250*
	(0.139)	(0.133)	(0.145)	(0.138)
2 Years after	–0.017	–0.016	–0.034	–0.033
	(0.152)	(0.158)	(0.165)	(0.173)
3 Years after	–0.014	–0.004	–0.034	–0.016
	(0.199)	(0.206)	(0.210)	(0.225)
4 Years after	0.183	0.197	0.161	0.183
	(0.209)	(0.217)	(0.220)	(0.239)
5 Years after	–0.103	–0.122	–0.145	–0.160
	(0.438)	(0.428)	(0.434)	(0.436)
Average Effects	–0.061	–0.057	–0.081	–0.077
	(0.146)	(0.152)	(0.158)	(0.165)
Control variables	Yes	Yes	Yes	Yes
2-digit HS linear trend	No	Yes	No	Yes
Manufacturing only	No	No	Yes	Yes
Number of observations	158,814	158,814	138,907	138,907
Effects jointly significant at 5%	No	No	No	Yes
Pre-trend significant at 5%	No	No	No	No

Source: Authors' calculation.

Notes: This table reports the coefficients β_e from DCDH22 estimators. The dependent variable is log of (Indonesia's export volume in kg + 1). Inferring the magnitude of the effects requires taking exponential over the estimated coefficients in this table. Standard errors are estimated using 100 bootstrap replications clustered at the 2-digit HS code level and reported in parentheses. To check for pre-trends at a 5% significance level, the results from joint-significance tests of all placebo estimators up until 3 years before the LCR implementation are summarized in the last row of the table. Average Effects reports the estimated average total effects of the treatment, i.e., the average of all the instantaneous and dynamic LCR effects across treated products. The results of joint-significance tests, which verify whether the contemporaneous and all dynamic treatment effects are jointly different from zero statistically at a 5% significance level, are provided in the table.

to 28% immediately following the implementation of LCR and the first year after, they must be interpreted in the context of the overall effects due to collinearity concerns.

However, when we only consider manufacturing products in the analysis, the results suggest a slightly different interpretation. Table 7.4 Column 4 shows that while the average effects of LCRs on the export volume of manufacturing products are not statistically significant, the joint-significance test of treatment effects for this product group rejects the hypothesis that all the estimated contemporaneous and dynamic effects, taken together, are statistically equal to zero among manufacturing products at a 5% significance level. Overall, these findings suggest that the imposition of LCRs tends to have minimal, if not somewhat negative, effects on exports, particularly those of manufacturing products. Additionally, we present the estimated trajectory of exports of manufacturing products after the implementation of LCRs in the manufacturing sector in Figure 7.2. The event-study plot indicates an initial

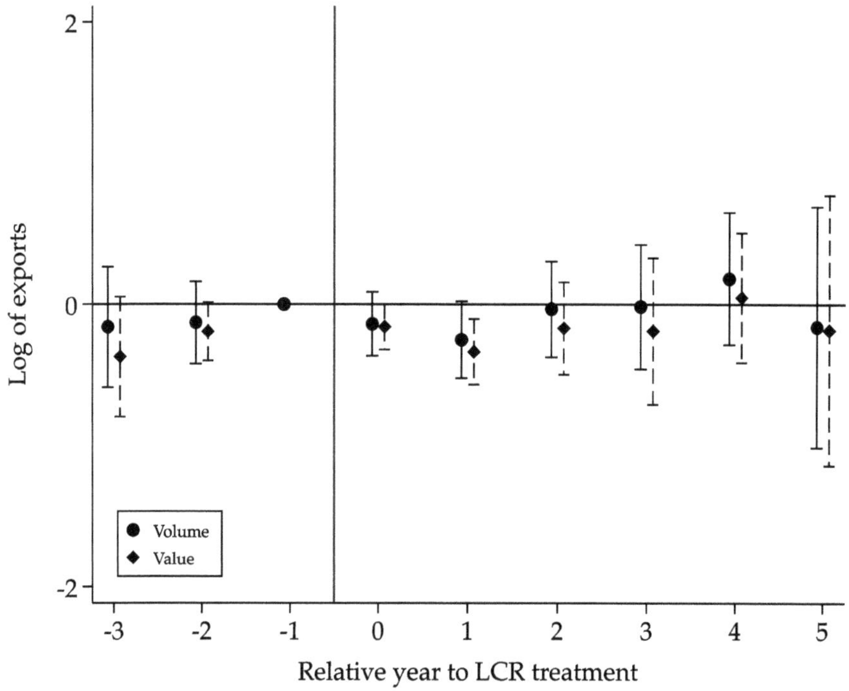

Figure 7.2 Effects of LCRs on Manufacturing Exports

Source: Authors' estimation.

Notes: This figure presents the dynamic effects of being exposed to an LCR on log of export volume and export value of manufacturing products based on DCDH22 DID estimators. The reported specifications include control variables and 2-digit HS linear trends. Standard errors are estimated using 100 bootstrap replications clustered at 2-digit HS code level. 95% confidence intervals are displayed for each year.

significant decline in manufacturing exports within a year of the LCR implementation, after which the effects gradually dissipate toward zero.

The imposition of an LCR requires firms to use a certain proportion of locally sourced inputs in their production processes, which can increase production costs and reduce their competitiveness in the export market. For example, Scheifele et al. (2022) state that LCRs have not resulted in a significant increase in exports for most countries, except for a few that had already developed export potential and capabilities in related fields prior to the imposition of LCRs. They argue that significant capability gaps at the technological frontier contribute to the failure of most LCR policies to enhance export performance. This factor may partly explain the absence of favorable effects of LCRs on Indonesia's exports, as observed in Table 7.4.

Tables 7.5 and 7.6 present the estimated impacts of LCRs on export volume and value, categorized by product groups. In both tables, the negative effects of LCRs on exports among all products and manufacturing products are consistent with the estimates of consumer goods and intermediate goods (Columns 4 and 5) and medium-tech goods (Column 10), despite the lack of statistical significance. Taken together, Table 7.5 Column 6 and Table 7.6 Column 6 suggest that while LCRs may have a positive association with the export volume of downstream products, they exert negative effects on the export values of these products. Similarly, Table 7.5 Column 9 and Table 7.6 Column 9 show that, on average, LCRs are associated with higher export volume but lower export value of high-tech products, indicating a potential loss in competitiveness in the export market. However, these associations are mostly not statistically significant.

Interestingly, Tables 7.5 and 7.6 Columns 7 and 8 indicate different patterns between product groups with high and low links to LCR sectors in response to the LCRs imposed on them. The two product groups exhibit opposite signs in the estimated LCR effects. Specifically, our findings suggest that exposure to LCRs has a negative and significant association with the export volume and value of products highly linked to other sectors with LCRs. In contrast, LCRs have positive but statistically insignificant associations with the exports of products with low links to other sectors with LCRs. These contrasting results provide suggestive evidence of a domestic reallocation of resources toward meeting LCRs requirements, as we have also observed earlier in the case of imports.

Both Table 7.5 Column 7 and Table 7.6 Column 7 suggest that local producers facing increased demand for their products due to LCRs in other sectors may have shifted their focus from exports to domestic markets to meet higher domestic demand resulting from other LCRs imposed in industries that use their products as inputs. This phenomenon is more pronounced for products with higher links to other sectors with LCRs than those with lower links. In line with a similar finding earlier, the results in our chapter indicate that LCRs negatively affected both imports and exports of products with high links

Table 7.5 Dynamic Effects of LCRs on Export Volume, by Product Group

	(1)	(2)	(3)	(4)	(5)	(6)	(7)	(8)	(9)	(10)
	All products	*Manufacturing*	*Capital goods*	*Consumer goods*	*Inter-mediate goods*	*Down-stream*	*High link to LCR sectors*	*Low link to LCR sectors*	*High-tech products*	*Medium-tech products*
0 Years after	–0.117	–0.139	0.441***	–0.373	–0.384	0.146	–0.458***	0.025	0.264	–0.275
	(0.115)	(0.116)	(0.104)	(0.272)	(0.260)	(0.255)	(0.116)	(0.144)	(0.617)	(0.271)
1 Year after	–0.235*	–0.250*	0.148	–0.321	–0.428	–0.059	–0.632***	0.128	–0.065	–0.268
	(0.133)	(0.138)	(0.249)	(0.340)	(0.322)	(0.637)	(0.166)	(0.148)	(0.905)	(0.219)
2 Years after	–0.016	–0.033	0.378***	–0.228	–0.103	0.199	–0.298**	0.363	0.076	–0.076
	(0.158)	(0.173)	(0.124)	(0.416)	(0.324)	(0.331)	(0.131)	(0.350)	(0.998)	(0.387)
3 Years after	–0.004	–0.016	0.612***	–0.454	–0.127	0.387*	–0.278	0.310	0.903	–0.185
	(0.206)	(0.225)	(0.103)	(0.527)	(0.354)	(0.221)	(0.301)	(0.265)	(0.895)	(0.507)
4 Years after	0.197	0.183	0.519*	0.010	0.032	0.459	–0.024	0.551	0.025	0.164
	(0.217)	(0.239)	(0.312)	(0.397)	(0.304)	(0.363)	(0.234)	(0.509)	(0.759)	(0.512)
5 Years after	–0.122	–0.160	0.403	–1.296	0.401	0.178	–0.240	0.558	2.402	0.099
	(0.428)	(0.436)	(0.516)	(0.880)	(0.753)	(0.520)	(0.380)	(1.127)	NA	(0.873)
Average Effects	–0.057	–0.077	0.493***	–0.375	–0.192	0.246	–0.358**	0.320	0.301	–0.141
	(0.152)	(0.165)	(0.122)	(0.372)	(0.257)	(0.224)	(0.148)	(0.303)	(0.771)	(0.395)
Number of products	9,342	8,171	2,381	2,774	4,213	3,788	3,827	3,874	677	2,118
Products with LCRs (%)	7.9	8.0	11.2	11.4	5.3	10.4	13.0	4.5	6.8	12.1
Number of observations	158,814	138,907	40,477	47,158	71,621	64,396	65,059	65,858	11,509	36,006
Effects jointly significant at 5%	No	Yes	Yes	No	No	No	Yes	No	No	No
Pre-trend significant at 5%	No	No	No	No	Yes	No	No	Yes	No	Yes

Source: Authors' calculation.

Notes: This table reports the DCDH22 estimators of the effects of being exposed to the first LCR up until 5 years after the LCR's starting implementation date for separate product groups. Detailed definitions of the product groups are available in Table 7.A3. The dependent variable is log of (Indonesia's export volume in kg + 1). Inferring the magnitude of the effects requires taking exponential over the estimated coefficients in this table. Standard errors are estimated using 100 bootstrap replications clustered at 2-digit HS code level and reported in parentheses. To check for pre-trends at a 5% significance level, the results from joint-significance tests of all placebo estimators up until 3 years before the LCR implementation are summarized in the last row of the table. Average Effects reports the estimated average total effects of the treatment, i.e., the average of all the instantaneous and dynamic LCR effects across treated products. The results of joint-significance tests, which verify whether the contemporaneous and all dynamic treatment effects are jointly different from zero statistically at a 5% significance level, are provided in the table.

Table 7.6 Dynamic Effects of LCRs on Export Value, by Product Group

	(1)	(2)	(3)	(4)	(5)	(6)	(7)	(8)	(9)	(10)
	All products	*Manufacturing*	*Capital goods*	*Consumer goods*	*Inter-mediate goods*	*Down-stream*	*High link to LCR sectors*	*Low link to LCR sectors*	*High-tech products*	*Medium-tech products*
0 Years after	–0.141	–0.159*	0.229***	–0.382*	–0.309	0.007	–0.386***	0.019	0.292	–0.286
	(0.088)	(0.082)	(0.057)	(0.223)	(0.265)	(0.114)	(0.069)	(0.080)	(0.397)	(0.191)
1 Year after	–0.315***	–0.335***	–0.252**	–0.377	–0.403	–0.358	–0.519***	0.067	–0.430	–0.504**
	(0.093)	(0.118)	(0.118)	(0.376)	(0.269)	(0.604)	(0.169)	(0.154)	(0.629)	(0.257)
2 Years after	–0.148	–0.169	0.003	–0.371	–0.145	–0.135	–0.269**	0.277	0.032	–0.362
	(0.164)	(0.167)	(0.205)	(0.321)	(0.241)	(0.352)	(0.121)	(0.434)	(0.587)	(0.459)
3 Years after	–0.173	–0.189	0.149	–0.455	–0.149	–0.020	–0.351	0.199	0.325	–0.419
	(0.266)	(0.265)	(0.211)	(0.502)	(0.357)	(0.457)	(0.356)	(0.374)	(0.528)	(0.609)
4 Years after	0.057	0.048	0.318	–0.060	–0.058	0.320	–0.135	0.470	–0.554	0.046
	(0.232)	(0.235)	(0.369)	(0.255)	(0.221)	(0.405)	(0.190)	(0.617)	(0.494)	(0.551)
5 Years after	–0.153	–0.184	0.110	–0.889	–0.016	0.053	–0.199	0.564	0.798	0.124
	(0.483)	(0.488)	(0.768)	(0.552)	(0.606)	(0.848)	(0.301)	(1.414)	NA	(1.039)
Average Effects	–0.161	–0.181	0.108	–0.389	–0.212	–0.045	–0.340**	0.253	–0.017	–0.323
	(0.169)	(0.171)	(0.264)	(0.291)	(0.209)	(0.337)	(0.145)	(0.378)	(0.428)	(0.487)
Number of products	9,342	8,171	2,381	2,774	4,213	3,788	3,827	3,874	677	2,118
Products with LCRs (%)	7.9	8.0	11.2	11.4	5.3	10.4	13.0	4.5	6.8	12.1
Number of observations	158,814	138,907	40,477	47,158	71,621	64,396	65,059	65,858	11,509	36,006
Effects jointly significant at 5%	Yes	Yes	Yes	Yes	No	No	Yes	No	Yes	No
Pre-trend significant at 5%	No	No	No	No	Yes	No	No	Yes	No	Yes

Source: Authors' calculation.

Notes: This table reports the DCDH22 estimators of the effects of being exposed to the first LCR up until 5 years after the LCR's starting implementation date for separate product groups. Detailed definitions of the product groups are available in Table 7.A3. The dependent variable is log of (Indonesia's export value in USD + 1). Inferring the magnitude of the effects requires taking exponential over the estimated coefficients in this table. Standard errors are estimated using 100 bootstrap replications clustered at the 2-digit HS code level and reported in parentheses. To check for pre-trends at a 5% significance level, the results from joint-significance tests of all placebo estimators up until 3 years before the LCR implementation are summarized in the last row of the table. Average Effects reports the estimated average total effects of the treatment, i.e., the average of all the instantaneous and dynamic LCR effects across all products. The results of joint-significance tests, which verify whether the contemporaneous and all dynamic treatment effects are jointly different from zero statistically at a 5% significance level, are provided in the table.

to other LCR sectors, providing suggestive evidence of the trade-repressing tendency of LCRs.

We find no discernible effects of LCRs on exports of high-tech or medium-tech products. The estimates have large standard errors, and any positive impact on high-tech exports may have been driven by problematic Year 5 estimates. Overall, we observe a minimal impact of LCRs on the exports of either high-tech or medium-tech products.

Finally, somewhat surprisingly, Table 7.5 Column 3 shows that LCRs are significantly and positively associated with exports of capital goods. Table 7.A4 provides further insights into the purportedly positive effects of LCRs on capital goods exports by presenting the estimated effects using different definitions of capital goods. Regardless of the definition used, the estimated effects of LCRs on exports remain positive, albeit with varying magnitudes and levels of significance.

5.3 *Alternative model and definition of LCRs*

In this subsection, we present the estimated effects of LCRs on trade using a different model and definition of LCRs and examine how the results differ. Specifically, we begin by reporting the results of the static model of LCRs and then exclude several non-mandatory LCRs from the analysis.

5.3.1. *Static model*

All the results we have considered so far revolve around the dynamic effects of LCR policy on trade flows. In this subsection, we report the results from running the static analog of equation (1) to study the contemporaneous effects of LCRs. While this approach may not capture the post-treatment dynamics of the outcomes, it provides valuable information on the expected magnitude of the treatment effect, as argued by Borusyak et al. (2022). We report the results from the static model estimation in Table 7.A5 for all four trade flows.

The results suggest that LCRs tend to have a negative but generally insignificant association with both imports and exports. However, for certain product groups, LCRs are found to have statistically significant effects on exports. For example, LCRs are significantly associated with a 15% decrease in the export value of manufacturing products and a 24% decrease in the export value of consumer goods. These findings are consistent with the results from the dynamic model, which also illustrate the trade-repressing tendency of LCRs among products with high links to LCR sectors.

The results from the static model also indicate the trade-repressing effects of LCRs among products with high links to other sectors with LCRs. Specifically, the presence of LCRs is significantly associated with a 33% reduction in export volume and a 30% reduction in export value of such products. The estimated static effects of LCRs on imports among products with high links to LCR sectors are also negative, though statistically insignificant.

Similar to previous findings, the results also indicate a positive and significant association between LCRs and exports of capital goods. By magnitude, the effects on capital goods' export value are about 30 percentage points lower than the effects on their export volume. This supports our earlier discussion on the possible trade-off between LCRs' positive effects on exports of some product groups and their negative impacts on competitiveness. Overall, the results in Table 7.A5 are generally consistent with those from the dynamic model discussed earlier in this chapter. They indicate minimal, if not somewhat negative, effects of LCRs on most imports and negative effects of LCRs on exports, except for capital goods.

5.3.2. *Excluding soft LCRs*

So far, we have examined the impact of *any* LCRs that exist in Indonesia, whether mandatory or non-mandatory. In this section, we alter the definition of LCR policy treatment. Specifically, we keep only mandatory or *strict* LCRs with a specific level of requirement (typically a minimum percentage (%) level that is required to come from local sources) and exclude *soft* LCRs, which refer to non-mandatory policies or regulations that only call for the prioritization of the use of domestic inputs without any specific level of requirement, from our analysis. We then re-estimate (1) to examine any divergence in the results due to the different types of LCR policies implemented. The results from DCDH22 estimators on the entire sample are presented in Table 7.A6.

The baseline results generally show a positive association between LCRs and imports and a negative association between LCRs and exports. However, when analyzing only strict LCRs, the results suggest that LCRs are associated with lower imports and even lower exports. One possible explanation for this is that policymakers may combine LCRs with other protectionist import measures, such as hefty tariffs on imported goods, to encourage the absorption of locally produced goods in domestic markets. For example, high tariffs on imported automobiles may make locally made automobiles more affordable and appealing to consumers, reducing the need for imports. However, it is worth noting that the average effects of LCRs on imports remain statistically insignificant, even after excluding soft LCRs.

At the same time, forcibly increased usage of domestic inputs through imposing mandatory LCRs could potentially limit access to high-quality and diversified inputs, which may increase domestic production costs and erode the domestic product's competitiveness in the global market. This could result in lower exports than the baseline results, as shown in Table 7.A6 Column 4, and potentially lead to a wider trade deficit.

6 Robustness check

We then conduct some sensitivity checks to verify if our findings are robust to several potential disturbances in the dataset. In this section, we report the results from five types of adjustments made to our main dataset, which includes all products.

Table 7.7 Columns 2 and 3 present the results from the first two adjustments. In these specifications, our concern is that products intermittently imported or exported by Indonesia might skew the overall results. For such products, there are multiple years in which they record no trade at all. These products might have caused some dramatic swings or volatility in the trade data from year to year, which may have distorted the overall estimated effects of LCRs. To address this concern, we remove products with only intermittent trade and examine how the estimated effects differ from the baseline results.

Table 7.7 Column 2 presents the results from regressions where we only include products with non-zero trade flows in at least 14 out of 17 years within the 2004–2020 period. In Column 3, we further restricted our analysis to only products with non-zero trade flows in every single year from 2004–2020. We conduct the removal of intermittently traded products separately for each of the trade flows (export volume and import volume).

For specifications reported in Table 7.7 Columns 4 and 5, we examine whether extreme year-on-year changes in trade flows distort the estimated effects of LCRs. We remove observations with annual growth at the 99th percentile or higher. We execute this idea in our dataset in two specific ways. In the first approach, reported in Column 4, we remove from the regression *observations for entire products* (i.e., all 17 years of them) that experienced positive growth spikes at the 99th percentile or higher magnitude at least twice within the 2004–2020 period. In the second approach, whose result is reported in Column 5, we simply remove from the regressions *any observations* that clock in year-on-year growth in trade flow with a magnitude at the 99th percentile or higher.

Another concern is that the estimated effects of LCRs earlier may have been driven by products with relatively small amounts of trade, i.e., those constituting minimal shares in Indonesia's overall trade basket. To partially mitigate this concern while being mindful not to drop too many products, we rank all products in terms of their total trade flows from 2004–2020 and only keep products at the 35th percentile or higher in the regression. This means that only about two-thirds of all products remain in the regressions. The results from this exercise are reported in Table 7.7 Column 6.

Overall, none of the proposed adjustments alters the overall effects of LCRs all that much, although magnitudes and statistical significance in some cases may differ. The signs of the estimated effects mostly remain the same. The top panel of Table 7.7 reports that the estimated overall effects of LCRs on imports remain positive but statistically insignificant. The positive magnitudes of the average effects would have been higher if not for the sizeable negative Year 5 estimates.

The results of our robustness check for exports are presented in the bottom panel of Table 7.7. Similar to our findings for imports, we observe that none of the modifications we make to our dataset significantly affects the estimated

Table 7.7 Dynamic Effects of LCRs on Trade Volume under Robustness Specifications

	(1)	(2)	(3)	(4)	(5)	(6)
	Baseline DCDH22	*Only mostly + trade products*	*Only always + trade products*	*Remove outlier-99 products (1st def.)*	*Remove outlier-99 products (2nd def.)*	*Only keep top traded products*
Import Volume						
0 Years after	–0.095	–0.061	0.040	–0.087	–0.110	–0.036
	(0.129)	(0.105)	(0.088)	(0.132)	(0.133)	(0.096)
1 Year after	0.272	0.298	–0.073	0.232	0.254	0.082
	(0.314)	(0.297)	(0.278)	(0.264)	(0.277)	(0.293)
2 Years after	0.063	0.106	–0.063	0.009	0.067	0.004
	(0.321)	(0.303)	(0.469)	(0.296)	(0.297)	(0.330)
3 Years after	0.623*	0.679	0.444	0.617*	0.593*	0.544
	(0.371)	(0.417)	(0.496)	(0.366)	(0.352)	(0.381)
4 Years after	0.314*	0.262	0.513	0.311	0.263	0.405**
	(0.189)	(0.174)	(0.342)	(0.196)	(0.218)	(0.204)
5 Years after	–0.431	–0.357	–0.734	–0.432	–0.460	–0.614
	(0.384)	(0.427)	(0.863)	(0.393)	(0.412)	(0.445)
Average Effects	0.193	0.220	0.108	0.176	0.173	0.140
	(0.208)	(0.194)	(0.271)	(0.195)	(0.198)	(0.214)
Export Volume						
0 Years after	–0.117	–0.015	0.112	–0.062	–0.069	–0.156
	(0.115)	(0.090)	(0.178)	(0.123)	(0.128)	(0.124)
1 Year after	–0.235*	–0.135	–0.379	–0.219*	–0.202	–0.210
	(0.133)	(0.160)	(0.285)	(0.126)	(0.128)	(0.140)
2 Years after	–0.016	0.057	–0.195	–0.032	–0.003	0.058
	(0.158)	(0.139)	(0.217)	(0.162)	(0.167)	(0.167)

(*Continued*)

Table 7.7 (Continued)

	(1)	(2)	(3)	(4)	(5)	(6)
	Baseline DCDH22	*Only mostly + trade products*	*Only always + trade products*	*Remove outlier-99 products (1st def.)*	*Remove outlier-99 products (2nd def.)*	*Only keep top traded products*
3 Years after	–0.004	0.048	–0.112	–0.014	0.004	0.041
	(0.206)	(0.193)	(0.212)	(0.214)	(0.227)	(0.219)
4 Years after	0.197	0.209	–0.125	0.196	0.185	0.226
	(0.217)	(0.214)	(0.240)	(0.223)	(0.231)	(0.233)
5 Years after	–0.122	–0.108	0.111	–0.137	–0.185	–0.014
	(0.428)	(0.431)	(0.456)	(0.443)	(0.463)	(0.470)
Average Effects	–0.057	0.014	–0.115	–0.047	–0.043	–0.022
	(0.152)	(0.129)	(0.197)	(0.164)	(0.169)	(0.162)
Effects on imports JS at 5%	Yes	No	No	Yes	Yes	Yes
Effects on exports JS at 5%	No	No	No	No	Yes	No
Pre-trend significant at 5%	No	No	No	No	No	No

Source: Authors' calculation.

Notes: This table compares the DCDH22 estimators of the effects of being exposed to the first LCR up until 5 years after the LCR's starting implementation date under several robustness specifications to the baseline result in Column 1. All regressions in this table incorporate control variables and 2-digit HS linear trends. The dependent variable is log of (Indonesia's import volume or export volume in kg + 1). Inferring the magnitude of the effects requires taking exponential over the estimated coefficients in this table. Standard errors are estimated using 100 bootstrap replications clustered at the 2-digit HS level and reported in parentheses. To check for pre-trends at a 5% significance level, the results from joint-significance tests of all placebo estimators up until 3 years before the LCR implementation are summarized in the last row of the table. Average Effects reports the estimated average total effects of the treatment, i.e., the average of all the instantaneous and dynamic LCR effects across treated products. The results of joint-significance tests, which verify whether the contemporaneous and all dynamic treatment effects are jointly different from zero statistically at a 5% significance level, are provided in the table. JS stands for Jointly Significant.

effects of LCRs on exports. Overall, our analysis indicates that LCRs tend to have minimal or, in some cases, negative effects on exports, particularly in the immediate aftermath and after the first year of their introduction. Our analysis suggests that outliers and intermittently traded products do not appear to significantly impact the magnitudes of the estimated LCR policy effects. However, we recognize that the existence of significant pre-trends may be a more salient issue in this context. Therefore, caution is necessary when interpreting some of the estimated results in our chapters, particularly those with significant pre-trends.

Taken together, our findings are generally in line with most of the earlier studies on the effects of LCRs. For example, Hufbauer et al. (2013) argue that LCRs increase production costs and impair efficiency, resulting in inferior competitiveness and decreased trade flows. Similarly, Deringer et al. (2018) find that LCRs implemented in Brazil, Russia, India, and China resulted in a decline in their exports of heavy vehicles. Furthermore, using CGE analysis on a Russian case study, Stone et al. (2014) conclude that LCRs have a negative impact on the economy as a whole, including higher prices and decreased total exports.

7 Conclusion

LCR is a widely used policy instrument in many countries, including Indonesia. However, empirical studies on the impact of LCRs on trade flows using observational data are limited. Our study contributes to the existing literature by analyzing Indonesia's trade data from 2004–2020 to investigate how the imposition of an LCR on a product affects the trajectory of its trade flows up to 5 years after its implementation. To this end, we construct a comprehensive dataset of all LCRs that have been or are currently in effect in Indonesia during this period. We utilize a difference-in-differences (DID) estimator developed by de Chaisemartin and D'Haultfœuille (2022a) to estimate the impact of LCRs on four trade flows (export volume, export value, import volume, and import value) under an event-study framework.

Our findings suggest that exposure to LCRs is weakly associated with an increase in a product's imports within 5 years of implementation. The joint-significance tests confirm that the contemporaneous effect and all dynamic effects of LCRs on imports differ from zero. This, coupled with the positive yet statistically insignificant average effects, suggests that, on average, the introduction of LCRs tends to slightly raise imports of the products on which they are imposed. In contrast, LCRs are, on average, associated with a decrease in export volume and value up to 5 years following implementation, particularly among manufacturing products. However, caution is warranted when interpreting the results, as most of the estimated effects on imports or exports are not statistically significant for most years and product groups.

Taken as a whole, our findings provide suggestive evidence for the following three points. First, the results suggest that LCRs may have negative effects on the competitiveness of local producers. This is evident from the divergence in the effects of LCRs on the export volume and value of various product groups. While LCRs may have helped increase the volume of exports, they may not have contributed to technological upgrades or enhanced competitiveness in the export market. Moreover, LCRs may not have added value to the traded goods, resulting in an overall negative effect on exports' value.

Second, our analysis of product groups with high and low links to LCR sectors indicates that LCR implementation may have led to the reallocation of domestic resources to meet the LCR requirements. We estimate a reduction in imports and exports among product groups that are heavily used as inputs by other industries with LCRs. This suggests that resources originally allotted for exports may have been redirected toward supplying other domestic industries, particularly those affected by the LCR policy.

Third, our findings suggest no evidence that the LCR policy is effective in promoting an export-oriented development strategy in general or boosting Indonesia's export ability. In fact, we find that LCRs tend to be associated with poorer export outcomes for the affected products in the short and medium run, with a few exceptions.

While our study finds that LCRs tend to have negative or minimal effects on trade flows, none of our findings in this chapter rule out the possibility that LCRs may bring favorable outcomes. For example, LCRs may be intended to promote domestic job creation or stimulate local production in certain industries. Our analysis does not explore these potential benefits and trade-offs, as they fall outside the scope of our study. However, our results do suggest that, at least in the short and medium runs, LCRs may lead to decreased export growth. Policymakers need to carefully consider such a trade-off in LCRs when considering their implementation.

We acknowledge several limitations of our study, which future research may address. First, our study employs a binary measure of LCRs and does not account for their varying degrees of stringency or restrictiveness. Future studies could develop more nuanced measures of LCRs and investigate how their effects vary across different levels of stringency. Second, our analysis is limited to LCRs on products within the HS code system, and as a result, we were unable to analyze the impacts of LCRs in the services sector or those related to government procurement. Future research could extend our analysis to cover other sectors or develop alternative approaches to include LCRs not covered by the HS code system. Finally, it would be valuable to examine the effectiveness of various incentives for local sourcing, as they could complement LCRs as a policy instrument.

Acknowldegement

The authors would like to acknowledge and thank David Sanotona, Muhammad Raihan Ramadhan, Militcyano Sapulette, Catherin Nur Safitri, Michelle Chandra Kasih, and Ivana Markus for outstanding research assistance, and Clément de Chaisemartin, Gene M. Grossman, Lili Yan Ing, Mélitine Malézieux, Pyan Amin Muchtar, and Chandra Tri Putra for valuable insights and helpful suggestions. The Ministry of Trade Republic of Indonesia kindly provided the trade data, both aggregate and by trading partner, used in this study.

Notes

1 Negara (2016) provides an excellent historical overview of LCRs in Indonesia.
2 This tendency is stronger under a more concentrated industrial structure, such as an oligopoly or monopoly.
3 These effects largely depend on substitution possibilities in production, the supply condition of domestic intermediates, and the market structure of the intermediate goods industry (Grossman, 1981).
4 We also include the rules of origin (RoOs) of free trade agreements in our literature survey as a particular form of LCRs. RoOs can be understood as regional value content requirements. Some of their theoretical predictions or empirical findings at the regional level might be analogous to the case of LCRs at the national level.
5 The list of LCRs and the affected products is based on Munadi, et.al., (2022).
6 We are aware that a 20% LCR imposed on a particular industry may not be as severe as a 20% LCR imposed on another industry. Consequently, we neither infer the severity levels of LCRs from their percentage requirements nor assign LCRs with higher percentage requirements more weight in our dataset.
7 We do not perform this averaging procedure on binary gravity variables that indicate whether Indonesia shares (i) a border, (ii) colonial links, or (iii) a common language with its top three trading partners.
8 The static analog of TWFE regression simply takes the form of $Y_{it} = \alpha_i + \alpha_t + \beta D_{it} + \gamma X_{it} + v_{it}$ with D_{it} being a binary variable for the policy treatment that is equal to 1 if a product *i* is being treated at time *t* and 0 otherwise.
9 Initial LCR treatment means the first time the product *i* was exposed to any LCR within our analysis period. A product that receives initial LCR treatment in year *g* is considered to belong to group *g*.
10 The parallel trend assumption requires that the difference in the outcome variable between the treatment and control groups would have remained constant over time if the treatment group had not received the treatment (Angrist and Pischke, 2009; Bertrand et al., 2004; and Wooldridge 2010).
11 Sector-specific linear trend allows for differential trends in the outcome variable across sectors within treatment and control groups (Bertrand et al. (2004) and Callaway and Sant'Anna (2021).
12 It is challenging to estimate the effects of LCRs beyond 5 years because many products were exposed to LCRs for the first time in 2015, and the dataset ends in 2020. Thus, much fewer observations can be used to estimate the LCR effects after six years and beyond. In all dynamic regressions in this chapter, we estimate the effects of LCRs up to 5 years after their implementation and placebo estimators up until 3 years prior to their implementation to check for significant pre-trends.
13 In a staggered treatment design, treatment can only increase and do so at most once. LCR policy treatment is non-staggered since treatment can increase or decrease multiple times for an affected product. This is because regulations containing LCRs were in some cases repealed (i.e., treatment decreases/switches off), and new regulations containing LCRs on certain products were in some cases added on top of existing ones (i.e., treatment increases more than once).
14 One source of bias is that OLS estimators do not satisfy the no-sign reversal property if the treatment effects are heterogeneous across groups *g* or time *t*. Specifically, one could have the treatment's instantaneous and dynamic effects to be positive in every (*g*,*t*) cell, but the expectations of those regression coefficients are negative.

References

Angrist, Joshua D., and Jörn-Steffen Pischke (2009). *Mostly Harmless Econometrics.* Princeton, NJ: Princeton University Press.

Antras, Pol, and Davin Chor (2013). *Organizing the Global Value Chain.* Econometrica 81(6): 2127–2204.

Araújo, Sónia, and Dorothee Flaig (2017). *Trade Restrictions in Brazil: Who Pays the Prices?* Journal of Economic Integration 32(2): 283–323.

Athukorala, Prema-chandra, and Arianto A. Patunru (2022). *Domestic Value Added, Exports, and Employment: An Input-Output Analysis of Indonesian Manufacturing.* Bulletin of Indonesian Economic Studies, DOI: 10.1080/00074918.2022.2134554.

Augier, Patricia, Michael Gasiorek, and Charles Lai Tong (2005). *The Impact of Rules of Origin on Trade Flows.* Economic Policy 20(43): 567–624.

Bertrand, Marianne, Esther Duflo, and Sendhil Mullainathan (2004). *How Much Should We Trust Differences-in-Differences Estimates?* The Quarterly Journal of Economics 119(1): 249–275.

Borusyak, Kirill, Xavier Jaravel, and Jann Spiess (2022). *Revisiting Event Study Designs.* Unpublished Working Paper 2108.12419, arXiv.org, revised April 2022.

Callaway, Brantly, and Pedro Sant'Anna (2021). *Difference-in-Differences with Multiple Time Periods.* Journal of Econometrics 225: 200–230.

Conconi, Paola, Manuel Garcia-Santana, Laura Puccio, and Roberto Venturini (2018). *From Final Goods to Inputs: The Protectionist Effect of Rules of Origin.* American Economic Review 108(8): 2335–2365.

de Chaisemartin, Clément, and Xavier D'Haultfœuille (2020). *Two-Way Fixed Effects Estimators with Heterogenous Treatment Effects.* American Economic Review 110(9): 2964–2996.

de Chaisemartin, Clément, and Xavier D'Haultfœuille (2022a). *Difference-in-Differences Estimators of Intertemporal Treatment Effects.* NBER Working Paper 29873. March 2022.

de Chaisemartin, Clément and Xavier D'Haultfœuille (2022b). *Two-Way Fixed Effects and Differences-in-Differences with Heterogenous Treatment Effects: A Survey.* The Econometrics Journal, 2022. utac017, https://doi.org/10.1093/ectj/utac017.

Deringer, Hanna, Fredrik Erixon, Philipp Lamprecht, and Erik Van der Marel (2018). *The Economic Impact of Local Content Requirements: A Case Study of Heavy Vehicles.* ECIPE Occasional Paper No. 1/2018, European Centre for International Political Economy (ECIPE), Brussels.

Flaig, Dorothee, and Susan F. Stone (2023). *Localisation Measures: A Global Perspective.* Chapter 2 in *Local Content Requirements: Promises and Pitfalls* (eds. Lili Yan Ing and Gene M. Grossman). New York, NY: Routledge.

Goodman-Bacon, Andrew (2021). *Difference-in-Differences with Variation in Treatment Timing.* Journal of Econometrics 225(2): 254–277.

Grossman, Gene M. (1981). *The Theory of Domestic Content Protection and Content Preference.* The Quarterly Journal of Economics 96(4): 583–603.

Hayakawa, Kazunobu, and Tadashi Ito (2019). *Local Procurement and Firm Performance: Pure Local Inputs and Semi Local Inputs.* Journal of Southeast Asian Economies 35(1): Special Issue: Commemorating the 50th Anniversary of the ISEAS – Yusof Ishak Institute: 101–110.

Hufbauer, Gary Clyde, Jeffrey Schott, Cathleen Cimino, Martin Vieiro, and Erika Wada (2013). *Local Content Requirements: A Global Problem.* Policy Analysis in

International Economics September 2013. Washington, DC: Peterson Institute for International Economics.
Korinek, Jane and Isabelle Ramdoo (2017). *Local Content Policies in Mineral-Exporting Countries.* OECD Trade Policy Paper No. 209. Paris: OECD Publishing. http://dx.doi.org/10.1787/4b9b2617-en
Lin, Shiue-Hung, and Yungho Weng (2020). *Can Strengthening the Local Content Requirements Meet a Government's Need to Raise Industrial Productivity and Production.* Journal of Applied Economics 23(1): 316–328.
Madan, Vibhas (1998). *Transfer Prices, Tariffs, and Content Restrictions.* Review of International Economics 6(4): 625–637.
Munadi, E., L. Y. Ing, D. Christian, and D. Sanotona (2022). The List of Indonesia's Laws and Regulations Containing LCRs and the Affected Products, from January 2009 to March 2022. Unpublished.
Negara, Siwage D. (2016). *Assessing the Impact of Local Content Requirements on Indonesia's Manufacturing.* Chapter __ in *The Indonesian Economy: Trade and Industrial Policies* (eds. Lili Yan Ing, Gordon Hanson, and Sri Mulyani Indrawati). New York, NY: Routledge.
OECD (2016). *The Economic Impact of Local Content Requirements.* Trade Policy Note, February 2016. Paris: OECD Publishing.
Qiu, Larry D., and Zhigang Tao (2001). *Export, Foreign Direct Investment, and Local Content Requirement.* Journal of Development Economics 66: 101–125.
Scheifele, Fabian, M. Bräuning, and Benedict Probst (2022). *The Impact of Local Content Requirements on the Development of Export Competitiveness in Solar and Wind Technologies.* Renewable and Sustainable Energy Reviews 168(3): 112831. DOI: 10.1016/j.rser.2022.112831
Stone, Susan, Dorothee Flaig, and Frank van Tongeren (2014). *Modelling Local Content Requirements: Quantitative Restrictions in a CGE Model (Presented at the 17th Annual Conference on Global Economic Analysis, Dakar, Senegal).* Purdue University, West Lafayette, IN: Global Trade Analysis Project (GTAP). www.gtap.agecon.purdue.edu/resources/res_display.asp?RecordID=4497
Stone, Susan, James Messent, and Dorothee Flaig (2015). *Emerging Policy Issues: Localisation Barriers to Trade.* OECD Trade Policy Papers No. 180, OECD Publishing, Paris, https://doi.org/10.1787/5js1m6v5qd5j-en
Sun, Liyang, and Sarah Abraham (2021). *Estimating Dynamic Treatment Effects in Event Studies with Heterogenous Treatment Effects.* Journal of Econometrics 225(2): 175–199.
Sytsma, Tobias (2019). *Rules of Origin Liberalization with Multi-Product Firms: Theory and Evidence from Bangladeshi Apparel Exporters* (September 11, 2019). Available at SSRN: http://dx.doi.org/10.2139/ssrn.3452286.
Trefler, Daniel (1993). *Trade Liberalization and the Theory of Endogenous Protection: An Econometric Study of U.S. Import Policy.* Journal of Political Economy 101(1): 138–160.
Veloso, Francisco M. (2006). *Understanding Local Content Decisions: Economic Analysis and an Application to the Automotive Industry.* Journal of Regional Science 46(4): 747–772.
Weiss, Miriam (2016). *The Role of Local Content Policies in Manufacturing and Mining in Low- and Middle-Income Countries.* UNIDO Working Paper 19/2016. Department of Policy, Research and Statistics.
Wooldridge, Jeffrey M. (2010). *Econometric Analysis of Cross-section and Panel Data.* Cambridge, MA: MIT Press.

Table 7.A1 List of LCRs in the Dataset

DocID		*8-digit HS codes affected*	*Starting implementation date*	*Broad sectors or industries affected*
2	MEMR Reg. 15/2013	102	2013	Upstream oil and gas equipment
5	MoI Reg. 15/2016 Jo. 6/2018, 24/2020	20	2016	Electricity infrastructure, tower, conductor
10	MoI Reg. 34/2017 Jo. 5/2018	250	2017	Automotive: Vehicles with 4 wheels or more
21	MCI Reg. 27/2015 Jo. 13/2021	24	2015	LTE-based telecommunication equipment
27	Government Reg. 76/2014	37	2014	Arms and defence equipment
74	MCI Reg. 26/2013 Jo. 9/2014, 4/2019	4	2013	Internet protocol set top box, TV
78	MCI Reg. 7/2009	24	2009	Telecommunication equipment, wireless broadband
79	MCI Reg. 32/2013	24	2014	Digital TV receivers
82	Presidential Reg. 55/2019	4	2019	Electric vehicles
83	MoI Reg. 61/2009	20	2009	Containers for liquified gas, stove gas accessories, etc.
84	MCI Reg. 30/2009 Jo. 11/2010 Jo. 6/2017	44	2009	Internet protocol set top box, TV
87	MoI Reg. 80/2014 Jo. 34/2015, 22/2016, 70/2016	279	2015	Automotive: Vehicles with 4 wheels or more
88	Presidential Inst. 6/2016 + MoH Reg. 17/2017	157	2016	Pharmaceuticals and medical devices
96	Presidential Reg. 146/2015	80	2015	Upstream oil and gas (esp. refineries)
129	Law 16/2012	37	2012	Arms and defence equipment
131	Law 22/2001 Jo. 11/2020	66	2001	Upstream and downstream oil and gas

Source: Munadi, et. al (2022).

Abbreviations: Reg. = Regulation; Inst. = Instruction; Jo. = Juncto; MEMR = Ministry of Energy and Mineral Resources; MoI = Ministry of Industry; MCI = Ministry of Communication and Informatics; MoH = Ministry of Health

Notes: The term Jo. (juncto) in this table is used loosely to represent some but not necessarily all updated versions of the preceding regulation. We only report relevant versions of updated regulations which still contain LCR stipulations. In some cases, we assign a single DocID for multiple regulatory documents if the LCR stipulations in each document are largely identical and/or cover similar sets of products.

Table 7.A2 List of Control Variables Used in the Regressions

#	*Name of Variable*	*Definition*	*Calculated separately for each trade flow?*	*Source**
1	ln_avpop	Log of average population of Indonesia's top 3 trade partners	Yes	EIU
2	ln_avrdd	Log of average real domestic demand of Indonesia's top 3 trade partners	Yes	EIU
3	ln_avexgs	Log of average exports of goods and services in 2010$ of Indonesia's top 3 trade partners	Yes	EIU
4	ln_avimgs	Log of average imports of goods and services in 2010$ of Indonesia's top 3 trade partners	Yes	EIU
5	ln_avgdp	Log of average real GDP in 2010$ of Indonesia's top 3 trade partners	Yes	EIU
6	ln_avgdppc	Log of average GDP per capita of Indonesia's top 3 trade partners	Yes	EIU
7	ln_avdist	Log of average distance between most populated cities in km of Indonesia and top 3 partners	Yes	CEPII
8	avgdpgr	Average of real GDP growth (%) of Indonesia's top 3 trade partners	Yes	EIU
9	avmfnp	Average MFN tariff rate (%) imposed by Indonesia's top 3 trade partners	Yes	WITS
10	avatrp_w	Average applied tariff rate on World, imposed by Indonesia's top 3 trade partners	Yes	WITS
11	avatrp_i	Average applied tariff rate on Indonesia, imposed by Indonesia's top 3 trade partners	Yes	WITS
12	reer	Average Real Effective Exchange Rate Index (2010=100) of Indonesia's top 3 trade partners	Yes	IMF
13	allborder	=1 if all top 3 trade partners share any geographical border with Indonesia, =0 if not	Yes	CEPII

(*Continued*)

Table 7.A2 (Continued)

#	*Name of Variable*	*Definition*	*Calculated separately for each trade flow?*	*Source**
14	colonial	=1 if all top 3 trade partners share colonial links with Indonesia, =0 if not	Yes	CEPII
15	com_lang	=1 if all top 3 trade partners share common languages with Indonesia, =0 if not	Yes	CEPII
16	lpi	Average Logistic Performance Index of Indonesia's top 3 trade partners	Yes	World Bank
17	brer	Average bilateral real exchange rate of Indonesia's top 3 trade partners	Yes	World Bank
18	bwlinkage	Backward linkage index of each product, calculated by Indonesia's Input-Output tables.	No	BPS
19	fwlinkage	Forward linkage index of each product, calculated by Indonesia's Input-Output tables.	No	BPS
20	downindex	Downstream index of each product, calculated by Antras and Chor (2013) method and IO tables of Indonesia. Closer to 1 (0) means more downstream (upstream).	No	BPS
21	linktoLCRsec	Link to other sectors with LCRs, i.e., share of output of each product used as inputs for other sectors/ industries with LCRs at the same year, as calculated from Indonesia's Input-Output (IO) tables.	No	BPS

Source: Authors' compilation

Table 7.A3 Definition of Product Groups/Subsamples

#	*Name of group*	*Definition*	*#HS Codes (8-digit)*	*#Products with LCRs*
1	All products	All product codes, 8-digit HS2012.	9,342	740
2	Manufacturing	Similar to (1), but excluding products with 2-digit HS codes 01–14 and 25–27.	8,171	653

#	*Name of group*	*Definition*	*#HS Codes (8-digit)*	*#Products with LCRs*
3	Capital goods	UNCTAD-SoP4: Capital Goods. Retrieved from WITS.	2,381	266
4	Capital goods: Non-machinery	Similar to (3), but excluding products with 2-digit HS codes 84–85.	634	218
5	Machinery and Transport SITC	Products with SITC Rev.3 codes beginning with 7. Transformed to HS2012 by HS-to-SITC3 concordance available in WITS.	2,290	358
6	Capital goods non-transport BEC	Products whose Broad Economic Categories (BEC) Rev.5 description is Capital goods (except for transport equipment). Retrieved from WITS, and transformed to HS2012 by HS-to-BEC concordance available in WITS.	1,086	82
7	Consumer goods	UNCTAD-SoP3: Consumer Goods. Retrieved from WITS.	2,774	315
8	Intermediate goods	Products that belong in either Global Value Chain group or UNCTAD SoP2: Intermediate Goods classifications available in WITS.	4,213	225
9	Downstream	Products whose 2004–20 mean of share of output sold as final goods lie at the 60th percentile or higher. Calculated from Indonesia's Input-Output (IO) tables.	3,788	394
10	High Link to LCR sectors	Products whose 2004–20 mean of *LinktoLCRsectors* lie at the 60th percentile or higher. *LinktoLCRsectors* is the share of output of each product sold as an intermediate input for other sectors with LCRs in each year, based on Indonesia's IO tables. We then take 2004–20 average of this variable and rank them for all products.	3,827	496
11	Low Link to LCR sectors	Products whose 2004–20 mean of *LinktoLCRsectors* lie at the 40th percentile or under.	3,874	176
12	High-tech products	Products that belong in High Tech group based on SITC Rev.3. Retrieved from WITS, and transformed to HS2012 by HS-to-SITC3 concordance available in WITS.	677	46

(*Continued*)

Table 7.A3 (Continued)

#	*Name of group*	*Definition*	*#HS Codes (8-digit)*	*#Products with LCRs*
13	Medium-tech products	Products that belong in Medium Tech group based on SITC Rev.3. Retrieved from WITS, and transformed to HS2012 by HS-to-SITC3 concordance available in WITS.	2,118	256

Source: Authors' compilation.

Table 7.A4 Dynamic Effects of LCRs on Exports of Capital Goods

	(1)	*(2)*	*(3)*	*(4)*
	Capital goods	*Capital goods: Non-machinery*	*Machinery and transport SITC*	*Capital goods non-transport BEC*
Export Volume				
0 Years after	0.441***	0.339	0.052	0.508**
	(0.104)	(0.282)	(0.228)	(0.250)
1 Year after	0.148	–0.276	–0.126	0.352
	(0.249)	(0.296)	(0.273)	(0.474)
2 Years after	0.378***	0.394	0.284	0.161
	(0.124)	(0.344)	(0.181)	(0.446)
3 Years after	0.612***	0.600***	0.600***	0.621
	(0.103)	(0.201)	(0.228)	(0.541)
4 Years after	0.519*	0.862*	0.700**	0.364
	(0.312)	(0.442)	(0.289)	(0.415)
5 Years after	0.403	1.115	0.230	–0.051
	(0.516)	(1.016)	(0.419)	(0.528)
Average Effects	0.493***	0.586*	0.314*	0.377
	(0.122)	(0.353)	(0.173)	(0.366)
Export Value				
0 Years after	0.229***	0.291**	–0.051	0.314
	(0.057)	(0.114)	(0.172)	(0.307)
1 Year after	–0.252**	–0.293	–0.418*	0.012
	(0.118)	(0.300)	(0.218)	(0.409)
2 Years after	0.003	0.130	0.041	–0.186
	(0.205)	(0.436)	(0.281)	(0.406)
3 Years after	0.149	0.259	0.213	0.045
	(0.211)	(0.488)	(0.379)	(0.435)
4 Years after	0.318	0.668	0.476	0.169
	(0.369)	(0.560)	(0.474)	(0.339)
5 Years after	0.110	0.983	0.244	–0.200
	(0.768)	(1.488)	(0.692)	(0.497)
Average Effects	0.108	0.368	0.062	0.053
	(0.264)	(0.536)	(0.296)	(0.300)
Number of products	2,381	634	2,290	1,086

	(1)	(2)	(3)	(4)
	Capital goods	*Capital goods: Non-machinery*	*Machinery and transport SITC*	*Capital goods non-transport BEC*
Effects on export volume JS at 5%	Yes	No	Yes	Yes
Effects on export value JS at 5%	Yes	No	No	No
Pre-trend significant at 5%	No	Yes	No	No

Source: Authors' calculation.

Notes: This table reports the DCDH22 estimators of the effects of being exposed to the first LCR up until 5 years after the LCR's starting implementation date under several definitions of capital goods. Detailed definitions of the product groups are available in Table 7.A3. The dependent variable is log of (Indonesia's exports (either volume in kg or value in USD) + 1). Inferring the magnitude of the effects requires taking exponential over the estimated coefficients in this table. Standard errors are estimated using 100 bootstrap replications clustered at the 2-digit HS code level and reported in parentheses. To check for pre-trends at a 5% significance level, the results from joint-significance tests of all placebo estimators up until 3 years before the LCR implementation are summarized in the last row of the table. Average Effects reports the estimated average total effects of the treatment, i.e., the average of all the instantaneous and dynamic LCR effects across treated products. The results of joint-significance tests, which verify whether the contemporaneous and all dynamic treatment effects are jointly different from zero statistically at a 5% significance level, are provided in the table. JS stands for Jointly Significant.

Table 7.A5 Static Effects of LCRs on Trade

	Import Volume	*Import Value*	*Export Volume*	*Export Value*
All products	–0.095	–0.062	–0.117	–0.141
	(0.129)	(0.150)	(0.115)	(0.088)
Manufacturing	–0.089	–0.025	–0.139	–0.159*
	(0.137)	(0.150)	(0.116)	(0.082)
Capital goods	–0.178	–0.189	0.441***	0.229***
	(0.281)	(0.304)	(0.104)	(0.057)
Consumer goods	0.000	0.194	–0.342	–0.280*
	(0.290)	(0.235)	(0.264)	(0.164)
Intermediate goods	0.030	0.071	0.168	–0.251
	(0.173)	(0.211)	(0.197)	(0.262)
Downstream goods	–0.074	–0.090	0.146	0.007
	(0.237)	(0.269)	(0.255)	(0.114)
High link to LCR sectors	–0.240	–0.254	–0.406***	–0.354***
	(0.192)	(0.219)	(0.138)	(0.093)

Source: Authors' calculation.

Notes: This table reports the coefficients β_e of the DCDH22 estimators, which represent the static effects of being exposed to the first LCR. The dependent variable is log of (Indonesia's trade flow (either imports or exports, and either in volume in kg or value in USD) + 1). Inferring the magnitude of the effects requires taking exponential over the estimated coefficients in this table. Standard errors are estimated using 100 bootstrap replications clustered at the 2-digit HS code level and reported in parentheses.

Table 7.A6 Dynamic Effects of Mandatory LCRs on Trade Volume

	Import		*Export*	
	Baseline DCDH22	*Exclude soft LCRs*	*Baseline DCDH22*	*Exclude soft LCRs*
Effects on Volume				
0 Years after	–0.095	–0.103	–0.117	–0.200
	(0.129)	(0.162)	(0.115)	(0.186)
1 Year after	0.272	–0.084	–0.235*	–0.398**
	(0.314)	(0.303)	(0.133)	(0.178)
2 Years after	0.063	–0.476*	–0.016	–0.101
	(0.321)	(0.289)	(0.158)	(0.233)
3 Years after	0.623*	0.003	–0.004	–0.072
	(0.371)	(0.421)	(0.206)	(0.322)
4 Years after	0.314*	0.152	0.197	0.184
	(0.189)	(0.370)	(0.217)	(0.340)
5 Years after	–0.431	–0.419	–0.122	–0.122
	(0.384)	(0.507)	(0.428)	(0.428)
Average Effects	0.193	–0.167	–0.057	–0.147
	(0.208)	(0.232)	(0.152)	(0.235)
Only mandatory LCRs included	No	Yes	No	Yes
Effects jointly significant at 5%	Yes	No	No	Yes
Pre-trend significant at 5%	No	No	No	No

Source: Authors' calculation.

Notes: This table reports the DCDH22 estimators of the effects of being exposed to the first LCR up until 5 years after the LCR's starting implementation date under several variations of LCR definition. Baseline reports the results when all LCRs are considered. Exclusion of soft LCRs means that only mandatory LCRs are considered. We exclude four non-mandatory LCRs from our dataset to set up this comparison. The dependent variable is log of (Indonesia's trade (either imports or exports, and either in volume in kg or value in USD) + 1). Inferring the magnitude of the effects requires taking exponential over the estimated coefficients in this table. Standard errors are estimated using 100 bootstrap replications clustered at the 2-digit HS code level and reported in parentheses. To check for pre-trends at a 5% significance level, the results from joint-significance tests of all placebo estimators up until 3 years before the LCR implementation are summarized in the last row of the table. Average Effects reports the estimated average total effects of the treatment, i.e., the average of all the instantaneous and dynamic LCR effects across treated products. The results of joint-significance tests, which verify whether the contemporaneous and all dynamic treatment effects are jointly different from zero statistically at a 5% significance level, are provided in the table.

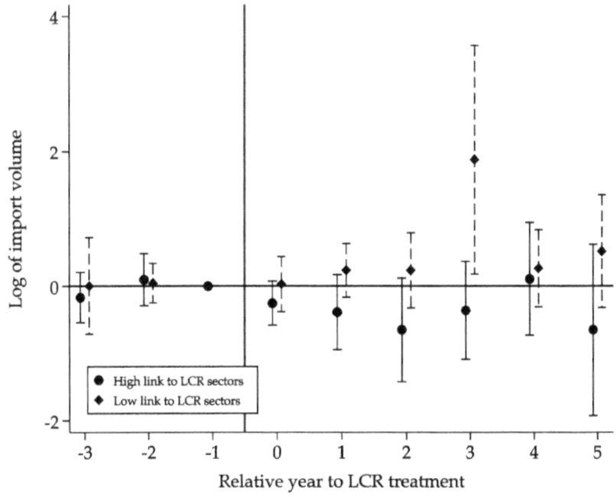

Figure 7.A1 Effects of LCRs on Import Volume, by Degree of Link to Other LCR Sectors

Source: Authors' estimation.

Notes: This figure presents the dynamic effects of being exposed to an LCR on log of import volume, based on separate DCDH22 estimations on the product group with a high link to LCR sectors (i.e., 2004–20 mean of *LinktoLCRsector* at the 60th percentile or above) and on the product group with a low link to other sectors with LCRs (i.e., 2004–20 mean of *LinktoLCRsector* at the 40th percentile or under). The reported specifications include control variables and 2-digit HS linear trends. Standard errors are estimated using 100 bootstrap replications clustered at 2-digit HS code level. 95% confidence intervals are displayed for each year.

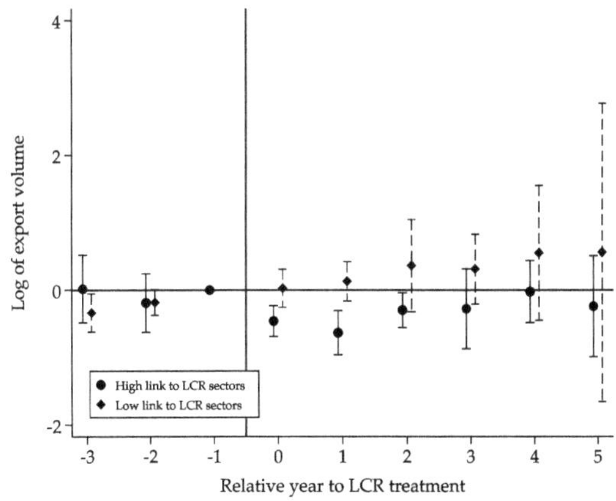

Figure 7.A2 Effects of LCRs on Export Volume, by Degree of Link to Other LCR Sectors

Source: Authors' estimation.

Notes: This figure presents the dynamic effects of being exposed to an LCR on log of export volume, based on separate DCDH22 estimations on the product group with a high link to LCR sectors (i.e., 2004–20 mean of *LinktoLCRsectors* at the 60th percentile or above) and on the product group with a low link to other sectors with LCRs (i.e., 2004–20 mean of *LinktoLCRsectors* at the 40th percentile or under). The reported specifications include control variables and 2-digit HS linear trends. Standard errors are estimated using 100 bootstrap replications clustered at 2-digit HS code level. 95% confidence intervals are displayed for each year.

Appendix Section 1

Construction of DCDH22 estimator

The difference-in-differences (DID) estimator developed by de Chaisemartin and D'Haultfœuille (2022a) provides an unbiased alternative to standard TWFE OLS estimation in cases where treatment timing varies and treatment effects are heterogeneous across groups or periods. It relies on three identifying assumptions: strong exogeneity and parallel trends for never-treated outcomes, sharp treatment design, and no anticipation effects. An important feature of our study is that the LCR policy treatment design is non-staggered.[13] In a recent survey, de Chaisemartin and D'Haultfœuille (2022b) argue that DCDH22 is the only currently available DID estimator that allows for dynamic effects and is applicable for binary, non-staggered treatment designs, such as the LCR policy.

The construction of the DCDH22 estimator specifically addresses the source of bias[14] in standard OLS TWFE estimators in cases where treatment effects are heterogeneous across groups. As explained by de Chaisemartin and D'Haultfœuille (2022a), in the case of non-staggered treatment design, the OLS TWFE estimators may utilize a *forbidden* comparison, i.e., comparing the outcome evolution of groups who were treated more and those who were treated less. Additionally, the presence of heterogeneous treatment effects and variation in treatment timing could give rise to negative weights for some individual groups, which may then render OLS TWFE estimators unable to identify convex combinations of treatment effects across groups or time. As a result, OLS TWFE estimators may fail to satisfy the no-sign reversal property. Such a failure may result in cases where treatment effects for all groups are positive, but the expectations of those regression coefficients are negative, making the estimated results misleading. DCDH22 estimator addresses this issue by leveraging both the never-treated product groups and the not-yet-treated product groups with the same initial treatment status as the treated groups to comprise valid control groups.

To produce the proposed DCDH22 estimator, we first need to record the year in which the treatment status of each treated product changes (i.e., from untreated to treated with an LCR) for the first time. We can then identify product groups g whose treatment status changed for the first time in year F_g. Recall that we are interested in capturing the dynamic effects of being exposed to an LCR up until e years after their implementation. Following de Chaisemartin and D'Haultfœuille (2022a and 2022b), consider the following two equations:

$$\delta_{g,e} = E\left(\Upsilon_{g,F_g+e} - \Upsilon_{g,F_g+e}\left(D_{g,1},\ldots,D_{g,1}\right)\right) \tag{2}$$

$$\beta_{g,e} = \Upsilon_{g,F_g+e} - \Upsilon_{g,F_g-1} - \left\{\frac{1}{N^{C}_{g,e}} \sum_{g':D_{g',1}=D_{g,1},F_{g'}>F_g+e} \left(\Upsilon_{g',F_g+e} - \Upsilon_{g',F_g-1}\right)\right\} \tag{3}$$

In (2), let $\delta_{g,e}$ denote the expected difference between the LCR-treated group g's actual trade outcome at year $F_g + e$ and the counterfactual trade outcome that would have prevailed had its treatment status remained unchanged from period 1 (i.e., year 2004) to year $F_g + e$. Moreover, $D_{g,t}$ represents the treatment status of product group g at time t. It is equal to 1 if the product is affected by LCR at time t and 0 if it is not affected by any LCRs at time t.

Moving on to (3), $\beta_{g,e}$ is the proposed DCDH22, which compares the $F_g - 1$-to-$F_g + e$ trade outcome evolution between group g (i.e., outside of curly bracket) and the control group g' whose treatment status has not changed yet at year $F_g + e$ but has the same treatment status with g at period 1 (year 2004) (i.e., inside of curly bracket). $N^C_{g,e}$ represents the number of control groups to compare the group g's outcome evolution e years after the treatment to.

Conditional on meeting the parallel trends assumption, de Chaisemartin and D'Haultfœuille (2022a) proved that $\beta_{g,e}$ is an unbiased estimator for $\delta_{g,e}$. The resulting coefficients, $\beta_{g,e}$, represent the estimated effects on trade outcome of having been exposed to an LCR for the first time e years ago for product group g. They can also be aggregated into an estimator of the effect of having been exposed to an LCR for $e + 1$ years. Another advantage of DCDH22 is that individual group effects $\beta_{g,e}$ (i.e., LCR effects on particular product groups) can be aggregated by weighted averaging procedure into the overall or total policy effects of LCRs, which represent the sum of both instantaneous and dynamic treatment effects. Estimation of DCDH22 can be implemented in Stata using the *did_multiplegt* command.

8 Quantifying the impacts of local content requirements

An analysis on Indonesia

Lili Yan Ing and Rui Zhang

1 Introduction

The fragmentation of the value chain across the globe increases the foreign content of goods produced in all countries. Policymakers have thus emphasized the importance of tracing how much local factors of production or locally produced inputs are used in the making of final goods and how effective the incentives provided to producers to encourage purchases from local suppliers are in promoting local production and employment. In various countries, we see the increasing use of local content requirements (LCRs) that require a minimum level of domestically produced inputs in the production or value added. Bilateral or regional free trade agreements or economic partnerships adopt LCRs (or regional content requirements) as well as RoOs (rules of origins) to prevent transshipment from non-member countries. Some host countries of foreign direct investment (FDI) also require a certain percentage of local factors of production and inputs to be used in producing final goods in order to boost the local economy through backward linkages. Thus, evaluating a commercial policy usually requires quantifying the impacts of LCR.

This chapter attempts to quantify the impacts of LCR on Indonesian manufacturing firms and sectors. We focus on a single regulation issued in May 2013 by the Ministry of Energy and Mineral Resources, whose primary goal is to promote the use of domestic content in upstream oil and gas business activities, protecting domestic sectors and employment from foreign competition. In 2012, the upstream oil and gas (OG henceforth) sector accounted for about 12% of Indonesia's value added, so it is an important sector of Indonesia's national economy. The LCR imposed by this regulation potentially affects all firms that supply inputs to the upstream OG sector in Indonesia, so it is of great policy interest to study the impacts of this regulation on the Indonesian economy.

We introduce LCR compliance decisions faced by manufacturing firms into the model developed by Blaum et al. (2018) and study the effects of the LCR on firms and sectors. Firms use both domestic content and foreign content in their production, and these inputs are assumed to be imperfect substitutes. An LCR specifies that at least a minimum percentage share (in value) of local

DOI: 10.4324/9781003415794-8

content should be used in local production. On the one hand, a failure to comply with the LCR results in an *ad valorem* non-compliance fee when a firm sells to the upstream OG sector. On the other hand, if the LCR is binding for the firm, compliance distorts the firm's sourcing decision and induces a cost penalty compared with the unit cost of unconstrained sourcing. An LCR-bound firm thus faces a trade-off between the non-compliance fee and the cost penalty due to compliance. The model allows firms to differ in their efficiency of using foreign content. Intuitively, if a firm is more dependent on foreign content, the cost penalty of compliance is higher, and the firm is less likely to comply. The model thus helps us to determine the cost penalty for each firm, given other firm characteristics.

The changes in costs and prices of compliers and non-compliers transmit to the sector-level price indexes, affecting the production costs of firms that find their LCR non-binding through the cross-sector input-output linkages. Following Dekle et al. (2007), we solve for the changes in firm-level unit costs, sales, employment, and sector-level price indexes in the equilibrium, so we can evaluate the impacts of the LCR imposition on the firm-level and sector-level outcomes.

We calibrate the initial equilibrium to the Indonesian economy prior to the LCR introduced in 2012. We then study the impacts of the LCR. Our findings are as follows. (1) Only 7% of manufacturing firms with low local content in the economy are constrained by the LCR. Among these LCR-bound firms, those that import relatively more are less likely to comply with the LCR. The compliers account for about 7% among the LCR-bound firms. (2) LCR does cause substantial responses and reallocation of firm-level sales to the OG sector. On average, the sales of compliers to the OG sector increase by 13%, and the sales of non-compliers to the OG sector decrease by 34% due to the non-compliance fees. (3) The changes in sales to non-OG sectors of different types of firms are between –0.5% and 0.1% and result in very small changes in firm-level sales and value added. Due to compliers' decisions to raise their local content, their employments, which constitute part of their local content, increase by 8% on average. At the national level, the effects on aggregate sales, value added, and employment are also small. (4) Although the LCR imposition causes the average local content of compliers to increase from 37% to 40%, it also raises costs of domestic inputs for all firms and leads to small declines in the local content of non-binding firms and non-compliers that are much more populous in the economy. The aggregate local content thus declines slightly from 83.96% to 83.95%, indicating a qualitatively unintended consequence of the LCR policy when domestic input costs are affected by the policy in general equilibrium, although the effect is quantitatively small in this case. (5) The price index increases for goods sold to the OG sector are much larger than the price index increases for goods sold to the non-OG sectors. As a result, domestic input costs and consumer prices increase by small amounts.

This chapter is closely related to the literature analyzing the implications of local and regional content requirements. Earlier theoretical investigations (e.g., Grossman, 1981; Krishna and Itoh, 1988; Ju and Krishna, 2005) suggest that the effects of LCR on domestic prices, resource allocations, and welfare hinge on specific assumptions, such as the form of the LCR, the market structure, and the degree of substitutions between inputs. Subsequent theoretical analyses also discuss the optimal LCR policy when such requirements apply to foreign investment firms in the domestic market (e.g., Lahiri and Ono, 1998; Qiu and Tao, 2001). Due to data limitations, empirical studies examining the effects of LCR, mostly those of RoOs, have only emerged in recent years. Conconi et al. (2018) shows that the RoOs of the North American Free Trade Agreement (NAFTA) cause the imports of intermediate inputs from non-NAFTA partner countries to Mexico to decline, a "trade diversion effect". Focusing on the NAFTA rules of origin on automobile parts, Yang (2021) shows that the trade diversion due to RoOs is non-linear in the restrictiveness of the rules, measured by the regional value content requirement. In the context of NAFTA and USMCA, Head et al. (2022) points out that as regional content requirement becomes stricter, intra-regional sourcing may eventually decline because more producers choose not to comply with the regional content requirement, generating a "Laffer curve" of regional content share. To complement the existing studies, we quantify the effects of Indonesia's LCR by accommodating firm-specific compliance decisions in an equilibrium model. Our quantitative results show that the effects of imposing the LCR are highly asymmetric across firms.

This chapter also connects to the literature on imported intermediate inputs, global sourcing, and firm-level production cost and efficiency. A number of empirical studies show that declining costs of imported intermediate goods due to trade liberalization lead to positive firm-level outcomes, such as increased productivity, new varieties, and export quality (see, for example, Amiti and Konings, 2007; Goldberg et al., 2010; Fan et al., 2015; De Loecker et al., 2016; Brandt et al., 2017). Our theoretical model follows Blaum et al. (2018) in treating domestic input and imported input made by the same sector as substitutes in a constant-elasticity-of-substitution (CES) production function. Using a similar way of modelling the role of imported intermediate inputs, Gopinath and Neiman (2014) and Antras et al. (2017) study the extensive margin of foreign sourcing in the product dimension and the country dimension. These studies mostly focus on the effects of foreign shocks common to domestic importing firms, such as tariff reductions, exchange rate movements, and foreign productivity shocks. We apply a similar framework to study a policy that is somewhat discriminatory across importing firms: For a given level of LCR, import-intensive firms suffer higher compliance costs and therefore are less likely to comply.

The rest of the chapter is structured as follows. Section 2 describes the regulation and LCR for Indonesia's upstream OG sector and reports data patterns. Section 3 introduces the LCR compliance decisions into a model of local and foreign sourcing. Section 4 describes how we calibrate the model. Section 5 reports and discusses the quantitative results. Section 6 concludes.

2 Indonesia's LCR for the upstream OG sector

Since 2010, Indonesia has used LCRs to regulate the local content of goods produced in Indonesia. The primary motivation for using LCR is to promote the purchase of domestic inputs and reduce the dependence on imported inputs, protecting domestic sectors and employment. In this chapter, we draw attention to one particular LCR introduced by the "Ministry of Energy and Mineral Resources (MEMR) Regulation No. 15 of 2013 concerning the Use of Domestic Products in Upstream Oil and Gas Business Activities" (referred to as the "MEMR regulation" henceforth). The MEMR regulation was designed to promote the use of domestic goods and services in Indonesia's upstream OG business activities. Upstream OG business activities are business activities focused or based on exploration and exploitation of oil and natural gas, and they account for a significant share of Indonesia's economy. In 2012, the upstream OG sector generates 8.3% of the gross output and 11.9% of the value added of Indonesia, whereas it only accounts for 4.5% of the intermediate input spending and 1% of the employment in the economy.[1]

As outlined in the MEMR regulation, the government of Indonesia requires every contractor, local producer, and supplier of goods and services involved in upstream OG operations to use domestic goods and services whenever possible. In addition, these parties are encouraged to maximize their use of domestic goods and services. In particular, it specifies the minimum percentages of local content that must be achieved in government procurement bidding by upstream OG contractors when they choose their suppliers of goods and services, and offers price preferences as rewards to firms that comply with the local content requirements or charges a non-compliance fee to firms that do not comply with the requirements.[2] Since the Indonesian government acts as the "owner" of the contract areas for exploration and exploitation of oil and natural gas resources, it appears reasonable to assume that firms not complying with the LCR suffer a price disadvantage when providing goods or service to the upstream OG business in Indonesia.

We focus on the impacts of the regulation on manufacturing firms. A manufacturing firm that may supply inputs to contractors in the upstream OG business activities is faced with a decision of whether to comply with the local content requirement. For example, drilling pipe is a necessary component to any drilling rig designed to extract oil from the ground, so it is an important input for the contractors in the upstream OG sector. A manufacturing firm producing drilling pipes may choose not to comply with the LCR if it heavily relies on imported inputs (e.g., imported steel) to produce drilling pipes. However, if the upstream OG sector is a major revenue source for this manufacturing firm, the firm may find complying with the LCR optimal because it cannot afford losing its competitiveness in such an important market.

A manufacturing firm may also lie about its compliance status to both avoid paying the non-compliance fee and escape the limits on the use of imported inputs. Such behavior, if discovered, results in an administrative sanction

Table 8.1 LCR Levels of Different Goods

	Target LCR level (%)		
Goods	*Short-term (2013–2016)*	*Medium-term (2017–2020)*	*Long-term (2021–2025)*
1. Drilling pipe			
a. High-grade	25	40	55
b. Low-grade	15	25	40
2. Distribution pipe (line pipe)			
a. Spiral/SAW	50	65	80
b. ERW	50	65	80
c. Seamless pipe	10	30	50
3. Drilling mud, cement and chemicals	40	55	70
4. Electrical submersible pump	15	25	35
5. Pumping unit	40	55	70
6. Machinery & equipment	20	30	40
7. Wellhead and X-mas tree			
a. Onshore	40	55	70
b. Offshore	15	30	40
8. Fuel oil (BBM)	60	75	95
9. Lubricant	50	60	70
10. Other goods	15	25	40

imposed by the Indonesian government. One of the most severe sanctions is a revocation of the Letter of Capability for Oil and Gas Supporting Business and a ban from supplying goods to the upstream oil and natural gas sector. Therefore, if the probability of getting caught is high, the manufacturing firm will not choose to lie about its compliance status.

What are the levels of LCR imposed by the MEMR regulation? Appendix I of the regulation provides the target levels of LCR applied to suppliers of different goods. Table 8.1 shows the target LCR levels. Suppliers of different goods are subject to different levels of LCR, and these goods are important inputs in the exploration and exploitation of OG resources. For example, as shown in the first row of Table 8.1, a producer of *high-grade drilling pipes* should demonstrate that at least 25% of its costs are of local content in order to receive a price preference or to avoid being charged a non-compliance fee of 15% as a supplier for contractors in the upstream OG business activities during the period of 2013–2016. The target LCR levels increase over time, revealing the motivation of the Indonesian government to promote increasing usage of domestic goods and labor.

2.1 Data and basic patterns

Since the MEMR regulation aims at promoting the use of local content, its effects hinge on how many manufacturing firms import inputs from abroad and how many of them may be constrained by the LCR. For this analysis, we use a micro-level data set of Indonesian manufacturing firms provided by Statistics Indonesia (BPS). The data set reports responses from an annual survey of large and medium-sized manufacturing firms, covering information on gross production output, number of workers, wages, capital stock, expenditure on domestic materials, and expenditure on foreign materials. The data set also provides information on production at the firm-product level.[3] We define 18 sectors in the economy, including agriculture, mining, service, and 15 manufacturing sectors.

We focus on the "long-term" LCR targets. To define the exact level of LCR faced by each manufacturing firm, we identify firms that produce goods listed in Table 8.1 (including "10. Other goods", for instance, motor vehicle) and match them to the corresponding LCR levels.[4] The majority of firms are classified into the "Other goods" category and are hence subject to a long-term LCR level of 40%.

A firm *i*'s local content λ_i is computed as

$$\lambda_i = \frac{c_{D,i} M_{D,i} + wL_i}{c_{F,i} M_{F,i} + c_{D,i} M_{D,i} + wL_i}, \tag{1}$$

where $c_{D,i}$ $M_{D,i}$, $c_{F,i}$ $M_{F,i}$ and wL_i are firm *i*'s expenditure on domestic materials, imported materials, and wage bill, respectively.

We first report some descriptive statistics to examine the stringency and the coverage of the LCR imposed by the MEMR regulation. Since the MEMR regulation went into effect in 2013, we focus on the firm-level information for 2012. The last row of Table 8.2 shows that among the 21, 078 manufacturing firms, the average local content is 91.3%, so an average manufacturing firm spends about 91% of its production costs on Indonesian-produced goods and Indonesian workers. Among these firms, only 21.5% are importers of inputs. We find that in 2012, only 6.7% of firms' local content is lower than their corresponding LCR.

Different sectors exhibit diverse behavior regarding their usages of local content. As shown in Table 8.2, firms operating in the sectors of "Coke & Refined Petroleum", "Chemicals & Medicine", "Basic Metals", "Electronic & Equipment", and "Other Transportation Equipment" import more and are more likely to be constrained by the LCR. These sectors are also more likely to supply inputs to the upstream OG sector. Therefore, we expect the LCR imposition to yield larger effects on firms operating in these sectors. On the other hand, sectors such as "Food & Beverages" and "Wood Products" have very high local content and are less likely to be suppliers of the upstream OG sector.

To further examine heterogeneity across sectors, we plot Table 8.2 Column 4 against Table 8.2 Column 2 in Figure 8.1. The downward-sloping relationship suggests that in sectors with lower average local content, more firms may be constrained by the LCR because the shares of firms relying on foreign inputs are larger.

Table 8.2 Firm-Level Local Content by Sector, 2012

	(1)	(2)	(3)	(4)
Manufacturing Sector	*No. of firms*	*Avg. local content (%)*	*Share of importers (%)*	*Local content < LCR (%)*
Food & Beverages	6,772	97.3	13.5	1.7
Textile & Apparel	3,910	90.3	21.2	6.7
Wood Products	1,015	97.3	16.1	1.6
Paper Products	447	89.8	22.1	7.8
Printing & Reproduction	461	96.6	18.9	1.3
Coke & Refined Petroleum	67	84.4	29.9	11.9
Chemicals & Medicine	1,053	75.4	46.0	20.7
Rubber & Plastic	1,553	88.7	26.4	8.0
Non-metallic Minerals	1,610	95.2	14.3	3.5
Basic Metals	241	75.3	47.3	23.7
Fabricated Metals	750	84.5	31.2	13.2
Electronic & Equipment	785	70.1	48.3	27.6
Motor Vehicles	267	77.5	40.4	18.7
Other Transportation Equipment	217	74.3	43.3	23.5
Other Manufacturing	1,930	93.3	19.1	4.9
All Firms	21,078	91.3	21.5	6.7

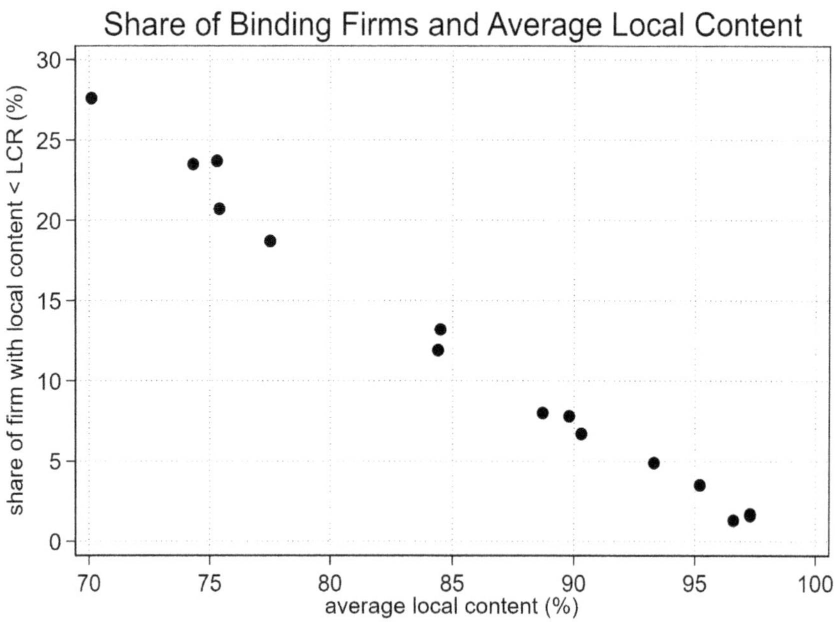

Figure 8.1 Share of Constrained Firms and Average Local Content

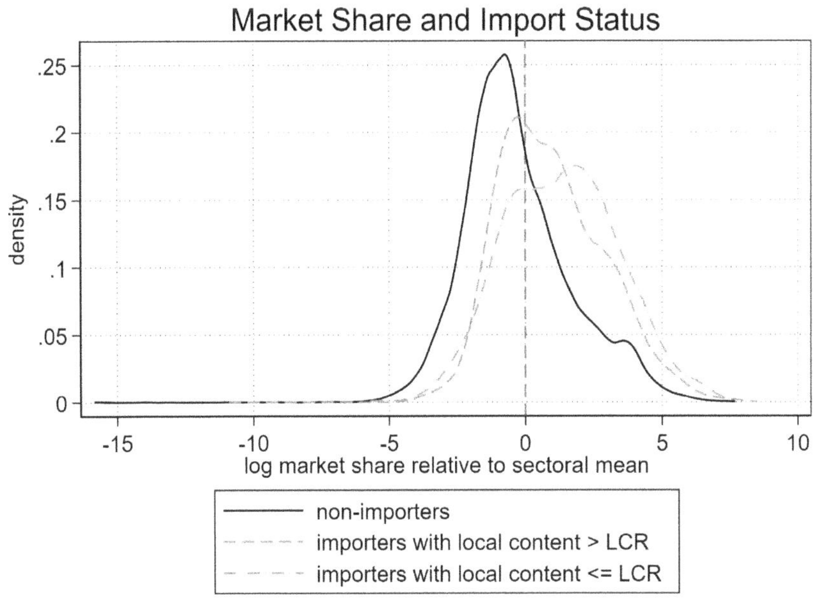

Figure 8.2 Market Share and Import Status

Empirical studies have found that firms that engage in international trade are usually larger firms. This is also true for Indonesian importers. Figure 8.2 plots the distributions of log market share (relative to the sectoral mean) for non-importers and importers. Clearly, importers have higher market shares than non-importers, consistent with the findings of the recent literature (e.g., Antras et al., 2017; Blaum et al., 2018). We also distinguish the distributions of importers with different levels of local content. The market shares of importers with local content lower than their LCR are slightly larger than those of other importers. It appears that firm size is negatively correlated with the likelihood of being constrained by the LCR.

We conclude this section by comparing the distributions of local content across firms before and after the LCR imposition. Figure 8.3 plots the distributions of local content in 2012 and 2014 for importing manufacturing firms. Comparing the two distributions, we notice that the probability density below 35% of 2014 is lower than that of 2012, while the probability density above 35% of 2014 is higher than that of 2012. This pattern seems to indicate that certain importers begin to comply with the LCR by increasing their local content, while there exists a large group of firms that choose not to comply with the regulation.

In sum, this section suggests that the impact of the LCR imposition may vary by sector. Certain sectors are more likely to be affected, because they host a large number of importing firms that rely heavily on imported inputs. It also shows that within a sector, larger manufacturing firms are more likely to be constrained by the LCR than smaller firms.

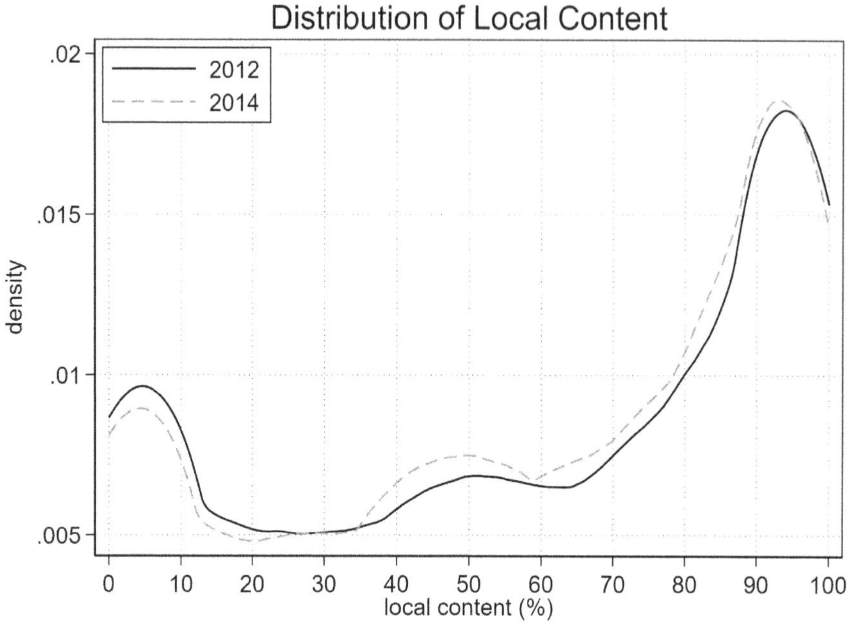

Figure 8.3 Distributions of Local Content for Importers

3 Model

In this section, we introduce the LCR compliance decision into a model with firm heterogeneity to describe the implications of the policy for Indonesian firms and for the economy. Following Antras et al. (2017) and Blaum et al. (2018), local content and foreign content are imperfect substitutes in a firm's production function. Local content consists of domestic inputs and labor, while foreign content only consists of imported inputs. The LCR specifies a threshold for the share of foreign content and introduces a cost penalty by distorting the firm's sourcing decision in the case of "binding compliance", under which the firm would have chosen a higher share of foreign content absent the LCR. A firm that complies with the LCR avoids paying an *ad valorem* non-compliance fee of 15% when supplying their goods to the upstream OG sector.

The cost changes of the LCR-bound firms transmit to the sector-level domestic price indexes and affect the input costs of other firms through the input-output linkages. We construct an equilibrium model to capture these features and use this model to evaluate the effects of the LCR imposition on firms and sectors.

3.1 Firm-level sourcing decision without LCR

We begin by describing firm-level sourcing decisions without LCR. We assume that a firm i combines local content $M_{D,i}$ and foreign content $M_{F,i}$ to produce output Y_i using a constant-elasticity-of-substitution (CES) aggregator,

$$Y_i = \varphi_i \cdot \left[\left(a_{D,i} \cdot M_{D,i} \right)^{\frac{\theta-1}{\theta}} + \left(a_{F,i} \cdot M_{F,i} \right)^{\frac{\theta-1}{\theta}} \right]^{\frac{\theta}{\theta-1}}, \tag{2}$$

where $\theta > 1$ is the elasticity of substitution between local content and foreign content for firms. The parameters $a_{D,i}$ and $a_{F,i}$ represent the efficiencies of firm i in using local content and foreign content, generating firm-specific domestic input share. The parameter φ_i is a Hicks-neutral productivity shifter that differs by firm. Denote the firm-specific costs of local content and foreign content as $c_{D,i}$ and $c_{F,i}$, the cost share of local content used by firm i is

$$\lambda_i = \frac{\left(c_{D,i} / a_{D,i} \right)^{1-\theta}}{\left(c_{D,i} / a_{D,i} \right)^{1-\theta} + \left(c_{F,i} / a_{F,i} \right)^{1-\theta}} = \frac{1}{1+\delta_i^{1-\theta}}, \quad \delta_i = \frac{c_{F,i} / a_{F,i}}{c_{D,i} / a_{D,i}}. \tag{3}$$

The parameter δ_i measures the firm-specific relative (efficiency-adjusted) cost of foreign content. An increase in international trade cost raises δ_i for all firms. The differences in δ_i across firms capture the fact that firms differ in their ability to source and use foreign content. Hence, without LCR, the unit cost of Y_i is

$$c_i = \frac{c_{D,i}}{\varphi_i a_{D,i}} \left(1 + \delta_i^{1-\theta} \right)^{\frac{1}{1-\theta}} = \frac{c_{D,i}}{\varphi_i a_{D,i}} \cdot \lambda_i^{\frac{1}{\theta-1}}. \tag{4}$$

The model is similar to that of Blaum et al. (2018). The main implication is that, conditional on the efficiency-adjusted cost of local content $c_{D,i}$ and productivity φ_i, the observed firm-level domestic input share λ_i is a sufficient statistic for the firm-level unit cost c_i. So given the cost of local content $c_{D,i}$, productivity φ_i, and the firm-level domestic input share λ_i, no additional information is needed in order to infer c_i.[5]

Furthermore, the local content $M_{D,i}$ is produced by local labor and composite domestic input. The production technology of $M_{D,i}$ is a CES aggregator given by

$$M_{D,i} = \left[\left(b_{L,i} \cdot L_i \right)^{\frac{\theta-1}{\theta}} + \left(Q_{D,i} \right)^{\frac{\theta-1}{\theta}} \right]^{\frac{\theta}{\theta-1}}, \tag{5}$$

where L_i is the amount of labor used and $Q_{D,i}$ is the amount of composite domestic input used by firm i. We describe the production of composite domestic input in Subsection 3.3. The parameter $b_{L,i}$ represents a firm-specific labor-augmented efficiency. For simplicity, we assume that the elasticity of substitution between labor and composite domestic input is also θ. Such a formulation indicates that a manufacturing firm is considering a "make or buy" decision when sourcing its local content. Meanwhile, we assume that the foreign content $M_{F,i}$ is only produced by the composite foreign input.

Using superscript k to denote the sector in which firm i operates, we have the following expressions for the costs of domestic and foreign content of firm i

$$c_{D,i}^{k} = \left[\left(P_D^k\right)^{1-\theta} + \left(w^k / b_{L,i}\right)^{1-\theta}\right]^{1/(1-\theta)} = P_D^k\left(\gamma_i\right)^{\frac{1}{\theta-1}},$$

$$c_{F,i}^{k} = P_F^k. \tag{6}$$

In the expressions above, P_D^k and P_F^k are the price indexes of composite domestic input and composite foreign input for firms in sector k. The variables w^k and γ_i denote the sector-specific wage and the cost share of composite domestic input in firm i's total cost of local content.

3.2 *The impacts of LCR on unit cost*

Next, we discuss how the LCR affects firm-level sourcing decisions and their unit costs. Suppose that a firm is subject to a LCR level of $\underline{\lambda}_i$, that is, it requires that at least $\underline{\lambda}_i$ share of firm i's content should be spent on local content to avoid being charged a non-compliance fee. If the LCR is binding for firm i (so $\lambda_i \leq \underline{\lambda}_i$) and the firm decides to comply with it, its sourcing decision is determined by

$$\frac{M_{D,i}}{M_{F,i}} = \frac{\underline{\lambda}_i}{1-\underline{\lambda}_i}\frac{c_{F,i}}{c_{D,i}}. \tag{7}$$

Such a sourcing decision implies the following unit cost of Υ_i,[6]

$$\kappa_i \cdot c_i, \tag{8}$$

where

$$\kappa_i = \left[\underline{\lambda}_i\left(\frac{\lambda_i}{\underline{\lambda}_i}\right)^{\frac{1}{\theta}} + \left(1-\underline{\lambda}_i\right)\left(\frac{1-\lambda_i}{1-\underline{\lambda}_i}\right)^{\frac{1}{\theta}}\right]^{\frac{\theta}{1-\theta}}, \quad \lambda_i \leq \underline{\lambda}_i. \tag{9}$$

When firm i complies with the binding LCR, its foreign sourcing decision is distorted. Hence, it is subject to a cost penalty κ_i if its "unconstrained" local content λ_i is lower than the one required by the LCR. It can be shown that

$\kappa_i \geq 1$ and that $\kappa_i = 1$ if and only if $\lambda_i = \underline{\lambda}_i$, namely, when the unconstrained local content coincides with the required LCR level.[7]

If $\lambda_i > \underline{\lambda}_i$, the LCR is non-binding for firm i and would not affect its sourcing decision, so its unit cost continues to be equal to c_i. On the other hand, if $\lambda_i \leq \underline{\lambda}_i$ and the firm chooses not to comply with the LCR, its unit cost remains equal to c_i. However, it is subject to an ***ad valorem*** non-compliance fee when selling to the upstream OG sector, specified in the later discussion.

Therefore, when an LCR is present, firm i's unit cost C_i is

$$C_i = \begin{cases} c_i, & i \in \Omega_{\mathrm{NB}} \cup \Omega_{\mathrm{NC}}, \\ \kappa_i \cdot c_i, & i \in \Omega_{\mathrm{C}}, \end{cases} \tag{10}$$

where Ω_{NB} is the set of firms that find the LCR to be non-binding, Ω_{NC} is the set of firms that choose not to comply with the LCR, and Ω_{C} is the set of firms that choose to comply with a binding LCR.

3.3 *Demand and firm size*

We next discuss the demand faced by firm i in the economy. We use superscripts to denote sectors. To model the demand faced by firm i in sector s from another sector k, we assume that in each sector k, there exist perfectly competitive producers of a composite domestic input. These composite domestic input producers first purchase outputs supplied by firms in sector s and combine these outputs to produce $Q_D^{k,s}$, a composite domestic input produced using sector-s outputs. The production technology of $Q_D^{k,s}$ is a CES aggregator given by

$$Q_D^{k,s} = \left[\sum_{i \in \Omega^s} \left(z^{k,s} \cdot q_i^{k,s} \right)^{\frac{\sigma^s - 1}{\sigma^s}} \right]^{\frac{\sigma^s}{\sigma^s - 1}}, \sigma^s > 1 \tag{11}$$

The variable $q_i^{k,s}$ refers to the quantity of goods produced by firm i in sector s and purchased by sector k, while the variable $z^{k,s}$ refers to the attractiveness or quality of that variety perceived by sector k.[8] The set Ω^s is the set of active varieties/firms in sector s.[9]

The composite domestic input producers of sector k further combine $Q_D^{k,s}$ across s to generate a composite domestic input Q_D^k for firms in sector k using the following Cobb-Douglas production function,

$$Q_D^k = \prod_s \left(Q_D^{k,s} \right)^{\beta_D^{k,s}}, \tag{12}$$

where $\beta_D^{k,s}$ is the cost share of outputs produced by sector s in sector k's total domestic input expenditure. We assume $\Sigma_s \beta_D^{k,s} = 1$.

The demand for firm *i*'s output by composite domestic input producers of sector *k* is

$$q_i^{k,s} = \left(p_i^s\right)^{-\sigma^s} \left(z^{k,s}\right)^{\sigma^s - 1} \left(P_D^{k,s}\right)^{\sigma^s - 1} X^{k,s}, \tag{13}$$

where $X^{k,s}$ is sector *k*'s total input expenditure spent on goods produced by sector *s*. The price index of $Q_D^{k,s}$ is

$$P_D^{k,s} = \left[\int_{i \in \Omega^s} \left(p_i^s / z^{k,s}\right)^{1-\sigma^s}\right]^{1/\left(1-\sigma^s\right)}. \tag{14}$$

The price index of the composite domestic input for firms in sector *k*, Q_D^k, is

$$P_D^k = \prod_s \left(\frac{P_D^{k,s}}{\beta_D^{k,s}}\right)^{\beta_D^{k,s}}. \tag{15}$$

Similarly, in each sector *k* also exist perfectly competitive producers of composite foreign input. We denote the price index of composite foreign input for firms in sector *k* as P_F^k. We assume that P_F^k is not affected by the LCR.

Firm *i* is a monopolistic competitor. Therefore, firm *i*'s price p_i^s, sales $Y_i^{k,s}$, and profit $\pi_i^{k,s}$ generated by selling to sector *k* are as follows,[10]

$$p_i^s = \frac{\sigma^s}{\sigma^s - 1} C_i,$$

$$Y_i^{k,s} = \left(\frac{\sigma^s}{\sigma^s - 1}\right)^{1-\sigma^s} \left(\frac{C_i}{z^{k,s}}\right)^{1-\sigma^s} \left(P_D^{k,s}\right)^{\sigma^s - 1} X^{k,s},$$

$$\pi_i^{k,s} = \frac{Y_i^{k,s}}{\sigma^s}. \tag{16}$$

Besides selling goods to different domestic sectors, a manufacturing firm also sells its goods to domestic final consumers. We assume that the final consumption demand is also CES,

$$q_i^{F,s} = \left(p_i^s\right)^{-\sigma^s} \left(z^{F,s}\right)^{\sigma^s - 1} \left(P^{F,s}\right)^{\sigma^s - 1} X^{F,s}, \tag{17}$$

where the superscript *F* stands for final demand. The price index is

$$P_D^{F,s} \equiv \left[\int_{i \in \Omega^s} \left(p_i^s / z^{F,s}\right)^{1-\sigma^s}\right]^{1/\left(1-\sigma^s\right)} + \left[\int_{i \in \Omega^{s*}} \left(p_i^s / z^{F,s}\right)^{1-\sigma^s}\right]^{1/\left(1-\sigma^s\right)}, \tag{18}$$

where Ω^{s*} is the set of foreign manufacturing firms in sector *s* that serve Indonesian consumers.

3.4 *Compliance decision*

A manufacturing firm that chooses not to comply with the LCR is subject to a noncompliance fee, which is an *ad valorem* fee charged by the government in the procurement process of the upstream OG sector. In particular, if a firm i does not comply with the LCR, its price is inflated by a factor of $\tau > 1$ when selling to the upstream OG sector.

$$p_i^{k,s} = \begin{cases} \dfrac{\sigma^s}{\sigma^s - 1}\tau C_i, & \text{if } s = \text{OG}, \\ \dfrac{\sigma^s}{\sigma^s - 1} C_i, & \text{if } s \neq \text{OG} \end{cases} \tag{19}$$

The potential firm-level profit, in the event of non-compliance, would be

$$\pi_{\text{NC},i}^{\text{S}} = \left(c_i\right)^{1-\sigma^s} \left[\Gamma^{\text{OG},s} \left(z^{\text{OG},s}\right)^{\sigma^s - 1} \tau^{1-\sigma^s} + \sum_{k \neq \text{OG}} \Gamma^{k,s} \left(z^{k,s}\right)^{\sigma^s - 1} \right], \tag{20}$$

where the constant $\Gamma^{k,s} = \dfrac{(\sigma^s - 1)^{\sigma^s - 1}}{(\sigma^s)^{\sigma^s}} \left(P_D^{k,s}\right)^{\sigma^s - 1} X^{k,s}$ collects several sector-specific constants and variables.

If firm i chooses to comply with the LCR, it avoids paying the non-compliance fee of selling to the upstream OG sector but incurs a cost penalty κ_i. In this event, its firm-level profit would be

$$\pi_{\text{C},i}^{\text{S}} = \left(\kappa_i c_i\right)^{1-\sigma^s} \left[\sum_k \Gamma^{k,s} \left(z^{k,s}\right)^{\sigma^s - 1} \right]. \tag{21}$$

A firm complies with the LCR if and only if

$$\pi_{\text{C},i}^{\text{S}} > \pi_{\text{NC},i}^{\text{S}} \Leftrightarrow S^{\text{OG},s} > \frac{1 - \kappa_i^{1-\sigma^s}}{1 - \tau^{1-\sigma^s}}, \tag{22}$$

where

$$S^{\text{OG},s} = \frac{\Gamma^{\text{OG},s} \left(z^{\text{OG},s}\right)^{\sigma^s - 1}}{\sum_k \Gamma^{k,s} \left(z^{k,s}\right)^{\sigma^s - 1}}$$

is the firm's share of sales generated by sales to the upstream OG sector and measures the importance of the upstream OG sector as a market for firm i that operates in sector s. Note that $S^{OG,s}$ does not differ by i because we assume that $z^{k,s}$ does not vary by i.

Inspecting (22), we find that the likelihood of compliance is increasing in $S^{OG,s}$ and τ: A larger size of the upstream OG sector as a market and a higher non-compliance fee both induce a stronger incentive to comply. Meanwhile, a higher compliance cost penalty κ_i due to strong dependence on foreign content reduces willingness to comply.[11] For any given values of $S^{OG,s}$ and τ, there exists a cutoff $\tilde{\lambda}_i$ such that for firms with unconstrained local content λ_i lower than the cutoff value $\tilde{\lambda}_i$, non-compliance dominates compliance.[12]

For a firm with its unconstrained local content higher than the LCR level $\underline{\lambda}_i$, the LCR is not binding and hence does not distort its sourcing decisions. Its profit is simply

$$\pi^s_{NB,i} = \left(c_i\right)^{1-\sigma^s} \left[\sum_k \Gamma^{k,s} \left(z^{k,s}\right)^{\sigma^s - 1} \right]. \tag{23}$$

Firm i's compliance decision and the associated profit is determined by

$$\pi^s_i = \begin{cases} \pi^s_{C,i'}, & \lambda_i < \underline{\lambda}_i \text{ and } S^{OG,s} > \dfrac{1-\kappa_i^{1-\sigma^s}}{1-\tau^{1-\sigma^s}} \\ \pi^s_{NC,i'} & \lambda_i < \underline{\lambda}_i \text{ and } S^{OG,s} \leq \dfrac{1-\kappa_i^{1-\sigma^s}}{1-\tau^{1-\sigma^s}} \\ \pi^s_{NB,i}, & \lambda_i \geq \underline{\lambda}_i. \end{cases} \tag{24}$$

3.5 *Equilibrium*

We are now ready to describe the equilibrium and compare the equilibria without and with the LCR. We denote a variable in the initial equilibrium without LCR as x, and its counterpart in the equilibrium with LCR as x'. Following Dekle et al. (2007), we denote the relative change of a variable as $\hat{x} = x'/x$. We assume that firms can hire labor without any frictions at a given sector-specific wage rate w^s as in Blaum et al. (2018).

In the equilibrium, the price index of $Q_D^{k,s}$, the composite domestic input produced by sector k using sector-s outputs, depends on individual prices of all firms in sector s. The LCR raises the prices of compliers by distorting their foreign sourcing decisions and the prices of non-compliers due to the non-compliance fee. The prices of composite domestic inputs also affect the sourcing and compliance decisions of all firms. The goods market clearing condition suggests that demands for outputs produced by each sector consist of intermediate input demands from other sectors and the final consumption demand.

Proposition 1 defines the two equilibria without and with the LCR. See Appendix A.1 for a detailed description of the two equilibria.

Proposition 1 (Equilibria without and with LCR). *Given exogenous variables* φ_i, $z^{k,s}$, $a^k_{D,i}$, $a^k_{F,i}$, $b_{L,i}$, P^k_F, w^k, $\beta^{k,s}_D$, $X^{F,k}$, *and* $\underline{\lambda}_i$, *and parameter* θ *and* σ^s, *the equilibrium without LCR is a vector of price indexes* $\{P^{k,s}_D\}$ *that satisfies equations (A1) and (A4) for all k and s. The equilibrium with LCR is a vector of price indexes* $\{P^{k,s'}_D\}$ *that satisfies equation (A2), (A3), and (A5) for all k and s.*

Proposition 2 formulates the equilibrium in relative changes and investigates the impacts of the LCR when other exogenous variables (e.g., φ_i, $a^k_{D,i}$, and $a^k_{F,i}$) are fixed. See Appendix A.2 for a detailed description of the equilibrium in relative changes.

Proposition 2 (Equilibrium in relative changes). *Given endogenous variables* $\{\lambda_i, \gamma_i, \Upsilon^{k,s}_i, X^{k,s}\}$, *exogenous variables* $\{X^{F,s}\}$, *policy variables* $\{\tau, \underline{\lambda}_i\}$, *and parameters* $\{\theta, \sigma^s, \beta^{k,s}_D\}$, *a relative change of the equilibrium caused by the LCR is a vector of price index changes* $\hat{P}^{k,s}_D$ *that satisfies (A3), (A6), (A7), (A8), (A9), (A10), (A11), and (A12).*

According to Proposition 2, once we calibrate and obtain the values of $\{\lambda_i, \gamma_i, \Upsilon^{k,s}_i, X^{k,s}\}$, $\{X^{F,s}\}$, $\{\tau, \underline{\lambda}_i\}$, and $\{\theta, \sigma^s, \beta^{k,s}_D\}$, we can evaluate the effects of imposing the MEMR LCR on firms and the economy.

4 Calibration

We calibrate the model to the Indonesian economy before the imposition of MEMR LCR regulation, the year 2012. We use two main data sources. The first data source is the Indonesian manufacturing firm survey data provided by the BPS, which is already described in the previous "2.1 Data and Basic Patterns" section. The second data source is the World Input-Output Table (WIOT), which we use to obtain the input-output coefficients and calibrate the basic features of non-manufacturing sectors. Since the upstream OG business sector mainly conducts exploration and exploitation of OG resources, it matches well with the "mining sector" in the WIOT classification. So we use the "mining sector" in the WIOT classification to define the OG sector.

4.1 Local content and domestic input share

The calculation of firm-level local content λ_i and LCR level $\underline{\lambda}_i$ for manufacturing firms has been discussed in Section 2.1. However, since the BPS firm survey data only covers the manufacturing sector, we still need information for non-manufacturing sectors in the economy, including the agriculture sector, the OG (mining) sector, and the service sector. Because we do not have firm-level information for these three sectors, we assume that firms in these sectors are identical. The levels of local content in the agriculture, OG, and service sectors in Indonesia are calibrated using the WIOT information.

For manufacturing firms, the calculation of γ_i follows (1). Similarly, we use the information in WIOT to calibrate γ_i for the agriculture, OG, and service sectors in Indonesia.

4.2 *Sales to different sectors*

By definition, $Y_i^{k,s}$ is firm *i*'s value of sales to sector *k*. The superscript *s* denotes the sector in which firm *i* operates. Because our model assumption indicates that the share of sales generated by sales to sector *k*, $S^{k,s}$, is the same across all firms in sector *s*, we can calculate $S^{k,s}$ for each $\{k, s\}$ pair using the information from the WIOT data and impute firm *i*'s sales to sector *k* (including sales to final consumers) as follows:

$$Y_i^{k,s} = S^{k,s} \times Y_i, \tag{25}$$

where Y_i is firm *i*'s total sales. This imputation also indicates that the market share of firm *i* in sector *k*'s total input purchase from sector *s* is independent of *k*, that is, $m_i^{k,s} = m_i^s$.

Our theoretical analysis suggests that the share of sales generated by sales to the OG sector, $S^{OG,s}$, is critical for the firm-level compliance decisions. Table 8.3 shows the values of $S^{OG,s}$ for different supplying sector *s*. A larger

Table 8.3 Share of Sales to Upstream OG Sector

Selling sector	*Share of sales to OG (%)*
Agriculture	0.01
Oil & Gas	17.23
Food & Beverages	0.09
Textile & Apparel	0.14
Wood Products	0.03
Paper Products	1.04
Printing & Reproduction	0.39
Coke & Refined Petroleum	2.96
Chemicals & Medicine	2.65
Rubber & Plastic	0.08
Non-metallic Minerals	0.00
Basic Metals	0.10
Fabricated Metals	0.09
Electronic & Equipment	3.56
Motor Vehicles	1.04
Other Transportation Equipment	0.18
Other Manufacturing	1.77
Service	4.05

value of $S^{OG,s}$ indicates that sales to the OG sector constitute a major revenue source for sector *s*, so other things being equal, firms in sector *s* are (on average) more likely to comply with the LCR. We notice that sales to the upstream OG generally account for a small share of the total sales for a sector *s*, except for the OG sector itself (17.23%). This should not be surprising given that only 4.5% of the intermediate input spending in Indonesia occurs in the OG sector. In other words, the OG sector does not appear to be a major revenue source for other sectors in the economy. The small values of $S^{OG,s}$ indicate that manufacturing firms may find it generally unattractive to distort their sourcing decisions merely to increase their sales to the OG sector, and those that do so may already be quite close to the required LCR levels so their compliance costs are small.

4.3 *Production-function parameters*

We use the following formula to calibrate the elasticity of substitution σ^s for sector *s*:

$$\frac{\sum_{i\in\Omega^s} Y_i}{\sum_{i\in\Omega^s}\left(c_{D,i}M_{D,i}+c_{F,i}M_{F,i}+wL_i\right)}=\frac{\sigma^s}{\sigma^s-1},$$

where Y_i is the total sales of firm *i*, and $c_{D,i}\,M_{D,i} + c_{F,i}\,M_{F,i} + wL_i$ is the production cost paid by firm *i*. Table 8.4 shows the calibrated value of σ^s by sector. A higher profit margin would thus translate to a lower value of σ^s.

Table 8.4 Calibrated Value of σ^s

Sector	σ^s
Agriculture	2.40
Oil & Gas	1.64
Food & Beverages	4.40
Textile & Apparel	3.73
Wood Products	3.46
Paper Products	4.57
Printing & Reproduction	5.55
Coke & Refined Petroleum	3.13
Chemicals & Medicine	5.12
Rubber & Plastic	7.34
Non-metallic Minerals	4.66
Basic Metals	5.04
Fabricated Metals	4.52
Electronic & Equipment	5.68
Motor Vehicles	3.39
Other Transportation Equipment	4.21
Other Manufacturing	4.24
Service	4.80

To calibrate the input-output coefficients $\beta_D^{k,s}$, we use the information from the WIOT data to compute the cost share of domestic input produced by sector s in sector k's total domestic input expenditure. For the elasticity of substitution between local content and foreign content in the production function, we assign $\theta = 2.38$, a preferred estimate obtained by Blaum et al. (2018) using French firm-level data. The calibrated value suggests that local labor, composite domestic input, and composite foreign input are substitutes. The non-compliance fee $\tau - 1$ is 0.15, consistent with the MEMR regulation.

4.4 *Aggregate domestic input expenditure*

Finally, we need to calibrate the aggregate domestic input expenditure $X^{k,s}$, which is defined by the system of equations (A4) in the initial equilibrium before the LCR imposition. For a given purchasing sector k, $X^{k,s}/X^{k,s'} = \beta_D^{k,s}/\beta_D^{k,s'}$, so the calibration of $X^{k,s}$ boils down to finding a vector of E^k such that $X^{k,s} = \beta_D^{k,s} \times E^k$ is consistent with (A4).

To calibrate $X^{k,s}$, we first compute $X^{F,s}$, the final consumption expenditure on goods produced by sector s in Indonesia, using the WIOT data. Holding the final consumption demand $X^{F,s}$ constant, we then solve the system of equations (A4) for $X^{k,s}$.

5 Quantitative results

In this section, we discuss the quantitative results of the LCR policy. With our calibration strategy, the model matches exactly the data in the year 2012, the initial equilibrium without the MEMR LCR. We use the quantitative model to perform a model-based evaluation of the effects of imposing the long-term LCR targets, so we introduce the LCR into the initial equilibrium and hold fixed other exogenous variables, such as firm productivity, firm-specific cost of foreign content, and foreign input price index. Therefore, the results reported in this section should be interpreted as reflecting the pure effects of the LCR policy when other exogenous components in the model are not changed.

Since the goals of the policy are to promote usage of domestic content and to protect domestic sectors and employment, we report the compliance statuses of different manufacturing firms and their characteristics, the effects of the LCR on sales, value added, and employment, and the resulting changes in firm-level and aggregate local content. Finally, we quantify the effects of the LCR on domestic composite input costs and consumers' welfare.

5.1 *Firm-level compliance decisions*

There are three groups of firms after the LCR imposition: (1) the non-binding firms that find the LCR constraint to be non-binding, (2) the compliers that find the LCR constraint binding and decide to comply with the regulation, and (3) the non-compliers that also find the LCR constraint binding but decide not to comply with the regulation. Table 8.5 shows the number of firms falling into each category. The last row of Table 8.5 shows that over 93% of manufacturing firms find the LCR to be non-binding. For the remaining 7% that find the LCR to be binding, only about 7% of them choose to comply with the LCR. We also find that the shares of firms falling into different compliance statuses vary by sector. A very tiny fraction of firms in the sectors of "Food & Beverage", "Wood Products", and "Printing & Reproduction" find the LCR binding because sales to the upstream OG sector only account for a very small fraction of their total sales. The LCR is more binding for firms in the sectors of "Coke & Refined Petroleum", "Chemicals & Medicine", "Basic Metals", "Fabricated Metals", "Electronic & Equipment", "Motor Vehicles", and "Other Transportation Equipment", where more firms exhibit stronger dependence on foreign inputs and lower local content. Finally, while the vast majority of the firms constrained by LCR choose not to comply, in the "Chemicals & Medicine" and "Electronic & Equipment" sectors, 13% of the LCR-bound firms comply with the regulation. As shown in Table 8.3, these are two manufacturing sectors that generate relatively larger fractions of their revenues from sales to the upstream OG sector (2.56% and 3.56%, respectively).

What are the characteristics of the firms constrained by the LCR? We examine this question by comparing the characteristics of firms with different compliance statuses, as shown in Table 8.6. First, we notice that compliers and non-compliers are, on average, much larger than non-binding firms. While the average market share (defined as firm-level sales divided by the sales of all firms

Table 8.5 Firm-Level Compliance Decisions

Sector	*Number of:*		
	Non-binding firms	*Compliers*	*Non-compliers*
Food & Beverages	6,655	6	111
Textile & Apparel	3,648	7	255
Wood Products	999	0	16
Paper Products	412	0	35
Printing & Reproduction	455	0	6
Coke & Refined Petroleum	59	0	8
Chemicals & Medicine	835	28	190
Rubber & Plastic	1,427	1	125
Non-metallic Minerals	1,553	0	57
Basic Metals	184	0	57
Fabricated Metals	651	6	93
Electronic & Equipment	567	29	189
Motor Vehicles	217	4	46
Other Transportation Equipment	166	2	49
Other Manufacturing	1,835	12	83
All	19,663	95	1,320

in the same sector) of compliers and noncompliers before the LCR imposition are 0.27% to 0.28%, the average market share of nonbinding firms before the LCR imposition is only 0.07%. Moreover, LCR-bound firms use imported inputs more intensively than non-binding firms. As shown in the second row of Table 8.6, the average local content (domestic input and labor cost divided by total input and labor cost) of non-binding firms before the LCR imposition is 96.9%, while the average local content of compliers and non-compliers before the LCR imposition are 37.1% and 11.9%, respectively. So LCR-bound firms are larger and import much more than non-binding firms to begin with, and non-compliers rely on foreign inputs more than compliers. Intuitively, firms better at using imported inputs are affected by the LCR more than firms that barely use imported inputs. Among these firms, those that import relatively less find it easier to comply with the regulation.

The imposition of the LCR affects all firms by raising their domestic input costs. The third row of Table 8.6 shows the average change in unit cost, $\hat{C}_i$, without taking into account either the cost penalties due to distorted sourcing decisions or the non-compliance fees. The effects are quite small. On average, the unit costs of non-binding firms increase by 0.07%, while the unit costs of compliers and non-compliers increase by 0.04% and 0.01%, respectively. Non-binding firms suffer relatively more from the rising domestic input costs because most of their inputs are sourced domestically.

The last row of Table 8.6 shows the average cost penalties, κ_i, for different types of firms were they choose to comply with the LCR, i.e., the cost of compliance. A value of $\kappa = 1$ indicates no cost penalty. Since the non-binding firms can comply with the LCR without changing their foreign sourcing decisions, their cost penalties are by definition equal to 1. We find that the average cost penalty of compliers is also extremely close to 1,[13] indicating that their "unconstrained" local content is only slightly lower than the one required by the LCR. In fact, the average local content of compliers before the LCR imposition is 37.1%, very close to the level of LCR faced by most firms (40%). In this case, it makes sense for these firms to slightly distort their sourcing decisions just to avoid the non-compliance fee of selling to the upstream OG sector. For non-compliers, the cost penalty of distorting their sourcing decisions to meet

Table 8.6 Firm Characteristics by Compliance Status

Firm type:	*Compliers*	*Non-binding firms*	*Non-compliers*
Before LCR imposition:			
Average market share per firm (%)	0.27	0.07	0.28
Average local content (%)	37.1	96.9	11.9
After LCR imposition:			
Average change in unit cost (%)	0.04	0.07	0.01
Average cost penalty κ	1.00	1	1.24

the LCR is substantial. The average κ for non-compliers is 1.24, meaning that on average, complying with the LCR would inflate these firms' unit cost by about 24% and seriously undermine their cost competitiveness. Notice that the average local content of the non-compliers before the LCR imposition is only 11.9%, so the cost to comply for these firms is significant, inducing them to give up compliance.

To summarize, we find that larger firms that use imported inputs more intensively are more likely to be constrained by the LCR. Among these LCR-bound firms, those that import relatively more are less likely to comply with the LCR.

5.2 *The impacts on sales, value added, and employment*

We examine the impacts of the MEMR LCR on firm-level and aggregate outcomes. A failure to comply with the LCR results in a firm being charged a non-compliance fee of 15% when selling to the upstream OG sector, so we first examine sales to the non-OG sector and the OG sector separately. Table 8.7 shows the results. Sales to non-OG sector are almost not affected by the LCR, as the average changes in sales to the non-OG sector are –0.5%, –0.2%, and 0.1% for compliers, non-binding firms and non-compliers, respectively.

Significant changes and reallocation appear in the sales to the OG sector. First, as shown in the third row of Table 8.7, non-compliers suffer an average decline of their sales to the OG sector of 34.0%, caused by the non-compliance fee. Second, both compliers and non-binding firms increase their market shares in the OG sector after the LCR imposition. On average, compliers and non-binding firms experience an increase of their sales to the OG sector by 13.3% and 5.8%, respectively. The last row of Table 8.7 shows the changes in total sales of each firm type. The total sales to the OG sector of non-compliers decrease by 24.3%, while the total sales to the OG sector of compliers increase by 14.6%. So the LCR does cause substantial responses of sales to the OG sector.

Next, we examine the change of firm-level sales, value added, and employment for different firm types. Firm-level sales sum up a firm's sales to the non-OG and the OG sectors. The upper panel of Table 8.8 shows the results.

Table 8.7 Changes in Sales to Different Sectors

Firm type:	*Compliers*	*Non-binding firms*	*Non-compliers*
		To non-OG sector:	
Average change in sales (%)	−0.5	−0.2	0.1
Change in total sales (%)	−0.2	−0.3	0.1
		To OG sector:	
Average change in sales (%)	13.3	5.8	−34.0
Change in total sales (%)	14.6	0.1	−24.3

The average change in firm-level sales for all types of firms is about –0.2%. Likewise, the average changes in firm-level value added are also small, ranging from –0.2% to 0.1%. Such small effects can be explained by the fact that on average, sales to the OG sector only account for a small fraction of a typical manufacturing firm's total sales (see Table 8.3). Turning to the employment effects, we find that the average change in firm-level employment of compliers is 8%. Such an increase is due to compliers' increases in their local content, which include the labor they hire, to the LCR levels. In contrast, non-binding firms and non-compliers see very limited average changes in their employments. We observe similar patterns when aggregating sales, value added, and employment for different firm types: Only the total employment of compliers exhibits a significant increase due to the compliance decisions, while other variables experience very small changes.

The lower panel of Table 8.8 shows that the LCR imposition leads to declines in total sales, total value added, and total employment in the whole economy by 0.2%, 0.2%, and 0.1%, respectively. The aggregate effects are hence small. The effects on the OG sector are slightly more significant, causing its total OG sales and value added to decrease by 0.5% and 0.4% and its total employment to increase by 0.1%.

An important motivation to impose LCR is to increase the usage of local content. So we also examine the changes in average and aggregate local content. The results are shown in Table 8.9. For comparison, we report the local content levels both before and after the LCR imposition ("without LCR" and "with LCR"). Columns 1 and 2 are average local content of different firm types. On average, the LCR imposition causes the average local content

Table 8.8 Changes in Sales and Value Added

Firm type:	*Compliers*	*Non-binding firms*	*Non-compliers*
Average change in:			
Firm-level sales (%)	−0.2	−0.2	−0.2
Firm-level value added (%)	0.1	−0.2	−0.2
Firm-level employment (%)	8.0	−0.1	−0.2
Change in:			
Total sales (%)	0.1	−0.2	−0.1
Total value added (%)	0.1	−0.2	−0.1
Total employment (%)	10.8	−0.1	−0.2
		All firms	
Change in the whole economy:			
Total sales (%)		−0.2	
Total value added (%)		−0.2	
Total employment (%)		−0.1	
Change in the OG sector:			
Total sales (%)		−0.5	
Total value added (%)		−0.4	
Total employment (%)		0.1	

Table 8.9 Changes in Firm-Level and Aggregate Local Content

Firm type:	*(1)*	*(2)*	*(3)*	*(4)*
	Avg. local content (%)		*Agg. local content (%)*	
	without LCR	*with LCR*	*without LCR*	*with LCR*
Compliers	37.13	40.00	36.09	40.00
Non-binding firms	96.92	96.91	91.01	91.00
Non-compliers	11.92	11.91	11.69	11.66
The whole economy			83.96	83.95
OG sector			87.91	87.83

of compliers to increase from 37.13% to 40%. As indicated by the theoretical analysis, compliers choose the exact level required by the LCR to minimize the compliance cost. Since the level of LCR faced by most manufacturing firms is 40%, the average local content also settles at the 40% level.

Non-binding firms and non-compliers both experience a slight decrease in their average local content, as shown in Columns 1 and 2 of Table 8.9. Although the decline in local content is quantitatively small and could be considered insignificant, the fact that firms are reducing their local content implies an unintended consequence of imposing a local content requirement induced by general equilibrium. Because the LCR restricts the use of imported inputs, it often leads to higher prices for domestic producers. If other domestic firms rely on the outputs of these producers, the cost of domestic inputs will also increase. Non-binding firms and non-compliers face higher costs for domestic inputs, which may discourage their use of these inputs, resulting in a decrease in their local content.

Changes in the aggregate local content of different firm types, as shown in Columns 3 and 4 of Table 8.9, reveal that the increase in local content of compliers is counterbalanced by the small decrease in local content of the more numerous non-binding firms and noncompliers. Consequently, the overall local content in the economy and the local content in the OG sector remain almost unchanged. The slight decline in local content resulting from higher domestic input costs outweighs the increase in local content resulting from compliance. While the overall impact of Indonesia's MEMR LCR appears negligible, this general equilibrium effect could potentially undermine the policy's original intent if the LCR were more binding and extensive.

5.3 *The impacts on prices and welfare*

We conclude the quantitative analysis by reporting the effects of the LCR imposition on aggregate prices and consumers' welfare. The previous results about changes in local content indicate that the LCR increases domestic input costs. Since the non-compliance fee only applies to sales to the OG sector, Table 8.10 shows the changes in the aggregate price indexes of goods sold to non-OG sectors and to OG sector separately. For example, the fourth row of Table 8.10 shows that the aggregate price index of goods produced by the "Textile & Apparel" sector and sold to the non-OG sectors increases by 0.03%, while the aggregate price index of goods produced by the "Textile & Apparel" sector and sold to the OG sectors increases by 3.98%.

Looking across different sectors, we find that the price increases of goods sold to the OG sector are much larger than the price increases of goods sold to the non-OG sectors. In particular, the prices of goods produced by "Coke & Refined Petroleum", "Basic Metals", "Other Transportation Equipment", "Motor Vehicles", "Electronic & Equipment", and "Fabricated Metals" all increase by more than 4%. The significant increases of prices of goods sold to the OG sector are mostly due to the non-compliance fees paid by the non-compliers.

Table 8.10 Changes in Price Indexes of Goods Sold to Different Sectors

Change in price index (%):	*(1)*	*(2)*
	To non-OG	*To OG*
Selling sector:		
Agriculture	0.01	0.01
Oil & Gas	0.44	0.44
Food & Beverages	0.02	0.75
Textile & Apparel	0.03	3.98
Wood Products	0.04	0.65
Paper Products	0.05	1.19
Printing & Reproduction	0.05	0.24
Coke & Refined Petroleum	0.21	6.46
Chemicals & Medicine	0.13	3.96
Rubber & Plastic	0.06	0.61
Non-metallic Minerals	0.19	2.86
Basic Metals	0.16	5.64
Fabricated Metals	0.12	4.07
Electronic & Equipment	0.04	4.15
Motor Vehicles	0.06	4.34
Other Transportation Equipment	0.03	5.32
Other Manufacturing	0.06	2.03
Service	0.05	0.05

On the other hand, prices of goods sold to the non-OG sectors all increase by less than 0.5%, so these prices are only slightly affected by the LCR imposition.

Table 8.11 shows the changes in the domestic input costs faced by different sectors. The domestic input cost faced by a firm in sector k is a weighted average of domestic price indexes across all sectors weighted by $\beta_D^{k,s}$. The parameter $\beta_D^{k,s}$ describes the intensity at which goods produced by sector s are used as inputs in the production of sector k. As shown in Table 8.11 Column 1, the effects of the LCR imposition on domestic input costs are generally quite small. Not surprisingly, the "Oil & Gas" sector experiences the largest increase in its domestic input cost (0.79%) because the LCR targets the goods supplied to this sector. The "Coke & Petroleum" sector sees the second largest increase in its domestic input cost (0.39%) due to its heavy reliance on the OG goods as its inputs. Table 8.11 Column 2 also shows the "tradeable" domestic input costs, which only concern the non-service inputs. The effects on the domestic tradeable input costs are usually larger. For instance, the domestic tradeable input cost of the "Oil & Gas" sector increases by 1.29%.

Finally, we examine the effect of the LCR imposition on domestic price faced by Indonesian consumers. The change in domestic consumer price is a Cobb-Douglas weighted-average of the price changes of different sectors shown in Table 8.11, where the Cobb-Douglas weights are the expenditure shares of each sector in the final consumption. The last row of Table 8.11 shows the results. The changes in aggregate consumer prices of all goods and tradeable goods are both about 0.04%.

Overall, the LCR imposition causes significant increases only in the prices of goods supplied to the upstream OG sector but has very limited impacts on prices of goods supplied to the other sectors. The resulting increases in domestic input costs and consumer prices are also quite small.

Table 8.11 Changes in Domestic Input Costs and Consumer Price

Sector	*(1)*	*(2)*
	Change in domestic input cost (%)	
	All inputs	*Tradeable inputs*
Agriculture	0.04	0.04
Oil & Gas	0.79	1.29
Food & Beverages	0.02	0.02
Textile & Apparel	0.06	0.06
Wood Products	0.04	0.04
Paper Products	0.06	0.06
Printing & Reproduction	0.06	0.08
Coke & Refined Petroleum	0.39	0.43
Chemicals & Medicine	0.20	0.26
Rubber & Plastic	0.08	0.09
Non-metallic Minerals	0.26	0.35
Basic Metals	0.28	0.36
Fabricated Metals	0.20	0.28
Electronic & Equipment	0.05	0.06
Motor Vehicles	0.06	0.07
Other Transportation Equipment	0.06	0.07
Other Manufacturing	0.07	0.10
Service	0.10	0.15
	Change in domestic price (%)	
	All goods	*Tradeable goods*
Final Consumption	0.04	0.04

6 Conclusions

In this chapter, we develop a model to quantify the impacts of local content requirements (LCRs). We focus on Indonesia's LCR regulation that promotes the use of domestic content in its upstream OG sector. We introduce the LCR compliance decisions faced by manufacturing firms into the foreign sourcing model developed by Blaum et al. (2018). An LCR-bound firm weighs the cost penalty of complying with LCR and the non-compliance cost to make its compliance decision. Domestic price indexes are affected by LCR in the equilibrium, so firms that are not bound by LCR also adjust their local content.

We calibrate the model to the Indonesian economy and quantify the impacts of the LCR regulation. The LCR causes substantial responses and reallocation of firm-level sales to the OG sector, but yields only small effects on aggregate sales, value added, and employment. Although the LCR imposition induces the average local content of compliers to increase, it also raises costs of domestic inputs and leads to declines in the local content of non-binding firms and non-compliers, resulting in a slightly lower aggregate local content. Therefore, an attempt to increase aggregate local content by imposing LCR may result in unintended consequences.

Acknowledgment

We are grateful to Oscar Fernando, James Losar, and Michelle Limenta for helping us better understand the regulation from the legal perspective and to Gene Grossman for his constructive suggestions. We thank Statistics Indonesia (BPS) for providing data on Manufacturing Survey and Ernawati Munadi, David Sanotona, and ERIA team for providing data on LCR. All errors are ours.

Notes

1 From 2005 to 2014, the sector's share in Indonesia's economy has been quite stable. For example, the share of value added generated by the upstream OG sector is 10% to 12% during this period.
2 According to the MEMR regulation, a price preference is "an adjustment value or normalization of the price against bid price in the procurement of goods and/or service."
3 A "product" is defined as a unique Kode Klasifikasi Industri (KKI) 9-digit code.
4 If multiple products produced by a firm are subject to different levels of LCR, we use their maximum for simplicity.
5 For simplicity, we do not endogenize $P_F/a_{F,i}$. Gopinath and Neiman (2014) and Antras et al. (2017) specify two different channels through which $P_F/a_{F,i}$ may respond to changes in the import environment.
6 To calculate the unit cost in this case, one simply needs to calculate $c_{D,i}\,M_{D,i} + c_{F,i}\,M_{F,i}$ subject to the following two constraints:

$$\left(c_{D,i}\cdot M_{D,i}\right)/\left(c_{F,i}\cdot M_{F,i}\right)=\underline{\lambda}/(1-\underline{\lambda})\text{ and}$$

$$\left[\left(a_{D,i}\cdot M_{D,i}\right)^{\frac{\theta-1}{\theta}}+\left(a_{F,i}\cdot M_{F,i}\right)^{\frac{\theta-1}{\theta}}\right]^{\frac{\theta}{\theta-1}}=1.$$

7 To see this, notice that $\partial\left(\kappa_i\right)^{\frac{1-\theta}{\theta}} / \partial\lambda_i = 0$ and $\partial^2\left(\kappa_i\right)^{\frac{1-\theta}{\theta}} / \partial\left(\lambda_i\right)^2 = \frac{1-\theta}{\theta}$ $\left[(\underline{\lambda})^{-1} + (1-\underline{\lambda})^{-1}\right] < 0$ when $\lambda_i = \underline{\lambda}$. Recall that $\theta > 1$

8 In principle, we can allow $z^{k,s}$ to differ by i, namely, firms may differ in their attractiveness perceived by sector k. However, calibrating a model with this dimension of firm heterogeneity will require information on individual firms' sales to different sectors, which is not available in our data.

9 For simplicity, we assume that all active firms in sector s sell to sector k, because we do not observe what sectors a particular firm sells to, which may require information on firm-to-firm transactions.

10 Theoretically, it is plausible to allow a firm to set differential prices to different sectors. However, we do not observe this information in the data.

11 Another potential option for a manufacturing firm is to misreport its compliance status in order to avoid the non-compliance fee without distorting its sourcing decision. Such a decision is only relevant for an LCR-bound firm. We assume that the probability of uncovering the misreporting is μ. In the event of getting caught, the firm faces an administrative sanction, resulting in a zero or even negative profit. Therefore, as long as the enforcement of the regulation is effective enough (meaning that the value of μ is high enough), This "lie to comply" option becomes unattractive to LCR-bound firms. So we do not consider this possibility in the theoretical model.

12 The underlying parameter governing the unconstrained local content is δ_i, the firm-specific efficiency-adjusted cost of foreign content. A higher value of δ_i corresponds to a lower value of the unconstrained local content λ_i.

13 In fact, the average cost penalty of compliers is 1.00125, so it appears 1.00 when being rounded to two decimal places.

References

Amiti, M., Konings, J., 2007. Trade liberalization, intermediate inputs, and productivity: Evidence from Indonesia. *American Economic Review* 97, 1611–1638.

Antras, P., Fort, T.C., Tintelnot, F., 2017. The margins of global sourcing: Theory and evidence from us firms. *American Economic Review* 107, 2514–2564.

Blaum, J., Lelarge, C., Peters, M., 2018. The gains from input trade with heterogeneous importers. *American Economic Journal: Macroeconomics* 10, 77–127.

Brandt, L., Van Biesebroeck, J., Wang, L., Zhang, Y., 2017. WTO accession and performance of Chinese manufacturing firms. *American Economic Review* 107, 2784–2820.

Conconi, P., Garćia-Santana, M., Puccio, L., Venturini, R., 2018. From final goods to inputs: The protectionist effect of rules of origin. *American Economic Review* 108, 2335–2365.

Dekle, R., Eaton, J., Kortum, S., 2007. Unbalanced trade. *American Economic Review* 97, 351–355.

De Loecker, J., Goldberg, P.K., Khandelwal, A.K., Pavcnik, N., 2016. Prices, markups, and trade reform. *Econometrica* 84, 445–510.

Fan, H., Li, Y.A., Yeaple, S.R., 2015. Trade liberalization, quality, and export prices. *Review of Economics and Statistics* 97, 1033–1051.

Goldberg, P.K., Khandelwal, A.K., Pavcnik, N., Topalova, P., 2010. Imported intermediate inputs and domestic product growth: Evidence from India. *The Quarterly Journal of Economics* 125, 1727–1767.

Gopinath, G., Neiman, B., 2014. Trade adjustment and productivity in large crises. *American Economic Review* 104, 793–831.

Grossman, G.M., 1981. The theory of domestic content protection and content preference. *The Quarterly Journal of Economics* 96, 583–603.

Head, K., Mayer, T., Melitz, M., 2022. The Laffer curve for rules of origin. https://scholar.harvard.edu/sites/scholar.harvard.edu/files/melitz/files/hmm_roo_laffer_shared.pdf

Ju, J., Krishna, K., 2005. Firm behaviour and market access in a free trade area with rules of origin. *Canadian Journal of Economics/Revue Canadienne d'économique* 38, 290–308.

Krishna, K., Itoh, M., 1988. Content protection and oligopolistic interactions. *The Review of Economic Studies* 55, 107–125.

Lahiri, S., Ono, Y., 1998. Foreign direct investment, local content requirement, and profit taxation. *The Economic Journal* 108, 444–457.

Qiu, L.D., Tao, Z., 2001. Export, foreign direct investment, and local content requirement. *Journal of Development Economics* 66, 101–125.

Yang, C., 2021. Rules of origin and auto-parts trade. https://chenying-yang.com/RoO_autoparts.pdf

Appendix A

Appendix: Describing the full equilibrium

A.1 Equilibria with and without LCR

In the equilibrium without LCR, the domestic price index of composite input purchased by sector k from sector s, $Q_D^{k,s}$, is given by

$$P_D^{k,s} = \frac{\sigma^s}{\sigma^s - 1}\left[\sum_{i \in \Omega^s}\left(\frac{C_i^s}{z^{k,s}}\right)^{1-\sigma^s}\right]^{\frac{1}{1-\sigma^s}}. \tag{A1}$$

In contrast, the same price index in the equilibrium with LCR is given by:

$$P_D^{k,s'} = \frac{\sigma^s}{\sigma^s - 1}\left[\sum_{i \in \Omega_{NB}^s \cup \Omega_C^s}\left(\frac{C_i^{s'}}{z^{k,s}}\right)^{1-\sigma^s} + \sum_{i \in \Omega_{NC}^s}\left(\frac{\tau C_i^{s'}}{z^{k,s}}\right)^{1-\sigma^s}\right]^{\frac{1}{1-\sigma^s}}, k = \text{OG}$$

$$P_D^{k,s'} = \frac{\sigma^s}{\sigma^s - 1}\left[\sum_{i \in \Omega^s}\left(\frac{C_i^{s'}}{z^{k,s}}\right)^{1-\sigma^s}\right]^{\frac{1}{1-\sigma^s}}, k \neq \text{OG}, F \tag{A2}$$

$$P_D^{k,s'} = \frac{\sigma^s}{\sigma^s - 1}\left[\sum_{i \in \Omega^s}\left(\frac{C_i^{S'}}{z^{k,s}}\right)^{1-\sigma^s} + \sum_{i \in \Omega^{s*}}\left(\frac{C_i^S}{z^{k,s}}\right)^{1-\sigma^s}\right]^{\frac{1}{1-\sigma^s}}, \quad k = F$$

where $\Omega_{NB}^s, \Omega_C^s$ and Ω_{NC}^s denote the sets of firms that find their LCR non-binding, firms that decide to comply with their binding LCR, and firms that decide not to comply, respectively. We can characterize the compliance decision of firm i based on

$$i \in \begin{cases} \Omega_{\mathrm{NB}}^{s'}, \text{ if } \lambda_i' \geq \underline{\lambda}_i, \\ \Omega_{\mathrm{C}}^{s'}, \text{ if } \lambda_i' < \underline{\lambda}_i \text{ and } S^{\mathrm{OG},s'} > \dfrac{1-\kappa_i'^{1-\sigma^s}}{1-\tau^{1-\sigma^s}} \\ \Omega_{\mathrm{NC}}^{s'}, \text{ if } \lambda_i' < \underline{\lambda}_i \text{ and } S^{\mathrm{OG},s'} \leq \dfrac{1-\kappa_i'^{1-\sigma^s}}{1-\tau^{1-\sigma^s}}, \end{cases} \tag{A3}$$

where

$$\hat{S}^{\mathrm{OG},s} = \frac{\Gamma^{\mathrm{OG},s'}\left(z^{\mathrm{OG},s}\right)^{\sigma^s-1}}{\Sigma_k \Gamma^{k,s'}\left(z^{k,s}\right)^{\sigma^s-1}} = \frac{\hat{\Gamma}^{\mathrm{OG},s}}{\Sigma_k S^{k,s}\hat{\Gamma}^{k,s}},$$

and $\hat{\Gamma}^{k,s} = \left(\hat{P}_D^{k,s}\right)^{\sigma^s-1} \hat{X}^{k,s}$

Input demands for goods produced by sector s depend on the sizes of other sectors k and the input-output linkage between k and s. Meanwhile, we assume that the final consumption expenditures $X^{F,s}$ are fixed. So the input market clearing condition is

$$X^{k,s} = \beta_D^{k,s}\left[\sum_{i\in\Omega^k}\sum_n \lambda_i\gamma_i\left(\frac{\sigma^k-1}{\sigma^k}\right)^{\sigma^k}\left(\frac{C_i}{z^{n,k}}\right)^{1-\sigma^k}\left(P_D^{n,k}\right)^{\sigma^k-1}X^{n,k}\right], \tag{A4}$$

and

$$\begin{aligned} X^{k,s'} = {} & \beta_D^{k,s}\left[\sum_{i\in\Omega^k}\sum_{n\neq\mathrm{OG}} \lambda_i'\gamma_i'\left(\frac{\sigma^k-1}{\sigma^k}\right)^{\sigma^k}\left(\frac{C_i'}{z^{n,k}}\right)^{1-\sigma^k}\left(P_D^{n,k'}\right)^{\sigma^k-1}X^{n,k'}\right] \\ & +\beta_D^{k,s}\left[\sum_{i\in\Omega_{\mathrm{NC}}^k} \lambda_i'\gamma_i'\left(\frac{\sigma^k-1}{\sigma^k}\right)^{\sigma^k}\left(\frac{\tau C_i'}{z^{\mathrm{OG},k}}\right)^{1-\sigma^k}\left(P_D^{\mathrm{OG},k'}\right)^{\sigma^k-1}X^{\mathrm{OG},k'}\right] \\ & +\beta_D^{k,s}\left[\sum_{i\in\Omega_{\mathrm{NB}}^k\cup\Omega_{\mathrm{C}}^k} \lambda_i'\gamma_i'\left(\frac{\sigma^k-1}{\sigma^k}\right)^{\sigma^k}\left(\frac{C_i'}{z^{\mathrm{OG},k}}\right)^{1-\sigma^k}\left(P_D^{\mathrm{OG},k'}\right)^{\sigma^k-1}X^{\mathrm{OG},k'}\right] \end{aligned} \tag{A5}$$

Combining the conditions shown, we can define the two equilibria without and with the LCR.

Proposition 1 (Equilibria without and with LCR). *Given exogenous variables φ_i, $z^{k,s}$, $a^k_{D,i}$, $a^k_{F,i}$, $b_{L,i}$, P^k_F, w^k, $\beta^{k,s}_D$, $X^{F,k}$, and $\underline{\lambda}_i$, and parameter θ and σ^s, the equilibrium without LCR is a vector of price indexes $\{P^{k,s}_D\}$ that satisfies equations (A1) and (A4) for all k and s. The equilibrium with LCR is a vector of price indexes $\{P^{k,s'}_D\}$ that satisfies equation (A2), (A3), and (A5) for all k and s.*

A.2 Equilibrium in relative changes

We investigate the impacts of the LCR imposition by formulating the equilibrium in relative changes. The relative change of price index is:

$$\left(\widehat{P}^{k,s}_D\right)^{1-\sigma^s} = \sum_{i\in\Omega^s_{NB}} m^{k,s}_i \left[\widehat{P}^s_D \widehat{\gamma}_i^{\frac{1}{\theta-1}} \widehat{\lambda}_i^{\frac{1}{\theta-1}}\right]^{1-\sigma^s} + \sum_{i\in\Omega^s_C} m^{k,s}_i \left[\widehat{P}^s_D \widehat{\gamma}_i^{\frac{1}{\theta-1}} \widehat{\lambda}_i^{\frac{1}{\theta-1}} \kappa'_i\right]^{1-\sigma^s}$$
$$+ \sum_{i\in\Omega^s_{NC}} m^{k,s}_i \left[\widehat{P}^s_D \widehat{\gamma}_i^{\frac{1}{\theta-1}} \widehat{\lambda}_i^{\frac{1}{\theta-1}} \tau\right]^{1-\sigma^s}, k = \text{OG},$$

$$\left(\widehat{P}^{k,s}_D\right)^{1-\sigma^s} = \sum_{i\in\Omega^s_{NB}\cup\Omega^s_{NC}} m^{k,s}_i \left[\widehat{P}^s_D \widehat{\gamma}_i^{\frac{1}{\theta-1}} \widehat{\lambda}_i^{\frac{1}{\theta-1}}\right]^{1-\sigma^s}$$
$$+ \sum_{i\in\Omega^s_C} m^{k,s}_i \left[\widehat{P}^s_D \widehat{\gamma}_i^{\frac{1}{\theta-1}} \widehat{\lambda}_i^{\frac{1}{\theta-1}} \kappa'_i\right]^{1-\sigma^s}, k \neq \text{OG}, F$$

$$\left(\widehat{P}^{k,s}_D\right)^{1-\sigma^s} = \sum_{i\in\Omega^s_{NB}\cup\Omega^s_{NC}} m^{k,s}_i \left[\widehat{P}^s_D \widehat{\gamma}_i^{\frac{1}{\theta-1}} \widehat{\lambda}_i^{\frac{1}{\theta-1}}\right]^{1-\sigma^s}$$
$$+ \sum_{i\in\Omega^s_C} m^{k,s}_i \left[\widehat{P}^s_D \widehat{\gamma}_i^{\frac{1}{\theta-1}} \widehat{\lambda}_i^{\frac{1}{\theta-1}} \kappa'_i\right]^{1-\sigma^s} + \left(1 - \sum_{i\in\Omega^{s*}} m^{k,s}_i\right), k = F, \quad \text{(A6)}$$

where $m^{k,s}_i = \Upsilon^{k,s}_i / X^{k,s}$ is the market share of firm i in sector k's total input purchase from sector s, or the market share of firm i in the final consumption demand. The change in output prices of non-binding firms arises from the general equilibrium effect that affects the domestic composite input prices. For instance, non-binding firms reduce domestic input usages when the domestic composite input prices increase. In addition to the general equilibrium effect, the compliance cost penalties κ_i' directly inflate the output prices of the complying firms. Meanwhile, non-compliers are charged an *ad valorem* non-compliance fee of τ when selling to the upstream OG sector, which also increases their prices.

According to the Cobb-Douglas formulation, the relative change in the cost of domestic composite input is

$$\widehat{P}_D^{s} = \Pi_n \left(\widehat{P}_D^{s,n} \right)^{\beta_D^{s,n}}. \tag{A7}$$

Looking into the change in the local content $\hat{\lambda}_i$ of firm i and assuming that foreign composite input cost P_F^k is not affected by the LCR, we notice that

$$\hat{\lambda}_i = \frac{\left[\gamma_i \left(\widehat{P}_D^{k} \right)^{1-\theta} + \left(1-\gamma_i\right) \right]^{\frac{1-\theta}{1-\theta}}}{\lambda_i \left[\gamma_i \left(\widehat{P}_D^{k} \right)^{1-\theta} + \left(1-\gamma_i\right) \right]^{\frac{1-\theta}{1-\theta}} + \left(1-\lambda_i\right)}, \tag{A8}$$

which depends on $\widehat{P}_D^{k}$ given λ_i, γ_i, and θ. Hence, we can get $\lambda_i' = \hat{\lambda}_i \lambda_i$. With λ_i' in hand, we can also calculate κ_i':

$$\kappa_i' = \left[\underline{\lambda} \left(\frac{\lambda_i'}{\underline{\lambda}} \right)^{\frac{1}{\theta}} + \left(1-\underline{\lambda}\right) \left(\frac{1-\lambda_i'}{1-\underline{\lambda}} \right)^{\frac{1}{\theta}} \right]^{\frac{\theta}{1-\theta}}. \tag{A9}$$

The change in domestic input share within firm i's local content is

$$\hat{\gamma}_i = \frac{\left(\widehat{P}_D^{k} \right)^{1-\theta}}{\gamma_i \left(\widehat{P}_D^{k} \right)^{1-\theta} + \left(1-\gamma_i\right)}. \tag{A10}$$

So we can rewrite the relative change in firm-level unit cost as

$$\widehat{C}_i = \begin{cases} \widehat{P}_D^{k} \hat{\gamma}_i^{\frac{1}{\theta-1}} \hat{\lambda}_i^{\frac{1}{\theta-1}}, & \text{if } i \in \Omega_{NC}^{k\,\prime} \cup \Omega_{NB}^{k\,\prime} \\ \kappa_i \widehat{P}_D^{k} \hat{\gamma}_i^{\frac{1}{\theta-1}} \hat{\lambda}_i^{\frac{1}{\theta-1}}, & \text{if } i \in \Omega_C^{k'} \end{cases} \tag{A11}$$

The total expenditure on domestic input in the LCR equilibrium can be written as:

$$X^{k,s}\widehat{X}^{k,s} = \beta_D^{k,s}\frac{\sigma^k - 1}{\sigma^k}\left[\sum_{i\in\Omega^k}\sum_{n\neq \mathrm{OG}}\lambda_i'\gamma_i'\Upsilon_i^{n,k}\widehat{C}_i^{1-\sigma^k}\widehat{P}_D^{n,k\sigma^k-1}\widehat{X}^{n,k}\right.$$

$$+\tau^{1-\sigma^s}\sum_{i\in\Omega_{\mathrm{NC}}^k}\lambda_i'\gamma_i'\Upsilon_i^{\mathrm{OG},k}\widehat{C}_i^{1-\sigma^k}\widehat{P}_D^{\mathrm{OG},k\sigma^k-1}\widehat{X}^{\mathrm{OG},k}$$

$$\left.+\sum_{i\in\Omega_{\mathrm{NB}}^k\cup\Omega_{\mathrm{C}}^k}\lambda_i'\gamma_i'\Upsilon_i^{\mathrm{OG},k}\widehat{C}_i^{1-\sigma^k}\widehat{P}_D^{\mathrm{OG},k\sigma^k-1}\widehat{X}^{\mathrm{OG},k}\right], \qquad \text{(A12)}$$

which helps to define $\widehat{X}^{k,s}$ given other variables. The following proposition describes the relative change of the equilibrium caused by the LCR imposition.

Proposition 2 (Equilibrium in relative changes). *Given endogenous variables* $\left\{\lambda_i, \gamma_i, \Upsilon_i^{k,s}, X^{k,s}\right\}$, *exogenous variables* $\{X^{F,s}\}$, *policy variables* $\{\tau, \underline{\lambda}_i\}$, *and parameters* $\left\{\theta, \sigma^s, \beta_D^{k,s}\right\}$, *a relative change of the equilibrium caused by the LCR is a vector of price index changes* $\widehat{P}_D^{k,s}$ *that satisfies (A3), (A6), (A7), (A8), (A9), (A10), (A11), and (A12).*

Once we calibrate and obtain the values of $\{\lambda_i, \gamma_i, \Upsilon_i^{k,s}, X^{k,s}\}$, $\{X^{F,s}\}$, $\{\tau, \underline{\lambda}_i\}$, and $\{\theta, \sigma^s, \beta_D^{k,s}\}$, we can evaluate the effects of imposing the MEMR LCR on firms and the economy.

Index

For Product Safety Concerns and Information please contact our EU representative GPSR@taylorandfrancis.com
Taylor & Francis Verlag GmbH, Kaufingerstraße 24, 80331 München, Germany

www.ingramcontent.com/pod-product-compliance
Ingram Content Group UK Ltd.
Pitfield, Milton Keynes, MK11 3LW, UK
UKHW020148200926
475702UK00016B/2602
9781032542218